Lecture Notes in Computer S

Edited by G. Goos, J. Hartmanis and J. van Leeuwen

Springer

Berlin
Heidelberg
New York
Barcelona
Hong Kong
London
Milan
Paris
Singapore
Tokyo

David Kotz Friedemann Mattern (Eds.)

Agent Systems, Mobile Agents, and Applications

Second International Symposium
on Agent Systems and Applications
and Fourth International Symposium
on Mobile Agents, ASA/MA 2000
Zurich, Switzerland, September 13-15, 2000
Proceedings

Springer

Series Editors

Gerhard Goos, Karlsruhe University, Germany
Juris Hartmanis, Cornell University, NY, USA
Jan van Leeuwen, Utrecht University, The Netherlands

Volume Editors

David Kotz
Dartmouth College, Department of Computer Science
6211 Sudikoff Lab, Hanover, NH 03755-3510, USA
E-mail: dfk@cs.dartmouth.edu

Friedemann Mattern
ETH Zürich, Institute for Information Systems
Haldeneggsteig 4, 8092 Zürich, Switzerland
E-mail: mattern@inf.ethz.ch

Cataloging-in-Publication Data applied for

Die Deutsche Bibliothek - CIP-Einheitsaufnahme

Agent systems, mobile agents, and applications : proceedings / Second
International Symposium on Agent Systems and Applications and Fourth
International Symposium on Mobile Agents, ASA, MA 2000, Zürich,
Switzerland, September 13 - 15, 2000. David Kotz ; Friedemann Mattern
(ed.). - Berlin ; Heidelberg ; New York ; Barcelona ; Hong Kong ;
London ; Milan ; Paris ; Singapore ; Tokyo : Springer, 2000
  (Lecture notes in computer science ; Vol. 1882)
  ISBN 3-540-41052-X

CR Subject Classification (1998): C.2.4, D.1.3, D.2, D.4.4-7, I.2.11, K.6.5

ISSN 0302-9743
ISBN 3-540-41052-X Springer-Verlag Berlin Heidelberg New York

This work is subject to copyright. All rights are reserved, whether the whole or part of the material is
concerned, specifically the rights of translation, reprinting, re-use of illustrations, recitation, broadcasting,
reproduction on microfilms or in any other way, and storage in data banks. Duplication of this publication
or parts thereof is permitted only under the provisions of the German Copyright Law of September 9, 1965,
in its current version, and permission for use must always be obtained from Springer-Verlag. Violations are
liable for prosecution under the German Copyright Law.

Springer-Verlag Berlin Heidelberg New York
a member of BertelsmannSpringer Science+Business Media GmbH
© Springer-Verlag Berlin Heidelberg 2000
Printed in Germany

Typesetting: Camera-ready by author, data conversion by DA-TeX Gerd Blumenstein
Printed on acid-free paper   SPIN 10722434   06/3142   5 4 3 2 1 0

Preface

This volume contains the proceedings of the Second International Symposium on Agent Systems and Applications and the Fourth International Symposium on Mobile Agents. ASA/MA 2000 took place in Zurich, Switzerland, at the ETH (the Swiss Federal Institute of Technology) on September 13–15, 2000.

In the age of information overload, *agents* have become an important programming paradigm. Agents can act on behalf of users to collect, filter, and process information. They can act autonomously and react to changing environments. Agents are deployed in different settings, such as industrial control, Internet searching, personal assistance, network management, games, and many others.

In our increasingly networked world, *mobile code* is another important programming paradigm. In distributed applications mobile code can improve speed, flexibility, structure, security, or the ability to handle disconnection. Mobile code has been applied to mobile computing, wireless networks, active networks, manufacturing, network management, resource discovery, software dissemination and configuration, and many other situations.

Mobile agents combine the features of agents and mobile-code technologies, and present their own set of challenges. Their use is increasingly explored by an expanding industry.

A full understanding of the capabilities and limits of these technologies (agents, mobile code, and mobile agents) is an open research topic in several communities. This symposium showcases experimental research as well as experiences gained while developing, deploying, and using applications and systems that meet real user needs. Authors were encouraged to include some sort of a quantitative analysis of their application or system. Deployment experience papers were asked to either contain quantitative analysis or a concrete, detailed discussion of the lessons learned from real-world applications or systems. We also encouraged authors of accepted papers to make the source code available, and if possible, to demonstrate the technology.

ASA/MA 2000 is a joint symposium on Agent Systems and Applications (ASA) and Mobile Agents (MA), reflecting the joint interests of those two communities. We retain, in name, the autonomy of those two conferences, although in practice we have a single program and a single program committee. ASA/MA 2000 continues the tradition of last year's symposium (the First International Symposium on Agent Systems and Applications and the Third International Symposium on Mobile Agents, 3–6 October 1999, Palm Springs, California, proceedings published by IEEE), which in turn continued the series of International Mobile Agents Workshops MA'98 (Stuttgart, Germany) and MA'97 (Berlin, Germany). Further information on the ASA/MA 2000 Symposium may be found on the Symposium web site www.inf.ethz.ch/ASA-MA/.

The program committee of ASA/MA 2000 chose the best possible papers from five main areas:

- agent applications
- agent systems
- multi-agent systems

- mobile agents
- mobile code

with a focus on the following topics:

- development tools
- security
- scalability
- fault tolerance
- communication, collaboration and coordination
- languages
- standards
- design patterns

- applications in mobile computing and wireless networks
- applications in electronic markets and commerce
- applications in active networks
- market-based control
- resource management
- agent societies and ensembles
- World-Wide-Web integration

We received 107 submissions from authors all over the world, and chose 20 papers for inclusion in the symposium. It was a difficult choice, based on 537 reviews produced by the program committee and by a collection of 32 outside referees. Each paper was reviewed by at least three people, and in some cases four or five people. The typical paper was reviewed by two program committee members and one outside reviewer. The submission and reviewing process was managed with the WIMPE conference-management package written by David Nicol at Dartmouth College. It is an invaluable tool, extremely useful for online paper submission and reviewing.

The program committee met in Boston on 1 May to examine all of the reviews and select the final 20 papers. Using the numerical rankings as a guide, we discussed each paper, and occasionally re-read a paper, until we were sure that we had the best selection. Two papers had been co-authored by program committee members who were present at the meeting; during the discussion of their papers they were asked to leave the room. One such paper was accepted one was not.

Every accepted paper was assigned a member of the program committee to supervise the revision process, to make sure that the referees' comments were addressed and to add additional feedback on the later drafts of the paper. This extra measure of quality control leads, we believe, to the very strong set of papers you see here.

In addition to the papers contained in these proceedings, the symposium program included invited presentations, tutorials, workshops, and a poster session. We chose not to accept any submitted papers directly into the poster session. Instead, a separate "Call for Posters" was sent in July to allow all authors, as well as anyone with late-breaking projects, to participate.

We would like to express our appreciation to the authors of the submitted papers, and we deeply thank all members of the program committee and the external reviewers for their effort and their valuable input. We would also like to express our thanks to Springer-Verlag for the excellent cooperation, to IBM who sponsored the event, and to the organizing staff at ETH Zurich, in particular Jürgen Bohn and Marc Langheinrich.

July 2000   David Kotz, Friedemann Mattern

Organization

The Joint Symposium on Agent Systems and Applications / Mobile Agents (ASA/MA 2000) took take place in Zurich, Switzerland on September 13–15, 2000. It was organized by ETH Zurich, the Swiss Federal Institute of Technology.

Executive Committee

Conference Chair:	Friedemann Mattern (ETH Zurich, Switzerland)
Program Chair:	David Kotz (Dartmouth College, USA)
Finance Chair:	Günter Karjoth (IBM Zurich, Switzerland)
Technical Editor:	Jürgen Bohn (ETH Zurich, Switzerland)
Publicity, Registration, and	
Local Arrangements Chair:	Marc Langheinrich (ETH Zurich, Switzerland)

Program Committee

Geoff Arnold (Sun Microsystems, USA)
Jeff Bradshaw (The Boeing Company, USA)
David Chess (IBM Research, USA)
Dag Johansen (University of Tromsø, Norway)
Jeff Kephart (IBM Research, USA)
David Kotz (Dartmouth College, USA)
Danny Lange (General Magic, USA)
Dejan S. Milojicic (HP Labs, USA)
Moira Norrie (ETH Zurich, Switzerland)
Gian Pietro Picco (Politecnico di Milano, Italy)
Radu Popescu-Zeletin (Technical University Berlin, Germany)
Kurt Rothermel (University of Stuttgart, Germany)
Christian Tschudin (Uppsala University, Sweden)
Giovanni Vigna (UC Santa Barbara, USA)
Jan Vitek (Purdue University, USA)
Mary Ellen Zurko (Iris Associates, USA)

Steering Committee

Fred Douglis (AT&T Labs, USA)
Robert Gray (Dartmouth College, USA)
Danny Lange (General Magic, Inc., USA)
Friedemann Mattern (ETH Zurich, Switzerland)
Dejan S. Milojicic (HP Labs, USA)
Kurt Rothermel (University of Stuttgart, Germany)

Referees

Stefan Arbanowski
Geoff Arnold
Joachim Baumann
Jeff Bradshaw
Jonathan Bredin
Ciaran Bryce
Cora Burger
Daniel Burroughs
Guanling Chen
David Chess
George Cybenko
Fawzi Daoud
Kurt Geihs
Bob Gray
Mark Greaves
Martin Hofmann
Fritz Hohl
Dag Johansen
Günter Karjoth
Stamatis Karnouskos

Charlie Kaufman
Jeffrey Kephart
Harumi Kuno
Ernö Kovacs
Danny Lange
Keith Marzullo
Sven van der Meer
Dejan Milojicic
N. C. Narendra
Moira Norrie
Mitsuru Oshima
Todd Papaioannou
Joseph Pasquale
Gian Pietro Picco
Bob Pinheiro
Radu Popescu-Zeletin
Apratim Purakayastha
Pierre Alain Queloz
Mudumbai Ranganathan
Kurt Rothermel

Peter Sewell
Stephan Steglich
Markus Strasser
Rahul Sukthankar
Niranjan Suri
Wolfgang Theilmann
Anand Tripathi
Volker Tschammer
Christian Tschudin
Tuan Tu
Venu Vaseduvan
Giovanni Vigna
Jan Vitek
Kenneth Whitebread
Pawel Wojciechowski
Franco Zambonelli
Michael Zapf
Mary Ellen Zurko

Sponsoring Institutions

IBM Zurich Research Laboratory, Switzerland
ETH Zurich, Switzerland
General Magic, Inc., USA

Table of Contents

Mobile Agent Applications

Applications of Multi-agent Systems

Communication and Mobility Control

Cooperation and Interaction

Invited Talk (Abstract):

Data or Computation – Which Should We Move?

Colin G. Harrison

IBM T. J. Watson Research Center
Yorktown Heights, NY 10598, U.S.A.

Abstract. The evolution of system architectures has been shaped by the varying evolutions of the costs of system operations. That is: the cost of computation, the cost of storage, the cost of communication, and the cost of operational management. In recent years the costs of computation and storage have continued to drop exponentially (at least). Communication costs have traditionally remained high relative to other costs and this has had a profound influence on the structure of system architectures, favouring centralized information systems with remote clients. But these costs too are in steep decline and in recent years end-to-end latencies in the Internet have approached values that in client-server days could only be achieved within campus networks. These trends will change this architectural balance, making much more attractive the widespread distribution of application function – even function requiring significant bandwidth. The current impetus towards exploring this model of computation is the desire to create dynamic business architectures in which components or entire business processes are delivered as remote network services. In this approach the business process is modeled as a form of workflow and the computation proceeds by moving the business data successively through several remote transaction systems. We contrast this approach with that of mobile agents in which the transaction itself moves through the network and consider why the mobile agent approach is not being adopted for dynamic business architectures.

D. Kotz and F. Mattern (Eds.): ASA/MA 2000, LNCS 1882, pp. 1-1, 2000.
© Springer-Verlag Berlin Heidelberg 2000

Strong Mobility and Fine-Grained Resource Control in NOMADS[1]

Niranjan Suri[1], Jeffrey M. Bradshaw[1, 2], Maggie R. Breedy[1], Paul T. Groth[1],
Gregory A. Hill[1], and Renia Jeffers[2]

[1] Institute for Human and Machine Cognition, University of West Florida, USA
{nsuri,jbradshaw,mbreedy,pgroth,ghill}ai.uwf.edu
[2] Intelligent Agent Technology, Phantom Works, The Boeing Company, USA
{jeffrey.m.bradshaw,teresa.z.Jeffers}boeing.com

Abstract. NOMADS is a Java-based agent system that supports strong mobility (i.e., the ability to capture and transfer the full execution state of migrating agents) and safe agent execution (i.e., the ability to control resources consumed by agents, facilitating guarantees of quality of service while protecting against denial of service attacks). The NOMADS environment is composed of two parts: an agent execution environment called Oasis and a new Java-compatible Virtual Machine (VM) called Aroma. The combination of Oasis and the Aroma VM provides key enhancements over today's Java agent environments.

1 Introduction

Mobile agent systems may be classified into two categories: those that support strong mobility and those that do not. Systems that provide strong mobility are able to capture and transfer the full execution state of the migrating agent. Systems that support only weak mobility do not transfer the execution state but rather restart execution of the agent on the remote system.

The Mobile Agent List [7] identifies over 60 mobile agent systems with the overwhelming majority being Java-based. Examples of well-known Java-based systems include Aglets [10], D'Agents [6], Voyager [14], and Concordia [12]. Because Sun's Java Virtual Machine (VM) does not allow execution state capture, very few of the Java-based mobile agent systems provide strong mobility. Those that do fall into two categories: systems using a modified Java VM and systems using a preprocessor approach.

Sumatra [1] and Ara [11,15] are two systems that use a modified Java VM to provide strong mobility. One problem with this approach is that the modified VM

---

[1] This research is supported in part by DARPA's Control of Agent-Based Systems (CoABS) program (Contract F30602-98-C-0170), the NASA Aviation Extranet JSRA (Contract NCA2-2005), and the National Technology Alliance (NTA).

D. Kotz and F. Mattern (Eds.): ASA/MA 2000, LNCS 1882, pp. 2–15, 2000.

cannot be redistributed due to licensing constraints.[2] A second problem is that both of these systems were based on Java Developer Kit (JDK) 1.0.2 VM, which did not use native threads. Since JDK 1.2 and JDK 1.3 VMs rely on native threads, modifying the newer VMs to capture execution state would be more difficult.

The WASP system [5] uses a preprocessor approach to provide strong mobility. The advantage of the preprocessor approach is the ability to work with the standard JDK VM. However, one of the disadvantages of the preprocessor approach is the overhead introduced by the additional code added by the instrumentation process. Another disadvantage is that capturing execution state of multiple threads requires that each thread periodically poll the other threads to see if any of them have requested a state capture operation. This polling adds additional overhead and complicates the task of writing agents with multiple threads.

Our approach in NOMADS was to develop a custom VM (called Aroma) that has the ability to capture thread execution state. Since the Aroma VM does not use any source code from Sun's VM implementation, there are no licensing constraints on redistributing the NOMADS system. Implementing the state capture in the VM gives us the capability to transparently handle multiple threads and to support additional kinds of mobility such as forced mobility.

Another important feature of the NOMADS system is dynamic resource control. Early versions of Java relied on the sandbox model to protect mobile code from accessing dangerous methods. In contrast, the security model in the Java 2 release is *permission-based*. Unlike the previous "all or nothing" approach, Java applets and applications can be given varying amounts of access to system resources based upon policies. Because these policies are external to the programs, the policies can be created and modified as appropriate by a developer, system or network administrator, the end user, or even a Java program. The policy-based approach is a major advance but current policies and underlying Java mechanisms do not address the problem of resource control. For example, while it may be possible to prevent a Java program from writing to any directory except /tmp (an *access* control issue), once the program is given permission to write to the /tmp directory, no further restrictions are placed on the program's I/O (a *resource* control issue). As another example, there is no current Java policy or mechanism available to limit the amount of disk space the program may use or to control the rate at which the program is allowed to read and write from the disk drive.

One attempt to provide resource control in Java is JRes [4] which provides CPU, network, and memory control. JRes uses a preprocessor to instrument code, allowing it to take into account object allocations for memory control. A second attempt [9] uses a modified Java VM to provide CPU resource control and scheduling. The Ajanta mobile agent system [16] takes a different approach by using proxies between the Java agents and resources to account for and limit the resources used by the agents. In the case of NOMADS, the Aroma VM enforces all of the resource controls and therefore does not rely on any preprocessing or special API at the Java code level.

---

[2] Even the new Community Source licensing policy offered by Sun Microsystems does not allow redistribution of a modified VM without additional constraints such as licensing the Java Compatibility Kit with an annual cost and paying a royalty fee to Sun for each copy of the VM that is distributed.

Agents simply use the standard Java platform API. Also, the overhead introduced by the resource control code in NOMADS is very low since the resource control is implemented in native code inside the VM (see performance results in section 5).

The rest of this paper is organized as follows. The next section describes the capabilities of the NOMADS system and some potential applications. Section three describes the implementation of the Aroma VM and in particular the implementation of the state capture and resource control mechanisms. Section four describes the Oasis agent execution environment. Section five presents our performance results to date and compares NOMADS with other mobile agent systems. Finally, section six concludes the paper and briefly discusses our plans for future work.

2   NOMADS Capabilities

The NOMADS environment is composed of two parts: an agent execution environment called Oasis and the Aroma VM. The combination of Oasis and Aroma provides two key enhancements over today's Java agent environments:

1. *Strong mobility,* the ability to capture and transfer the full execution state of mobile agents. This allows agents to be moved "anytime" at the demand of the server or the agent rather than just at specific pre-determined points.
2. *Safe execution,* the ability to control the resources consumed by agents thereby facilitating guarantees of quality of service (QoS) while protecting against denial of service attacks. Adding these resource control capabilities to the access control mechanisms already provided by the new Java 2 security model allows mobile agents to be deployed with greater confidence in open environments. Also resource control is an essential foundation for future work on providing QoS guarantees.

2.1   Strong Mobility

Strong mobility simplifies the task of the agent programmer. Since strong mobility preserves the execution state, mobility can be invoked by the agent simply by calling the appropriate API anywhere in the code. The code fragment below shows a simple NOMADS agent that displays a message on one system, moves to another system, and displays another message.

```
public class Visitor extends Agent
{
    public static void main (String[] args)
    {
        System.out.println ("On source");
        go ("<destination host>");
        System.out.println ("On destination");
    }
}
```

The following code fragment shows an Aglets agent that performs the same task. Note that in this case a boolean variable has to be introduced external to the run()

method in order to store state information. This added complexity is not peculiar to Aglets but to any mobile agent system that does not provide strong mobility.

```
public class Visitor extends Aglet
{
    public void run()
    {
        if (_theRemote) {
            System.out.println ("On destination");
        }
        else {
            System.out.println ("On source");
            _theRemote = true;
            dispatch (destination);
        }
    }
    protected Boolean _theRemote = false;
}
```

Strong mobility is also vital for situations in which there are long-running or long-lived agents and, for reasons external to the agents, they need to suddenly move or be moved from one host to another. In principle, such a transparent mechanism would allow the agents to continue running without any loss of their ongoing computation and, depending on circumstances, the agents need not even be aware of the fact that they have been moved (e.g., in *forced mobility* situations). Such an approach will be useful in building distributed systems with complex load balancing requirements. The same mechanism could also be used to replicate agents without their explicit knowledge. Such transparent replication would allow the support system to replicate agents and execute them on different hosts for safety, redundancy, performance, or other reasons (e.g., isolating and observing malicious agents without their knowledge).

Exploiting Java's bytecode approach, NOMADS allows the execution state of an agent to be captured on one host of one architecture (say an Intel x86 running Windows NT) and restored on another host with a different architecture (such as a Sun SPARC running Solaris). While it is possible to achieve some measure of transparent persistence by techniques such as having a special class loader insert read and write barriers into the source code before execution, such an approach poses many problems [8]. First, the transformed bytecodes could not be reused outside of a particular persistence framework, defeating the Java platform goal of code portability. Second, such an approach would not be applicable to the core classes, which cannot be loaded by this mechanism. Third, the code transformations would be exposed to debuggers, performance monitoring tools, the reflection system, and so forth, compromising the goal of complete transparency. In contrast, NOMADS agents can run without changes in either the Aroma VM or a standard Java VM, though of course special strong mobility and safe execution features would only available in the former.

We note that the current version of NOMADS does not provide any mechanism to transparently access resources independent of agent mobility. We are currently working on transparently redirecting network and disk resources.

2.2 Safe Execution

Mechanisms for monitoring and controlling agent use of host resources are important for three reasons [13]. First, it is essential that access to critical host resources such as the hard disk be denied to unauthorized agents. Second, the use of resources to which access has been granted must be kept within reasonable bounds, making it easier to provide a specific quality of service for each agent. Denial of service conditions resulting from a poorly programmed or malicious agent's overuse of critical resources are impossible to detect and interrupt without monitoring and control mechanisms for individual agents. Third, tracking of resource usage enables accounting and billing mechanisms that hosts may use to calculate charges for resident agents.

The Aroma VM provides flexible and dynamic resource control for disk and network resources. Using Aroma, it is possible to limit both the rate and the quantity of resources that each agent is allowed to use. Resource limits that may be enforced include disk and network read and write rates, total number of bytes read and written to disk and network, and disk space. Note that disk space is different from disk bytes written because of seek operations and file deletions that may be performed on disk files. The rate limits are expressed in bytes/sec whereas the quantity limits are expressed in bytes.

Once an agent is authenticated, a policy file specifies the initial set of limits that should be enforced by Aroma. These limits are dynamically changeable through the Oasis administration program (discussed in section 4). Dynamically changing resource limits is also beneficial to prioritizing agents that are running on a host. In a related project, we are working on a high-level policy-based agent management system that resides on top of the low-level enforcement capabilities of the Aroma VM [2,3].

2.3 Miscellaneous Features

NOMADS provides a few other features to support agents and the tasks they may need to perform. A low-level messaging API is provided to allow an agent to send a message to another agent. Agents are assigned Universally Unique Identifiers (UUIDs) upon creation and the UUIDs are used to address agents when sending messages. Agents may also use alternate names for convenience. A directory service maps agent names to their UUIDs. Agents can use the standard Java Platform API for other operations such as creating new threads, synchronizing between threads, accessing files and networks, and for performing I/O.

3   Aroma Virtual Machine

The Aroma VM is a Java-compatible VM designed and implemented with the specific requirements of strong mobility and safe execution. The primary goals for Aroma were to support:

1. Capture of the execution state of a single Java thread, thread group, or all threads (complete process) in the VM
2. Capture of the execution state at fine levels of granularity (ideally, between any two Java bytecode instructions)
3. Capture of the execution state as transparently to the Java code executing in the VM as possible
4. Cross-platform compatibility for the execution state information (transferable between Aroma VMs on different architectures)
5. Flexibility in how much information is captured (in particular whether to include the definitions of Java classes)
6. Easy portability to a variety of platforms (at least Win32 and various UNIX/Linux platforms)
7. Flexible usage in different contexts and inside different applications
8. Enforcement of fine-grained and dynamically changing limits of access to resources such as the CPU, memory, disk, network, and GUI

In the current version of Aroma, the VM can only capture the execution state of all threads rather than just a designated subset. Also, at the present time, only the disk and network resource limits have been implemented. These limitations will be addressed in future versions of Aroma.

The Aroma VM is implemented in C++ and consists of two parts: the VM library and a native code library. The VM library can be linked to other application programs. Currently, two programs use the VM library – avm (a simple wrapper program that is similar to the java executable) and oasis (the agent execution environment). The VM library consists of approximately 40,000 lines of C++ code. The native code library is dynamically loaded by the VM library and implements the native methods in the Java API. Both the VM and the native code libraries have been ported to Win32, Solaris (on SPARC) and Linux (on x86) platforms. In principle, the Aroma VM should be portable to any platform that supports ANSI C++, POSIX or Win32 threads, and POSIX style calls for file and socket I/O. We plan to port the Aroma VM to WinCE-based platforms, and expect that a port to Macintosh OS X when it is available will be straightforward as well.

3.1 Aroma VM Interface

The interface to the Aroma VM provided by the VM library is fairly simple. The VM is usually in one of five states – uninitialized, initialized, ready, running, and paused. The first step after creating an instance of the VM is to initialize the VM. An instance of the VM may be initialized for one of two purposes: to execute a new Java program (agent) or to restore a previously captured execution state. After initialization, methods may be invoked to either specify a class name to execute (in the case of running a new program) or to restore execution state. If restoring execution state, the state information is read from a stream (which may point to memory, disk, or a network connection). At this point, the VM moves into the ready state.

Once the VM is in the ready state, further optional operations may be performed. These include setting resource limits, setting properties within the Java runtime environment, and redirecting console I/O.

The next step is to invoke the run() method of the VM which causes it to start executing the Java code. The VM creates a new native thread for each Java thread present in the VM and each native thread independently starts executing. Once this step is completed, the VM is in the running state.

While in the running state, methods are provided in the VM interface to set resource limits on an executing program, query the resource limits, and to query the current resource consumption. Finally, there are methods that request a state capture. The captured state is written to a stream (which may be in memory, on disk, or over a network). If a state capture operation is requested and successfully completed, the VM enters the paused state. At this point, either the execution can be continued or the VM (and consequently the program) may be terminated.

3.2   Capturing Execution State

Aroma is capable of capturing the execution state of all threads running inside the VM. This state capture may be initiated by either a thread running inside or outside the VM. The former is useful when the agent requests an operation that needs the execution state to be captured. The latter is useful when the system wants the execution state to be captured (for example, to implement forced mobility).

Java VMs have used two different approaches for implementing the multithreading provided by Java. One approach used in the early 1.0 versions of the JDK was to utilize a user-level threads package. The more recent approach has been to map Java threads to independent native operating system threads. Although using a user-level threads package would simplify the task of capturing thread state, we chose the latter approach. Choosing native threads made it simpler to write portable code across multiple platforms. We developed some straightforward thread and IPC abstractions that mapped easily to the Win32 thread model and to the POSIX thread model. This prevented us from having to either develop our own threads package (which would be platform specific and difficult to port) or use an existing threads package (which may or may not be available on different platforms). Also, mapping to native threads allows the VM to take advantage of the presence of multiple CPUs. Therefore, if a VM has two Java threads running (JT_1 and JT_2), then there are two native threads (NT_1 and NT_2) that correspond to JT_1 and JT_2. If the execution state of the VM is captured at this point and restored later (possibly on a new host), then two new native threads will be created (NT_3 and NT_4) to correspond to the two Java threads JT_1 and JT_2.

However, mapping Java threads to native threads complicates the mechanism of capturing the execution state. This is because when one Java thread (or some external thread) requests a state capture, the other concurrently running threads may be in many different states. For example, other Java threads could be blocked trying to enter a monitor, waiting on a condition variable, sleeping, suspended, or executing native code. We wanted to place as few restrictions as possible on when a thread's state may be captured so that we can support capturing execution state at fine levels of granularity. Therefore, the implementation of monitors was carefully designed to accommodate state capture. For example, if a Java thread is blocked trying to enter a monitor, then there is a corresponding native thread that is also blocked on some IPC primitive. If at this point the execution state is captured and restored later (possibly on a different system and of a different architecture), a new native thread must resume in the same blocked state that the original native thread was in when the state was captured. To support this capability, the monitors were designed in such a way that native threads blocked in monitors could be terminated and new native threads could take their "place" in the monitors at a later point in time. As an example, consider a native thread NT_1 on host H_1 that represents a Java thread JT_1. NT_1 could be blocked because JT_1 was trying to enter a monitor. The VM will allow another thread to capture the execution state at such a time and when the state is restored later, a new native thread NT_2 (on possibly a new host H_2) will be created to represent JT_1. Furthermore, NT_2 will continue to be blocked in the monitor in the same state as NT_1.

Another requirement is the need to support multiple platforms. In particular, to support capturing the execution state on one platform (such as Win32) and restoring the state on a different platform (such as Solaris SPARC). The Java bytecode format ensures that the definitions of the classes are platform independent so transferring the code is not an issue. For transferring the execution state, the Aroma VM assumes that the word size is always 32-bits and that the floating-point representations are the same. With these assumptions, the only other major issue is transferring state between little-endian and big-endian systems. The Aroma VM writes a parameter as part of the state information indicating whether the source platform was big- or little-endian. The destination platform is responsible for byte-swapping values in the execution state if necessary.

One limitation is that if any of the Java threads are executing native code (for example, by invoking a native method), then the VM will wait for the threads to finish their native code before initiating the state capture. This limitation is necessary because the VM does not have access to the native code execution stack.

It is important to note that the captured execution state does not include information about local system resources such as open files or network ports. We are working on higher-level services that will allow programs to transparently continue accessing network and disk resources.

3.3 Enforcing Resource Limits

The native code library is responsible for implementing the enforcement of resource limits. The current version is capable of enforcing disk and network limits. The limits may be grouped into three categories: rate limits, quantity limits, and space limits. Rate limits allow the read and write rates of any program to be limited. For example, the disk read rate could be limited to 100 KB/s. Similarly, the network write rate could be limited to 50 KB/s. The rate limits ensure that an agent does not exceed the specified rate for any I/O operations. For example, if a network write rate of 50 KB/s was in effect and a thread tried to write at a higher rate, the thread would be slowed down until it does not exceed the write rate limit.

Quantity limits allow the total bytes read or written to be restricted. For example, the disk write quantity could be limited to 3 MB. Similarly, the network read quantity could be limited to 1 MB. If an agent tried to read or write more data than allowed by the limit, the thread performing the operation would get an IOException.

The last category of limits is the space limit, which applies only to disk space. Again, if an agent tries to use more space than allowed by the disk space limit, then the VM will throw an IOException. Note that the disk space limit is different from the disk write quantity limit. If an agent has written 10 MB of data, it need not be the case that the agent has consumed 10 MB of disk space, since the agent might have written over the same file(s) or erased some of the files that it had written.

To enforce the quantity limits, the native code library maintains four counters for the number of bytes read and written to the network and the disk. For every read or write operation, the library checks whether performing the operation would allow the agent to exceed a limit. If so, the library returns an exception to the agent. Otherwise, the appropriate counter is incremented and the operation is allowed to proceed. To enforce the disk space limit, the library performs a similar computation except that seek operations and file deletions are taken into consideration. Again, if an operation would allow the agent to exceed the disk space limit, the library returns an exception and does not complete the operation.

To enforce the rate limits, the library maintains four additional counters for the number of bytes read and written to the network and the disk and four time variables, which record the time when the first operation was performed. Before an operation is allowed, the library divides the number of bytes by the elapsed time to check if the agent is above the rate limit. If so, the library puts the thread to sleep until such time that the agent is within the rate limit. Then, the library computes how many bytes may be read or written by the agent in a 100ms interval. If the operation requested by the agent is less than what is allowed in a 100ms interval, the library simply completes the operation and returns (after updating the counter). Otherwise, the library divides the operation into sub-operations and performs them in each interval. After an operation is performed, the library sleeps until the interval finishes. For example, if an agent requests a write of 10 KB and the write rate limit was 5 KB/s, then the number of bytes that the agent is allowed to write in a 100ms interval is 512 bytes. Therefore, the library would loop 20 times, each time writing 512 bytes and then sleeping for the remainder of the 100ms interval. One final point to make is that if a rate limit is changed then the counter and the timer are reset. This reset is necessary to make sure that the rate limit is an instantaneous limit as opposed to an average limit.

We are currently evaluating two different implementation schemes for the CPU resource control. The first approach is to have each native thread (that represents a Java thread) check the percentage of CPU used by that thread (by querying the underlying operating system) and then sleep if necessary. The check would be performed periodically after executing a certain number of Java bytecode instructions. The second approach is to have a separate monitoring thread that checks the CPU utilization of all the Java threads and then pauses the Java threads as necessary. In this case, the monitoring thread will be assigned high priority and will wake up periodically to perform its monitoring.

Although we have not started implementing the memory resource control, we expect that it will be fairly straightforward since the VM handles all object instantiations. The VM can maintain a counter variable that keeps track of memory usage and throw an exception (or take other appropriate action) when memory usage is exceeded.

4   Oasis Execution Environment

Oasis is an agent execution environment that embeds the Aroma VM. It is divided into two independent programs: a front-end interaction and administration program and a back-end execution environment. Figure 1 shows the major components of Oasis. The Oasis Console program may be used to interact with agents running within the execution environment. The console program is also used to perform administrative tasks such as creating accounts, setting policies, and changing resource limits. The Oasis process is the execution environment for agents. Among other things, it contains instances of the Aroma VM for running agents, a Policy Manager, a Dispatcher, one or more Protocol Handlers, and a Messaging Handler. Each agent executes in a separate instance of the Aroma VM, and can use multiple threads if desired. However, all the instances of the Aroma VM are inside the same Oasis process, which allows the VM code to be shared.

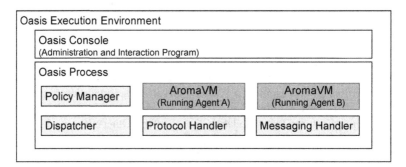

Fig. 1. The Oasis Execution Environment

The policy manager is a major component of the execution environment. It is responsible for establishing security and resource control policies for all agents. Policies address authentication and agent transfer, execution control, access control, and resource usage. As Figure 1 shows, a user or administrator may interact with the Oasis environment through a separate administration process that allows the user to examine and change various resource limits.

Oasis can support multiple protocol handlers. A protocol handler is responsible for transferring the state of an agent from one Oasis to another. The default protocol handler in Oasis implements a custom agent transfer protocol but new protocol handlers can be written to support other (standard) protocols. The default protocol handler is capable of compressing and decompressing agent state information on the fly while an agent is being transferred.

One important design choice was to run each agent within a separate instance of the Aroma VM. Such a design has both advantages and disadvantages. The advantage is that resource accounting and control is simplified. The disadvantage is increased overhead. We are working on the possibility of sharing class definitions between multiple Aroma VMs which should reduce the overhead significantly.

Agents can communicate by sending and receiving messages. Message transfer is implemented by a simple API that provides a sendMsg() and a receiveMsg() functions. Agents are addressed via UUIDs. The messages themselves can contain any serializable Java object. Oasis maintains message queues for each agent. The message queues are maintained outside the Aroma VM instances so that it is easy to handle situations where a message arrives while a VM's state is being captured.

One of the capabilities provided by Oasis is the dynamic adjustment of resource limits of agents. This causes a potential problem for certain kinds of resources when resource limits are lowered below the threshold already consumed by an agent. For example, an agent may have already used 10 MB of disk space and the resource limit might be reduced to 8 MB. The current implementation does not attempt to reclaim the 2 MB of disk space back from the agent. Instead, any future requests for disk space simply fail until the agent's disk usage drops below 8 MB. In the future, we would like to explore a mechanism to notify an agent about the change in resource limits (using a callback function) and allow the agent a fixed amount of time for the agent to comply with the changed limits or perhaps to negotiate some compromise. If the agent does not comply then Oasis has the option of terminating the agent or transmitting the agent back to its home or to some other designated location.

5   Performance

This section describes some initial performance results of NOMADS. The performance measurements are divided into two categories: performance of agent mobility and performance of resource limits. We have not yet collected any data but superficial comparisons indicate that the Aroma VM is significantly slower than Sun's Java VM. Once we have completed implementation of necessary features, we will focus more attention on performance optimization and testing.

5.1   Agent Mobility Performance[3]

We compared the mobility performance of NOMADS with three other Java-based systems including Aglets 1.1b2 [10], Concordia 1.14 [12], and Voyager 3.2 [14]. For each platform, we wrote a simple mobile agent that carried a payload of a specified size. The objective was to measure the round-trip time of each agent (i.e., the time taken for the agent carrying the payload to move from the source host to the destination and return back to the source. In our experiments, the independent variables were the system type and the agent payload size (0, 16 KB, and 64 KB). In the case of NOMADS, an additional independent variable was the compression of agent state information. The dependent variable was the round-trip time for the agent.

---

[3] The design of the mobility performance measurement experiments used here were based on earlier work done in conjunction with other members of the DARPA CoABS program, at Dartmouth College, Boeing, and Lockheed-Martin. In particular, Robert Gray at Dartmouth was instrumental in designing and conducting the original set of mobility experiments.

The equipment used for the experiments were two Pentium III systems operating at 650 MHz with 256 MB RAM each running Windows NT 4.0 with Service Pack 6. The systems were on an isolated 100 Mbps Fast Ethernet network. Aglets, Concordia, and Voyager were all running on JDK 1.2.2. The results are summarized in the table 1 below. The times reported for NOMADS-C are the times for NOMADS with compression enabled for agent transfer. All times are in milliseconds.

The results show that the performance of NOMADS ranges from 1.87 to 3.7 times slower than the other systems. NOMADS is slower because of the additional execution state information that is being transferred. The relative performance of NOMADS is better when the agents are larger (or are carrying a large payload). Another interesting result is the tradeoff between CPU-time and transfer time with and without compression. On a 100 Mbps network, enabling compression actually decreases performance because more time is spent in the compression and decompression phase than the actual transfer phase. We expect the compression feature would be more useful on a slower connection, such as one implemented on a wireless network. Finally, it is also interesting to note that the performance of NOMADS is virtually unchanged irrespective of the payload size. This can be explained by the fact that the size of the payload is insignificant when compared to the size of the agent state (which is several hundred KB).

We expect the performance of NOMADS to improve significantly after optimization. For example, currently, the state information transferred by NOMADS includes all the Java class definitions. We plan to optimize the system by not transferring the class definitions of those classes that are already available on the remote system. We also plan to support capturing the execution state of individual threads or thread groups, which should significantly improve performance.

Table 1. Comparison of Jump Agent Performance

	NOMADS	NOMADS-C	Aglets	Concordia	Voyager
0 KB	333.5	443.8	90.6	138.5	115.6
16 KB	337.4	446.7	100.8	147.7	124.7
64 KB	341.6	448.7	144.8	182.3	169.3

5.2   Resource Control Performance

To report on the performance of resource control in NOMADS, we measured the overhead imposed by the resource control code on the overall performance of I/O operations. We took four different performance measurements:
(a) The Java VM from Sun Microsystems
(b) The Aroma VM with no resource control code
(c) The Aroma VM with resource control code but no resource limit in place
(d) The Aroma VM with resource control code and a very high resource limit in place (i.e., one that will never be exceeded by the agent)

The measurements were taken using an agent that continuously writes data to the network. Two variants of the agent were used, one that wrote the data in 10 KB blocks and the other that wrote the file in 64 KB blocks. In each case, we measured the I/O rate in bytes per millisecond.

The results (summarized in table 2 below) show that the overhead imposed by the resource control code is minimal. Although we have not measured the overhead of the disk resource limits, we expect them to be very similar since the mechanism for enforcing the limits is the same.

Table 2. NOMADS Resource Control Performance Results

	10 KB	64 KB
Java VM	9532	9903
Aroma VM (with no resource control code)	8772	9650
Aroma VM (with code but no limit)	8746	9656
Aroma VM (with code but very high limit)	8702	9655

6   Conclusions

We have described our motivations for developing a mobile agent system that provides strong mobility and safe execution. We have also described the initial design and implementation of the Aroma VM and the Oasis agent execution environment. Initial performance results are promising. The speed of agent transfer using the current unoptimized NOMADS code ranges only from 1.87 to 3.7 times slower than the weak mobility systems evaluated and we have several ideas for significantly increasing performance. The overhead for resource control in our experiment was insignificant.

To date, both the Aroma VM and Oasis have been ported to Windows NT, Solaris (on SPARC), and Linux (on x86). The Aroma VM is currently JDK 1.2 compatible with some limitations and missing features, the major omission being support for AWT and Swing. The AWT implementation affords opportunities for evaluating resource management mechanisms for graphical resources. NOMADS may be downloaded at no cost for educational and research use from http://www.coginst.uwf.edu/nomads.

Work is currently underway on optimizing the transfer of execution state information, capturing execution state of individual threads and thread groups, implementing transparent redirection for both disk and network resources, and resource controls for CPU and memory. We are also working on sophisticated high-level agent management tools [2,3] that build on top of the resource control capabilities of NOMADS.

References

1.   Acharya, A., Ragnganathan, M., & Saltz, J. Sumatra: A language for resource-aware mobile programs. In J. Vitek & C. Tschudin (Ed.), *Mobile Object Systems.* Springer-Verlag.

2. Bradshaw, J. M., Greaves, M., Holmback, H., Jansen, W., Karygiannis, T., Silverman, B., Suri, N., & Wong, A. Agents for the masses: Is it possible to make development of sophisticated agents simple enough to be practical? *IEEE Intelligent Systems*(March-April), 53-63.

3. Bradshaw, J. M., Cranfill, R., Greaves, M., Holmback, H., Jansen, W., Jeffers, R., Karygiannis, T., Kerstetter, M., Suri, N. & Wong, A. Policy-based management of agents and domains, submitted for publication.

4. Czajkowki, G., & von Eicken, T. JRes: A resource accounting interface for Java. *Proceedings of the 1998 ACM OOPSLA Conference*. Vancouver, B.C., Canada.

5. Fünfrocken, S. Transparent migration of Java-based mobile agents: Capturing and reestablishing the state of Java programs. In K. Rothermel & F. Hohl (Ed.), *Mobile Agents: Proceedings of the Second International Workshop (MA 98)*. Springer-Verlag.

6. Gray, R. S. Agent Tcl: A flexible and secure mobile-agent system. *Proceedings of the 1996 Tcl/Tk Workshop,* (pp. 9-23).

7. Hohl, F. The Mobile Agent List. http://ncstrl.informatik.uni-stuttgart.de/ ipvr/vs/projekte/ mole/mal/mal.html.

8. Jordan, M., & Atkinson, M. *Orthogonal persistence for Java—A mid-term report*. Sun Microsystems Laboratories.

9. Lal, M. & Pandey, R. CPU Resource Control for Mobile Programs. *Proceedings of the First International Symposium on Agent Systems and Applications and the Third International Symposium on Mobile Agents (ASA/MA'99)*. IEEE Computer Society Press.

10. Lange, D. B., & Oshima, M. *Programming and Deploying Java Mobile Agents with Aglets*. Reading, MA: Addison-Wesley.

11. Maurer, J. *Porting the Java runtime system to the Ara platform for mobile agents*. Diploma Thesis, University of Kaiserslautern.

12. Mitsubishi. Concordia htttp://www.meitca.com/HSL/Projects/Concordia/ whatsnew.htm.

13. Neuenhofen, K. A., & Thompson, M. Contemplations on a secure marketplace for mobile Java agents. K. P. Sycara & M. Wooldridge (Ed.), *Proceedings of Autonomous Agents 98,* . Minneapolis, MN, , New York: ACM Press.

14. ObjectSpace. ObjectSpace Voyager http://www.objectspace.com/products/voyager.

15. Peine, H., & Stolpmann, T. The architecture of the Ara platform fro mobile agents. In K. Rothernel & R. Popescu-Zeletin (Ed.), *Proceedings of the First International Workshop on Mobile Agents (MA 97)*. Springer-Verlag.

16. Tripathi, A. & Karnik, N. Protected Resource Access for Mobile Agent-based Distributed Computing. In Proceedings of the ICPP Workshop on Wireless Networking and Mobile Computing, Minneapolis, August 1998.

Bytecode Transformation for Portable Thread Migration in Java

Takahiro Sakamoto, Tatsurou Sekiguchi, and Akinori Yonezawa

Department of Information Science, Faculty of Science, University of Tokyo
7-3-1 Hongo, Bunkyo-ku, Tokyo, Japan 113-0033
{takas,cocoa,yonezawa}@is.s.u-tokyo.ac.jp

Abstract. This paper proposes a Java bytecode transformation algorithm for realizing transparent thread migration in a portable and efficient manner. In contrast to previous studies, our approach does not need extended virtual machines nor source code of target programs. The whole state of stack frames is saved, and then restored at a remote site. To accomplish this goal, a type system for Java bytecode is used to correctly determine valid frame variables and valid entries in the operand stack. A target program is transformed based on the type information into a form so that it can perform transparent thread migration. We have also measured execution efficiency of transformed programs and growth in bytecode size, and obtained better results compared to previous studies.

1 Introduction

Mobile computation is a promising programming paradigm for network-oriented applications where running computations roam over the network. Various kinds of applications are proposed such as electric commerce, auction, automatic information retrieval, workflow management and automatic installation.

The ability to preserve execution states on migration is an important criterion of classifying programming languages for mobile computation [,]. Migration is called *transparent* if a mobile application is resumed at the destination site with exactly the same execution state as before [ ]. From the viewpoint of *programming* mobile applications, the notion of transparent migration is especially important since it allows the programmer to write mobile applications in the same way as writing ordinary non-mobile applications. It substantially supports the mobile application programmer to understand program behavior. Early mobile language systems such as Telescript [ ] and Agent Tcl [ ] had a mechanism of transparent migration.

Transparent migration, however, is not adopted in major Java-based mobile language systems (e.g., IBM Aglets [ ] and Voyager [ ]) though Java has been very popular among people who are interested in mobile computation. There is a difficulty in implementing transparent migration in Java. In order to move computation transparently, the call stack needs to be preserved across migration. But the Java security policy forbids Java bytecode itself to manipulate the stack.

D. Kotz and F. Mattern (Eds.): ASA/MA 2000, LNCS 1882, pp. 16– , 2000.
© Springer-Verlag Berlin Heidelberg 2000

Two different approaches have been proposed for realizing transparent migration in Java: extending a Java virtual machine and transforming source code.

Both approaches, however, have their own difficulties. The former approach requires mobile applications to run only on modified virtual machines. This nullifies one of the advantage of Java, which is *ubiquity of common virtual machines*. On the other hand, the latter approach is not applicable when source code is not available. In fact, Java source codes are often unavailable.

In contrast to the two approaches above, our approach can avoid these drawbacks by *bytecode transformation*. In our approach, bytecode instead of source code is transformed into the form that makes transparent migration possible.

Bytecode transformation has several advantages compared to source code transformation. The Java language forces clean programming, where only structured control transfer is allowed. When a method is resumed, we want to transfer the control to a suspended point in the method. A suspended point can be in a compound statement, but the Java language forbids a control transfer into a compound statement. In contrast, there is `goto` instruction in the Java bytecode set. The control can be transferred to any program point in a method if it is allowed by the bytecode verifier. The use of `goto` instruction can reduce the size of inserted code fragments for control transfer, and hopefully it can improve execution efficiency of transformed codes. Actually, as shown later, codes produced by our bytecode transformer show better execution efficiency on JDK 1.2.2 than those produced by a source code transformer [ ].

There are two difficulties in bytecode transformation. (1) Transformed codes must pass a bytecode verifier. (2) It is difficult to know the set of values to be saved and restored. In the bytecode level, values are passed by frame variables and the operand stack. There are neither variable declarations nor scoping rules. To obtain necessary information for bytecode transformation, we had to adopt a type system of Java bytecode [ ], and to devise a static program analyzer on it.

The rest of this paper is organized as follows: Sect.   gives an overview of our mobile agent system. Sect.   describes our implementation scheme for thread migration. Sect.   explains a static program analysis for the bytecode transformation. Sect.   describes our scheme of bytecode transformation for transparent thread migration and gives an example of a transformed bytecode. Sect.   shows some experiments with our current implementation of the bytecode transformation. Sect.   discusses related work. Sect.   concludes this paper.

2   Overview of Our Mobile Agent System

This section gives an overview of our model of mobile computation and our mobile agent system.

The model of mobile computation adopted in our mobile agent system is simple, plain and direct so that it accommodates wide applicable domains. The subject and the unit of mobility in our system are a *thread*. A thread migrates to a remote site, preserving its execution states such as the call stack and a part of the heap image. The thread at the departure site will vanish and an equivalent thread will appear at the destination. In this sense, our model of migration is similar to those of Arachne threads system [ ] and Emerald [ ] rather than major Java-based mobile agent systems.

In our system, a place or a location to which a mobile agent migrates is a *Java virtual machine*. A mobile agent (thread) hops around a group of Java virtual machines.

Basically, a heap image that a migrating thread can refer to is duplicated to the destination. This may cause a serious security flaw because a secret data may be duplicated to a remote site implicitly. Our mobile language system does not provide a protection mechanism for that kind of flaws, but our system can be *combined* with various proposed techniques [,] that prevent security flaws.

Though objects on a heap can be transmitted to a remote site, resources such as files, windows and sockets cannot be. These stationary resources, thus, cause a problem on migration if a mobile agent has references to them. We have two options for dealing with these resources. The first one is to force the programmer to use *transient* references for these stationary resources. A transient reference is automatically nullified on migration. The second one is to use the class library [ ] adapted for mobile environment instead of the default libraries in JDK. This class library shares a common interface with JDK and it enables transparent access of stationary resources. A stationary resource is either accessed remotely by Java RMI or duplicated automatically to a destination on migration.

The bytecode transformation scheme described in this paper can be used in the class loader for mobile code. A class loader fetches class files from both local and remote sites if they are not loaded yet into a Java virtual machine. When a class loader detects a class file not modified yet, our bytecode transformer automatically transforms it at load time into a form in which its execution states can be saved and restored.

3   How to Move a Thread Over the Network

Our basic mechanism of transparent thread migration on Java virtual machines is, in principle, similar to other schemes based on source-code-level transformation [, , , ,]. A thread migration is accomplished by three steps:

- The execution states of a target thread are saved at the departure site into a machine-independent data structure. The thread terminates itself when the migration succeeds.
- The data structure representing the execution states of a target thread and a part of the heap image are transmitted through the network to the destination site.
- A new thread is created at the destination. Equivalent execution states of the target thread are reconstructed for the new thread.

The above whole process is implemented by using only standard mechanisms of Java and Java RMI.

3.1   Saving Execution States

The execution states of a thread consist of those of the methods in execution. The execution states of a method consist of (1) a program counter, (2) valid local (frame) variables, and (3) valid entries in the operand stack. The execution states of the methods are encoded into a data structure. Note that we assume that each method is transformed so that it can save its execution state *when a special exception is thrown*. When a migration is in operation, an exception is thrown. If a method captures the exception, the method stores its execution state to a newly created state object defined for each method, and then it propagates the exception to the caller of the method. This process is repeated until the exception reaches the bottom of the stack.

3.2   Transmitting Execution States

When the exception is captured at the bottom of the call stack, all the state objects are transmitted to the destination site by using Java RMI. All values on the heap that can be reached from the target thread are also transmitted to the destination by a mechanism of Java RMI.

3.3   Restoring Execution States

The execution states of a target thread is reconstructed from the state objects. The call stack is reconstructed by calling the methods in the order in which they were invoked at the departure site. Each method is transformed in advance so that it can restore its execution state from the state object. When a method is called with the state object, it restores the values of the stack frame, and it continues execution from the suspended point.

4   Bytecode Analysis

To transform bytecode for transparent migration, we need information on a set of all *valid* frame variables and entries in the operand stack for each program point. A variable or a slot is valid if a value on it is available for every possible control flow. Types of frame variables and entries in the operand stack are also necessary. In addition, a transformed code must pass a Java bytecode verifier if the original code passes it. To obtain such necessary information on bytecode, we adopt a type system for Java bytecode.

4.1   A Type System for Java Bytecode

Our bytecode transformer exploits exactly the same information for bytecode verification [ ]. We adopt the formulation of bytecode verifier by Stata and Abadi [ ]. It is a type system for a small subset of Java bytecode called JVML0.

If a bytecode is well-typed, it tells that the bytecode is verifiable. A type judgment is written in their type system as follows:

$$F, S, i \vdash P.$$

where P denotes a sequence of instructions that constitutes a method. F is a mapping from a program point to a mapping from a frame variable to a type. S is a mapping from a program point to an ordered sequence of types. Finally i denotes a program point or an address of code. Intuitively, the map $F(i)$ gives a type of a local variable at program point i. The string $S(i)$ gives the types of entries in the operand stack at program point i.

These F and S are useful to our bytecode transformation since they contain typing information about valid local variables and entries in the operand stack, respectively.

When a type judgment $F, S, i \vdash P$ is true, it tells that program P is *verifiable* at program point i. The whole program is verifiable if the program is verifiable for every program point in it. This is denoted by $F, S \vdash P$.

The type reconstruction problem for JVML0 is to find appropriate F and S such that $F, S \vdash P$ is true for given P. It is actually a verification algorithm itself. We have implemented a type reconstruction algorithm for the extended JVML0 to be explained next.

4.2 Extending JVML0 to the Full Set of Java Virtual Machine

Since JVML0 includes only a small subset of the Java virtual machine, we have extended it so that it incorporates the full set of Java virtual machine except bytecode subroutines. In doing so, the following points are important.

Instruction. The Java virtual machine has around 200 instructions. A typing rule is defined for each instruction.

Type. Stata and Abadi's type system has only three kinds of types: an integer type, a reference type and a return address type. We have to add primitive types, and the notions of inheritance and subtyping to reference types. In order to pass a bytecode verifier, our bytecode transformer has to know the most specific type of a value when the value is restored from a state object.

Exception. Since Stata and Abadi's type system lacks the mechanism of throwing and catching exceptions, we have to add a facility of handling exceptions.

5 Bytecode Transformation

This section describes our bytecode transformation algorithm. It takes a method in bytecode and produces a method that has instructions for saving and restoring its execution state. Because the produced bytecode also consists of the standard JVM instructions, the transformed method including the state handling mechanism is compatible with any standard JVM and any JIT compiler.

5.1   Overview of Bytecode Transformation

The transformation algorithm changes the signature of a given method to take a state object as an extra parameter and inserts the following code fragments in the method:

- An exception handler for each method invocation. The occurrence of migration is notified by a special exception. The exception handler is responsible for saving an execution state. The program counter to be saved is known since an exception handler is unique for each suspended point. The set of valid local variables and their types (whether it is a primitive type or a reference type) are found by the bytecode analysis described in Sect.   (from F and S). Even if a migration takes place in a **try** statement with the **finally** clause, the **finally** clause is not executed on migration, because we do not insert a **jsr** instruction to the **finally** clause in the exception handler.
- Instructions for saving valid entries on the operand stack. The contents on the operand stack are defined to be discarded when an exception is thrown, which means that their values cannot be fetched from an exception handler. The basic idea for saving values on the operand stack is to make the copies of them in the extended local variables before the method invocations. The valid entries on the operand stack are found from S.
- Instructions at the head of the method that restore all valid frame variables. When the execution state of a method is restored, a state object is passed to the method in the extended parameter. The inserted code restores all valid frame variables at the suspended point. After restoring the frame variables, the control is transferred to the suspended point.
- Instructions that put a state object as an extra parameter for a method invocation instruction.

5.2   State Class

```
public class STSamplefoo extends javago.StackFrame
  implements java.io.Serializable {
    public int      M_EntryPoint;
    public int[]    ArrayI = new int[1];
    public long[]   ArrayL = new long[2];
    public float[]  ArrayF = new float[3];
    public double[] ArrayD = new double[4];
    public Object[] ArrayA = new Object[5];
}
```

Fig. 1. A state class

Our transformation algorithm defines a state class for each method. An execution state of a method is stored into an instance of the state class. Fig. shows all field variables of a state class, where the array sizes are the maximum numbers of the values of the corresponding type in the execution states. These numbers are found by the bytecode analysis. The type of a value to be saved is either one of the primitive types (`int`, `long`, `float`, and `double`) or a reference type (`Object`).

5.3 Extending Method Frame for Local Variables

The set of the local variables are extended for saving valid entries in the operand stack and some other purposes. The amount of local variables is determined by the information S, which is obtained by the bytecode analyzer, and another eight local variables are used for special purpose in our current implementation of transformation. These reserved frame variables are used to keep the state object for the current method, the state object for the caller of the current method, a special exception that notifies migration, and array references in the current state object (that is `ArrayI`, ..., `ArrayA` in Fig.).

5.4 Example of a Transformed Bytecode

```
public class test {
    public static int foo(int x, int y) {
        int z = x + y;
        may_migrate();
        return z;
    }
}
```

Fig. 2. A toy method that may cause a migration

We illustrate the bytecode transformation by using a toy method in Fig. . This method is compiled into the (pseudo) bytecode listed in the left part in Fig. , and it is transformed into the one listed in the right part. An address with a subscript or a prime denotes an inserted code.

When the **may_migrate** method wants to migrate, the method throws a special exception. The exception handler at line 4' catches the exception and saves the execution states (x, y and z). Then it propagates the exception to the caller method. On resumption, this method is invoked with a state object. It restores the execution state from the state object at line 0_3. The control is transferred to line 2' and then the execution state of the **may_migrate** method will be restored.

5.5 Which Method Should Be Transformed?

Since our bytecode transformer changes the signature of a method, the transformer must modify method invocation instructions accordingly. Some methods, however, preserve their signatures as mentioned in Sect.   . An important question, thus, arises: which method should be transformed? There are two solutions:

```
1: z = x + y;              0₁: if not resumption, jump to 1;
2: call may_migrate;       0₂: tablejump 0₃;
3: return z;               0₃: restore x,y,z; jump to 2';
                           1: z = x + y;
                           2': push state_object;
                           2: call may_migrate;
                           3: return z;
                           4': save x,y,z; throw;
```

Original bytecode.   Transformed bytecode.

Fig. 3. Original and transformed pseudo bytecode for the toy method

annotation by the programmer, and construction of a call graph. In the first solution, methods to be transformed are specified by the programmer. This scheme
is simple and able to realize the programmer's intention correctly, but it cannot
deal with class files written by others. In the second solution, every method that
contains migration instructions is transformed. Besides, every method that *indirectly* invokes migration instructions is also transformed. The second kind of
methods is found by constructing a call graph. Though this scheme can deal with
class files written by others, it requires *all* class files before starting execution.
It is difficult to achieve this requirement in cases that a mobile agent visits some
location for the first time and that two unknown agents meet somewhere.

Our solution is to predesignate the set of methods not to be modified. Our
transformer does not modify system classes and the signatures of callback methods in user code. This scheme does not need annotation nor a call graph, but an
implementor of the transformer must have a good knowledge of system classes.

5.6 Limitations

Our transformation algorithm and its current implementation has some limitations.

First, our current transformer cannot handle programs that may migrate
when a live return address of a subroutine is included in a local variable or
an entry of an operand stack. The reason is that a return address cannot be
saved arbitrarily under the restrictions of Java bytecode verifier. This limitation
matters when a migration occurs in a `finally` clause of a `try` statement.

We are planning to eliminate this limitation in future. The basic idea is to
keep traces of subroutine calls dynamically. The bytecode transformer inserts a
code fragment in subroutines that keeps the set of subroutines in execution and
their invocation order. When the execution state of a method is restored, the
subroutines that were in execution at the departure site are invoked explicitly
by the inserted code fragment. The code in the subroutines that were already
executed is skipped by dynamic checking. Perhaps, this scheme degrades execution performance because many code fragments are inserted that are always

executed, but this scheme lowers code growth in comparison to unfolding and it does not need to extend the exception table.

Second, as is mentioned in Sect.   , we do not transform system classes because they have tight connections with native code. This decision makes migration across callback methods impossible such as the `actionPerformed` and the `finalize`. The transformer preserves the signatures of these callback methods. In the callback methods, a null state object is passed to transformed methods.

Third, our transformation changes the signature of a method in order to pass a state object as an extra parameter. This induces some programs using reflection not to work correctly.

Fourth, our current implementation of transformation removes the line number table attribute of the target method, since debug information is no longer correct after transformation. This implies that it becomes unable to trace the execution of transformed methods with source-code debuggers. This limitation, however, can be easily eliminated by maintaining the line number table.

6   Experiments

This section shows some experiments with our current implementation of byte-code transformer for transparent thread migration. We measured the cost of the transformation process and evaluated the quality of transformed codes produced by our bytecode transformer from the viewpoints of execution efficiency and code size. The transformed codes are compared with (1) those produced by our source code transformer JavaGo [ ] and (2) the original code without transformation.

The implementation is written in Java using only standard libraries in JDK. The size of the source code is around 5000 lines. All the benchmark programs were generated as standalone applications in advance by this transformer.

6.1   Elapsed Time for Bytecode Transformation

Table 1. Elapsed time for bytecode transformation

program	# of methods	analysis(ms)	code insertion(ms)	total (ms)
fib	1	235	79	314
qsort	1	285	81	366
nqueen	1	267	80	347
_201_compress	23	3454	1349	4803

(JDK 1.2.2, Sun UltraSPARC 168MHz)

Table   shows the times consumed by our transformer to analyze and transform all methods of the sample programs, where _201_compress is a benchmark program included in SpecJVM98. These elapsed times are rather small, but our bytecode analyzer needs at least the same costs of bytecode verification.

6.2 Execution Efficiency of Transformed Programs

Table 2. Comparison of execution efficiency

	elapsed time (ms)					
	with JIT			without JIT		
program	original	JavaGo	ours	original	JavaGo	ours
fib(30)	111	263 (+137%)	173 (+56%)	870	2553 (+193%)	1516 (+74%)
qsort(400000)	214	279 (+30%)	248 (+16%)	2072	2856 (+38%)	2597 (+25%)
nqueen(12)	1523	2348 (+54%)	1731 (+14%)	30473	36470 (+20%)	30843 (+1.2%)
_201_compress	33685	61629 (+83%)	40610 (+21%)	365661	713936 (+95%)	433439 (+19%)

(JDK 1.2.2, Intel Celeron(TM) Processor 500MHz)

The elapsed times of transformed programs were measured and compared with those of the original programs. The purpose of this measurement is to identify the overheads induced by inserted code fragments in the original programs. Thus, migration does *not* take place during the execution of the benchmark programs. The results are shown in Table . As a comparison, the elapsed times of the transformed programs by JavaGo, which is a source code level transformer, is also listed in the table.

Most part of the overheads is due to the code fragments for saving the operand stack at suspended points. The overheads of the Fibonacci method is rather high because the method does almost nothing but invokes the method itself recursively. When the contents of a method is so small, the relative overheads of inserted code fragments tend to be high. This tendency is common to migration schemes based on program transformation. Our results, nevertheless, are better than those of JavaGo. In this experiment, the overheads induced by our bytecode transformation are always less than those induced by JavaGo. For quick sort and N-queen programs, the overheads were approximately 15% to the original programs when the applications were executed with Just-In-Time compilation.

6.3 Growth in Bytecode Size of Transformed Programs

Table 3. Comparison of bytecode size

	bytecode size (in bytes)		
program	original	JavaGo	Ours
fib	276	884 (3.2 times)	891 (3.2 times)
qsort	383	1177 (3.1 times)	1253 (3.3 times)
nqueen	393	1146 (2.9 times)	976 (2.5 times)
_201_compress	13895	22029 (1.6 times)	18171 (1.3 times)

The growth in bytecode size due to our bytecode transformation is shown in Table . To show the pure growth in the method body size, these sizes do not include that of the state classes. The growth rates for these programs are approximately three times. We think that these results would be the worst case because the relative amount of inserted code fragments tend to be high when an original method is small.

The size of bytecode produced by our transformation scheme is very similar to the size of bytecode produced by JavaGo scheme. But their characteristics are quite different each other. In case of JavaGo, the size of transformed bytecode is proportional to square of the deepest depth of loops. In contrast, the size of bytecode transformed by our transformation scheme is proportional to the number of suspended points.

7   Related Work

Telescript [ ] was an early interpreted programming language for mobile agents developed by General Magic Inc. The Telescript interpreter had a mechanism for transparent migration. Unfortunately, General Magic does not seem to develop Telescript anymore. Agent Tcl [ ] was also a mobile language system developed in the early stage of mobile computation. Agent Tcl also has a mechanism for transparent migration. It is useful to run existing Tcl scripts on a mobile environment.

However, this emphasis on transparent migration was not inherited by major Java-based mobile language systems because of the restrictions imposed by the Java virtual machine release policy. Shudo avoided the restrictions by extending a Java virtual machine and implemented a transparent thread migration system [ ]. Fünfrocken [ ] pointed out that an exception handling mechanism could be used for notifying occurrence of migration with low costs. He developed a scheme of transparent migration for standard Java, but his scheme had difficulties in resumption of control in a compound statement. Sekiguchi et al. eliminated these difficulties based on the idea of unfolding and developed a transparent migration system [ ] in Java. Their scheme enables transparent migration on any standard Java virtual machine with Java RMI. But it requires all Java source code that constitutes a mobile program. In Java, programs are always distributed in the form of bytecode, and source code may be unavailable.

Eddy Truyen et al. [ ] developed independently a Java bytecode transformer for transparent migration, which shares a large part with ours. Both perform bytecode verification to determine all valid values in a frame and insert code fragments in the target bytecode based on the analysis. The major difference between their scheme and ours is execution efficiency. They use `return` and `if` instructions to roll back the stack during saving state, while we use the mechanism of exception. The former scheme significantly degrades the efficiency. Taga measured execution overheads of that scheme [ ] (although it was performed in C++) and reports that the additional overheads are 27% – 137% of the original execution time compared to our scheme. In addition, their scheme uses a data area proper to a thread to pass state objects. Their scheme, therefore, can preserve the signature of transformed methods, but it also induces considerable performance loss. Truyen discusses execution efficiency and growth in bytecode size in a formal setting, while we measured with real applications.

8   Conclusion and Future Work

We have proposed a scheme for bytecode transformation that enables Java programs to save and restore their execution states including the call stack with low overheads. A bytecode transformer based on our scheme has actually been implemented. The transformer gives Java programs the ability of transparent migration. As is described in Sect. , the quality of the bytecode transformer is measured and we have obtained better results compared to existing schemes for transparent migration based on source code transformation. The latest implementation of the transformer described in this paper is widely available at http://www.yl.is.s.u-tokyo.ac.jp/amo/.

Further work is needed to eliminate the limitations mentioned in Sect.   due to bytecode subroutines. More programs can be transformed if these limitations are removed.

Acknowledgment

The authors would like to express our sincere thanks to Hidehiko Masuhara who contributed to much of the presentation of this paper.

References

1. Hirotake Abe, Yuuji Ichisugi, and Kazuhiko Kato. An Implementation Scheme of Mobile Threads with a Source Code Translation Technique in Java. In *Proceedings of Summer United Workshops on Parallel, Distributed and Cooperative Processing*, July 1999. (in Japanese).
2. Boris Bokowski and Jan Vitek. Confined Types. In *Intercontinental Workshop on Aliasing in Object-Oriented Systems in Association with ECOOP Conference*, 1999.
3. Luca Cardelli. Mobile Computation. In *Mobile Object System: Towards the Programmable Internet*, volume 1222 of *LNCS*, pages 3–6. Springer-Verlag, April 1997.
4. Gianpaolo Cugola, Carlo Ghezzi, Gian Pietro Picco, and Giovanni Vigna. Analyzing Mobile Code Languages. In *Mobile Object System: Towards the Programmable Internet*, volume 1222 of *LNCS*, pages 93–109, April 1996.
5. Bozhidar Dimitrov and Vernon Rego. Arachne: A Portable Threads System Supporting Migrant Threads on Heterogeneous Network Farms. In *Proceedings of IEEE Parallel and Distributed Systems*, volume 9(5), pages 459–469, 1998.
6. Stefan Fünfrocken. Transparent Migration of Java-Based Mobile Agents. In *MA '98 Mobile Agents*, volume 1477 of *LNCS*, pages 26–37. Springer-Verlag, 1998.   ,
7. Robert S. Gray. Agent Tcl: A Transportable Agent System. In *Proceedings of the CIKM Workshop on Intelligent Information Agents, Fourth International Conference on Information and Knowledge Management*, 1995.   ,
8. White J. E. *Telescript Technology: Mobile Agents*. White Paper. General Magic, Inc, 1996.   ,
9. Danny Lange and Mitsuru Oshima. *Programming and Deploying Java Mobile Agents with Aglets*. Addison-Wesley, 1998.

10. Tim Lindholm and Frank Yellin. *The Java Virtual Machine Specification Second Edition*. Addison-Wesley, 1999.
11. Andrew C. Myers. JFlow: Practical Mostly-Static Information Flow Control. In *Proceedings of the 26th ACM SIGPLAN-SIGACT on Principles of Programming Languages*, pages 228–241, January 1999.
12. Voyager Core Package Technical Overview, 1997. ObjectSpace Inc.
13. Tatsurou Sekiguchi, Hidehiko Masuhara, and Akinori Yonezawa. A Simple Extension of Java Language for Controllable Transparent Migration and its Portable Implementation. In *Coordination Languages and Models*, volume 1594 of *LNCS*, pages 211–226. Springer-Verlag, April 1999.   ,   ,   ,
14. Kazuyuki Shudo. Thread Migration on Java Environment. Master's thesis, University of Waseda, 1997.
15. Raymie Stata and Martín Abadi. A Type System for Java Bytecode Subroutines. SRC Research Report 158, Digital Systems Research Center, June 1998.   ,
16. B. Steensgaard and E. Jul. Object and Native Code Thread Mobility among Heterogeneous Computers. In *Proceedings of the ACM Symposium on Operating Systems Principles*, pages 68–78, 1995.
17. Volker Strumpen and Balkrishna Ramkumar. Portable Checkpointing for Heterogeneous Architectures. In *Fault-Tolerant Parallel and Distributed Systems*, chapter 4, pages 73–92. Kluwer Academic Press, 1998.
18. Nayuta Taga, Tatsurou Sekiguchi, and Akinori Yonezawa. An Extension of C++ that Supports Thread Migration with Little Loss of Normal Execution Efficiency. In *Proceedings of Summer United Workshops on Parallel, Distributed and Cooperative Processing*, July 1999. (in Japanese).   ,
19. Eddy Truyen, Bert Robben, Bart Vanhaute, Tim Coninx, Wouter Joosen and Pierre Verbaeten Portable Support for Transparent Thread Migration in Java. To appear in ASA/MA 2000.
20. Hiroshi Yamauchi, Hidehiko Masuhara, Daisuke Hoshina, Tatsurou Sekiguchi, and Akinori Yonezawa. Wrapping Class Libraries for Migration-Transparent Resource Access by Using Compile-Time Reflection. to appear in Proceedings of Workshop on Reflective Middleware, 2000. April.

Portable Support for Transparent Thread Migration in Java

Eddy Truyen[*], Bert Robben, Bart Vanhaute, Tim Coninx, Wouter Joosen
and Pierre Verbaeten

Departement Computerwetenschappen, K.U.Leuven
Celestijnenlaan 200A, B-3001 Heverlee, Belgium
{eddy, bartvh}@cs.kuleuven.ac.be
http://www.cs.kuleuven.ac.be/~xenoops/CORRELATE/

Abstract. In this paper, we present a mechanism to capture and reestablish the state of Java threads. We achieve this by extracting a thread's execution state from the application code that is executing in this thread. This thread serialization mechanism is implemented by instrumenting the original application code at the byte code level, without modifying the Java Virtual Machine. We describe this thread serialization technique in the context of middleware support for mobile agent technology. We present a simple execution model for agents that guarantees correct thread migration semantics when moving an agent to another location. Our thread serialization mechanism is however generally applicable in other domains as well, such as load balancing and checkpointing.

1   Introduction

Mobile agent technology is promoted as an emerging technology that makes it much easier to design, implement and maintain distributed systems. Adding mobility to the object-oriented paradigm creates new opportunities to reduce network traffic, overcome network latency and eventually construct more robust programs. Mobile agents are active, autonomous objects or object clusters, which are able to move between distributed locations (e.g. hosts, web servers, etc…) during their lifetime.

Java has been put forward as the platform for developing mobile applications. There are various features of Java that triggered this evolution. First, in a large number of application domains, Java's machine-independent byte code has solved a long-lasting problem known to agent-based systems, namely the fact that agents must be able to run on *heterogeneous* platforms. A Java program is compiled into portable byte code that can execute on any system, as long as a Java Virtual Machine (JVM) is installed on that system. Nowadays, JVM's are running on systems with different

---

[*] This research was supported by a grant from the Flemish Institute for the advancement of scientific-technological research in industry (IWT).

D. Kotz and F. Mattern (Eds.): ASA/MA 2000, LNCS 1882, pp. 29–43, 2000.

hardware and system software characteristics (ranging from off-the-shelf PC's to Smart Cards). Second, byte code is easily transportable over the net and can be downloaded whenever necessary by means of the customizable Java class loading mechanism [1]. This flattens the way for supporting *code mobility*. Third, Sun's powerful serialization mechanism allows migrating transparently data state of Java objects (i.e. the contents of instance variables), making *object state mobility* possible. Fourth, Java offers security concepts, allowing construction of secure agent execution environments [2].

Unfortunately, Java is not designed as an agent-based system programming language and therefore most agent-related functionality has to be added. Current research tackles this problem by offering this functionality in the form of *middleware support* for mobile agents. Conventional middleware technologies offer communication mechanisms and a programming model to application programmers for developing distributed applications. In order to support agent-based applications, such conventional middleware functionality is extended with mobile object semantics (e.g. semantics concerning the location of an object, etc.), mechanisms for migration of agents, infrastructure for receiving arriving agents, resource management, execution support, security etc. [3, 4]. In the past, research groups and companies have built various mobile agent systems, fully implemented in Java [2,5].

1.1   Problem Statement: Transparent Thread Migration in Java

Migration is a mechanism to continue the current execution of an agent at another location in the distributed system. To migrate an agent, some state information of the agent has to be saved and shipped to the new destination. At the target destination, the state of the agent is reestablished and finally the execution of the agent is rescheduled.

From the technical view, an agent consists of an object or a cluster of objects. In Java, each object consists of the following states:

- Program state: this is the byte code of the object's class.
- Data state: the contents of the instance variables of the object.
- Execution state: a Java object executes in one or more *JVM threads*. Each JVM thread has its own *program counter register* (pc register) and has a private *Java stack*. The Java stack is equivalent to the stack of conventional languages. A Java stack stores *frames*. A new frame is created each time a Java method is invoked. A frame is destroyed when its method completes. Each frame holds local variables and an operand stack for storing partial results and passing arguments to methods and receiving return values [6].

In order to migrate a thread, its execution must be suspended and its Java stack and program counter must be captured in a serializable format that is then send to the target location. At the target location, the stack must be reestablished and the program counter must be set to the old code position. Finally the thread must be rescheduled for execution. If migration exhibits this property it is called *transparent* or *strong* migration. If the programmer has to provide explicit code to read and reestablish the state of an agent, migration is called *non-transparent* or characterized as weak migration [7].

Although code migration and data migration is strongly supported in Java, thread migration is completely not supported by current Java technology. JVM threads are not implemented as serializable. Furthermore, the Java language does not define any abstractions for capturing and reestablishing the thread state information inside the JVM. Due to these technical obstructions, recent state-of-the art middleware support for Java-based mobile agents such as Mole is not able to provide agent applications with transparent thread migration. Weak thread migration is supported, but burdens the programmer with manually encoding the 'logical' execution state of an agent into the agent's data state [2].

1.2 Byte Code Rewriting of Application Code

We implemented a thread serialization mechanism by extracting the state of a running thread from the application code that is running in that thread. To achieve this, we developed a byte code transformer that instruments the application code by inserting code blocks that do the actual capturing and reestablishing of the current thread's state. We implemented this transformer using the byte code rewriting tool JavaClass[8], that offers a programming interface for byte code reengineering.

Our system makes it possible that running threads can be saved at any execution point, even at difficult points such as in the middle of evaluating an expression, or during the construction of an object. The implemented mechanism is fully implemented at the code level. As such, it does not require changes to the JVM.

We now give an overview of the remainder of this paper. In the next section we give an overview of our approach in the context of mobile agents. In section 3, we describe the implementation of how a thread's execution state can be captured and later reestablished. In the following two sections we give a quantitative analysis of our thread serialization mechanism and we discuss related work with regard to this. In section 6, we describe how our thread serialization mechanism can be used in other domains such as load balancing. In section 7, we describe the implementation status of the prototype and raise some final issues related to the subject of this paper. Finally, we conclude.

2   Overview of Our Approach

In this section we give a high-level overview of how our thread serialization mechanism is used for migrating mobile agents. We present a simple execution model for agents that guarantees correct thread migration semantics when moving an agent to another location.

2.1 Execution Model for Agents

In order to allow easy migration, a suitable model for executing agents must be deployed in the middleware layer of the agent system. Figure 1 gives an overview of this execution model [9]. We offer a complement to JVM threads at a higher abstraction level, namely *tasks*. A task is a higher-level construct for executing a computation (i.e. a sequence of instructions) concurrently with other computations. A task encapsulates a JVM thread that is used for executing that task. As such, a task's execution state is the execution state of a JVM thread in which the task is running.

An agent is implemented as a cluster of Java objects that cooperate together to implement its expected functionality. For executing its program, an agent owns a task that is exclusively used for that agent. This gives an important property to agents, namely that they are self-contained. They do not share any execution state. When migrating the agent its task is migrated with it, without impacting the execution of other agents. In principle, an agent may encapsulate multiple tasks in more intelligent execution schemes (e.g. a mobile agent that has one main task and several helper tasks).

A so-called `TaskScheduler` schedules the execution of tasks. The task scheduler controls what task is to execute next. As such, we can experiment with different scheduling policies, tailored to a specific application domain. When the scheduler starts a task, the task is assigned a JVM thread for executing itself. In principle, the execution model allows creating a new thread for each task, let the different threads run concurrently and rely on the efficient JVM implementation for context switching support.

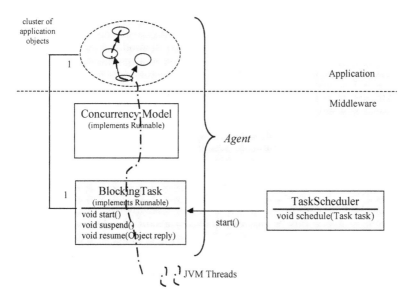

Fig. 1. Execution Model for Agents

It is important to realize that this execution model is transparently enforced upon the mobile agent application by the middleware layer. For example, the enforcement of synchronization constraints inherent to concurrent execution should ideally be realized within the middleware layer of the agent system. Tasks support this, since they are programmable entities: system developers (who build middleware) implement specialized tasks that offer primitives useful for constructing various powerful concurrency models with built-in support for specific synchronization mechanisms. For example in Figure 1, a `BlockingTask` is a specialized task derived from the base class `Task` that is used for implementing a concurrency model supporting synchronous invocation semantics between agents.

2.2   Serializable Tasks

A task is serializable at any execution point, making transparent thread migration possible. In opposition to the Java object serialization mechanism, task (de)serialization is not automatic but must be initiated by calling two special primitives, which are each defined as a method on `Task`. These primitives are meant for requesting capturing and reestablishment of a task's execution state. We illustrate the use of these primitives in the context of a migration scenario of an agent:

- `public void capture()`. This method must be called whenever the current executing task must be suspended and its execution state must be captured in a serializable format. For example, an agent that wants to migrate invokes this method (indirectly) on its task. After state capturing is finished, a migrator middleware component migrates the agent together with its serialized task to the target location. Notice that our task serialization mechanism requires that state capturing must be initiated within the execution of the task that is to be migrated.
- `public void resume()`. Invoking this method on a `Task` object, will reschedule the task with the task scheduler. When the task scheduler restarts the task (by calling `start()` on it), the execution state of the task is first reestablished before resuming execution. In the migration example, this method will be called by the peer migrator middleware component at the target location after it receives the migrating agent.

As a consequence, tasks are not serializable at each moment, but only after the execution state capturing process is finished and before the execution state reestablishment process is started.

Each task is associated with a separate `Context` object into which its thread execution state is captured, and from which its execution state is later reestablished. This context object can be serialized by means of the Java object serialization mechanism. To capture and reestablish a task's thread state, byte code instructions are inserted into the code of the encapsulating agent. These instructions capture the current Java stack and the last executed instruction (i.e. program counter index) into the task's context. Obviously, byte code instructions are also inserted that reestablish the original stack from the context and jump to the instruction where execution was suspended. The next section discusses this in detail.

3   Implementation of Thread Serialization

Each task is associated with a number of boolean flags that represent a specific execution mode of the task. A task can be in three different modes of execution:

- Running: the task is normally executing.
- Capturing: the task is in the process of capturing its current execution state into its context. When the task is in this mode, its flag isCapturing is set.
- Restoring: the task is in the process of reestablishing its previous execution state from its context. When the task is in this mode, its flag isRestoring is set.

In the rest of this section, we describe respectively the mechanisms behind the state capturing and reestablishing process. Finally we shortly describe the implementation of the byte code transformer itself.

3.1   Capturing Execution State

Whenever an agent wants to migrate, it calls indirectly on its task the operation capture() that suspends the execution of the agent and initiates the state capturing process by setting the flag isCapturing.

```
public void capture() {
    Context currentContext = getContext(Thread.currentThread());
     if (currentContext.isRestoring) {
       currentContext.isRestoring = false;
    } else   {
       currentContext.isCapturing = true;
       currentContext.pushThis(this);
    }
}
```

Fig. 2. Starting Capturing and Finishing Reestablishment

Since the execution state of an ongoing task is a sequence of stack frames located in the method call stack of the task's JVM thread, we traverse that stack and do state capturing for each stack frame. This is realized by subsequently suspending the execution of each method on the stack after the *last performed invoke-instruction (LPI)* executed by that method, and starting with the top frame's method.[1]

Figure 3 illustrates how this works. In this example, the method computeSerial() is the top frame's method. When control returns from capture(), a state capturing code block for the top frame is first executed. The frame is then discarded by suspending the execution of its corresponding method (i.e. computeSerial()) through an inserted return instruction, initiating the state

---

[1] The top frame is also called current frame [6] and corresponds with the method that invokes capture() - the current method.

capturing process for the previous frame on the stack (i.e. `myMethod()`). The same process is then recursively repeated for each frame on the stack.

For each method on the stack, we save the corresponding stack frame in the state it was before executing the method's LPI. An *artificial program counter* is also stored in the task's context. This is a cardinal index that refers to the LPI.

Our byte code transformer inserts a state capturing code block after every invoke-instruction occurring in the application code. These are all the code positions in a method `myMethod()` where control may be transferred back to, after the capturing of the called method `computeSerial()` is finished.

```
public class A {
   private B b = new B(..);
   public void myMethod() {        calling method
      int l = 0;
      java.util.Date today = ...;
      Vector v = new Vector();
      if (...) {
         boolean test = false;
         ...
      }
LPI →  int k = 5 * b.computeSerial(today);
      }
      ...
   }
}

public class B {
   ....

   public int computeSerial(Date date) {    top frame's method
      .....
LPI →  currentTask.capture();
      .....
      return ...;
   }
}
```

if isCapturing() {
store stackframe into context
store artificial PC as LPI-index
return;
}

go to previous stack frame

if isCapturing() {
store stackframe into context
store artificial PC as LPI-index
return;
}

Fig. 3. State Capturing

3.2 Reestablishing Execution State

Calling the operation `resume()` upon a suspended `Task` object reschedules this task with the task scheduler. Actual reestablishment of the task's execution state is however initiated when the task scheduler restarts the task. To reestablish the execution state, we just call again all the relevant methods in the order they have been on the stack when the state capturing took place. Figure 4 illustrates this for the same example as in section 3.1.

Our transformer inserts additional code in the beginning of each method body. This inserted code consists of several state reestablishing code blocks, one for each code position where the previous execution of the method may have been suspended; these code positions are the invoke-instructions that occur in the method body. In a switch instruction the appropriate state reestablishing code block is selected based on the stored LPI-index of the method. The chosen code block then restores the method's frame to its original state and restores the method's pc register by jumping to the method's LPI, skipping the already executed instructions. Executing its LPI initiates the reestablishing process of the next stack frame. Finally, during reestablishment of the top stack frame, the operation `capture()` is invoked by our inserted code for a second time. Now, this operation sets the `isRestoring` flag back to false, finishing the reestablishing process (see Figure 2).

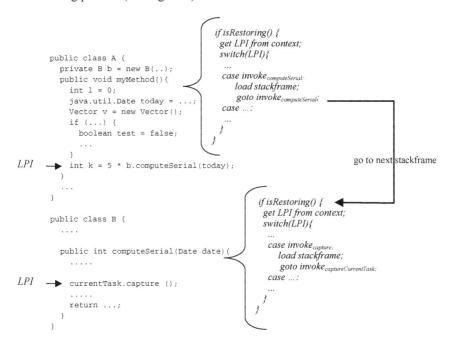

Fig. 4. State Reestablishment

3.3   Implementation of Transformer

In order to generate the correct state capturing and reestablishing code block for a invoke-instruction occurring in a method, we first need to know what's on the method's stack frame before that invoke-instruction is executed. That is, we need to analyze the type of the local variables visible in the scope of the instruction and the type of the values that are on the operand stack before the instruction is executed. This analysis is rather complex, since type information is not anymore explicitly represented in the byte codes of the method. The implementation of this analysis is based on a type inference process that is similar to the one used in the Java byte code verifier, as described in the Java Virtual Machine specification [6].

After the type inference analysis completes, our transformer starts rewriting the original application code method per method. Each method is rewritten invoke-instruction per invoke-instruction. Our transformer distinguishes between instance method invocations, static method invocations, super-calls and constructor invocation. For example, Figure 5 shows the information captured and reestablished when the method's LPI is an instance method invocation (`invokevirtual`).

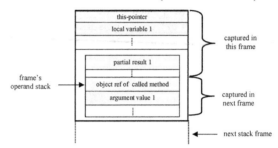

Fig. 5. Stack Frame before Invoking an Instance Method

4   Quantitative Analysis

Instrumenting and inserting code introduces time and space overhead. Since code is inserted for each invoke-instruction that occurs in the program, the space overhead is directly proportional to the total number of invoke-instructions that occur in the agent's application code. Note that JDK method calls are not instrumented (see section 7.2).

Per invoke-instruction, the number of additional byte code instructions is a function of the number of local variables in the scope of that instruction (L), the number of values that are on the operand stack before executing the instruction (V) and the number of arguments expected by the method to be invoked (A). Table 1 shows per invoke-instruction the file space penalty in terms of the number of additional byte code instructions.

Table 1. Space and Time Overheads

L	V	A	File space penalty + 2c (c<1) (max/avg #instr)	Overhead normal execution (# instr)	Duration capturing frame (# instr / avg. time)	Duration reestablishing frame (# instr/ avg. time)
0	0	0	14 / 14	4	71 / ≤0.001 ms	45 / ≤0.001 ms
1	0	0	19 / 18	4	105 / ≤0.001 ms	68 / ≤0.001 ms
0	1	0	17 / 16	4	104 / ≤0.001 ms	67 / ≤0.001 ms
0	0	1	15 / 15	4	71 / ≤0.001 ms	46 / ≤0.001 ms
5	1	2	44 / 41	4	274 / 0.002 ms	184 / ≤0.002 ms
3	3	3	41 / 38	4	272 / 0.002 ms	183 / ≤0.002 ms
5	5	5	59 / 54	4	406 / 0.007 ms	275 / 0.004 ms

The last three columns of the table show respectively the run-time overhead per invoke-instruction during normal execution and the overheads of the capturing and reestablishment of one stack frame. These run-time overheads are expressed as the number of additional byte code instructions executed, and as an average time measurement (expressed in milliseconds). Notice that run-time overhead during normal execution is constant per invoke-instruction.

To summarize, we give a more formal analysis of the different overheads (in terms of additional inserted byte code instructions):

- Maximum file space penalty = 14 +5L + 3V + A + 2c (c <1)
- Runtime overhead during normal execution = 4
- Maximum duration capturing frame = 71 + 34L + 33V
- Maximum duration reestablishing frame = 45 + 23L + 22V + A

In practice, file space penalty and run-time overhead is proportional to the number of nested method invocations. This is of course completely dependent on the complexity of the application under consideration. Table 2 shows experimental time and file space measurements for two sample programs. File space penalty is relatively high for these examples. This is because these sample programs are characterized by a high ratio between the number of invoke-instructions and the total number of byte code instructions. However in more 'normal' software development, we experienced for two in-house developed applications an average byte code blow-up factor of 30% and 37%.

Table 2. Experimental Data

	Overhead normal execution	*File space penalty*
Factorial(100)	28.8 ms – 28.4 ms: 1.5 %	1031KB – 498 KB: 107%
Fibonnaci(30)	430 ms – 340 ms: 27 %	1018KB – 494KB: 106%

All the above run-time tests were performed on a Pentium II 350 MHz, 64 Mbytes, Linux, Blackdown JDK1.2.2, JIT enabled.

Data overhead per captured stack frame is small since this consists of an integer index pointing to the last performed invoke-instruction (LPI), and the associated object reference in case of an instance method invocation.

5   Related Work

There are systems [11,12,13] that provide the required state capturing of Java programs. However they modified the Java VM. The big disadvantage of these systems is that the implemented support is not portable across existing Java platforms. We found that it is possible to capture execution state efficiently at the application code level, without requiring a modification of the JVM. This makes our thread serialization mechanism portable across standard Java platforms

Researchers at TU Darmstadt [7] have implemented a thread serialization mechanism that takes the same approach as we do. However, this is done by preprocessing the *source code* of the application, which is rather limited compared with byte code transformation. First, with source code transformation, it is not possible to extract the complete execution state of a running thread. It is for example not possible to inspect the values that are on the operand stack of the current executing method. Secondly, our thread serialization mechanism is more efficient in terms of space and time overhead, due to the higher precise control offered at the byte code level. For example, in [7] one reports a worst-case byte code blow-up factor of 470%, while we experienced a worst-case blow-up factor of 107% for a similar sample program. This difference in efficiency is because the low-level byte code instructions make it much easier to manipulate the control flow in a program. For example, to prevent re-execution of already executed method code during reestablishment we skip the already executed code with a simple `goto` instruction. This instruction is however not available at the source code level: in [7] one introduces instead a not small number of if-statements to organize the skipping of already executed code. Although this can be optimized using an unfolding technique [14], the general claim of improved efficiency with byte code transformations remains. Third, byte code transformation provides us with more flexibility. For example, with byte code transformations it is allowed to insert reestablishing code before the execution of the default super-call within a constructor, while this is not allowed at the source code level. Finally, several practical benefits arise from the use of byte code transformations: load-time modification and instrumentation of third party libraries (of which the source code is not a priori available) is possible at the byte code level, while it is not at the source code level.

The existing approaches that perform instrumentation at the source code level [7, 14] have used the exception throwing facility to capture execution state. We have chosen not to use the exception mechanism, since entries on the operand stack are discarded when an exception is thrown, which means that their values cannot be captured from an exception handler.

6   Thread Migration Initiated by an External Control Instance

Until now we have only illustrated a migration scenario, where migration is initiated by an agent itself. Another scenario is where migration of an agent is initiated by an external control instance such as a load balancer component.

Our current thread serialization implementation is more difficult to use for such systems. Remember that state capturing of a task can only be initiated within the execution of that task itself. This makes it difficult for the external control instance to initiate the state capturing process of another agent's task. This deficiency may be solved by associating with each task an additional fourth boolean flag, that signals an external thread serialization request when set to true. An additional byte code instruction that checks the value of this flag must then also be inserted after each candidate LPI.

Currently, we follow another working approach in stead that consists of using a more restricted variant of the agent execution model (see section 2.1). This rigid execution model requires that on each point of time only one task is running while all other active tasks in the application are temporarily suspended and captured in a serializable format.

As stated a general requirement for the agent execution model in section 2.1, also this variant execution model must transparently be enforced upon the application by a dedicated middleware implementation, relieving the agent programmer from any responsibility in complying with this variant execution model. This middleware implementation is based on an in-house developed meta-level architecture called Correlate with a generic Meta-Object Protocol (MOP) for run-time reflection [9]. Here, the middleware implementation is deployed at the meta-level, while the application logic of the agents resides at the base-level.

Not only task scheduling but also context switching is now controlled at the meta-level, without relying on the preemptive scheduling support of the JVM at all. There is only one JVM thread running in the system. All tasks are scheduled within this JVM thread by the task scheduler. To achieve context switching between tasks, we use our thread state capturing mechanism. That is, at each meta-level interception point (i.e. when meta-level logic takes control over base-level logic), we suspend and capture the currently executing agent and let the task scheduler decide which task is to be executed next, always using the one existing JVM thread. The Correlate MOP guarantees that all this happens transparently to the application logic and thus puts no responsibility on the agent programmer to call `capture()` for each separate interception point.

As such, the Correlate MOP allows us to implement at the meta-level an *automated* and *coordinated multitasking* scheme that satisfies the variant execution model. The external control instance is now implemented as a meta-level component. Whenever the external control instance is executing, it can safely assume that all other active tasks are a priori suspended in a serializable form. Although time-inefficient, this approach avoids polling of the external control instance to discover when an agent's task is ready for migration. We demonstrated a load balancing application using this variant execution model at OOPSLA'99 [10].

7   Discussion

In this section we discuss relevant issues that relate to the subject of this paper and we describe the implementation status of our current prototype.

7.1   A Classloader for Mobile Code

Since we perform a byte code level transformation, our thread serialization mechanism requires that all methods that might initiate state capturing must be transformed. Since mobile agent applications are in general of very dynamic nature, it is often not possible to predict on advance which classes need to be transformed and which classes not. This problem can be handled by deferring transformation until run-time. In Java, this can easily be realized by implementing a custom classloader for mobile code that automatically performs the transformation. In this regard, the overhead induced by the transformation process – which is not small for the current implementation - becomes a relevant performance factor.

7.2   Transforming the Java API Libraries

Since a mobile agent – like any Java program – may use the JDK libraries, the question arises whether it is necessary to transform these standard provided libraries too. From a technical point of view, this is only a problem when a library call causes a native method to be placed on the thread stack. We cannot handle this case, since we extract thread execution state at the byte code level.

In our current prototype we chose however not to transform the JDK libraries at all (nor the JDK method calls that happen from within the application code). In most cases this is indeed not necessary, since library calls do not initiate state saving by themselves. The exceptions to this are library calls that result in a callback to the application code [7]. For example when the agent programmer uses the Observer pattern with graphical packages such as Swing, callbacks occur. We believe however that using callbacks is a dangerous programming style for agents, since it may violate the thread encapsulation principle (see section 2.1).

7.3   Implementation Status of Current Prototype

An interesting problem with state capturing arises when so-called *non-initialized* values are on the stack. These values cannot be saved. This problem occurs when suspending the execution during the evaluation of the arguments for a constructor operation. In this case, a non-initialized object reference was earlier pushed on the operand stack by the byte code instruction `new`. Our transformer deals with this problem by taking the code block that computes the argument values, moving it before the `new` instruction and storing these values in temporal local variables. These temporal variables are then used for retrieving the argument values when invoking the constructor.

Although possible, we have not yet implemented state capturing during the execution of an exception handler. The major difficulty here is dealing with the `finally` statement of a `try` clause.

A third, more pragmatic issue is that our byte code transformer currently throws away all debugging information associated with a Java class. This affects of course the ability to debug a transformed class with the source-code debugger.

8   Conclusion

In this paper, we presented a portable mechanism for thread serialization in Java, enabling transparent migration of mobile agents. This mechanism is realized by capturing a thread's execution state at the byte code level. The implemented prototype is more efficient then similar approaches that extract thread state at the source code level. This prototype has been used at an OOPSLA'99 demonstration [10].

Acknowledgements

We would like to thank Erik Van Hoeymissen for his work on applying the thread serialization mechanism in the domain of load balancing. We also wish to thank Bo Nørregaard Jørgensen for the many fruitful discussions. Finally, we would like to express our appreciation to Danny Lange, Mitsuru Oshima and the anonymous reviewers for their useful suggestions to improve this paper.

References

1. S. Liang and G. Bracha. Dynamic Class Loading in the Java Virtual Machine. In Proceedings of the Conference on Object-Oriented Programming, Systems, Languages and Applications (OOPSLA'98), pp. 36-44, 1998.
2. M. Straßer, J. Baumann and F. Hohl. Mole - A Java based Mobile Agent System. In *M. Mühlhäuser: (ed.), Special Issues in Object Oriented Programming*, pp. 301-308, 1997.
3. Y. Berbers, B. De Decker, W. Joosen. Infrastructure for mobile agents. In Proceedings of the Seventh ACM SIGOPS European Workshop: System Support for Worldwide Applications, pp. 173-180, 1996.
4. S. Fünfrocken. Integrating Java-based Mobile Agents into Web Servers under Security Concerns. In *Proceeding of the IEEE Hawai'i International Conference on System Sciences,* 1998.
5. Mitsubishi Electric, Concordia online information, http://www.meitca.com/ HSL/Projects/ Concordia.
6. T. Lindholm and F. Yellin. *The Java Virtual Machine Specification.* Addison-Wesley, 1996.
7. S. Fünfrocken. Transparent Migration of Java-based Mobile Agents (Capturing and Reestablishing the State of Java Programs). In *Kurt Rothermel, Fritz Hohl (Eds.), Proceedings of the Second International Workshop on Mobile Agents (MA'98)*, pp. 26-37, 1998.
8. M. Dahm. Byte Code Engineering. In *Clemens Cap, editor, Proceedings JIT'99*, 1999.
9. B. Robben. Language Technology and Metalevel Architectures for Distributed Objects. Phd KULeuven, 1999. ISBN 90-5682-194-6.
10. E. Truyen, F. Matthijs, W. Joosen, B. Vanhaute, B. Robben, R. Slootmaekers, P. Verbaeten. Supporting Object Mobility - from Thread Migration to Dynamic Load Balancing. Demonstration at OOPSLA'99. (Correlate v3.3, Java prototype), www.cs.kuleuven.ac.be/~eddy/PUBLICATIONS/OOPSLADemoProceed.ps
11. M. Ranganathan, A. Acharya, S. D. Sharma and J Saltz. Network-aware Mobile Programs. Proceedings of the USENIX Annual Technical Conference, Anaheim, California, 1997.
12. H. Peine and T. Stolpmann. The architecture of the ara platform for mobile agents. In *Proceedings of the Second International Workshop on Mobile Agents (MA' 97)*, 1997.

13. S. Bouchenak. Pickling threads state in the Java system. In Proceedings of the third European Research Seminar on Advances in Distributed Systems (ERSADS'99), 1999.
14. T. Sekiguchi, H. Masuhara, and A. Yonezawa. A Simple Extension of Java Language for Controllable Transparent Migration and its Portable Implementation. In *Coordination Languages and Models,* volume 1594 of LNCS, pages 211-226, Springer-Verlag, April 1999.

Secure Mobile Agent-Based Merchant Brokering in Distributed Marketplaces

Günter Karjoth

IBM Research
Zurich Research Laboratory
gka@zurich.ibm.com

Abstract. Cooperating merchants establish a distributed marketplace under the auspices of an independent market authority. Each merchant's server is equipped with a trusted device, a smart card for example, provided by the market authority. The market authority plays the role of a trusted third party for the customer as well as for the merchants. This paper describes protocols that prevent the malicious alteration of the data collected by visiting mobile agents roaming through the marketplace without being detectable by subsequent servers or by the owner of the agent upon its return. Another protocol makes the trusted device a secure execution platform for routines provided by the agent owner.

1 Introduction

Researchers envision that electronic commerce on the Internet will provide software agents that search for information about products of interest to the user, compare prices and features, negotiate a fair price and possibly, if authorized by their user, make a purchase and authorize payment via credit card or a digital cash provider [ ].

When shopping on the Internet today, one can already take advantage of services that scour the Web to provide a list of online merchants and the prices they charge for a specific product, whether a book, CD, or video game. These services are realized by software agents, also called shopbots, that help one find a product at the lowest price possible. A shopbot program, for example BargainFinder or Jango (a commercial product based on the ShopBot [ ]), typically resides at a Web site. It sends out inquiries on behalf of a customer to other Web sites, collects the relevant information, and compiles a report tailored to the customer's requirements.

Mobile agents are software programs that live in computer networks, performing their computations and moving from server to server as necessary to fulfill their goals. As mobile agents have the advantages of reducing communication requirements and operating more flexibly than stationary agents, comparison shopping has also been employed for mobile agents [,]. XML as well as mobile agent technology may make comparison-shopping agents significantly more flexible, open-ended, and easier to implement [ ].

D. Kotz and F. Mattern (Eds.): ASA/MA 2000, LNCS 1882, pp. 44–   , 2000.
© Springer-Verlag Berlin Heidelberg 2000

However, mobile agents are exposed to a very serious security threat: malicious servers might endanger passing agents. In the comparison shopping scenario, servers might have an incentive to subvert the computation of a visiting agent, for example by removing cheaper offers. Thus, a mobile agent's user needs to be able to trust that either the agent cannot be subverted when visiting a malicious server or that illegal modifications can later be detected. Existing partial solutions to the malicious server problem can be distinguished as to whether they provide active or passive protection. Whereas the use of cryptography allows information to be hidden within the agent and its integrity to be checked, only the use of dedicated, trusted hardware appears able to prevent agent tampering.

Protocols to achieve forward integrity of partial results carried by free-roaming agents were first described by Yee [ ]: a malicious host cannot alter results collected at previous hosts. His protocols only use cryptographic techniques such as hashing and digital signatures. Karjoth *et al.* showed later how to make it impossible to forge a previous offer, even when it was made by oneself or by a colluding server [ ]. Loureiro *et al.* describe a protocol that allows merchants to change their offers during competitive brokering [ ].

Yee as well as Wilhelm *et al.* have proposed that mobile agent systems be endowed with trusted tamper-resistant hardware, which is not under the control of the local system and can host and execute agents [,]. The device issuer guarantees the integrity of the execution environment to the mobile agent owner. The secure coprocessor is only accessible via a well-defined interface and contains a private key not known to any other entity. The encryption of the agents under the public key of the receiving coprocessor protects against manipulation and disclosure when in transit. As mobile agents travel only in an encrypted state over the network and only execute within the coprocessor, the problem of general (multi-hop) security is reduced to client/server security. Of course, the manufacturer has to ensure adequate protection of the coprocessor's internals against malicious code it may execute. Others have noted that it is sufficient for many mobile agent applications that only some of the mobile agent operations, the security-sensitive ones, be executed within the protected environment. For example, Fünfrocken describes the employment of JavaCards, which allow Java code to be loaded and executed on a smart card, which is a resource-constrained, tamper-resistant but cheap hardware [ ].

This paper follows the latter approach. It describes a distributed marketplace, where all servers are equipped with trusted but resource-constrained devices. The protocols proposed take gradual advantage of services provided by the trusted devices. The first protocol uses the trusted devices only to execute cryptographic operations to seal and protect the results collected by the agent. The next protocol employs devices that compare a given offer with the current best

---

[1] In 1998, Sander and Tschudin attracted considerable attention in the mobile agent community when they proposed the technique of "computing with encrypted functions" to overcome the difficulty of mobile code protection [ ]. The challenge is to find a transformation for a program into an encrypted form such that it is still executable.

offer carried by the agent. Finally, the third protocol allows agents to download their own routines and data onto the devices. Thus, agents get the capability not only to compare and gather information on prices of goods, but also to pick a satisfying offer and decide to buy it. All protocols can be realized with a simple trusted smart card, in particular a JavaCard [ ], which provides only basic cryptography (signing, encryption, and secure storage of private keys) and limited computation capabilities.

The structure of the remainder of the paper is as follows. In Section , we describe the architecture of the distributed marketplace. In Section , we introduce a protocol for protecting the integrity of collected data. Section continues with a protocol that performs some decisions within the trusted devices. In Section , we describe a protocol that employs the agent's capability to download code on the trusted devices. In Section , we draw some conclusions.

2   Distributed Marketplace

To gain business advantages, merchants may join forces to establish a distributed marketplace for buyer and seller agents to meet and negotiate deals. To improve the marketplace's reputation, it may run under the supervision of a trusted organization, for example a financial institution, a non-profit corporation, or a guild formed by merchants. We refer to this organization as the market authority. We assume that it publishes guidelines of behavior that are binding for its members. In case of a dispute between a customer and a marketplace member, it may also serve as an arbitration board. In our setting, the market authority is a trusted third party for the customer as well as for merchants.

The marketplace consists of a number of server computers and the definition of allowable interactions and communication techniques. Each merchant's server is equipped with a trusted device that is provided by the market authority M. Trusted devices have a unique pair of public and private keys. The public key of the authority M is known to each trusted device in the marketplace. Thus, it serves as a trust authority whose signature certifies whether a given public key belongs to a trusted device that is part of the distributed marketplace. Customers may distrust potentially malicious merchants, but there is also mutual suspicion amongst the participating merchants in the market. The market authority guarantees to both parties that the installed devices are trustworthy, i.e. that the private keys never leave the device. Note that we require trusted hardware only at the merchant's server.

The market authority or some of the merchants may serve as "portals" into the marketplace. Targeted to mobile agents, the portal serves as a well-known entry into the marketplace and offers directory services to retrieve merchant addresses. This makes it easier for a customer to deal with large marketplaces, as only one address and corresponding public key has to be known. Fluctuations in the participating merchants are kept transparent. As Figure shows, the agent visits merchants within the marketplace that can contribute to its search for the best price.

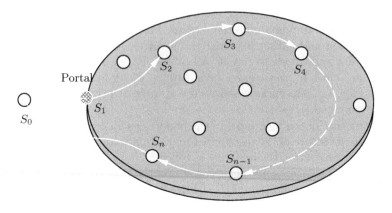

Fig. 1. Distributed marketplace with portal

The purpose of the marketplace is to let agents travel from server to server, collecting intermediate results. We do not care how much work had been done on a server prior to finding the result and whether the computation ran correctly as long as the computation is independent of input from previous servers. Comparison shopping is an application example, because the intermediate result, the price, is independent of previous price quotes. Offers of previously visited shops are kept confidential in order not to influence future price quotes. We do not consider the possibility that a server may learn about the prices of competitors by querying them directly. Other applications, for example a distributed auction, do not require data confidentiality and non-repudiation. Instead of closed bids and merchant anonymity, as in [,], multiple updates of the same merchant offer allow the implementation of several rounds of competing offers between bidders [ ].

The proposed protocols protect the flow of control for critical agent operations and preserve the privacy of data provided by the agent owner at agent initialization. Partial results collected by the agent and returned to the originator cannot be tampered with undetectably, and the agent's process of decision making cannot be influenced by manipulating the flow of control or internal control data.

For simplicity, we assume that server S_1 hosts a portal to the marketplace. In the following, we often do not distinguish between a merchant and its server, denoting both by S_i, $1 \leq i \leq n$. We consider itineraries where the merchants to be visited are not predetermined. Although all nodes are known, the agent is free to decide which n out of m nodes to visit and in what order. This means that at any place the agent can determine, based on its current state, the next hop or hops of the agent. However, although the agent might visit merchants not known at departure, these merchants must belong to the same marketplace. It is the market authority M that defines the members of the marketplace.

In a comparison shopping application, each server S_i represents a merchant and the intermediate results are the offers o_i of the merchants returned to the originator $S_0 = S_{n+1}$. We assume that offers include the name of the merchant. Depending on the application, an offer o_i might be encrypted and/or signed, denoted by O_i. If the details are not important, we refer to it as an encapsulated offer, an element of the append-only container carried by the agent.

Our protocols rely on certain cryptographic primitives. The agent owner provides its agent with a secret one-time key $\mathcal{K}$, and a message m encrypted under this key using a symmetric encryption algorithm (e.g., DES) is denoted $\{m\}_\mathcal{K}$. Encryption is probabilistic and secure against chosen plaintext attacks. Let $\mathcal{H}(m)$ be a one-way, collision-resistant hash function (e.g., SHA-1) that leaks no information (in a computational sense). It will take a message m of arbitrary length and produce a message digest of a specified size (160 bits if the SHA-1 is to be used). In particular, we use function $\mathcal{H}$ to generate hash chains that link the offers of the merchants.

Public-key cryptography is used to secure information sent to trusted devices and for verifiable signatures. A message m encrypted under the public encryption key of the trusted device $\mathcal{T}_i$ is denoted $\mathcal{ENC}_{\mathcal{T}_i}(m)$. Only device $\mathcal{T}_i$ can decrypt it with its private encryption key. A message signed by merchant S_i is denoted $\mathcal{SIG}_{S_i}(m)$. We assume that, given the signature $\mathcal{SIG}_{S_i}(m)$, anyone can extract m. In addition, the identity of merchant S_i can be deduced by examining the signature $\mathcal{SIG}_{S_i}(m)$. Finally, $[m]$ is a message m sent via an authenticated channel, and $Alice \rightarrow Bob$: m denotes Alice sending message m to Bob.

3   Price Collection

In [ ], Devanbu and Stubblebine describe protocols by which resource-limited, trusted processors can store stacks and queues on untrusted hosts while retaining only a constant amount of memory in the trusted processor. Whenever an operation on the data structure is performed, the trusted processor analyzes and certifies the values. For this purpose, it generates an initial secret value for each data instance on the host that never leaves the processor's memory. Hash chains link the initial secret with the elements added to or removed from the data instance. Whereas the initial secret identifies the instance, the last computed digest determines the instance's state. Both values are retained in the trusted processor's memory.

Our price collection protocol follows the above work but makes instances of the data structure movable. Whereas [ ] assumes that the key (the initial secret) associated with the instance of the data structure never leaves the trusted processor, in our approach we seal the key together with the last digest by encrypting them under the public key of the trusted device of the server that shall be visited next by the agent. As there is no pop operation, the append-only container carried by the agent is a special case of stacks and queues, and thus the security properties proved in [ ] also hold.

We assume there is an authenticated channel with message stream integrity whenever server S_i interacts with its trusted device T_i. The list $\boldsymbol{O_n}$ is a sequence of n pairs collected from servers $S_1, S_2, \ldots, S_n$. Each pair $O_i = \{\mathcal{SIG}_{S_i}(o_i)\}_\mathcal{K}$ consists of an offer o_i, signed by merchant S_i and encrypted under the list's secret key $\mathcal{K}$, and an integrity value (digest) h_i that links this pair with the previous pair in the list: $h_i = \mathcal{H}(O_{i-1}||h_{i-1})$.

On its itinerary, an agent carries a list of offer-digest pairs as well as the list's key and digest (encrypted under the public key of the designated trusted device) and the last digest of that list (encrypted under the list's key). The list's key and digest allow the receiving trusted device to verify the integrity of the list as well as to chain its merchant's offer to the list. When the agent returns home, the list's digest, encrypted under the list's key that is known to the agent owner, allows the agent owner to verify the integrity of the list.

We assume that the customer knows the public key of the market authority M, for example by possessing a certificate issued by a widely known and trusted certification authority. It also has a certificate issued by M that binds a public key to the trusted device of the portal. To initialize the agent, the agent owner generates a random, secret value $\mathcal{K} = h_0$, the list's key, and hashs it. This digest $\mathcal{H}(h_0)$ is later used to identify the offer collection. Next, the owner encrypts key and digest under the public key of the trusted device of the first merchant, $\mathcal{ENC}_{T_1}(\mathcal{K}, \mathcal{H}(h_0))$, and sends the agent off. The protocol flow is defined in Figure . Arrows indicate the direction of transmission, and the encapsulated offer O_0 is null.

$$S_{i-1} \longrightarrow S_i : \quad \boldsymbol{O_{i-1}}, \mathcal{ENC}_{T_i}(\mathcal{K}, h_i)$$

$$S_i \longrightarrow T_i : \quad [\mathcal{ENC}_{T_i}(\mathcal{K}, h_i), \mathcal{SIG}_{S_i}(o_i), \mathcal{SIG}_M(T_{i+1})]$$

$$T_i \longrightarrow S_i : \quad [\mathcal{ENC}_{T_{i+1}}(\mathcal{K}, h_{i+1}), \{h_{i+1}\}_\mathcal{K}, O_i, h_i]$$

$$\text{where} \quad O_i = \{\mathcal{SIG}_{S_i}(o_i)\}_\mathcal{K},$$

$$h_{i+1} = \mathcal{H}(O_i||h_i)$$

$$S_i \longrightarrow S_{i+1} : \quad \boldsymbol{O_{i-1}}||\langle O_i, h_i \rangle, \mathcal{ENC}_{T_{i+1}}(\mathcal{K}, h_{i+1})$$

$$S_n \longrightarrow S_{n+1} : \quad \boldsymbol{O_{i-1}}||\langle O_i, h_i \rangle, \{h_{i+1}\}_\mathcal{K}$$

Fig. 2. Price collection protocol $(1 \leq i \leq n)$

When the agent arrives at server S_i, it requests an offer for a certain product. The server passes its signed offer $\mathcal{SIG}_{S_i}(o_i)$ to its trusted device T_i, together with the encrypted key and digest of the agent's offer list and the public key of the trusted device of the next server to be visited by the agent, signed by the market authority.

The server's trusted device $\mathcal{T}_i$ first verifies the signature on the next server's public key to check whether this trusted device belongs to the marketplace. If so, it creates the encapsulated offer O_i by encrypting the received offer $\mathcal{SIG}_{S_i}(o_i)$. Next, it calculates the new integrity value $h_{i+1} = \mathcal{H}(O_i||h_i)$, the encapsulated offer concatenated with the last digest. Finally, the $\mathcal{T}_i$ returns to S_i the key and new digest $\mathcal{ENC}_{\mathcal{T}_{i+1}}(\mathcal{K}, h_{i+1})$, the encrypted new digest $\{h_{i+1}\}_\mathcal{K}$, and the new offer-digest pair O_i, h_i.

Now server S_i appends the received offer-digest pair to the agent's offer list and sends the agent to the next server S_{i+1}.

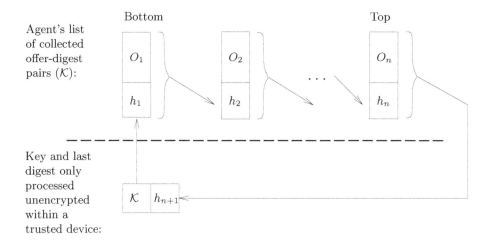

Fig. 3. A secure implementation of an offer collection o_1 to o_n

When the agent returns to the originating host, it has collected n offers. It carries the list of offer-digest pairs $\boldsymbol{O_n}$, the encrypted digest $\mathcal{ENC}_{\mathcal{T}_{n+1}}(\mathcal{K}, h_{n+1})$, and the encrypted last digest $\{h_{i+1}\}_\mathcal{K}$. To verify the integrity of the collected offers, the agent originator determines the agent's identity and retrieves the secret key $\mathcal{K}$ that corresponds to the returned agent instance. Next, the agent owner decrypts the last digest and extracts the integrity value h_{n+1}. Based on key $\mathcal{K}$, the agent owner checks the integrity of the encapsulated offers in $\boldsymbol{O_n}$ by recursively recalculating the hash chain to check whether the result matches the received integrity value h_{n+1}:

$$h_1 = \mathcal{H}(\mathcal{K})$$
$$h_{i+1} = \mathcal{H}(O_i||h_i).$$

After the integrity of the collected data has been proved, the agent owner opens the individual offers using the secret key as the decryption key. Finally, for the best offer o_i, the agent owner checks whether the signature $\mathcal{SIG}_{S_i}(o_i)$ is correct; i.e. whether it binds merchant S_i to the contained offer o_i.

The data structure maintained by the price collection protocol is illustrated in Figure . The arrows show the inputs to the computed digest. The key and last digest of the container are always maintained in the $\mathcal{T}$ devices. Updates are only done within a $\mathcal{T}$ device, and the key and last digest only leave a $\mathcal{T}$ device in encrypted form, expressed by the dashed box in the figure. Thus, if the container's key and last digest are retained in the trusted device or transmitted only in encrypted form, then a tampering of the container can always be detected.

Variations

The merchant might delegate signing its offer to the trusted device. This functionality might either be implemented as another function of the device, for example in the case of a multi-application smart card, or integrated into the price collection protocol.

The load of the agent to be carried around can be reduced if it is not important to know at which merchant the hash chain over the collected offers broke. In that case it is not necessary to include the hash values $h_1, \ldots, h_n$ in the list $\boldsymbol{O_n}$.

When the encryption of the merchant's offer is made optional, it would implement open bidding. Then, to give the merchant the ability to bid several times, one may allow the offer list to carry several offers from the same merchant, or one uses the technique described in [ ]. For the latter, however, it is required that the agent owner share a secret with any merchant the agent might visit.

4   Best Offer

In the case of an exhaustive comparison shopping itinerary, the agent's offer list may grow considerably. However, if the customer is interested only in getting the best offer it is sufficient that the agent carry only the currently best offer. This can be done safely if the offer comparison takes place *inside the trusted device* to shield it from malicious servers. Furthermore, the encrypted form of the stored best offer should always change whenever it has been compared with a new offer at a different server, so that no information about the decision result can leak. The protocol is given in Figure .

Compared with the previous protocol, the agent only carries the present best offer O_i instead of the complete offer list $\boldsymbol{O_i}$. To provide some feedback on the quality of the returned offer, we extend the offer structure as follows:

$$Offers(o) - \text{number of offers compared,}$$
$$Lowest(o) - \text{offer with the lowest price,}$$
$$Average(o) - \text{average price.}$$

To initialize the agent, its owner generates a random number $\mathcal{K}$. This time $\mathcal{K}$ serves as key to 'sign' the best offer. The initial value of the best offer O_0 is $\{0, max\_price, 0\}_{\mathcal{K}}$ where max_price is the highest value that can be stored. The

$$S_{i-1} \longrightarrow S_i : O_{i-1}, \; \mathcal{ENC}_{T_i}(\mathcal{K}, h_i)$$

$$S_i \longrightarrow T_i : \quad [\mathcal{ENC}_{T_i}(\mathcal{K}, h_i), \; O_{i-1}, \; \mathcal{SIG}_{S_i}(o_i), \; \mathcal{SIG}_M(T_{i+1})]$$

$$T_i \longrightarrow S_i : \quad [\mathcal{ENC}_{T_{i+1}}(\mathcal{K}, h_{i+1}), \{h_{i+1}\}_\mathcal{K}, O_i]$$

$$\text{where} \;\; h_{i+1} = \mathcal{H}(O_i \| \mathcal{K})$$

$$O_i = \{\#\text{offers}, \text{lowest}, \text{average}\}_\mathcal{K}$$

$$\text{and} \quad \#\text{offers} = \text{Offers}(O_{i-1}) + 1$$

$$lowest = \begin{cases} \mathcal{SIG}_{S_i}(o_i) & \text{if } o_i < Lowest(O_{i-1}); \\ Lowest(O_{i-1}) & \text{otherwise.} \end{cases}$$

$$average = \frac{Offers(O_{i-1}) \cdot Average(O_{i-1}) + o_i}{\#\text{offers}}$$

$$S_i \longrightarrow S_{i+1} : O_i, \; \mathcal{ENC}_{T_{i+1}}(\mathcal{K}, h_{i+1})$$
$$S_n \longrightarrow S_{n+1} : O_i, \; \{h_{i+1}\}_\mathcal{K}$$

Fig. 4. Best offer protocol $(1 \leq i \leq n)$

agent owner computes the digest $h_1 = \mathcal{H}(O_0)$ over the initial best offer and encrypts the offer digest $\mathcal{ENC}_{T_i}(\mathcal{K}, h_1)$ for the first merchant to be visited.

At each merchant site, the trusted device T_i always updates the fields containing the number of merchants already visited (#offers) and the current average price of the product (average). If the merchant's price is lower than the current best price (lowest) then this field is updated, too. Finally, trusted device T_i encrypts the updated best offer, using key $\mathcal{K}$.

Variations

When the agent is initialized, the originator may limit the number of merchants to be visited and the minimum price the agent should find.

Again, if the offers are not encrypted, the protocol would implement open bidding.

In the described protocol for best offer collection, there is no problem if a merchant makes more than one offer as only the offer with the lowest price will be stored. However, there are malicious ways to change the accompanying values. For example, if a malicious merchant makes a number of additional offers with unacceptably high prices, the agent would return an incorrect value for the average price of the desired good. To prevent these and other attacks, for example black-box testing, the trusted device may keep a log of recent queries and associated agent identifiers.

5   Secure Decision Making

A marketplace provides a set of predefined services such as comparison shopping. These services are parameterized and might be based on advanced theories [ ]. However, making the best choice may not depend only on the price but also on other balancing factors such as availability or quality. In this section we describe how trusted devices can provide protected areas in which agents can review the collected data and take decisions based on that information. For example, an agent can securely evaluate its data, autonomously decide to buy the best offer, and execute the necessary steps. The ability to provide a trusted computation platform secures other classes of interactions in a market, such as negotiation and deal settlement.

Consider an agent that contains code to calculate some function F. To prevent modification by an adversary, the code is signed and optionally encrypted. When the code is downloaded, the trusted device checks the integrity of function F's code by verifying its signature and makes the code available for execution. Furthermore, function F and its input should be linked; i.e. a malicious merchant should not be able to supply data not intended for the task of the agent. Assume that an agent shall iteratively compute $x_{i+1} = F(x_i, y_i)$ on servers S_1 to S_n, where the agent owner provides x_1 and each server S_i provides y_i. Then a malicious server might feed the trusted device either with wrong input x_i' or with a different function F'.

The secure decision protocol in Figure   preserves the integrity and confidentiality of an agent owner-supplied function, ties this function with the agent, and securely links the computed values. To achieve these properties, the protocol uses the agent owner's secret one-time key K to bind the agent's code part (F) with its computation data (x_i). At the beginning, the agent owner sends the code together with the secret key to the market authority. After inspection of the code, the market authority encrypts the code under the secret key and signs the encrypted data. Next, the agent owner sends to the first merchant S_1 the signed and encrypted code, the initial offer O_0 encrypted under the secret key K, and the secret key K encrypted under the public key T_1 of the trusted device of merchant S_1.

On server S_i, the agent forwards to the trusted device T_i the received data together with the merchant's offer o_i. Trusted device T_i first verifies the signature on the encrypted code. Next, it decrypts the secret key K with its private key. Using K, it decrypts the code of function F as well as the data of offer O_{i-1}. Finally, the device returns the result of the execution of $O_i = F(O_{i-1}, o_i)$ en-

---

[2] The market authority may perform a number of checks to ensure that the code is well-behaved, ranging from manual inspection to automatic verification as simple as standard bytecode verification.

Set up:

$$S_0 \longrightarrow M : \quad \mathcal{ENC}_M(F, K)$$

$$M \longrightarrow S_0 : \quad \mathcal{SIG}_M(\{F\}_K)$$

Round trip:

$$S_{i-1} \longrightarrow S_i : \mathcal{ENC}_{\mathcal{T}_i}(K), \ \{O_{i-1}\}_K, \ \mathcal{SIG}_M(\{F\}_K)$$

$$S_i \longrightarrow \mathcal{T}_i : \quad [\mathcal{ENC}_{\mathcal{T}_i}(K), \ \{O_{i-1}\}_K, \ \mathcal{SIG}_M(\{F\}_K), \ \mathcal{SIG}_M(\mathcal{T}_{i+1}), \ o_i]$$

$$\mathcal{T}_i \longrightarrow S_i : \quad [\mathcal{ENC}_{\mathcal{T}_{i+1}}(K), \ \{O_i\}_K]$$
$$\text{where} \quad O_i = F(O_{i-1}, o_i)$$

$$S_i \longrightarrow S_{i+1} : \mathcal{ENC}_{\mathcal{T}_{i+1}}(K), \ \{O_i\}_K, \ \mathcal{SIG}_M(\{F\}_K)$$
$$S_n \longrightarrow S_{n+1} : \{O_i\}_K$$

Fig. 5. Secure decision protocol $(1 \le i \le n)$

crypted under the secret key K together with the secret key itself encrypted under the public key $\mathcal{T}_{i+1}$ of the next merchant's trusted device.

Compared with the approach described in [ ], trusted devices are relieved from the task of encrypting the code for the next device on the itinerary of the agent.

6   Conclusion

We presented a distributed marketplace that provides a context in which mobile agents can securely collect information, conduct negotiations, and make agreements. The market authority plays the role of a trusted third party, which is vital to the security of the marketplace. By providing the trusted devices, it guarantees to customers as well as participating merchants the sanctity of security-sensitive agent operations.

Our protocols require trusted hardware only at the merchant's site. To securely transport information collected by an agent, it must not be stored in the encrypted code part of the agent as in [ ], avoiding re-encryption of the code part. Instead, cryptographic computations performed within the trusted devices securely link the collected results with the help of a secret key chosen by the agent owner. Compared with software-only solutions [,], agents carry less data.

If dynamic download of code is supported, agent owners can equip their agents with specialized routines without running the risk of espionage or manipulation of the flow of control by a malicious server. To protect competitive multiple issuer negotiation, Vogler *et al.* distribute the negotiation function between two cooperating agents [   ]. The security-sensitive functions and data are contained in one agent (the "protected" agent), which is executed only on trusted processors. It interacts with another agent, which moves from merchant to merchant. The agent domain of [   ] reflects to some extent our marketplace but differs in that there is only one trusted processor per domain. Thus, our local interactions with a smart card perform better than the remote interactions between a cooperating agent pair.

The distributed marketplace described here does not rely on a public-key infrastructure. It provides a "lightweight" infrastructure itself. For example, if merchants are organized in the form of a Web ring, it is sufficient for each server to hold the certificate of the next merchant's site.

There are a number of additional mechanisms that can help further improve the trust in and reputation of a marketplace. The market authority might periodically monitor the participating merchants' behavior. For example, the results of "detection agents" introduced into the marketplace might indicate truncation attacks of malicious merchants if expected offers are missing. Based on the trusted devices, the market authority may also keep audit logs about the execution of mobile agents, as proposed, for example, by Vigna [   ] and others. To overcome the resource constraints of the trusted device, the audit log can be kept securely on the merchant's server using the same technique as for the agent's offer list.

Acknowledgments

This work was partially supported by the Defence Evaluation & Research Agency (DERA) under the Beacon programme. It represents the views of the author. This work has greatly benefited from early discussions with Jürgen Bohn on smart card-based comparison shopping protocols. He also implemented a variant of the price collection protocol in his Master's thesis. Thanks to Thomas Eirich, Stefan Pleisch, and Michael Waidner for their detailed comments.

References

1. M. Baentsch, P. Buhler, T. Eirich, F. Höring, and M. Oestreicher. JavaCard – from hype to reality. *IEEE Concurrency*, 7(4):36–43, 1999.
2. P. Dasgupta, N. Narasimhan, L. E. Moser, and P. M. Melliar-Smith. MAgNET: Mobile agents for networked electronic trading. *IEEE Transactions on Knowledge and Data Engineering*, 11(4):509–525, 1999.
3. P. T. Devanbu and S. G. Stubblebine. Stack and queue integrity on hostile platforms. In *IEEE Symposium on Research in Security and Privacy*, pages 198–207. IEEE Computer Society Press, 1998.

4. B. Doorenbos, O. Etzioni, and D. Weld. A scalable comparison-shopping agent for the world-wide web. In *AGENTS-97*, 1997.
5. S. Fünfrocken. Protecting mobile web-commerce agents with smartcards. In *Joint Symposium on Agent Systems and Applications and on Mobile Agents (ASA/MA 99)*, pages 90–102. IEEE Computer Society Press, 1999.   ,
6. Q. Huai and T. Sandholm. Mobile agents in an electronic auction house. *IEEE Internet Computing*, 4(2):80–86, 2000.
7. G. Karjoth, N. Asokan, and C. Gülcü. Protecting the computation results of free-roaming agents. In K. Rothermel and F. Hohl, editors, *Second International Workshop on Mobile Agents (MA '98)*, Lecture Notes in Computer Science 1477, pages 195–207. Springer, 1998.   , ,
8. S. Loureiro, R. Molva, and A. Pannetrat. Secure data collection with updates. In *1st Asia-Pacific Conference on Intelligent Agent Technology*, Hong Kong, 1999.
   ,   ,
9. P. Maes, R. Guttman, and A. Moukas. Agents that buy and sell: Transforming commerce as we know it. *Communications of the ACM*, 42(3), 1999.
10. T. Sander and C. Tschudin. Towards mobile cryptography. In *IEEE Symposium on Research in Security and Privacy*, pages 215–224. IEEE Computer Society Press, 1998.
11. T. Sandholm. eMediator: A next generation electronic commerce server. Fourth International Conference on Autonomous Agents (AGENTS 2000), Barcelona, Spain, June 2000.
12. G. Vigna. Cryptographic traces for mobile agents. In G. Vigna, editor, *Mobile Agents and Security*, Lecture Notes in Computer Science 1419, pages 137–153. Springer, 1998.
13. J. Vitek and C. Jensen, editors. *Secure Internet Programming: Security Issues for Mobile and Distributed Objects*, Lecture Notes in Computer Science 1603. Springer, 1999.
14. H. Vogler, A. Spriestersbach, and M.-L. Moschgath. Protecting competitive negotiation of mobile agents. IEEE Workshop on Future Trends of Distributed Computing Systems (FTDCS 99), pages 145–150. IEEE Computer Society Press, 1999.
15. B. Whitaker. Intelligent agents for electronic commerce. *NCR Technical Journal*, 1999.
16. U. G. Wilhelm, S. Staamann, and L. Buttyàn. Introducing trusted third parties to the mobile agent paradigm. In Vitek and Jensen [ ], pages 471–491.
17. B. S. Yee. A sanctuary for mobile agents. In Vitek and Jensen [ ], pages 261–273.
   ,   ,

Solving Fair Exchange with Mobile Agents

Henning Pagnia[1], Holger Vogt[1]*, Felix C. Gärtner[1]*, and Uwe G. Wilhelm[2]

[1] Computer Science Dept., Darmstadt Univ. of Technology
D-64283 Darmstadt, Germany
{pagnia,holgervo,felix}@informatik.tu-darmstadt.de
[2] Operating Systems Laboratory, Communication Systems Department, Swiss
Federal Institute of Technology
1015 Lausanne, Switzerland
Uwe.Wilhelm@epfl.ch

Abstract. Mobile agents have been advocated to support electronic commerce over the Internet. While being a promising paradigm, many intricate problems need to be solved to make this vision reality. The problem of *fair exchange* between two agents is one such fundamental problem. Informally speaking, this means to exchange two electronic items in such a way that neither agent suffers a disadvantage. We study the problem of fair exchange in the mobile agent paradigm. We show that while existing protocols for fair exchange can be substantially simplified in the context of mobile agents, there are still many problems related to security which remain difficult to solve. We propose three increasingly flexible solutions to the fair exchange problem and show how to implement them using existing agent technology. The basis for ensuring the security properties of fair exchange is a tamper-proof hardware device called a trusted processing environment.

1   Introduction

Ever since their emergence, mobile agents have been advocated to revolutionize the way in which we go shopping on the Internet. Instead of having to surf endlessly through the World Wide Web (WWW) and digesting huge amounts of possibly untrustworthy information, personalized mobile agents autonomously gather information about items we want to buy. Once they have found the WWW page, the piece of software or the latest hit single which we were looking for, the agent can perform the purchase on behalf of the user and – to our enjoyment – carry the item back home.

While being a promising paradigm, many technical aspects must be solved to make this vision reality. First of all, there are substantial security issues involved. For example, vendors which let mobile agents visit their WWW servers are usually not willing to execute arbitrary (possibly malicious) agent code on

---

* This author's work was supported by the Deutsche Forschungsgemeinschaft (DFG) as part of the two PhD programs (Graduiertenkollegs) "Enabling Technologies for Electronic Commerce" and "ISIA" at Darmstadt University of Technology.

D. Kotz and F. Mattern (Eds.): ASA/MA 2000, LNCS 1882, pp. 57–   , 2000.
© Springer-Verlag Berlin Heidelberg 2000

their local machine. Solutions to this problem have been proposed and have even been introduced into modern programming languages like Java. However, the converse of protecting the host from the agent is also a problem: agents often carry precious data such as personal information, electronic money, or (minor) company secrets. It must be ensured that such items cannot be stolen by other agents or robbed by visited hosts, and that agents cannot be kidnapped. From the existing solutions [, , ,] we have chosen to pursue one which is based on trusted hardware, such as the trusted processing environment (TPE) described by Wilhelm *et al.* [ ].

However, the ability to protect the agent from fellow agents or hosts alone does not solve the manyfold problems associated with electronic business transactions on the WWW. For many transactions it is still necessary to provide mechanisms for executing an exchange of digital items in a fair manner. Intuitively, fairness means that either both participants receive their desired item or (in case of an unsuccessful exchange) nobody wins or loses something valuable. A naive protocol to perform such an exchange could be the following: an agent wishing to buy the soundtrack of "My Fair Lady" from a music vendor could proceed to the vendor's host, receive the audio file, pay for it electronically and travel back home again. There are two obvious problems with this simple protocol: 1) the agent could leave the vendor's host before paying, and 2) the vendor could hinder the agent from leaving the host after having paid. Obviously, both outcomes of the transaction are unfair.

The situation can be improved if the host contains or is connected to a TPE which is trusted. In such a scenario, the vendor places its own local agent onto the TPE and then both customer and vendor agent start to exchange their items fairly. But how to proceed? Assume for example, that the vendor agent first delivers the data file to the customer agent. Who can now prevent the customer agent from leaving the TPE? On the other hand, if the customer first hands the money to the vendor, who can guarantee that the vendor will readily hand over the data file? If a data file is returned, who guarantees that it is in fact the soundtrack of "My Fair Lady"? And how is it possible for customer and vendor to check the integrity of the exchanged item without revealing it to the other? The core problem encountered here is usually called the problem of *fair exchange*.

Due to its importance in electronic commerce, the problem of fair exchange has received increasing attention in recent years and a number of papers have been published in this area (see for example the papers by Asokan *et al.* [ ], Franklin and Reiter [ ] or Vogt *et al.* [ ]). In almost all of these papers, the problem has been studied in a general message-passing network scenario which makes solutions to the problem rather complex (if not impossible [ ]). This results from the possible occurrence of communication faults or malicious process behavior (e.g., intentionally stopping to proceed in the protocol or sending corrupted messages). We will show that protocols to solve fair exchange can be substantially simplified when adapting them to the agent scenario. To our knowledge, fair exchange in this context has not been addressed in the literature yet.

In this paper, we consider the following scenario: two agents, A and B, meet on a trusted host (implemented by a TPE) to exchange two items in a fair manner. We propose three novel solutions to the fair exchange problem in the mobile agent environment which are both practical and efficient, we sketch how they can be implemented in existing agent platforms, and we discuss their relative merits and shortcomings.

We proceed as follows: In Section   we introduce the concept of a TPE which is the basic building block of our solutions. In Section   we define the fair exchange problem and state why the mobile agent scenario bears the potential of simple solutions to a difficult problem. We then present these solutions in Sections   and . Finally, we summarize and discuss our results in Section .

2   Trusted Processing Environment

The necessity to protect mobile agents from their execution environment has been addressed in several publications [, , ,]. Here, different solutions have been proposed for the problem of protecting the data of a mobile agent from undesired disclosure and its code from undesired interference. We have chosen to pursue the approach identified by Wilhelm *et al.* in [ ], which relies on the usage of trusted and tamper-resistant hardware. This approach proposes to formalize the guarantees into a policy that is associated with the underlying hardware. Such a policy consists of a set of rules prescribing the behavior of the hardware for all relevant situations. A similar protection and the enforcement of a meaningful policy are either very difficult or impossible to achieve in any of the other mentioned approaches. We will first explain the overall approach by introducing the trusted processing environment (TPE) and then explain some of the policies that can be enforced by a TPE.

2.1   Trusted and Tamper-Resistant Hardware

As noted above, the basic idea of the TPE is to rely on trusted and tamper-resistant hardware to protect a mobile agent from interference by the owner of the TPE. This implies that we have to trust the manufacturer of the TPE to properly design and produce its TPEs, which is a basic assumption underlying the entire approach (a more extensive discussion of this assumption can be found in [ ]). Thus, we assume that the host computer which is under the control of the TPE owner, cannot interfere with the task of the TPE other than through a restricted interface. This interface is completely controlled by the TPE and allows, for instance, to upload and remove agents or to interact with agents on the TPE. The TPE (see Figure) is a complete computer and provides an agent execution environment which cannot be inspected or tampered with. It is designed as a closed system that contains its entire operating code (i.e., operating system, virtual machine for mobile agents, I/O interface for external interactions, and cryptographic library) in non-volatile protected memory (e.g., internal ROM) that allows a secure boot of the system. Finally, the TPE contains the private key K_{TPE}^{-1} of a cryptographic key pair (K_{TPE}, K_{TPE}^{-1}). K_{TPE}^{-1} is generated by the TPE and is known to no principal other than the TPE itself – including the TPE's physical owner. The secrecy of this private key, ensured by the tamper-resistance of the TPE, is a crucial requirement for TPE usage to enforce a particular behavior. The actual guarantees towards the physical protection offered by the TPE are the following:

1. The TPE is tamper-resistant and its private key has not been compromised.
2. The virtual machine inside the TPE correctly implements the specification of the programming language used by the mobile agent.
3. The cryptographic library implements the cryptographic algorithms correctly.
4. Any access to or manipulation of data on the TPE is under the control of the operating system.
5. The operating system protects a mobile agent from other agents on the same TPE.

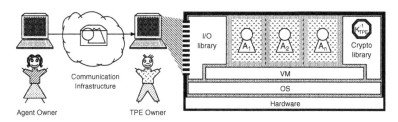

Fig. 1. Mobile agents on the trusted processing environment (TPE)

The protection offered by the TPE and its conformance to a particular policy is ensured by the manufacturer, which provides the TPE owner with an appropriate certificate. This certificate contains information about the TPE, such as manufacturer, type, the provided guarantees, the enforced policy, and the public key (K_{TPE}). Thus, in order to securely send a mobile agent to a particular TPE, in principle the following steps have to be taken. The sender has to obtain the certificate of the TPE, verify the policy enforced by the TPE, assess the assurance in the tamper-resistance of the TPE, and send the mobile agent encrypted with the public key of the TPE to the TPE owner. This guarantees that the information within the mobile agent cannot be accessed or tampered with while the mobile agent is in transit. Once the mobile agent has arrived on the TPE, it is protected by the tamper-resistance of the TPE and the policy implemented in the TPE as described next.

2.2   Using the TPE

As we have previously stated, the presented approach was primarily conceived to provide a well defined protection to a mobile agent. A detailed discussion of the many possible protection goals and the corresponding policies is outside the scope of this presentation (for further information see [ ]). We will only discuss the policy rules that are most relevant to the problem of fair exchange and point out how mobile agents can take advantage of them. We now assume a TPE that enforces the following rules:

(R1) The code of an agent will never be disclosed or altered by the TPE and any invocation of the agent's methods will be executed exactly according to the code of the agent.

(R2) The data of an agent can exclusively be accessed and manipulated through the interface of the agent. If the agent does not provide methods to directly access a particular data item, its value can at most be inferred from the responses to other method invocations.

(R3) The TPE will protect the mobile agent from any interference from other agents on the same TPE (other than calls to the mobile agent's public interface).

(R4) Prior to a migration, an agent will obtain the certificate of the designated receiver's TPE. The agent can decide whether it wants to be transferred and the current TPE will honor the agent's decision. For the transfer, the agent will be encrypted with the public key of the receiver's TPE.

(R5) The TPE establishes a unique identifier for each mobile agent on the TPE and provides an invokee with the ID of the invoker. The TPE invokes a method exclusively and unaltered on the mobile agent with the ID provided in the invocation.

(R6) The TPE provides an operation that, given the ID of a mobile agent A, returns the cryptographic hash of the immutable part of A. The TPE will query A if it approves of this operation.

(R7) The TPE guarantees the survival of a mobile agent despite the possibility of a temporary hardware failure.

This policy allows a mobile agent, for instance, to rely on its own code in order to hide parts of its state (e.g., cryptographic keys), to control its migration to other TPEs, and to ensure the confidentiality, integrity, and authenticity of local method invocations. Provided that the policy of the TPE will be enforced (which is ensured by the manufacturer), it is quite obvious how the mobile agent can implement these protection goals. A very interesting protection goal in the context of fair exchange can be realized based on rule R6, which allows a mobile agent to determine whether it interacts with an agent executing some specific code. This mechanism is called *authentic code* [ ]. The underlying idea is that the implementation of a mobile agent can be analyzed in order to ensure that it correctly implements a well-defined behavior. An owner will then configure his mobile agent to only interact with a mobile agent that is identical to the one he has previously analyzed. This allows a mobile agent, for instance, to disclose a

---

[1] Of course, the effort to analyze an agent can be very high. However, since such an agent must only be analyzed once and can then be used *many* times, the effort is often justified.

particular piece of information exclusively to an agent with a completely known behavior. We will discuss this issue in more detail in Section   .

3   The Fair Exchange Problem in the Mobile Agent Scenario

While the notion of fairness in electronic commerce feels rather simple to understand, it is quite difficult to formalize [ ]. In the context of a fair exchange, fairness intuitively means that either both participants receive their desired item or (in case of an unsuccessful exchange) nobody wins or loses something valuable. This means that if, for example, Alice and Bob want to exchange items, a system must *not* allow, for example, that Bob can obtain access to Alice's item while Alice cannot access Bob's item. More specifically, a system that implements a *fair exchange protocol* between Alice and Bob must ensure three conditions [, p. 9]:

1. Effectiveness: If Alice and Bob behave correctly and if the protocol terminates, then Alice will have Bob's item and vice versa.
2. Timeliness: The protocol will eventually terminate.
3. Fairness (see below).

We will now discuss the third condition in more detail. Fair exchange protocols must particularly protect against the situation in which either party refuses to cooperate in order to gain an advantage. Existing fair exchange protocols are rather complicated due to the asynchronous nature of the underlying network: problems occur because in this system model communication can be interrupted, or nodes can crash. Hence, a proper termination of the exchange process cannot be guaranteed. In order to overcome this restriction different notions of fairness have been introduced [ ]:

a) *Strong fairness*: When the protocol has completed, either Alice has Bob's item or Bob has gained no additional information about Alice's item, and vice versa [, p. 9]. In other words: A participant who behaves correctly does not suffer a disadvantage, i.e., it is never the case that Alice receives Bob's item but Bob does not receive Alice's item, or vice versa.

b) *Weak fairness*: Either strong fairness is achieved, or a correctly behaving participant Alice can prove to an arbiter that Bob has received (or still can receive) Alice's item without any further intervention from Alice [, p. 9] (no matter whether Bob behaves correctly or not), and vice versa.

Strong fairness is achieved on protocol completion usually by using a trusted third party which first collects the items to be exchanged and then (after checking their validity) swaps them. Weak fairness is reached if either the exchange process terminates in the way as described above or both parties collected sufficient proofs in order to enforce the exchange after protocol completion with the help of an outside arbiter.

It can be shown that it is impossible to reach strong fairness in an asynchronous system without a trusted third party [ ]. It turns out that even by involving a trusted third party (TTP) strong fairness cannot be guaranteed in an asynchronous system without making special assumptions. Assume that the TTP has collected the items from the two exchange parties Alice and Bob. Next, the TTP forwards Bob's item to Alice but crashes before it sends the other item to Bob. (Alternatively, one can assume that the communication link to Bob breaks down.) Now, Alice has received the item but Bob has not. Hence, the exchange did not terminate in a fair way. Fair exchange protocols therefore are implemented with reliable communication and persistent TTPs. Exploiting these properties, they define strong fairness to be reached if both parties *eventually* receive the item [ ].

As discussed in Section   a TPE must provide solutions to many of the problems which also have to be solved for a TTP, particularly reliability and persistency. This means, that the TPE must ensure that agents cannot die due to node crashes [ ] and that agents migrate in a reliable "exactly-once" fashion from host to host [ ]. For performing fair exchange, we let all three parties involved (TTP, Alice, and Bob) reside on the same node. In this scenario neither can communication break down nor can a single party crash. If the TPE node crashes before fair exchange was committed, then all parties are destroyed, thereby resetting the exchange process. If it crashes after the exchange has been performed then the TPE must ensure that the agents are correctly recovered. Because of these properties the mobile agent scenario is so well-suited for solving fair exchange.

Still, for items which might expire or items whose value decreases by time (e.g., stock quotes or time table information) the exchange is problematic: One party might receive the item in time whereas the other party receives it after its expiration, rendering the item useless. Thus, the so achieved degree of fairness might still be unsatisfactory.

4   Fair Exchange Using Designated TPE Functionality

4.1   The Basic Protocol

We propose the use of mobile agents meeting at a special-purpose TPE. This TPE offers designated fair exchange functions and is thus extended by new methods which we introduce in Section   . Alice sends its mobile agent A to the TPE while Bob sends agent B. Each agent carries the item which is intended to be exchanged and includes a routine for checking the expected item. When the agents meet, the TPE must ensure that they play fair, i.e., only if the items were exchanged successfully and both agents are content, the agents are allowed to move on. Furthermore, none of the agents must be allowed to communicate with any other party except for their exchange partner. This prevents that a party might gain an advantage by forwarding the newly received item to an outside party before the exchange is committed.

The protocol we propose is as follows: As shown in Figure   one can think of the two agents (A and B) to be locked in an empty room with a single door but no windows. After the agents have entered the room they are not released unless both signal that the exchange was successful. The agents will only do this if they have checked the exchanged items and are content with what they received. The exchange is assumed to be completed only if both have signaled a "Commit" message. Otherwise the door remains locked. If either agent decides "Abort" then both agents will be destroyed.

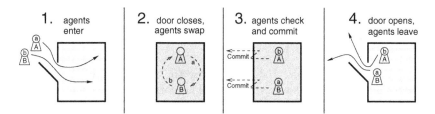

Fig. 2. Fair exchange in a locked room

Defining a fair exchange protocol for this scenario is much simpler than in the distributed scenario. The reason for this is that the agents are isolated during the exchange process. Consequently, swapping the items does not need to take place atomically provided that in the meantime neither agent is capable of spreading information to the outside. Opening the door finally results in simultaneously releasing the two agents and effectively re-enables their ability to communicate. Now that the items have been exchanged, the agents should be retransmitted to their owner. This however, is no longer part of the fair exchange protocol but is under control of the agent platform. The exchange protocol guarantees that the agents swap the items in a fair manner. But it has not to deal with the way both agents take the received items back to their owner. The reason for this is that mobile agents are allowed to visit an arbitrary number of sites before returning to their owner and hence, an agent might have more tasks to fulfill after having executed the exchange. Therefore, the exchange process has to be regarded complete as soon as the items have been exchanged between the agents.

4.2   Implementing the Protocol Using a Designated TPE

The TPE offers fair exchange functionality through three publicly accessible methods:

- `BeginFairExchange(AgentId id)`
- `CommitFairExchange()`
- `AbortFairExchange()`

Figure   shows a possible implementation of these methods in pseudocode. Their semantics is as follows: Upon invocation of `BeginFairExchange(B)`, the TPE guarantees that the invoking agent can only invoke its own local methods as well as communication with agent B. Note that the agent that enters the room first is blocked until its partner has arrived. Each agent is then allowed to make one call of either `CommitFairExchange()` or `AbortFairExchange()`. These restrictions are maintained by the TPE until one of the following cases arises:

1. Both the invoking agent *and* agent B invoke `CommitFairExchange()`. In this case execution resumes normally.
2. At least one of the two agents invokes `AbortFairExchange()`. In this case both agents are terminated and a notification about this fact is sent to the parent of the agents (either the agent owner or the mobile agent that spawned the participating agent).

The solution is fair because there is no way to "smuggle" an item out of the room without the other party's consent. The corresponding security property that there is no flow of information from inside the room to the outside during the exchange process.

Instead of terminating both participating agents in case 2, the agents could as well be reset into the state they were in before invoking `BeginFairExchange()`. However, this involves technically complex mechanisms to ensure that agents do not enter an infinite loop. To us, it seems simpler to send out "one-time" agents to perform the fair exchange and destroy the agents in case the exchange fails.

5   Fair Exchange Without Extending Existing TPE Functionality

TPEs are complex devices which are not easy to manufacture and require a complex certification infrastructure. Therefore, adding specific pieces of hard- or software to the TPE, as proposed in the previous section, might not always be a suitable solution. In this section we show that under certain assumptions the exchange functionality placed within the TPE can be incorporated into a specialized agent. This solution avoids the use of a designated special-purpose TPE but also has inherent problems because the exchange agent has to be flexible and trustworthy at the same time. In Section   we study these problems in more detail and discuss some solutions in Section   . Subsequently, we present two increasingly flexible solutions for fair exchange in Sections   and   .

5.1   The Check-Routine Problem

The simplest solutions to the fair exchange problem which do not alter TPE functionality are based on the concept of a *fair exchange agent* (FEA). A FEA is an agent that acts as a trusted intermediate to the two agents A and B which want to perform a fair exchange. If such an intermediate is available, the exchange can proceed as follows: A and B both send their item to the FEA. The

Agent code of A:

```
 ⋮
BeginFairExchange(B);
send(B, itemA);
receive(B, itemB);
if (checkB(itemB) == OK)
   CommitFairExchange();
else
   AbortFairExchange();
endif;
 ⋮
```

Agent code of B:

```
 ⋮
BeginFairExchange(A);
send(A, itemB);
receive(A, itemA);
if (checkA(itemA) == OK)
   CommitFairExchange();
else
   AbortFairExchange();
endif;
 ⋮
```

Methods provided by the TPE:

```
method BeginFairExchange(AgentId you) is
begin
   d[me] := UNCERTAIN;
   if NOT(is_waiting(you))
      wait(me);
   else
      close_door;    -- block communication
      wakeup(you);
   endif;
end;

method CommitFairExchange() is
begin
   d[me] := COMMIT;
   if (d[you] == UNCERTAIN))
      wait(me);
   elseif (d[you] == COMMIT))
      open_door;    -- resume communication;
      wakeup(you);
   endif;
end;

method AbortFairExchange() is
begin
   d[me] := ABORT;
   destroy(you);
   destroy(me);
end;
```

Fig. 3. Possible implementation of the fair exchange policy

FEA checks whether A has sent the item which B wants to have and vice versa. If both checks succeed, the FEA forwards A's item to B and B's item to A. This type of protocol is a *fair exchange protocol with an active trustee*.

In contrast to the solution presented in Section , the validity check of the items must occur within the FEA itself (and *not* in A and B) in order to ensure fairness. But note that because the items in consideration for exchange will usually be different ones in each instance of the problem, the activity of checking the items will be different every time the FEA is used. Thus, prior to executing fair exchange, both A and B must indicate to the FEA how it should check the other's item for validity.

The simplest solution would be for both A and B to devise a specific **check** method which takes the other's item as an input and returns **true** only if the item actually has the desired features. This approach is rather flexible because it enables to check an item in all ways allowed by the underlying programming language. For example, it would be possible to calculate cryptographic checksums over the entire item or over parts of it, it could compare parts of the item with some test data, or it could perform file format checks (e.g., "is the data a JPEG image?").

Subsequently, agent A devises a method checkB and B devises a method checkA. Both A and B send the code of this methods to the FEA before the fair exchange takes place. Within the fair exchange protocol, the FEA uses checkB to check the item sent by B and checkA to check the item sent by A. Only if both methods return true will the FEA complete the exchange.

The problem with this solution stems from its flexibility: If arbitrary code is allowed within the check routines, it is possible to cheat. To understand this, imagine that A devises a routine checkB(item) which first sends item to itself (i.e., to A) and then returns false. As a result, the exchange is in danger of ending in an unfair situation where A has obtained B's item but B has not received A's item. Consequently, it is necessary to guarantee that nothing "bad" happens within the check routines.

The bad things which may happen within the check routines are similar to those which were forbidden within the fair exchange policy described in Section : there must be no flow of information from inside the check routine to another agent. This should include information flow through hidden channels [ ], which is particularly difficult.

5.2   Solving the Check-Routine Problem

This section contains a discussion of four possible solutions for the check routine problem. It depends on the application scenario which one should be selected.

Parameterized check routines. One solution is to use a predefined check routine from a specialized library. For example, the FEA could provide a set of publicly accessible methods, e.g., to check whether a file represents a valid JPEG image. In this case an agent could simply send the identifier of the desired check routine to the FEA prior to the exchange.

Alternatively, the FEA could offer a generic check routine which is parameterized with a predefined range of values. This could be, for example, a routine which scans the input for a set of keywords (the parameter of the routine would be the set of words). Extending this idea, the generic check routine would take an expression in a formal "item description" language as an argument. A drawback of this approach is that this requires the definition of a rather complex language which is sufficiently expressive in order to allow the check for all relevant item properties.

---

[2] A problem which arises in the context of electronic money is that it is impossible to prevent double spending without online access to a bank. This means that the check routine *must* make an online query when checking the money. In this case we can only ensure that the amount of information flow out of the check routine is bounded.

Syntactic check. Instead of using generic `check` routines, A and B could still be allowed to write their own methods. In this case it must be possible to automatically verify that their respective routines play according to the rules. For example, by automatically scanning the agents' code before invoking it, it is possible to check whether a method contains the invocation of a `send` command. If no other way exists to smuggle information out of the `check` function, then fairness can be guaranteed. However, for leaking information usually other possibilities than using the `send` command exist. Fraudulent agents are likely to garble their harmful actions within innocent looking code and preventing agents from performing such malicious actions solely by using syntactic checks is a difficult task.

Mutual code checking. Instead of the FEA having to validate the `check` routines, this task can be transferred to the participating agents. This means that A validates B's `checkA` routine and vice versa. This solution makes the task easier for the FEA, but has its own limitations. Consider for example the following scenario: A is looking for a text containing a set of keywords and so it devises a method `checkB` which simply scans the item for these words. The code of this method is sent to B so that B can validate that nothing bad happens therein. But knowing the code of `checkB`, B can easily fool A by piecing together an arbitrary text containing these keywords. While not being unfair in a formal sense, the disclosure of its `check` routine lowers an agent's confidence in the quality of the received item.

The described scenario is by no means exotic: it always occurs when in addition to syntactic checking an agent wants to perform "semantic" checking by using heuristics. Instances of this problem are, e.g., plausibility checks on a credit card number or simple spot checks on mass-produced articles. Disclosure of the `check` routines bears the potential of cheating as explained above.

Sandboxing. A more powerful solution for verifying that the check routine well-behaves is to monitor its execution. Any attempt to execute an unfair command will be recognized at run-time. It will result in an immediate termination and rejection of the check routine. This approach for protecting the participating parties from malicious code is comparable with the sandbox model for Java applets. In contrast to the syntactic check, sandboxing is more immune against innocent looking, obfuscated code which is intended to deceive the other party. Another advantage of this security concept is that the timely termination of the check routines can also be monitored. If the execution time exceeds a previously defined time limit, the FEA stops computation and aborts the exchange. A limitation of sandboxing is its limited flexibility: Any command must either be allowed or forbidden. If for example communication is forbidden, then the client has no means to, e.g., obtain certificates from a key server.

5.3   Using Authentic Code

In this section we propose a novel solution for fair exchange which is not based on a designated TPE but instead uses a trusted third agent. The trust in such an agent is based on rule R6 of Section   : The agents A and B first cooperate to build a new agent (see below) and they both check whether this agent executes the exchange in a fair way. Then one of them starts this newly constructed agent, and the other party can query the cryptographic hash value of this agent. If it matches the hash of the previously checked agent, the started agent and the checked agent are both identical with overwhelming probability. This means that the started agent can be trusted to guarantee fairness.

The construction of this fair exchange agent consists of two parts: The basic functionality for the fair exchange is always the same and can be implemented by taking an appropriate piece of code out of a publicly available library (a pseudocode implementation is given in Figure   ). As all parts of such a public library usually have been examined in advance, they don't have to be checked again when they are used for the construction of the fair exchange agent. The second part of the fair exchange agent consists of the check routines. These are exchanged between the agents A and B and must then be carefully examined as described in the paragraph about mutual code checking in Section   . Only if the check routines turn out to be fair, they are built into the fair exchange agent.

```
begin
  receive(A, itemA) || receive(B, itemB);
  if ((checkA(itemA) != OK) OR (checkB(itemB) != OK))
    send (A, ''ABORT'') || send (B, ''ABORT'');
  else
    send (A, itemB) || send (B, itemA);
  endif;
end;
```

Fig. 4. The pseudocode of a generic fair exchange agent

The advantage of this approach is that the agents A and B are able to solve the fair exchange problem without further assistance. They can trust their newly constructed fair exchange agent because of the following two reasons: First, the code is known to both agents and has been checked for malicious instructions. Second, they can be sure that the fair exchange agent they use is identical with the previously examined code.

5.4   Using an Independent Fair Exchange Agent

The solution which uses authentic code for providing trust in the FEA has some drawbacks: The construction of the complete FEA might cause of lot of communication between the two agents A and B, and checking the fairness of the newly constructed agent might require a huge amount of computation. Apart from that, some properties (like the termination of the FEA) cannot be entirely validated and authentic code is not available on every platform for mobile agents.

A different solution for fair exchange uses a certified "freelance", i.e., independent FEA (IFEA), which acts as an active TTP: The IFEA is an agent which receives both items, checks them and performs the swap, if the items have the desired properties. In contrast to the solution with authentic code, the agents A and B needn't know the code of the IFEA in order to trust it. Instead, they have to trust the party which has created the IFEA. This trust can be established by a certificate which is issued by this party for its IFEA. This certificate ensures that the party has instructed the IFEA to perform an exchange in a fair way. The agents A and B must then only be able to verify the certificate provided with the IFEA.

When the agents A and B decide to start a fair exchange of their items, the IFEA is probably already running. Therefore it has to be very flexible in exchanging all kinds of items. This can be achieved if an agent which wants to exchange an item sends its code for item checking to the IFEA. This again leads to the problem of detecting malicious check routines which is discussed in detail in Section   . In contrast to the solution with authentic code, the burden of solving the **check** routine problem (with one of the approaches from Section   ) is now placed on the IFEA.

In the faultless case both check routines will usually accept the items which have been delivered to the IFEA. The IFEA forwards the items to the agents A and B and finishes the exchange by performing a reset. Now the IFEA can again be used for another fair exchange.

6   Summary and Conclusions

Due to its omnipresence, the fair exchange problem is an important problem in electronic commerce. It is at the core of almost every application processing electronic business transactions and by no means a problem solved easily. Fair exchange protocols must be devised carefully in order to cope with the many fault-tolerance and security problems encountered in today's networks.

In this paper we have shown that protocols for fair exchange can be substantially simplified by adopting the mobile agent paradigm of electronic commerce. The simplifications stem from the fact that many of the fault-tolerance and security problems which are present in the general network case can be ignored in the mobile agent scenario. For example, in the mobile agents paradigm it is assumed that agents can roam the network in a fault-tolerant manner, that their cargo is protected from disclosure and that the environment has the power to reset or terminate agents violating accepted behavioral policies.

The three solutions we have proposed are summarized in Table   . Algorithmically, solution 1 is probably the simplest one, but it involves adding functionality to a TPE. This might be prohibitively expensive since TPEs are complex devices which must be certified. Solutions 2 and 3 build upon existing TPE functionality, but both involve solutions to the check routine problem described in Sections   and   . Solution 2 places this burden upon the individual agents, i.e., they have to be able to analyze/monitor each other's **check** routine. This

Table 1. Summary of the three solutions

Solution	Section	What is revealed in advance?	Trust ensured by?
1. Change the TPE		nothing	TPE policy
2. Authentic Code		check routine	FEA code analysis and TPE (through authentic code)
3. Independent FEA		nothing	Trust in IFEA owner

solution works because both parties can trust in the authenticity of the FEA, which is guaranteed by the authentic code policy of the TPE. Solution 3 relieves the participating agents from solving the check routine problem by utilizing specialized agents to perform this task. Consequently, this solution seems to be the most "agent-friendly" way to offer a fair exchange service over an existing TPE infrastructure. However, the specialized FEAs have to be certified, a cost which must not be underestimated. In contrast, solution 2 does not involve (additional) certification overhead.

A point which is of interest to researchers studying fair exchange in the asynchronous network case is the following: Because the agent execution environment solves many of the fault-tolerance and security problems at hand, our solutions only need to solve the remaining exchange and security functionality. In this sense, they crystallize the "essence" of these parts of the exchange problem. Encapsulation of this functionality in program modules could lead to a more modular way of building fair exchange protocols [ ].

The solutions we have presented are both practical and efficient. They are practical because they can be implemented using existing or devised agent technology. They are efficient because all computations are local to one network host and solution 1 (Section) requires only two agent interactions (which is minimal). The efficiency of solutions 2 (Section) and 3 (Section) is only bounded by the amount of computation necessary to solve the check routine problem.

Still some questions remain: For example, despite the fact that we achieve strong fairness in our protocols, it is usually a user concern that a well-behaving participant can still prove that it has acted according to the protocol. How can this feature be added to our solutions? Future work will evaluate the applicability of our solutions in agent-based online shops.

Acknowledgments

We wish to thank Wolfgang Theilmann for his comments on a previous version of this paper and the anonymous referees for their useful feedback.

References

1. N. Asokan. *Fairness in electronic commerce.* PhD thesis, University of Waterloo, May 1998.

2. N. Asokan, M. Schunter, and M. Waidner. Optimistic protocols for fair exchange. In T. Matsumoto, editor, *4th ACM Conference on Computer and Communications Security*, pages 8–17, Zurich, Switzerland, Apr. 1997. ACM Press.

3. D. E. Denning. A lattice model of secure information flow. *Communications of the ACM*, 19(5):236–243, May 1976.

4. M. K. Franklin and M. K. Reiter. Fair exchange with a semi-trusted third party. In T. Matsumoto, editor, *4th ACM Conference on Computer and Communications Security*, pages 1–5,7, Zurich, Switzerland, Apr. 1997. ACM Press.

5. F. C. Gärtner, H. Pagnia, and H. Vogt. Approaching a formal definition of fairness in electronic commerce. In *Proceedings of the International Workshop on Electronic Commerce (WELCOM'99)*, pages 354–359, Lausanne, Switzerland, Oct. 1999. IEEE Computer Society Press.

6. F. Hohl. Time limited blackbox security: Protecting mobile agents from malicious hosts. In Vigna [   ], pages 92–113.   ,

7. D. Johansen, K. Marzullo, F. B. Schneider, K. Jacobsen, and D. Zagorodnov. NAP: Practical fault-tolerance for itinerant computations. In M. G. Gouda, editor, *Proceedings of the 19th IEEE International Conference on Distributed Computing Systems*, pages 180–189, Austin, Texas, June 1999. IEEE Computer Society Press.

8. H. Pagnia and F. C. Gärtner. On the impossibility of fair exchange without a trusted third party. Technical Report TUD-BS-1999-02, Darmstadt University of Technology, Department of Computer Science, Darmstadt, Germany, Mar. 1999. Available at http://www.informatik.tu-darmstadt.de/BS/Gaertner/publications/TUD-BS-1999-02.ps.gz. A substantially revised version is available upon request from the authors.   ,

9. V. Roth. Mutual protection of co-operating agents. In J. Vitek and C. Jensen, editors, *Secure Internet Programming: Security Issues for Mobile and Distributed Objects*, volume 1603 of *Lecture Notes in Computer Science*, pages 277–287. Springer-Verlag, New York, NY, USA, 1999.   ,

10. K. Rothermel and M. Straßer. A Fault-Tolerant Protocol for Providing the Exactly-Once Property of Mobile Agents. In *Proc. 17th IEEE Symposium on Reliable Distributed Systems 1998 (SRDS'98)*, pages 100–108, Los Alamitos, California, 1998. IEEE Computer Society Press.

11. T. Sander and C. F. Tschudin. Protecting mobile agents against malicious hosts. In Vigna [   ].   ,

12. S. Schneider. Formal analysis of a non-repudiation protocol. In *PCSFW: Proceedings of The 11th Computer Security Foundations Workshop*, pages 54–65. IEEE Computer Society Press, 1998.

13. G. Vigna, editor. *Mobile Agents and Security*, volume 1419 of *Lecture Notes in Computer Science*. Springer-Verlag, Berlin, 1998.

14. H. Vogt, H. Pagnia, and F. C. Gärtner. Modular fair exchange protocols for electronic commerce. In *Proceedings of the 15th Annual Computer Security Applications Conference*, pages 3–11, Phoenix, Arizona, Dec. 1999. IEEE Computer Society Press.   ,

15. U. G. Wilhelm. *A Technical Approach to Privacy based on Mobile Agents protected by Tamper-resistant Hardware*. PhD thesis, École Polytechnique Fédérale de Lausanne, Switzerland, May 1999.

16. U. G. Wilhelm, L. Buttyàn, and S. Staamann. On the problem of trust in mobile agent systems. In *Symposium on Network and Distributed System Security*, pages 114–124. Internet Society, Mar. 1998.   ,

Principles of Mobile Maude*

Francisco Durán, Steven Eker, Patrick Lincoln, and José Meseguer

SRI International
Menlo Park, CA 94025, USA

Abstract. Mobile Maude is a mobile agent language extending the rewriting logic language Maude and supporting mobile computation. Mobile Maude uses reflection to obtain a simple and general declarative mobile language design and makes possible strong assurances of mobile agent behavior. The two key notions are *processes* and *mobile objects*. Processes are located computational environments where mobile objects can reside. Mobile objects have their own code, can move between different processes in different locations, and can communicate asynchronously with each other by means of messages. Mobile Maude's key novel characteristics include: (1) reflection as a way of endowing mobile objects with "higher-order" capabilities; (2) object-orientation and asynchronous message passing; (3) a high-performance implementation of the underlying Maude basis; (4) a simple semantics without loss in the expressive power of application code; and (5) security mechanisms supporting authentication, secure message passing, and secure object mobility. Mobile Maude has been specified and prototyped in Maude. Here we present the Mobile Maude language for the first time, and illustrate its use in applications by means of Milner's cell-phone example. We also discuss security and implementation issues.

1 Introduction

Use of the Internet has exploded in recent years, and current technological trends may lead to new systems and business models based substantially on mobile code and mobile agents [,]. It seems likely that within a few years most major Internet sites will be hosting some form of mobile code or mobile agents. As more and more applications come to depend on mobile code, new risks for unintentional or malicious failures and for compromises of vital information must be avoided. Declarative mobile languages seem particularly promising to achieve high levels of confidence and security in mobile computing. This is because, by being directly based on formalisms with a precise semantics, there is a much shorter conceptual distance between the formal properties that must be ensured and the code. Furthermore, such formalisms can be *intrinsically concurrent*, further facilitating the programming and reasoning tasks.

One approach recently favored in declarative mobile language design is using *mobile calculi* that extend or modify the π-calculus [ ] with new features,

---

* Supported by DARPA through Rome Laboratories Contract F30602-97-C-0312, by ONR Contract N00014-99-C-0198, and by NSF Grant CCR-9505960.

D. Kotz and F. Mattern (Eds.): ASA/MA 2000, LNCS 1882, pp. 73– , 2000.
© Springer-Verlag Berlin Heidelberg 2000

including mechanisms for encryption and security. Calculi of this kind include, among others, the Spi Calculus [ ], the Join Calculus [ ], and the Ambient Calculus [ ]. In addition, there is a broader body of work favoring declarative approaches, including work in the related field of coordination languages [ ] and UNITY-based mobility [ ]. There has also been a great expansion of the capabilities and security of agent-based languages such as Ajanta [ ], OAA [ ] and D'Agents [ ].

Mobile Maude is an extension of Maude [ ] supporting mobile computation that uses reflection in a systematic way to obtain a simple and general declarative mobile language design. The formal semantics of Mobile Maude is given by a rewrite theory in rewriting logic. However, the fact that such a rewrite theory is executable (as exploited in the current simulator) does not overly constrain later implementation choices for a Mobile Maude system. We comment on such choices in Section . The two key notions of Mobile Maude are *processes* and *mobile objects*. Processes are located computational environments where mobile objects can reside. Mobile objects have their own code, can move between different processes in different locations, and can communicate asynchronously with each other by means of messages. Mobile Maude's key novel characteristics include:

- *Based on rewriting logic*, a simple first-order formalism that is intrinsically concurrent and has a clear mathematical semantics [ ].
- *Extends Maude*, a high performance interpreter and compiler implementation of rewriting logic.
- *Object-oriented and asynchronous*, with (mobile) objects as first-class entities in the language, and with direct support for asynchronous message-passing communication.
- *Reflective*: using rewriting logic reflection, the application code in a mobile object (a rewrite theory $\mathcal{R}$) is metarepresented as *data*, as a term $\overline{\mathcal{R}}$. This endows mobile objects with powerful "higher-order" capabilities within a simple first-order framework.
- *Simple rewriting semantics without loss in expressiveness*: the semantics of mobility is defined in an application-independent way by a small set of rewrite rules axiomatizing Mobile Maude's *system code*; however, *application code* inside mobile objects can be defined in Maude with great freedom and expressiveness.
- *Secure*, with underlying encryption primitives supporting authentication, secure message passing, and secure object mobility.

The above characteristics distinguish Mobile Maude from mobility calculi and from the other languages described above, and offer some novel advantages not available in such languages. In this paper, after briefly introducing rewriting logic, Maude, and reflection (Section 2) we give an overview of Mobile Maude and its rewriting semantics based on the current Mobile Maude simulator (Section 3) and discuss a simple mobile phone application (Section 4). Section 5 then discusses the design of Mobile Maude's security infrastructure; and Section 6 outlines our implementation plans. We end with some concluding remarks.

2 Rewriting Logic, Maude and Reflection

Rewriting logic [ ] is a very simple logic in which the state space of a distributed system is formally specified as an algebraic data type by means of an equational specification consisting of a signature of types and operations Σ and a collection of conditional equations E. The *dynamics* of such a distributed system is then specified by rewrite rules of the form $t \rightarrow t'$, where t, t' are Σ-terms, that describe the *local, concurrent transitions* possible in the system, namely, when a part of the distributed state fits the pattern t, then it can change to a new local state fitting the pattern t'. A *rewrite theory* is a triple (Σ, E, R), with (Σ, E) an equational specification axiomatizing a system's distributed state space, and R a collection of rewrite rules axiomatizing the system's local transitions.

Maude [ ] is a high-level reflective language and high-performance interpreter and compiler supporting rewriting logic specification and programming for a wide range of applications. Maude integrates an equational style of functional programming with an object-oriented programming style for highly concurrent object systems. Modules are rewrite theories whose basic axioms are rewrite rules.

2.1 Object-Oriented Modules

In Maude, object-oriented systems are specified by object-oriented modules in which *classes* and *subclasses* are declared. Each class is declared with the syntax

$$\texttt{class } C \mid a_1 : S_1, \ \ldots, \ a_n : S_n$$

where C is the name of the class, and for each $a_i : S_i$, a_i is an attribute identifier, and S_i is the sort (type or domain) over which the values of such an attribute identifier must range. Objects of a class are then record-like structures of the form

$$< O : C \mid a_1 : v_1, \ \ldots, \ a_n : v_n >$$

with O the name of the object, $v_1, \ldots, v_n$ the current values of its attributes, and with v_i of sort S_i for $1 \leq i \leq n$. Objects can interact with each other in a variety of ways, including the sending of messages. The state of a concurrent object system is called a *configuration*. Typically, a configuration is a multiset of objects and messages. The multiset union operator for configurations is denoted with empty syntax (juxtaposition). It is associative and commutative so that order and parentheses do not matter, and so that rewriting is multiset rewriting supported directly in Maude. The *dynamic behavior* of a concurrent object system is then axiomatized by specifying each of its basic concurrent transition patterns by a corresponding labeled rewrite rule that rewrites a multiset of objects and messages into a new multiset of objects and messages, perhaps including new object identifiers and new messages.

2.2   Reflection and the META-LEVEL

Rewriting logic is reflective in the precise sense that there is a finitely presented rewrite theory $\mathcal{U}$ which is *universal*, that is, for any finitely presented rewrite theory $\mathcal{R}$ (including $\mathcal{U}$ itself) we have the following equivalence:

$$\mathcal{R} \vdash t \longrightarrow t' \iff \mathcal{U} \vdash \langle \overline{\mathcal{R}}, \overline{t} \rangle \longrightarrow \langle \overline{\mathcal{R}}, \overline{t'} \rangle$$

where $\overline{\mathcal{R}}$, $\overline{t}$, and $\overline{t'}$ are terms representing, respectively, $\mathcal{R}$, t, and t' as data elements of $\mathcal{U}$.

Reflection is systematically exploited in the Maude design and implementation [ ], providing key features of the universal theory $\mathcal{U}$ in a built-in module called META-LEVEL. In particular, META-LEVEL has sorts Term and Module, so that the representations $\overline{t}$ and $\overline{\mathcal{R}}$ of a term t and a module $\mathcal{R}$ have sorts Term and Module, respectively. Furthermore, META-LEVEL provides key metalevel functions for rewriting and evaluating terms at the metalevel, namely, meta-apply, meta-reduce, and meta-rewrite [ ].

3   Mobile Maude

We explain below the design of processes and mobile objects and their rewriting semantics, based on a formal specification of Mobile Maude written in Maude. Note that this specification is executable.

3.1   Processes and Mobile Objects

The key entities in Mobile Maude are processes and mobile objects; both are modeled as distributed objects in classes P and MO, respectively. Processes are *located* computational environments *inside which* mobile objects can reside, can execute, and can send and receive messages to and from other mobile objects located in different processes. Mobile objects carry their own internal state and code (rewrite rules) with them, can move from one process to another, and can communicate with each other by asynchronous message passing. Figure   shows several processes in two locations, with (mobile) object o_3 moving from one process to another, and with object o_1 sending a message to o_2. The *names* of processes range over the sort Pid, whereas the names of mobile objects range over the sort Mid and have the form o(PI,N) with PI the name of the object's *parent* process, in which it was created, and N a number.

The class P of Mobile Maude processes is declared as follows,

```
class P | cnt: MachineInt, cf: Configuration, guests: Set[Mid],
          forward: PFun[MachineInt, Tuple[Pid, MachineInt]].
```

---

[1] The key operator for the sort Term is of the form _[_]: Qid TermList -> Term where the sort Qid of quoted identifiers is used to metarepresent operator names. Then a term such as, for example, X + Y is metarepresented as '_+_['X,'Y] .

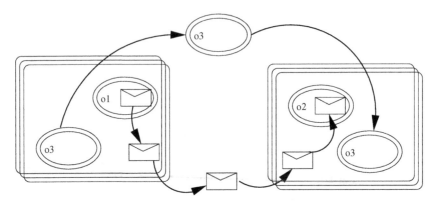

Fig. 1. Object and message mobility

Note the interesting fact that the attribute cf is itself a *configuration*, that is, a multiset of objects and messages. This means that processes exist as objects of an *outer* configuration of processes (plus messages and possibly mobile objects in transit) but also contain "in their belly" an *inner* configuration consisting of mobile objects and messages currently residing inside the process. Mobile objects can *move* from one process to another. For this reason, each process keeps information about the mobile objects currently in its belly in the guests attribute.

Since mobile objects may move from one process to another, reaching them by messages is nontrivial. The solution adopted in Mobile Maude is that, when a message's addressee is not in the current process, the message is forwarded to the mobile object's parent process. Each process stores forwarding information about the whereabouts of its children in its forward attribute, a partial function in PFun[MachineInt, Tuple[Pid, MachineInt]] that maps child number n to a pair consisting of the name of the process in which the object currently resides, and the number of "hops" to different processes that the mobile object has taken so far. The number of hops is important in disambiguating situations when old messages (containing old location information) arrive after newer messages containing current location. The most current location is that associated with the largest number of hops. Whenever a mobile object moves to a new process, the object's parent process is always notified. Note that this system does not guarantee message delivery in the case that objects move more rapidly than messages.

Mobile objects are specified as objects of the following class MO,

```
class MO | mod: Module, s: Term, p: Pid, hops: MachineInt, mode: Mode.
```

Note that the sorts Module and Term, associated to the attributes mod and s, respectively, are sorts in the module META-LEVEL, that is imported by the specification of Mobile Maude. They metarepresent Maude modules and terms in such modules. The mobile object's *module* must be object-oriented, and the mobile object's *state* must be the metarepresentation of a pair of configurations meaningful for that module and having the form C & C', with C' a multiset of *outgoing messages* that must be pulled out, and C containing unprocessed *incoming messages* and an *inner object*, with the *same identity* as that of the mobile object containing it. Therefore, we can think of a mobile object as a *wrapper* that encapsulates the state and code of its inner object and mediates its communication with other objects and its mobility. For this reason, Figure depicts mobile objects by two concentric circles, with the inner object and its incoming and outgoing messages contained in the inner circle. The process where the object currently resides is stored in the p attribute. The number of "hops" from one process to another is stored in the hops attribute. Finally, an object's mode is only active inside the belly of a process: moving objects are idle.

3.2   Mobile Maude's Rewriting Semantics

The entire semantics of Mobile Maude can be defined by a relatively small number of rewrite rules written in Maude. Such a specification is executable and can be used as a Mobile Maude simulator. We should think of such rules as a specification of the *system code* of Mobile Maude, that operates in an application-independent way providing all the object and process creation, message passing, and object mobility primitives (for our design of the actual system code see Section). By contrast, all *application code* is encapsulated in a metarepresented form within mobile objects and is executed at the metalevel inside such objects.

We give the flavor of Mobile Maude's rewriting semantics by commenting on four rules: three for object mobility, and one for mobile object execution. Other rules in the same style deal with message communication, mobile object and process creation, and so on. (See   .)

The three rules below govern object mobility. Such mobility is initiated by the mobile object's inner object, which puts the metarepresentation 'go[T'] in the second component (i.e., as an outgoing message) of the state. The term T' metarepresents the name of the process where the object wants to go. The rule message-out-move indicates how such a name is decoded by the downPid function, and shows in its righthand side the mobile object ready to go—which is indicated by being enclosed inside a go operator. Here and in what follows, mathematical variables (M, T, T', C, SMO etc.) are written in capitals, but their sort declarations are omitted. SMO, for example, stands for a set of mobile object ids.

```
rl [message-out-move]: < M: MO | s: '_&_[T, 'go[T']], mode: active >
  => go(downPid(T'),< M: MO | s: '_&_[T, {'none}'MsgSet], mode: idle >).

rl [go-proc]: < PI: P | cf: C go(PI', < M: MO | >), guests: M . SMO >
 => if PI =/= PI'
    then < PI: P | cf: C, guests: SMO > go(PI',< M: MO | >)
    else
      < PI: P | cf: C < M: MO | p: PI, mode: active >, guests: SMO >
    fi.
```

```
rl [arrive-proc]: go(PI,< o(PI', N): MO | hops: N' >)
   < PI: P | cf: C,guests: SMO,forward: F >
 => if PI == PI' then
      < PI: P | cf: C < o(PI', N): MO | p: PI,hops: N' + 1,
                       mode: active >, guests: o(PI', N) . SMO,
                       forward: F [ N -> (PI, N' + 1) ] >
      else < PI: P | cf: C < o(PI', N): MO | p: PI, hops: N' + 1,
                              mode: active >, guests: o(PI', N) . SMO >
            to PI' @ (PI, N' + 1) { N } fi.
```

The rule **go-proc** then initiates the move of the object from its current process (PI) to another process PI' by extracting it from PI and putting it in the outer configuration. The **arrive-proc** rule then finishes the motion by inserting the mobile object inside the belly of the target process in active mode and with updated information about its current process and number of hops, and includes the object's name in the set of current guests. However, if the destination process happens to be the parent process, then the forwarding information has to be updated; otherwise, the parent process has to be informed of the mobile object's whereabouts by means of the message to PI' @ (PI, N' + 1) { N }.

The execution of mobile objects uses reflection and is accomplished by the following rule which simply invokes **meta-rewrite**. This rule can be modified to limit resources used in execution of each meta-rewrite and to enforce fairness.

```
rl [do-something]: < M: MO | mod: MOD, s: T, mode: active >
   => < M: MO | s: meta-rewrite(MOD, T, 1) >
```

4   A Mobile Cell Phone Example

In [ ], Milner presents a simple mobile telephones example to illustrate the π-calculus. We use a variant of this example to illustrate how mobile *application code* can be written in Maude and can be wrapped in mobile objects. As already explained in Section   , Mobile Maude *systems code* is specified by a relatively small number of rules for processes, mobile objects, mobility, and message passing. Such rules work in an *application-independent* way. Application code, on the other hand, can be written as Maude object-oriented modules with great freedom, except for being aware that, as explained in Section   , the top level of the state of a mobile object has to be a pair of configurations, with the second component containing outgoing messages and the first containing the inner object and incoming messages.

The example includes a set of *cars*, with mobile phones in them, which move around a large geographical area. The mobile phones are always in contact with one of the *bases*, which communicate among themselves through a control *center*. When the center detects that a car is approaching a new base, it sends messages to the base currently in contact with the car asking it to release the car, and to the new base, asking it to get in contact with it.

We represent cars, bases, and centers as objects of respective classes `Car`, `Base`, and `Center`. Such objects in the application code will then be embedded as *inner objects* of their corresponding mobile objects. We assume that the mobile objects encapsulating different bases are located in different process, and that the mobile object encapsulating a car is in the process of the base it is currently in contact with. We also assume that there is a single mobile object encapsulating the center, which is located in a different process. The center causes a car mobile object to move from the process of the base it is currently in contact with to the process of the new base it switches to.

An object of the `Car` class has two attributes, `base`, storing the name of the base it is currently in contact with, and `phone-book`, a set storing the names of other cars it knows about and can call.

```
class Car | base: Oid, phone-book: Set[Oid] .
```

An object of the `Base` class has two attributes, `cars`, storing the names of the cars the base is in contact with, and `center`, the name of the center.

```
class Base | cars: Set[Oid], center: Oid .
```

The center is an object of class `Center`. The connection information is a partial function, mapping each car name to the base it is currently in contact with, stored in the `cntrl` attribute. In addition, the center stores the names of all bases and cars in the `bases` and `cars` attributes.

```
class Center | cntrl: PFun[Oid, Oid], bases: Set[Oid], cars: Set[Oid] .
```

Cars talk to each other through their respective bases, with the center mediating the conversations between cars in different bases. For simplicity, we model any words said to a car object O by means of the term `talk(O)`. Mobile Maude can model binding and rebinding of resources in mobile systems. A car object can initiate a conversation by choosing another car name in its phone book and placing a message addressed to its current base with such a request in the outgoing messages part of the state, according to the rule

```
rl [talk]: < O: Car | base: O', phone-book: O'' + OS > C & none
                => < O: Car | > C & (to O': talk(O'')).
```

Other rules then govern the handling of the request by the base, which forwards it to the other car if it is also in contact with it, or otherwise asks the center to forward it to the appropriate base. Such car talking rules, and the entire example, can be found in   .
We focus instead on the application code rules that—when such code is encapsulated in corresponding mobile objects—cause car mobile objects to move from one process to another. We assume that, by some other mechanism not modeled here, the center can know the positions of the cars and the bases, and therefore can detect that a car is approaching a new base different from the one it is in contact with, and can then start the switching of the connections. The

center then sends a **release** message to the base connected to such a car and an **alert** message to the new base. When a base receives a **release** message it sends a **switch** message to the car with the identifier of its new base. When a base receives the **alert** message it saves the identifier of the new car connected with it. The reception of a **switch** message by a car causes it to connect to a new base, by updating its **base** attribute, and by placing the **go** command in the outgoing messages part of the state, causing the mobile object encapsulating the car to move to the process in which the new base is located (see rule **message-out-move** in Section   ). Note that **crl** is a conditional rule, that is, a rule that is only enabled when the condition is true. As before, sort declarations for the variables (O, O', OS, OS', C, etc) are omitted.

```
crl [switch]: < O: Center | cntrl: PF,bases: O' + O''' + OS,
                             cars: O'' + OS' > C & none
   => < O: Center | cntrl: PF[O'' -> O'] > C & (to O': alert(O''))
      (to O''': release O'' to O') if PF[O''] == O'''.

rl [release]: < O: Base | cars: O' + OS >
              (to O: release O' to O'') C & none
   => < O: Base | cars: OS > C & (to O': switch(O'')).

rl [alert]: < O: Base | cars: OS > (to O: alert(O'))
   => < O: Base | cars: O' + OS >.

rl [move]: < O: Car | > (to O: switch(o(PI, N))) C & none
   => < O: Car | base: o(PI, N) > & go(PI).
```

5 Mobile Maude Security

In Mobile Maude, like in all mobile-agent systems, four key security issues should be addressed: protecting an individual machine (physical machine or in general any execution environment) from malicious agents, protecting a group of machines from various forms of attack, protecting agents from malicious hosts, and protecting groups of agents from one-another. For example, to protect an individual machine from malicious agents, we employ cryptographic authentication of the agent's authority, resource constraints and fairness management based on the agent's identity, and secure execution environments that provide strong partitioning (if not some level of noninterference) and enforce the decisions of the resource manager. No mobile agent systems today meet the strongest form of all these security needs. Mobile Maude will provide a platform with some of these kinds of secure services built-in, and the Maude reflective framework provides an excellent vehicle for experimentation with techniques to provide a complete secure solution for mobile agents. Specifically, Mobile Maude supports the privacy of data through encryption, the authentication of communications through a public-key infrastructure service, the security of mobility (built on both of the above), and the reliability and integrity of computation by means of redundant checks.

5.1   Mobile Maude Security Infrastructure

The security features of Mobile Maude are provided as optional features for those applications which require one or more properties of security, privacy, authenticity, and integrity. The Mobile Maude object system is used to define subclasses of Mobile Maude objects, processes, and locations which can provide the required features as needed. For example, the birthplace of an object acts as the authoritative signature key repository, and birthplaces are authenticated in a hierarchy back to a predefined set of primordial sources of trust. Thus to authenticate a message, a receiver can contact the birthplace of the sending object, and securely obtain the public key of that object, and then authenticate that the message was properly signed using PGP or similar secure signature scheme. This is similar to the Telescript [ ], D'Agents [ ], and IBM Aglets [ ]. In Aglets, for example, migrating Java code is cryptographically signed and then standard Java security resource mechanisms are enforced. In Mobile Maude the communication to the birthplace must also be carried out using authentication, and thus authentication keys for all birthplaces must be obtained from the roots of trust entrusted with public keys. When a Maude mobile object changes locations, its entire state can be signed by the originating process and encrypted using the public key of the destination process. In this way, as the object moves over untrusted communication paths, the object cannot be altered or interrogated, and can maintain valuable secrets (such as it's own signature keys).

5.2   Secure Message Passing and Mobility

There are several approaches to providing security for messages and mobility in a mobile context. A simple and efficient but relatively insecure approach is security by obscurity, where processes or objects are inaccessible if one does not know their name. By hiding the name of a location, process, or object, only those objects which already know the name can communicate with it. We adopt in addition the encryption of messages and objects in transit. Objects and processes that send or receive messages encrypt the communication and forward it so that malicious network manipulation cannot read or modify the communicated content.

5.3   Resource Bounds and Fairness

Another key aspect of Mobile Maude is the provision of fairness and other guaranteed bounds on resource allocation. The fairness provided by Mobile Maude prevents some kinds of denial-of-service attacks by ensuring that all processes are allowed to make progress, even in the presence of large numbers of spurious messages or objects. However, more aggressive bounds on object-generation and message-generation can be provided and can be combined with authentication techniques to ensure even stronger guarantees on performance.

6 Implementation Approaches

The implementation of Mobile Maude presents several technical challenges. One of the interesting notions is that rewriting logic allows one to specify something at a high level of abstraction, while also allowing one to refine toward an efficient implementation. That is, Mobile Maude is both a formal system specified via a rewrite theory and an implementation of such a system. Of course, although the rewriting logic specification is executable this leaves open many possibilities for a concrete real implementation. The current Maude specification built on top of Maude 1.0.5 is executable and can be used as a simulator. We have thought through the detailed design of, and plan to implement a specific efficient single-host implementation of Mobile Maude.

For the single-host executable implementation, we will build upon the forthcoming Maude 2.0 interpreter/compiler, utilizing the builtin object system, for object/message fairness. Maude is implemented as a high performance interpreter (up to 2.98 million rewrites per second on a 667Mhz Xeon) and as a compiler (up to 15 million rewrites per second on a 667MHz Xeon). The Mobile Maude system code will still be written entirely in Maude, and thus locations and processes will be encoded as Maude terms. This implementation effort will be completed rapidly once Maude 2.0 is available, by simplifying and extending the existing specification.

For the second implementation effort, we will focus on true distributed execution. We will define and build a very simple Mobile Object Transfer Protocol (MOTP) 0.1 on top of TCP/IP. We will implement Mobile Maude servers written in Maude, using the built-in string handling and internet socket modules planned for Maude 2.0. The Maude 2.0 socket modules will support non-blocking client and server TCP sockets (at the OS level) and will make use of the concurrency inherent in the Maude object-message model rather than relying on threads as found in legacy programming languages. In this implementation effort, a Mobile Maude server will run on top of a Maude 2.0 interpreter, keeping track of the current locations of mobile objects created on a host, handle change of location messages, reroute messages to mobile objects and run the code of mobile objects by invoking the metalevel. In this implementation, processes could be actual, if forking new interpreters or JIT Maude compilation is made available in Maude 2.0, or could be simulated (i.e. encoded as Maude terms). The total implementation effort here is moderate — over and above the effort need to implement Maude 2.0, since much of the infrastructure including implementation of MOTP 0.1 will be done using the Maude 2.0 language implementation.

7 Concluding Remarks

We have presented the basic concepts of Mobile Maude, a new declarative mobile language design extending Maude and based on rewriting logic reflection. We have explained the language's semantics based on its current specification, which serves also as a simulator for the language. We have also illustrated the use of Maude with a simple mobile cell phone application. Security and implementation issues have also been discussed. Much work on implementation, security infrastructure, formal methodology, and applications remains ahead.

Mobile Maude's simple declarative semantics together with its security infrastructure offers the promise of being able to reach high levels of assurance about the language itself and about specific applications through the use of a variety of formal methods. This promise has to be fulfilled by developing adequate formal methodologies, and by demonstrating how it can be attained in practice for substantial applications. The encouraging experience using a flexible range of formal methods in Maude (see the surveys [,]) and the formal tools already available [ ] and planned for the future will help in this task.

Acknowledgement

We would like to thank the reviewers for many insightful comments on this paper.

References

1. M. Abadi and A. Gordon. A calculus for cryptographic protocols: the spi calculus. *Information and Computation*, 148:1–70, 1999. An extended version of this paper appears as Research Report 149, Digital Equipment Corporation Systems Research Center, January 1998.
2. L. Cardelli and A. Gordon. Mobile ambients. In M. Nivat, editor, *Proceedings of FoSSaCS'98: Foundations of Software Science and Computational Structures*, number 1378 in Lecture Notes in Computer Science, pages 140–155. Springer-Verlag, 1998. To appear in TCS July 2000.
3. P. Ciancarini and A. W. (eds.). *Coordination Languages And Models*, volume 1594. Springer LNCS, 1999.
4. M. Clavel, F. Durán, S. Eker, P. Lincoln, N. Martí-Oliet, J. Meseguer, and J. Quesada. Maude: specification and programming in rewriting logic. SRI International, January 1999, $\cdot$, ,
5. M. Clavel, F. Durán, S. Eker, and J. Meseguer. Building equational proving tools by reflection in rewriting logic. In *Proc. of the CafeOBJ Symposium '98, Numazu, Japan.* CafeOBJ Project, April 1998. $\cdot$
6. G. Denker, J. Meseguer, and C. Talcott. Formal specification and analysis of active networks and communication protocols: the Maude experience. In *Proc. DARPA Information Survivability Conference and Exposition DICEX 2000, Vol. 1, Hilton Head, South Carolina, January 2000*, pages 251–265. IEEE, 2000.
7. C. Fournet and G. Gonthier. The reflexive cham and the join-calculus. In *Proceedings of 23rd ACM Symposium on Principles of Programming Languages*, pages 52–66. ACM, 1996.
8. R. S. Gray, D. Kotz, G. Cybenko, and D. Rus. D'Agents: Security in a multiple-language, mobile-agent system. In G. Vigna, editor, *Mobile Agents and Security*, LNCS 1419, pages 154–187. Springer-Verlag, 1998. ,
9. D. Kotz and R. S. Gray. Mobile agents and the future of the Internet. *ACM Operating Systems Review*, 33(3):7–13, August 1999.

10. D. Lange and M. Oshima. *Programming and Deploying Java Mobile Agents with Aglets.* Addison-Wesley, 1998.
11. D. B. Lange and M. Oshima. Seven good reasons for mobile agents. *Communications of the Association for Computing Machinery*, 42:88–89, March 1999.
12. D. Martin, A. Cheyer, and D. Moran. The open agent architecture: A framework for building distributed software systems. *Applied Artificial Intelligence*, 13:91–128, 1999. Available via
13. J. Meseguer. Rewriting logic and Maude: a wide-spectrum semantic framework for object-based distributed systems. To appear in *Proc. FMOODS 2000* Kluwer, 2000.
14. J. Meseguer. Conditional rewriting logic as a unified model of concurrency. *Theoretical Computer Science*, 96(1):73–155, 1992.   ,
15. R. Milner, J. Parrow, and D. Walker. A calculus of mobile processes (Parts I and II). *Information and Computation*, 100:1–77, 1992.   ,
16. G. Roman, P. McCann, and J. Plun. Mobile UNITY: Reasoning and specification in mobile computing. *ACM Transactions on Software Engineering and Methodology*, 6:250–282, July 1997.
17. A. Tripathi, N. Karnik, M. Vora, T. Ahmed, and R. Singh. Mobile agent programming in ajanta. In *Proceedings of the 19th International Confernce on Distributed Computing Systems (ICDCS '99)*, 1999.
18. J. White. Telescript technology: the foundation for the electronic marketplace. General Magic White Paper, General Magic, Inc., 1994.

Secure Dynamic Reconfiguration of Scalable CORBA Systems with Mobile Agents*

Fabio Kon, Binny Gill, Manish Anand,
Roy Campbell, and M. Dennis Mickunas

Department of Computer Science
University of Illinois at Urbana-Champaign

Abstract. As various Internet services, e-commerce, and information systems permeate our lives, their continual availability becomes a dominant issue. But continuing software evolution requires system reconfiguration. Running systems must upgrade their components or change their configuration parameters. In addition, Internet services often need to serve thousands or millions of users. This scenario raises three conflicting issues: availability, configurability, and scalability.

We propose the use of mobile reconfiguration agents for the efficient, secure, and scalable dynamic reconfiguration of Internet systems. We describe a CORBA object-oriented framework that supports dynamic reconfiguration and allows customization to different kinds of computing environments ranging from PDAs and embedded systems with limited resources to powerful workstations.

1 Introduction

The scope of Internet services continues to expand, stretching to new fields and encompassing more and more human activities in the virtual world of the web. Activities such as management of bank accounts, reading news, accessing medical information, filing income taxes, submitting articles to scientific conferences, getting weather and natural disaster information, and consolidating votes in elections or referenda stress the importance of service availability, reliability, and security. However, the rapid evolution of software requires frequent code updates and reconfiguration. Maintaining the flexibility and rapid growth of these systems while ensuring the service requirements on such a scale as the Internet is a challenging problem.

A flexible service can adapt to meet changing requirements and resource availability. However, flexibility usually conflicts with availability. A service provider must often shut down, reconfigure, and restart a service in order to update or reconfigure it. But, disruption may result in business loss, as in the case of e-commerce, or it may put lives in danger, as in the case of systems delivering

* This research is supported by the National Science Foundation, grants 98-70736 and EIA99-72884EQ. Fabio Kon is supported in part by CAPES-Brazil, proc. 1405/95-2.

D. Kotz and F. Mattern (Eds.): ASA/MA 2000, LNCS 1882, pp. 86–   , 2000.
© Springer-Verlag Berlin Heidelberg 2000

disaster information. Research in dynamic configuration [ ] seeks solutions to this problem. By breaking a complex system into smaller components and by allowing the dynamic replacement and reconfiguration of individual components with minimal disruption of system execution, it is possible to combine high degrees of flexibility and availability.

Scalability also conflicts with flexibility and it is usually not addressed by research in dynamic configuration. Services such as video on demand, on-line bookstores, and search engines must maintain a high level of parallelism in order to fulfill their demand. World-wide services with high-bandwidth requirements such as on-line sales of software must be readily available in different countries. The problem is that reconfiguring and updating a distributed collection of servers is troublesome. It may lead to wasted bandwidth – as duplicated information is sent through the same Internet lines – and it introduces several problems related to consistency and fault-tolerance. In this paper, we present an architecture that solves the problems of availability, flexibility, and scalability in an integrated and secure way.

2   Application Scenarios

The application of mobile agents to a variety of distributed computations can improve performance significantly. It also provides a uniform way to deal with code mobility and disconnected operations. We now look at two different uses of mobile agents for dynamic configuration.

Multimedia Distribution System. We first identified the need for mobile reconfiguration agents for Internet systems when we developed a component-based system for scalable distribution of multimedia streams [ ]. This system realizes distribution using a network of *Reflectors* spread across a wide area. Each Reflector works as a relay, receiving input multimedia packets from a list of trusted sources and forwarding these packets to other Reflectors or to end-user clients. The communication between each pair of reflectors can use a variety of protocols depending upon the situation.

Our experience with this system ranges from point-to-point audio conferencing to live broadcast of video and audio through a network of more than 30 Reflectors delivering multimedia streams to millions of users across five continents [ ]. The difficulty in carrying out those experiments, managing more than 30 Reflectors in a wide-area network, exposed the necessity of flexible mechanisms for runtime reconfiguration as well as agent-based tools for optimizing bandwidth utilization in code distribution and component reconfiguration.

Using the Reflector system, we carried out the live broadcast of the NASA Mars Pathfinder mission from a PC station at the Jet Propulsion Laboratory, a broadcast that lasted for several months. During that period, we found programming errors in the Reflector code and were forced to update the executable code in all the machines manually. In addition, system reconfigurations, like increasing the maximum number of allowed clients or adding new multimedia channels, were also cumbersome since the administrator had to connect to each of the Reflectors separately.

In the following sections we present our solution to the problems mentioned above. We reorganized the Reflector code to permit the dynamic replacement of some of its fundamental components. Thus, using the reconfiguration agent infrastructure described in sections   and   , Reflector administrators are now able to distribute new implementations of Reflector components and to replace old implementations by new ones on-the-fly.

Mobile Computing and Factory Control Systems. Mobile reconfiguration agents also aid in industrial settings where embedded software systems control factory machinery. The administrator can walk on the factory floor, inspecting the physical machinery while using a PDA to inspect the state of the digital control devices by contacting them through infra red or wireless connections. Using a graphical management tool, the administrator may create agents that visit the controllers in that section and return the collected information to the PDA. Using this information, the administrator can then create appropriate agents and inject them into the network, reconfiguring the system to optimize production.

3   Configurable Middleware

To support dynamic (re)configuration of distributed component-based systems, we built *dynamicTAO* [ ], a CORBA ORB that enables on-the-fly reconfiguration of its internal engine. *dynamicTAO* exports an interface for loading and unloading components into the ORB runtime and for inspecting the ORB configuration state. It can also be used for dynamic reconfiguration of applications running on top of the ORB and even for the reconfiguration of non-CORBA applications.

The *dynamicTAO* architectural framework is depicted in figure . The *Persistent Repository* stores component implementations in the local file system organizing them in hierarchical *categories*. It offers methods for manipulating categories and the implementations of each category. Once a component implementation is stored in the local repository, it can be dynamically loaded into the system runtime. A *Network Broker* receives reconfiguration requests and forwards them to the *Dynamic Service Configurator*, which supplies common operations for dynamic configuration of components at runtime.

We delegate some of the basic configuration tasks to components of the ACE framework [ ] such as the ACE_Service_Config – used to process startup configuration files and manage dynamic linking – and the ACE_Service_Repository – used to manage loaded implementations.

System administrators or "intelligent" reconfiguration software can drive the reconfiguration of applications running on top of *dynamicTAO* by connecting to a network broker using a given TCP/IP port or a CORBA IDL interface. This scheme uses the Distributed Configuration Protocol (DCP) (see   ), which defines commands for code distribution, inspection of dynamic state, reconfiguration of runtime software architecture, and reconfiguration of running components. Figure   shows the *DynamicConfigurator* IDL interface that supports DCP.

The first nine operations shown in figure   are used to inspect the dynamic structure of a particular domain and to retrieve information about the different abstractions. In our model, a *category* represents the type of a component and each category typically contains different *implementations*, i.e., dynamically loadable code stored in the local persistent repository. Once an implementation is loaded into the system runtime, it becomes a *loaded implementation* and can be associated with a logical *component* in the application domain. Finally, components have *hooks* which represent inter-component dependencies, reflecting the runtime software architecture of the application and its underlying ORB.

The `load_impl` operation dynamically loads a component implementation from the ORB persistent repository into the system runtime and starts running it. `hook_impl` attaches it to a hook in one of the components in the domain. `remove_impl` finalizes and unloads a component from the runtime and `configure_impl` is used to send component-specific configuration messages to a given component. `upload_impl` allows a remote entity to store code for an implementation in the persistent repository, so that it can later be linked to a running process. `download_impl` allows a remote client to retrieve the code for an implementation from the ORB persistent repository.

4   *dynamicTAO* Reconfiguration Agents

Our initial version of *dynamicTAO* and its DCP implementation required a point-to-point connection between the administrative tool and an application process in order to configure that particular application process. But this approach did not scale. If a system administrator needed to upgrade a certain component of an on-line service composed of 30 replicas, it was necessary to connect to each replica separately, upload the new implementation of the component, and reconfigure the replica.

As a first solution to this problem we considered implementing a management front-end that would allow administrators to type sequences of reconfiguration

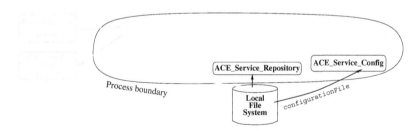

Fig. 1. *dynamicTAO* components

```
interface DynamicConfigurator                  void hook_impl (in string loadedImpl,
{                                                               in string compName,
  typedef sequence<string> sList;                               in string hookName);
  typedef sequence<octet> implCode;
                                                void suspend_impl   (in string loadedImpl);
  sList list_categories ();                     void resume_impl    (in string loadedImpl);
  sList list_impls (in string categName);       void remove_impl    (in string loadedImpl);
  sList list_loaded_impls ();                   void configure_impl (in string loadedImpl,
  sList list_domain_components ();                                   in string message);
  sList list_hooks (in string compName);
  string get_impl_info   (in string implName);  void upload_impl    (in string categName,
  string get_comp_info   (in string compName);                      in string impName,
  string get_hooked_comp (in string compName,                       in implCode binCode);
                          in string hookName);  void download_impl  (in string categName,
  string get_latest_vers (in string categName);                     inout string impName,
                                                                    out implCode binCode);
  long load_impl (in string categName,          void delete_impl    (in string categName,
                  in string impName,                                 in string impName);
                  in string params)           };
```

Fig. 2. The *DynamicConfigurator* interface

actions that would be sent to a list of application nodes. Although this approach would improve scalability by simplifying the work of the administrator, it would not solve the problem of bandwidth waste, i.e., sending large amounts of duplicated information across long-distance Internet lines.

The solution we adopted was to allow administrators to organize the nodes of their Internet systems in a hierarchical manner for reconfiguration purposes. The administrator specifies the topology of the distributed service as a directed graph and creates a *mobile reconfiguration agent* which is injected into the network. The reconfiguration agent then visits the nodes of this graph of interconnected ORBs. Each ORB first replicates and forwards the agent to neighboring nodes, then executes the agent locally, processing its reconfiguration commands, and, finally, collects the reconfiguration results, sending them back to the neighboring agent source.

Using this approach, the administrator can organize the reconfiguration hierarchy to optimize the data flow between distant application nodes. The reconfiguration commands are executed in parallel in the various nodes, improving response time. If desired, the graph may contain different levels of redundancy so that the system can tolerate the failure of some of the nodes in the reconfiguration network. To enhance scalability and decentralize administration, different administrative domains may select a *Domain Representative* for the purpose of receiving reconfiguration agents. The global administrator only needs to include the *Domain Representative* in the distribution graph. It is then the responsibility of the representative to forward the agent to the relevant nodes in its domain.

In this model, the agent behavior is defined by its reconfiguration script and graph, which are specified by the administrator. In Section   , we describe how we extend our model to support *autonomous* agents that decide by themselves which nodes to visit and which reconfigurations to perform. Overall, our goal was to develop a flexible infrastructure that could support different flavors of reconfiguration agents.

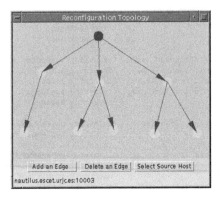

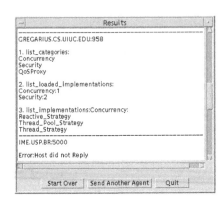

(a) Creating the graph edges   (b) Results returned by agent

Fig. 3.

4.1   Implementation

Our implementation of the mobile reconfiguration agent infrastructure consists
of (1) extensions to the original implementation of *dynamicTAO* for receiving,
processing, and forwarding reconfiguration agents, and (2) a Java graphical front-
end for specifying reconfiguration graphs and for assembling and sending reconfiguration agents. The administrator selects those ORBs that will be part of the
reconfiguration graph and, using the mouse, draws directed edges connecting
the graph nodes as shown in figure   . Once the reconfiguration graph is established, the graphical front-end assists the administrator in building a script
of DCP commands that are codified into a reconfiguration agent. Finally, the
administrator instructs the tool to send the agent to the initial node in the graph.

Each agent contains (1) a copy of the reconfiguration graph (so that different
agents can operate on different graphs at the same time), (2) a script of DCP
commands to be interpreted on each node in the graph, and (3) a unique sequence
number which is used to avoid processing duplicated copies of the same agent on
the same node. When the agent comes back to the administrator node, the results
returned by all the nodes in the reconfiguration graph are finally displayed to the
administrator through the graphical front-end. The system also draws attention
to the nodes that did not reply within a given timeout. Figure   shows the
results returned by an agent containing three DCP inspection commands (also
called an *inspection agent*).

Our agent dissemination system can be seen as a simple, lightweight implementation of reliable multicast over TCP/IP. We intentionally adopted this
simple and reliable solution for agent transmission because it lets us concentrate
on the dynamic configuration aspects of the problem. However, depending upon
the topology of the reconfiguration network (for example, if the nodes have many
output edges), it may be worthwhile to use other underlying protocols such as
IP-Multicast for distributing agents. In that case, however, the complexity of the
middleware would be much higher since it would have to guarantee reliability
over a non-reliable protocol.

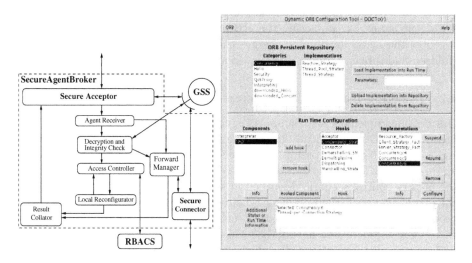

(a) The Secure Agent Broker   (b) The *Doctor* configuration tool

Fig. 4.

4.2   Security

To provide security, our architecture supports access control, authentication, and encryption by using our group's CORBA implementation of the standard General Security Services (GSS) API [ ]. We adopted the Role-Based Access Control model (RBAC) because it is more flexible and easier to manage than the traditional DAC approach used in systems like Unix and Windows [ ].

We extended *dynamicTAO* to include an instance of a *SecureAgentBroker*, a subclass of the *Network Broker* that supports secure reconfiguration agents. As shown in figure   , it uses a component implementing the *GSS API* and a *Role-Based Access Control Service (RBACS)*. The administrator who wishes to inject a reconfiguration agent into the network establishes a secure connection with the root node in the distribution graph by using a GSS-enhanced version of the administrative front-end. We use the GSS encryption mechanisms for data privacy and integrity. Thus, unauthorized principals are not able to decrypt the agent or tamper with it. The system ensures authenticity by using credentials and delegated credentials supplied by the GSS. The RBACS provides mechanisms by which the *SecureAgentBroker* enforces access control. Thus, the system is able to recognize multiple roles such as, for example, *admin*, *user*, and *alien*. The *admin* might have all the rights for reconfiguration and inspection; the *user*, only inspection; and the *alien* might have no rights.

Whenever a *SecureAgentBroker* needs to forward a reconfiguration agent to another node, it first establishes a secure connection with it. Then, it forwards the encrypted agent along with the credential and role name of the original author of the agent. On receiving a reconfiguration agent, the broker decrypts it and checks for integrity and authenticity by using the GSS API. It then forwards the agent to other nodes as dictated by the distribution tree accompanying the

agent. The *Access Controller* checks the authorization for each DCP command
the agent issues by contacting the RBACS. If the access is valid, the broker
executes the agent locally and merges the results with the results from all its
children nodes before forwarding the collated results to its parent.

4.3 Plugging Different Interpreters – Java Agents

Our default implementation supports agents with simple reconfiguration scripts
based on the DCP protocol. On the one hand, this allowed us to write an extremely lightweight interpreter that processes the agents efficiently. This is very
appropriate for PDAs and embedded systems that can be found, for example, in
the factory control scenario described in section . On the other hand, it limits
the expressiveness and autonomy of the reconfiguration agents. By using a more
powerful language for reconfiguration such as Java, the administrator is able to
write more sophisticated agents that can use the agent and ORB state to make
decisions about their actions. To achieve that, we organized our infrastructure as
an object-oriented framework to which different kinds of agent interpreters and
mechanisms can be plugged. For example, by plugging a Java Virtual Machine,
we added support for Java agents.

We encapsulated Sun's JVM into a component that can be dynamically
loaded into the *dynamicTAO* domain; this component exports an interface that
contains operations for loading and interpreting Java bytecode. In addition to
the reconfiguration topology graph, that now can be modified on-the-fly, the
Java agent carries its dynamic state from node to node and it contains Java
bytecode that is interpreted inside a sand-box so that its actions can be limited.
By using the *DynamicConfigurator* IDL interface (see figure), the Java bytecode
can issue inspection and reconfiguration commands to the ORB domain. Based
on the result of these commands the agent can (1) update the state it carries
from node to node, (2) change its behavior to adapt to the environment and user
preferences on each node, and (3) modify the reconfiguration graph, deciding to
migrate to a different set of nodes. In that manner, our framework offers both
simple agents based on DCP scripts for environments with limited resources and
powerful Java agents that can carry state and modify its behavior along the way.

4.4 A Discussion on Fault-Tolerance and Consistency

Our experience with distributed computer systems has shown that several applications do not require strict consistency between the components in the different
nodes. When deploying the multimedia distribution system described in section
for example, we were able to use different versions of Reflector components simultaneously. In many cases, even if a component update was successful in part
of the nodes and failed in another part, the distributed system could continue
working gracefully until all the updates were achieved manually.

To keep the system small and efficient, we opted not to provide strong guarantees about the execution of the reconfiguration commands in the current implementation. On a single node, some reconfiguration commands may fail while

others succeed; it is the responsibility of the agent to catch the exceptions raised by the failed commands and treat them accordingly. Also, reconfiguration commands may succeed on some nodes and fail on others. To cope with these errors, the system detects the failures and the graphical front-end (shown in figure   ) displays to the administrator where they occurred and the respective diagnosis messages. Then, using a separate tool called *Doctor* (the Dynamic ORB Configuration Tool in figure   ), the administrator can connect to the node where the failure occurred, inspect its state and reconfigure the node manually. By navigating through ORB and application components interactively, the administrator can investigate the causes of the errors, and fix them.

On the other hand, it is possible to achieve the effects of atomic transactions using the functionality we are offering through the Java agents. On an individual node, the Java agent can be programmed to store the previous state of the system before starting to make any changes. Should an error occur during the reconfiguration process on that node, the Java code can catch the exceptions and bring the configuration back to the initial state.

To achieve the effects of atomic transactions on the distributed system as a whole, one can use a different technique. According to our experience, reconfiguration failures usually happen when a new component is loaded (and the dynamic loader cannot link it) or when the new component is initialized (and it fails to locate the functions or allocate the resources it needs). Thus, we instruct the administrator to separate its reconfiguration in two phases resembling the two-phase commit protocol for atomic transactions [ ]. First, the administrator sends an agent to load all the required components and to initialize them by executing the *load_impl* operation (and, if needed, *configure_impl*). If an error occurs, the administrator chooses between sending a new agent to unload the new components from all the nodes or using *Doctor* to fix the individual errors. If the component implementations are loaded and initialized successfully in all the nodes, the administrator sends a new agent to attach them to the proper applications and ORB components, which would correspond to the *commit* phase of the two-phase commit protocol.

We found this to be sufficient for most of the application scenarios with which we work. However, some other applications require more strict guarantees of the ACID properties [ ] for atomic transactions. For example, if we want to reconfigure the marshalling and unmarshaling components in all the ORBs in a distributed system, it is important to guarantee an *all-or-nothing* property in the transactions. If an ORB replaces its marshalling mechanism and one of the ORBs to which it sends requests does not change its unmarshaling mechanism, they might no longer be able to communicate. To support that, one could extend our infrastructure by using standard transaction mechanisms for distributed systems [ ] and recent protocols for mobile agent fault-tolerance [ ].

5   Experimental Results

We have used our infrastructure in a variety of systems including Solaris 7, IRIX 6.5, Linux Red Hat 6.1, and Windows NT and 98. To evaluate the response time and relative performance gains made possible by our infrastructure, we established an intercontinental testbed with the collaboration of researchers in Brazil and Spain. The testbed consisted of three groups of machines: two Sun Ultra-60 and one Ultra-5 machines running Solaris 7 at   , three 333MHz PCs running Linux RedHat 6.1 at   , and three 300MHz PCs running Linux RedHat 6.1 at   .

The machines inside each group were connected by 100Mbps Fast Ethernets while the groups were connected among themselves through the public Internet. We executed several instances of a test application running on top of *dynamic-TAO* and injected different kinds of agents in this network.

To avoid drastic oscillations in the available Internet bandwidth and latency, and to minimize undesired interference, we carried out the experiments during the night . The average bandwidth and round-trip latency between our lab at   and   were 76KBps and 170*ms*, respectively. Between our lab and   , 32 KBps and 270*ms*, respectively.

In our first set of experiments, we measured the total round-trip time for executing five inspection commands (*list_categories*, *list_impl*, *list_loaded_impl*, *list_domain_components*, and *get_comp_info*) using different techniques. By sending the five commands to a single remote node using an agent, we obtained a 68% performance improvement compared to sending a separate request for each command without using agents (362 *ms* against 1128 *ms*). When sending agents to the nine nodes using the distribution tree shown in figure   , we obtained a 60% performance improvement compared to a point-to-point approach (847 *ms* against 2127 *ms*).

To measure how the benefits of using a distribution tree varies with the size of the agent, we sent a series of agents carrying the code for components of different sizes to be installed in the remote nodes. As shown in figure   , as the size of the component being uploaded increases, the relative gain of using a distribution tree instead of point-to-point connections increases significantly. This happens because the agent "multicast" mechanism minimizes the use of the public Internet, which is the bottleneck in this experiment. In the graphs, each value is the arithmetic mean of 10 runs of each experiment and the vertical bars represent the standard deviation. Finally, figure   shows the comparative performance between the agent approach and conventional client/server requests as the number of requests increases from one to eight. The client/server times were measured by building an application that sends the commands contained in the agent as separate requests transmitted sequentially via TCP/IP connections. Since the overhead of processing this kind of agent (around 1*ms*) is negligible compared to the latency of long distance Internet lines, the performance of both

---

[1] When we ran the experiments during times of high network traffic and congestion, the performance numbers were even more in favor of our mobile agents approach.

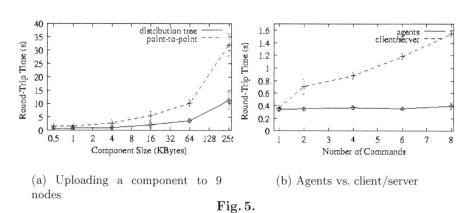

(a) Uploading a component to 9 nodes

(b) Agents vs. client/server

Fig. 5.

approaches when sending a single command is roughly the same. As we increase the number of commands in each experiment, the total completion time for the agent barely varies while the completion time for the client/server application increases rapidly as expected.

Although our implementation could still be improved significantly with more tuning and optimizations, these preliminary results are very encouraging. They demonstrate clearly that mobile agents can provide extreme performance improvements for the reconfiguration of wide-area distributed systems.

6   Related Work

Previous and ongoing research in dynamic configuration [ ] use architectural description languages, connectors, and dataflow models to represent the structure of complex applications and, in some cases, use configuration languages to specify dynamic modifications in this structure.

This paper shows how we combine two apparently unrelated research areas (mobile agents and dynamic configuration) to manage the dynamic reconfiguration of distributed applications in an efficient, scalable, and secure way.

Ranganathan et al. developed a middleware for reconfigurable distributed scripting [ ] that also involves agents and reconfiguration. However, while we use mobile agents to reconfigure scalable component-based applications, their work focuses on the dynamic reconfiguration of agent-based applications that use their middleware. Thus, our motivation and goals are different.

One of the most common concerns related to mobile agents is security. Requirements include the authentication of the involved parties and the protection of the execution environments from malicious agents. Albeit, the most challenging issue, the protection of the mobile agents from the execution environments, is still mostly unresolved. Methods based on provably-secure languages and proof-carrying code [ ] have been proposed to provide protection for execution environments. JavaSeal [ ] shows how to isolate agents from one another. Protecting the agent from malicious hosts is, in general, more difficult and can be partially solved by approaches like the time-limited black-box security and clueless agents [ ].

Our approach is to provide secure communication channels for the agents to traverse, protecting them from external attacks. The hosts use Role-Based Access Control [ ] to limit what the agents can do.

Baldi and Picco presented an elaborated quantitative model for mobile code performance [ ]. Puliafito, Riccobene, and Scarpa carried out an analytical comparison among the client-sever, remote evaluation, and mobile agents paradigms [ ]. Their results help evaluating under which circumstances the use of mobile agents is beneficial.

Ismail and Hagimont carried out an empirical performance evaluation of their infrastructure for Java mobile agents, comparing them to Aglets [ ] and to approaches based on RMI. Their experiments focused on single-hop agents on *intra*-continental networks. Our experiments involved single- and multi-hop agents on *inter*continental networks. Both works demonstrated that the mobile agent model can lead to significant performance improvements.

7   Conclusions

As Internet services become pervasive in our society, we become more and more dependent on their availability. However, software is in continuous evolution, which requires running systems to be updated and reconfigured on-the-fly with minimal disruption.

This paper proposes the use of mobile reconfiguration agents for secure, efficient, and scalable dynamic reconfiguration of Internet systems. We described a prototype implementation of such a mobile reconfiguration agent infrastructure based on a CORBA-compliant ORB supporting dynamic reconfiguration. Our framework can be customized either with efficient, lightweight agent interpreters – for environments with limited resources such as PDAs and embedded systems – or with more powerful interpreters such as the Java Virtual Machine.

Empirical results show that agents can improve the performance of distributed, dynamic reconfiguration greatly. We believe that, within a few years, the use of mobile agents for management and configuration of large-scale Internet systems will be a common practice.

Availability

The source code and documentation for *dynamicTAO*, DCP, and the mobile-agent-based reconfiguration engine is available at

.

Acknowledgments

The authors gratefully acknowledge Luiz Magalhães, Ramesh Chandra, Balaji Srinivasan, and Arun Viswanathan for early work on the reconfiguration agent infrastructure. We thank Francisco Ballesteros and Alexandre Oliva for giving access to their laboratories so that we could perform the wide-area experiments. Finally, we thank Geoff Arnold and the anonymous reviewers for their precious comments on the preliminary versions of this paper.

References

1. M. Baldi and G. Picco. Evaluating the Tradeoffs of Mobile Code Design Paradigms in Network Management Applications. In *Proc. 20th Int. Conf. Software Engineering*, pages 146–155, April 1998.
2. J. L. Eppinger, L. B. Mummert, and A. Z. Spector, editors. *CAMELOT and AVALON: A Distributed Transaction Facility*. Morgan Kaufmann Pub., 1991.
3. J. Gray and A. Reuter. *Transaction Processing: Concepts and Techniques*. Morgan Kaufmann Publishers, San Mateo, California, 1993.
4. L. Ismail and D. Hagimont. A Performance Evaluation of the Mobile Agent Paradigm. In *Proceedings of OOPSLA'99*, pages 306–313, Denver, November 1999.

5. P. Jain and D. C. Schmidt. Dynamically Configuring Communication Services with the Service Configuration Pattern. *C++ Report*, 9(6), June 1997.
6. F. Kon, R. Campbell, et al. A Component-Based Architecture for Scalable Distributed Multimedia. In *Proc. 14th ICAST*, pages 121–135, Naperville, April 1998.

7. F. Kon, M. Román, et al. Monitoring, Security, and Dynamic Configuration with the dynamicTAO Reflective ORB. In *Proceedings Middleware'2000*, number 1795 in LNCS, pages 121-143, New York, April 2000.
8. J. Linn. The Generic Security Service Application Program Interface (GSS API). Technical Report Internet RFC 2078, Network Working Group, January 1997.
9. G. C. Necula and P. Lee. Safe, Untrusted Agents Using Proof-carrying Code. In G. Vigna, editor, *Mobile Agents and Security*, LNCS 1419, pages 61–91. 1998.
10. A. Puliafito, S. Riccobene, and M. Scarpa. An Analytical Comparison of the Client-Sever, Remote Evaluation, and Mobile Agents Paradigms. In *Proc. ASA/MA'99*, pages 278–292, October 1999.
11. J. Purtilo, R. Cole, and R. Schlichting, editors. *Fourth International Conference on Configurable Distributed Systems*. IEEE, May 1998.   ,
12. M. Ranganathan, V. Schall, V. Galtier, and D. Montgomery. Mobile Streams: A Middleware for Reconfigurable Distributed Scripting. In *Proc. ASA/MA'99*, pages 162-175, October 1999.
13. R. S. Sandhu and E. J. Coyne and H. L. Feinstein and C. E. Youman. Role-Based Access Control Models. *IEEE Computer*, 29(2):38–47, February 1996.   ,
14. F. A. Silva and R. Popescu-Zeletin. An Approach for Providing Mobile Agent Fault Tolerance. In *Proc. Second Int. Workshop on Mobile Agents*, pages 14–25, September 1998.
15. G. Vigna, editor. *Mobile Agents and Security*, volume 1419 of *Lecture Notes in Computer Science*. Springer-Verlag, 1998.
16. J. Vitek and C. Bryce. The JavaSeal Mobile Agent Kernel. In *Proc. ASA/MA'99*, pages 103–116, October 1999.

The Bond Agent System and Applications

Ladislau Bölöni, Kyungkoo Jun, Krzysztof Palacz,
Radu Sion, and Dan C. Marinescu

Computer Sciences Department, Purdue University
West Lafayette, IN, 47907, USA
{boloni,junkk,palacz,sion,dcm}@cs.purdue.edu

Abstract. In this paper we present the basic design philosophy of the
Bond agent system, the multi-plane agent model and the component-
based architecture implementing the model. We discuss several applications of Bond agents: resource discovery, an adaptive video service, a
workflow management system, a system of agents for remote monitoring
of web servers, and a network of PDE solvers.

1 Introduction

We present some of the features of the Bond agent system and several applications of it. The original goal was to create an infrastructure for a Virtual
Laboratory and to support scheduling of complex tasks and data annotation
for data intensive applications. The Virtual Laboratory is expected to facilitate
remote control and monitoring of experiments, data analysis, replaying of a past
experiment, knowledge sharing among scientists scattered around the country.
Early on, we realized that, due to the complexity of the tasks involved, the infrastructure should support knowledge and workflow management and be based
upon a distributed object system. We created an agent model and a component-
based architecture to assemble the agents [ ].

Our thinking and design choices were influenced by existing systems and,
whenever possible, we adopted ideas and integrated implementations fitting our
agent model. We integrated with relative ease JESS, a Java Expert System Shell
from Sandia National Laboratory, [ ] and we are in the process of designing a
planning engine and integrating a knowledge management system.

Now we outline our views regarding several controversial issues in the area
of software agents and present our design choices. The intelligent agents and
the distributed objects and systems communities have slightly different views
regarding the future of software agents. The first group is primarily concerned
with intelligent agents and applications where agents are indispensable, e.g. space
exploration or robotics, where advanced planning and unrestricted autonomy are
necessary. The second group believes in agents with a wide range of intelligence
and autonomy capabilities, useful for the development of the next generation
Internet-based applications.

A recent paper by Nwana and Ndumu [ ] provides a lucid but somber analysis of the field. The authors review the promises and evaluate the progress of

D. Kotz and F. Mattern (Eds.): ASA/MA 2000, LNCS 1882, pp. 99– , 2000.
© Springer-Verlag Berlin Heidelberg 2000

the last few years in the field and conclude that, while progress has been made in several areas including information discovery, ontologies, agent communication, reasoning and coordination, monitoring and integration of agents and legacy software for the past five years, the progress in the software agents field has been by and large, slow and marred by recycling of concepts developed earlier. The stagnation of the field is attributed by the authors of the study to several causes: (a) lack of focus on problems that indeed require agent technology as opposed to problems that can be solved by traditional distributed system. (b) inability to identify a "killer application", and (c) a premature tendency towards formalization, attributable to many academic agent researchers that focus on manufactured agent applications rather than on realistic ones.

Our view regarding applications of software agents is different, we see a fair number of applications where software agents technology may have a significant impact though more traditional approaches are possible. The design of complex systems requires components with different degrees of autonomy, intelligence and mobility, any component may or may not be viewed as an agent depending upon the particular circumstances it is used. Agents could be used to support: (a) access to services from platforms ranging from supercomputers to hand-held devices, (b) composition and customization of services, (c) information discovery, (d) resource management, (e) negotiations and so on. At the same time, we regard the software engineering of agents as a major concern and believe that software agent technology should be integrated with other methods and technologies used to build complex open systems, including object-oriented technology, concurrency, distribution. If we have to use special agent communication and content languages, design our own societal services, use special toolkits for building agents, while waiting for someone to discover a "killer application", it is very likely that, after five years from now, an equally somber review of the field could be expected.

Another controversial aspect of agents is related to mobility. Code mobility is a long-term obsession of distributed system designers, has its roots in work done last decade at MIT on remote evaluation, on process migration research, fashionable two decades ago, and can be related to the Xerox Worm. Some question the usefulness of agent mobility, others point out the tremendous challenges posed by it, security being often at the top of the list, and argue that we should address first the very difficult problems posed by immobile agents [ ]. Systems like Voyager [ ] and IBM's Aglets [ ] were specifically designed to support agent mobility while others like Retsina [ ] or Zeus [ ] ignore it. Systems like AgentTCL [ ] and Bond support agent mobility.

We believe that there are applications where support for agent mobility is critical, the agent is an integral part of the model, e.g. in active networks [ ] [ ] [ ]. There are applications where mobile agents may have a significant advantage in terms of either functionality or performance compared with more traditional techniques: (a) extensible servers, applications where a user is represented by an agent installed at a remote server location, (b) data-intensive applications where it is impractical to move data, (c) applications in mobile computing area where the user is intermittently connected to the network and resources available on the network access device are insufficient, (d) dynamic deployment of software [ ].

2   The Bond Agent System

The Bond agent model is influenced by the definition of an agent given by Stan Franklin and Art Graesser [ ]: *an autonomous agent is a system situated within and part of an environment that senses that environment and acts on it, over time, in pursuit of its own agenda and so as to effect what it senses in the future.*

The agent execution model assumes that the agent has an explicit goal. Agents receive external events and generate actions. The actions of an agent are determined by the pursue of its goal, events may trigger immediate responses, but agents perform actions even without any external input. Since an agent can emulate every other execution model, some researchers are inclined to view every program as an agent. This approach does not lend itself to efficient implementations, the simpler the execution model the more optimal implementation is possible. For example, we can optimize the response time of a stateless server far better than of an agent with a complex state.

Bond is based upon the AM_1^{mp} model [ ]. We believe this model to be well suited to an object-oriented implementation, though less powerful than BDI. This model allows us to reason about agents while using an object-oriented programming style.

An important aspect of agent design is the communication style. Most agent systems use a message-oriented style although recently agents based upon CORBA MASIF specification [ ], e.g. Grasshopper [,] are emerging. Agents using message-oriented communication either rely on an agent communication language like KQML [ ] or FIPA [ ] or use free-format communication. Several agent toolkits use KQML, e.g., JATLite from Stanford [ ] and the Agent-Builder [ ], a commercial product. Other commercial products, e.g., Aglets [ ] or Voyager [ ] use free-format communication. The Bond agent system uses KQML. Like other agent system we take advantage of few performatives supported by KQML, internally a KQML message is represented by a table consisting of attribute name and value pairs. This approach allowed us to add to our system XML-based communication with ease. At this time, Bond agents can mix KQML or XML messages.

Another important consideration in the design of an agent system is mobility. Agent systems like Aglets from IBM, [ ], Telescript [ ] from General Magic consider migration a defining property of an agent and a basic design goal is to allow an agent to migrate at any time. In Bond, migration is considered a rare event in the life of an agent and migration is possible only under certain circumstances and we implement a *weak migration model.* We restrict the locations an agent may migrate to and the time when migration is possible. A Bond agent runs under the control of the agent factory and uses the communication substrate provided by a Resident, thus it cannot migrate freely to any site [ ]. An agent may move at the time of a transition from one state to another. If multiple planes are running concurrently then we have to wait until each plane reaches a transition. To migrate an agent we simply send the blueprint of the agent and the model including the current state of the agent to a new site, [ ]. The agent factory at the receiving end re-assembles the agent and when so instructed activates it from the state found in the model.

The statecharts model [ ] is used to specify embedded systems and UML [ ]-based systems. The parallelism in statecharts is expressed as *concurrent sub-states* while in Bond we support multiple simpler state machines. In statecharts transitions may have conditions and actions associated with them, while in our model, only states can generate actions and transitions are unconditional. In our model the structural components, the multiplane state machines, the active components, the strategies, and the model of the world are clearly separated. If we introduce a condition, a boolean function on the model associated with a transition, the state machine would be dependent on the model. If an action would be associated with a transition that would either imply that actions can be generated outside strategies, or alternatively, that there is a strategy which is not determined by the state vector. Both of these semantics are expressed in our model by *inserting an intermediate node* between the source and destination, the strategy of these node than performing the desired action or evaluating the condition. Thus, the multi-plane state machines in our model can be larger for the same task than the corresponding statecharts, but they are easier to analyze and generate, because of the simpler semantics. On the other hand, real time systems are easier to specify in the statecharts format. Another feature of statecharts, the possibility to define embedded sub-states is also missing in our system. Its functionality in most cases can be replaced by the state vector of the multi-plane state machine. We are investigating the benefits of sub-states; they improve the expressiveness of the system, make checkpointing, migration and agent surgery [ ] more difficult.

Now we present a component-based architecture for software agents. In this architecture an agent consists of a group of active objects linked together by a data structure, rather than a large monolithic code. The behavior of the agent is determined by the active and passive objects and the data structure. The active objects usually consist of compiled code, thus can be executed with little additional overhead. The data structure can be modified with ease allowing for flexible behavior. The four major components of an agent are: the model, the agenda, the state machines, and strategies.

The *model of the world* is a container object, it contains the information about the agent environment. There is no restriction on the format of this information: it can be a knowledge base or ontology composed of logical facts and predicates, a pre-trained neural network, a collection of meta-objects or different forms of handles of external objects (file handles, sockets, etc), or typically, a heterogeneous collection of all these. The model also stores information the agent has about itself, e.g., plans or intentions if the agent conforms to the BDI model.

The *agenda object* defines the goal of the agent. The agenda implements a boolean function and a distance function on the model. The boolean function shows if the agent accomplished its goal or not. The agenda acts as a termination condition for the agents, except for agents with a *continuous agenda* where their goal is to maintain the agenda as being satisfied. The distance function may be used by the strategies to choose their actions.

The *multi-plane state machine* of the agent is a data structure composed of a number of state machines arranged in *planes*. The state of each state machine is defined by the active node. The state of the agent is defined by a *vector of states*. An agent changes its state by performing *transitions*. In turn, transitions are triggered by internal or external *events*. External events are messages sent by other agents or programs. The set of external messages that trigger transitions of the agent's state machine defines the *control subprotocol* of the agent.

Each node of the multi-plane state machine has associated a *strategy object*. Strategy objects generate *actions* based upon the model and the agenda of the agent. Strategies do not reveal internal state information - their behavior is determined exclusively by the model and the agenda. The strategies must store their state in the model. Actions are considered atomic from the agent's point of view, external and/or internal events interrupt the agent only between actions. Each action is defined exclusively by the agenda of the agent and the current model. A strategy can terminate by triggering a transition or by generating an internal event. After the completion of a transition the agent moves into a new state where a different strategy defines its behavior.

Informally, a strategy is a function which takes as parameters the model of the world and the agenda of the agent and returns actions. From the implementation point of view, a strategy is a Java object with a function called `action()` that performs the actions needed at the given instance.

The strategies are activated: (a) in response to external events and (b) as the flow of control requires while pursuing the agent's agenda. *Messages* from remote applications, and *user interface events* like pressed keys, mouse-clicks are examples of external events. The strategies are activated by the event handling mechanism - the Java event system for GUI events, or the messaging thread for messages in case of external events, or by an *action scheduler*.

The state of the agent is defined by a *vector of states*, which implies that the behavior or the agent is determined by a *vector of strategies*.

This structure allows us to assign different strategies for handling different types of events - for example a strategy from one plane handles the messages, while the other plane is handling the user interface events. One of the planes may provide reasoning or planning functions, one the execution, another one carry out housekeeping operations. The strategies in these planes are activated by the action scheduler.

The multi-plane structure provides the means to express concurrent agent activities. The actual nature of the parallelism is determined by the scheduling mechanism used by the action scheduler. In case of a round-robin activation mechanism the actions belonging to different strategies are interleaved without overlapping while multi-threaded execution allows for truly concurrent actions. Other possible activation schemes are priority-based and preemptive.

The agents are described by their *active components* (the strategies) and the *structural components* - the multi-plane state machine.

A strategy should be compatible with the agent implementation language, Java in case of Bond. There are two requirements a software component should meet to be a valid strategy: it should allow its state to be linked to the model and it should break its behavior into actions. JavaBeans, ActiveX objects, C++ libraries or functions in interpreted languages can all be valid strategies. In the Bond system, besides Java-written strategies, we are currently supporting strategies written in Jess and Python through the JPython interpreter. Any other language can be used through the Java native interface.

The structural component of an agent, the multi-plane state machine, can be constructed as a program, but a more flexible approach is a textual description, interpreted by an *agent factory*. An agent description language called *Blueprint* was defined to describe the structure of an agent. We are now extending the blueprint agent description language to accommodate XML-based agent description. Other agent systems, e.g. Zeus [ ], use a visual programming interface to create agents.

3   Work in Progress

Knowledge Management. Bond adopts the knowledge model provided by the Open Knowledge Base Connectivity Protocol [ ]. This is achieved through integration with Protégé 2000, a knowledge modeling tool and programming library [ ]. Each instance of the base class of the Bond object hierarchy can be viewed as an instance frame conforming to one or more class frames; subsequently the own slots associated with each Bond object represent assertions about the object or about the abstract entity represented by it. The uses of knowledge management abstractions in Bond include descriptions of capabilities of strategies and agents, representation of properties registered with community services, planning operator pre- and postconditions and data structures used for communication with the inference engine. Thanks to the facilities of Protégé, knowledge represented in a running Bond system can be exported in the Resource Description Framework format and new Bond objects can be assembled from imported RDF descriptions.

Agent Management. The Microserver. Management, monitoring and debugging in multi-agent systems pose serious challenges. Agent debugging and monitoring should be done with as little intrusion as possible, agent management should be highly efficient, we need a uniform interface to access agent properties. We propose to enable dynamic access to running agents and their properties using a microserver. A *microserver* is a light thread managing predefined *access-points* to enable external access through an appropriate protocol, e.g., HTTP, to agent's properties. The *property access-point* enables public access to the agent properties. The *method invocation access-point* enables RMI-like calls to any

Bond object including agents. The task of the microserver is to translate from the internal object messaging protocol (inside the Java Virtual Machine) to the external (ex. HTTP) access protocol. The design of the formats and serialization of corresponding call arguments and results are especially challenging.

We integrated the HTTP microserver implementation as another communication engine in Bond. This approach is consistent with the overall Bond architecture. It allows direct browser access to any Bond object including the agent factory, as well as the ability to integrate the Bond framework with other systems using a microserver and a general purpose access-point. Another interesting issues to explore is the deployment of probes to access a Bond object. Probes are objects attached dynamically to Bond objects to augment their ability to understand new sub-protocols [ ], [ ], and support new functionality.

4   Applications

To test the limitations and the flexibility of our system, we developed several applications of the Bond agents ranging from a resource discovery agent to a network of PDE solver agents. We overview some of these applications.

Resource Discovery. The Bond agents for resource discovery and monitoring have distinct advantages over statically configured monitors which have to be re-designed and programmed if they are deployed to other heterogeneous nodes. Moreover the local monitors should be pre-installed [ ] [   ] [ ]. The dynamic composability and surgery of the Bond agents makes it possible to deploy monitoring agents on the fly with strategies compatible with target nodes, and modify them on demand either to perform other tasks or to operate on other heterogeneous resources.

We developed an agent-based resource discovery and monitoring system shown in Figure . Agents running at individual nodes learn about the existence of other agents by using *distributed awareness*, a distributed mechanism by which each node maintains locations of other nodes it has communicated with over a period of time and exchanges periodically this information among themselves [ ]. Whenever an agent, a *beneficiary agent*, needs detailed information about individual components of other nodes, it uses the distributed awareness information to identify a target node, then creates a blueprint of a monitoring agent capable of probing and reporting the required information on the target node, and sends the blueprint to an agent factory of it. The agent factory assembles the monitoring agent and launches it to work. A blueprint repository, which is either local or remote, stores a set of strategies. By sending a surgery script, the beneficiary agent can modify the agents as desired.

This solution is scalable and suitable for heterogeneous environments where the architecture and the hardware resources of individual nodes differ, the services provided by the system are diverse, the bandwidth and the latency of the communication links cover a broad range. On the other hand, the amount of resources used by agents might be larger than those required by other monitoring systems.

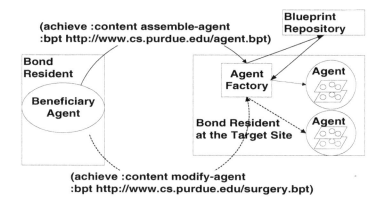

Fig. 1. The dynamic deployment and modification of monitoring agents. The Beneficiary agent sends either a blueprint (solid line) or a surgery script (dotted line) to an agent factory to deploy a monitoring agent or to modify an existing one. The agent factory assembles it with local strategies or ones from a remote blueprint repository

Adaptive Video Server. Adaptive MPEG agent system implements an architecture supporting server reconfiguration and resource reservations for a video application [ ]. Software agents provide feedback regarding desired and attained quality of service at the client side. Server agents respond by reconfiguring video streaming and reserving communication bandwidth and/or CPU cycles according to a set of rules. An inference engine, a component of the server agent, controls an adaptation mechanism. A native bandwidth scheduler and a CPU scheduler in Solaris 2.5.1 support QoS reservation

The architecture of the adaptive MPEG agent system is shown in Figure . An MPEG client agent is responsible for displaying a video stream and monitoring the reception of the video stream. When a client agent requests a video, an MPEG video server spawns an MPEG server agent which delivers and controls video streaming. Two communication channels exist between a client and its corresponding server side: a control channel for streaming commands and feedback from client to server, and a data channel for the streaming.

The MPEG server agent is configured to deliver an MPEG compressed video stream at start-up. As resource state of network bandwidth and CPU loads on the server and client change, the server agent can gracefully adapt by selecting one of three supported streaming modes: B/P frame dropping mode, Server decoding mode, and server decoding and dropping mode.

The application-specific program that adapts the current streaming mode to system resource state is written as a set of rules for the Java Expert System Shell (JESS) [ ]. Our adaptation design is based on the following considerations. There are three resources on an end-to-end streaming path: server CPU, network, and client CPU, any one of which is a potential bottleneck limiting per-

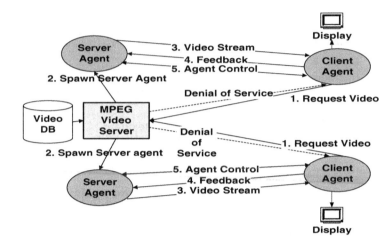

Fig. 2. The MPEG system consists of a server and a set of server agents and client agents. The server and client agents support video streaming and display functions respectively. With a set of rules, the server agents can respond to changing resource state by adapting the video streaming

formance. Once a bottleneck is identified, one of the following adaptation rules reacts accordingly: bandwidth reservation rule, CPU reservation rule, dropping rule, decoding rule, and decoded dropping rule.

The advantage of the agent-based MPEG system is greater flexibility and system reconfigurability. The rules governing the behavior of the agents can be modified dynamically. Moreover, the agents themselves can be modified to add another streaming modes by the surgery.

Agent-Based Workflow Management. Motivated by deficiencies of existing workflow management systems (WFMS) in the area of flexibility and adaptability to change we initiated work on building a workflow management framework on top of the Bond system [ ]. Usually in WFMS implementations agents enhance the functionality of existing WFMS and act as personal assistants performing actions on behalf of the workflow participants and/or facilitating interaction with other participants or the workflow enactment engine. We propose an agent–based WFMS architecture in which software agents perform the core task of workflow enactment. In particular we concentrate on the use of agents as *case managers*: autonomous entities overlooking the processing of single units of work. Our assumption is that an agent–based implementation is more capable of dealing with dynamic workflows and with complex processing requirements where many parameters influence the routing decisions and require some inferential capabilities. We also believe that the software engineering of workflow management systems is critical and instead of creating monolithic systems we should assemble them out of components and attempt to reuse the components.

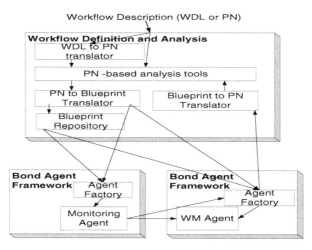

Fig. 3. Workflow management in Bond

Figure   illustrates the definition and execution of a workflow in Bond. The workflow management agent originally created from a static description can be modified based upon the information provided by the monitoring agent. Several workflows may be created as a result of mutations suffered by the original workflow [ ]. Once the new blueprint is created dynamically, it goes through the analysis procedure and only then it can be stored in the blueprint repository. The distinction between the monitoring agent and the workflow management agent is blurred, if necessary they can be merged together into a single agent.

We use Petri nets as an unambiguous language for specifying the workflow definition and provide a mechanism for enacting a large class of Petri net–based workflow definitions on the Bond finite state machine. For interoperatbility reasons we also supply a translator from the industry standard Workflow Process Definition Language [ ] to our internal representation.

Remote Web Server Monitoring. The widespread use of web servers for business-oriented activities requires service guarantees because large variations of response time or even a very short time service failure can make an enormous negative economic impact as estimated in [ ]. In addition to the service guarantee, the need for support for multiple classes of services based on QoS, various web-server farming, and security against denial-of-service will affect the future technologies related to web server configuration and management.

The agent-controlled management of web servers can facilitate the tasks of web administrators. One typical example of those tasks is the following; based on the report from commercial web monitoring service companies [ ] [ ], the web administrators reboot failed servers, improve revealed bottlenecks, and optimize systems. Intelligent agents can automate these tasks with a set of rules describing conditions and corresponding actions, which mainly control parameters of servers.

The architecture of agent-controlled web cluster is shown in Figure . Actual web servers are located behind a proxy, a frond-end server which dispatch requests to the web servers according to a *dispatching table* defined by a set of policies or load balancing algorithms. Only the proxy is exposed to outer world users. This is similar to other web cluster architectures but includes *adaptation* and *monitoring* agents.

The adaptation agent controls the web configuration, and uses a set of rules to modify the the dispatching table for load balancing, caching, QoS connection, and request filtering. The adaptation agent also communicates with its peers controlling other sites mirroring the service for global load balance and traffic optimization. The monitoring agents are mobile agents deployed to strategic locations on the Internet to collect performance data of the web service. They can measure response time, test new transaction, monitor errors or failures. The data provided by the monitoring agents are used by the adaptation agent to improve the web configuration.

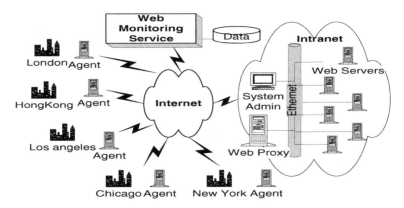

Fig. 4. Agent-based web management and monitoring system. The adaptation agent is responsible for controlling a set of web servers. It manages a dispatching table for load balancing and QoS-aware web service. The monitoring agents collect web-performance data in the perspective of human users

At the same time, we propose to develop the following agents: an agent simulating the web-surfing behavior of human users for customer-oriented data, an *interface agent* for administrators to manually configure web cluster, and an agent controlling monitoring agents by directing the geographic distribution of monitoring agents, the temporal activation patterns of the monitoring agents, and the workload caused by the monitoring agents.

A Network of PDE Solver Agents. Data parallelism is a common approach to reduce the computing time and to improve the quality of the solution for data-intensive applications. Often the algorithm for processing each data segment is rather complex and the effort to partition the data, to determine the optimal number of data segments, to combine the partial results, to adapt to a specific computing environment and to user requirements must be delegated to another program. Mixing control and management functions with the computational algorithm leads in such cases to brittle and complex software. We developed a network of PDE solver agents and discussed its application for modeling propagation and scattering of acoustic waves in the ocean [ ].

Agents with inference abilities coordinate the execution and mediate the conflicts while solving PDEs. Three types of agents are involved: one PDECoordinator agent, several PDESolver and PDEMediator agents. The PDECoordinator is responsible with the control of the entire application, a PDEMediator arbitrates between the two solvers sharing a boundary between two domains, and a PDESolver is a wrapper for the legacy application. Thus we were able to identify with relative ease the functions expected from each agent and write new strategies in Java. The actual design and implementation of the network of PDE solving agents took less than one month. Thus, the main advantage of the solution we propose is a drastic reduction of the development time from several months to a few weeks.

5   Summary

The main contribution of the Bond project is in the area of software engineering and component-based agent architectures. We introduced an agent description language called *Blueprint* and a multi-plane state machine agent model. An agent factory translates a blueprint into an internal data structure controlling the run-time behavior of the agent and allows Bond agents to be modified at run time and to migrate. The advantage of the reusable component approach is reduced development time, e.g. the network of PDE solvers discussed in Section   was designed as a two months class project while the initial implementation was a multi year project leading to a Ph.D. dissertation.

Our agent model allows us to integrate with ease components developed elsewhere, the inference engine Jess from Sandia National Laboratory and Protege, a knowledge management system from Stanford.

We are considering alternative semantics engines for the agent factories, one based upon a Petri Net enactment engine and one based upon statecharts. The Petri Net engine will be used for dynamic workflow management and will be integrated with a planning engine. We also support agent control via Web browsers.

We propose to use mixins consisting of agents and legacy programs as illustrated by several applications presented in Section   . Once we have all critical components in place we'll use this infrastructure for a Virtual Laboratory for Structural Biology.

Acknowledgments

The work reported in this paper was partially supported by grants from the National Science Foundation, MCB-9527131 and DBI 9986316, by the Scalable I/O Initiative, and by a grant from the Intel Corporation.

References

1. Keynote. URL http://www.keynote.com.
2. Service Metrics. URL http://www.servicemetrics.com.
3. Tivoli Enterprise Solutions. URL http://www.tivoli.com/products/solutions.

4. C. Bäumer, M. Breugst, S. Choy, and T. Magedanz. Grasshopper — A universal agent platform based on OMG MASIF and FIPA standards. In Ahmed Karmouch and Roger Impley, editors, *First International Workshop on Mobile Agents for Telecommunication Applications (MATA'99)*, pages 1–18, Ottawa, Canada, October 1999. World Scientific Publishing Ltd.
5. S. Bhattacharjee, K. L. Calvert, and E. Zegura. On Active Networking and Congestion. Technical Report GIT-CC-96-02, Georgia Institute of Technology. College of Computing.
6. L. Bölöni and D. C. Marinescu. An Object-Oriented Framework for Building Collaborative Network Agents. In H. N. Teodorescu, D. Mlynek, A. Kandel, and H.-J. Zimmerman, editors, *Intelligent Systems and Interfaces*, International Series in Intelligent Technologies, chapter 3, pages 31–64. Kluwer Publising House, 2000.
7. Ladislau Bölöni, Ruibing Hao, Kyungkoo Jun, and Dan C. Marinescu. An object-oriented approach for semantic understanding of messages in a distributed object system. In *Proceedings of the International Conference on Software Engineering Applied to Networking and Parallel/ Distributed Computing, Rheims, France*, May 2000.
8. Ladislau Bölöni and Dan C. Marinescu. Agent surgery: The case for mutable agents. In *Proceedings of the Third Workshop on Bio-Inspired Solutions to Parallel Processing Problems (BioSP3), Cancun, Mexico*, May 2000.
9. Ladislau Bölöni and Dan C. Marinescu. A component agent model - from theory to implementation. In *Proceedings of the AT2AI Workshop, Vienna, Austria, April 2000, to appear*, 2000.
10. M. Breugst, I. Busse, S. Covaci, and T. Magedanz. Grasshopper – A Mobile Agent Platform for IN Based Service Environments. In *Proceedings of IEEE IN Workshop 1998*, pages 279–290, Bordeaux, France, May 1998.
11. S. Chapin, D. Katramatos, J. Karpovich, and A. Grimshaw. Resource management in legion. In *Proceedings of the 5th Workshop on Job Scheduling Strategies for Parallel Processing in conjunction with the International Parallel and Distributed Processing Symposium*, April 1999.
12. Workflow Management Coalition. Interface 1: Process definition interchange process model, 11 1998. WfMC TC-1016-P v7.04.
13. R. Fikes and A. Farquhar. Distributed repositories of highly expressive reusable knowledge. Technical Report 97-02, Knowledge Systems Lab Stanford, 1997.
14. Tim Finin et al. Specification of the KQML Agent-Communication Language – plus example agent policies and architectures, 1993.
15. S. Fitzgerald, I. Foster, C. Kesselman, G. Laszewski, W. Smith, and S. Tuecke. A directory service for configuring high-performance distributed computations. In *Proceedings of the 6th IEEE Symp. on High-Performance Distributed Computing*, pages 365–375, 1997.
16. S. Franklin and A. Graesser. Is it an agent, or just a program? In *Proceedings of the Third International Workshop on Agent Theories, Architectures and Languages*. Springer Verlag, 1996.

17. E. Friedman-Hill. Jess, the Java expert system shell. Technical Report SAND98-8206, Sandia National Laboratories, 1999. ,

18. G. Glass. ObjectSpace voyager — the agent ORB for Java. *Lecture Notes in Computer Science*, 1368:38–??, 1998. ,

19. W. E. Grosso, H. Eriksson, R. W. Fergerson, J. H. Gennari, S. W. Tu, and M. A. Musen. Knowledge modeling at the millennium (the design and evolution of protege-2000). Technical report, Stanford Medical Informatics Institute, 1999.

20. D. Harel, A. Pnueli, J. P. Schmidt, and R. Sherman. On the Formal Semantics of Statecharts. In *2nd IEEE Symposium on Logic in Computer Science*, 1987.

21. Zona Research Inc. White Paper: The Economic Impacts of Unacceptable Web Site Download Speeds, 1999.

22. K. Jun, L. Bölöni, K. Palacz, and D. C. Marinescu. Agent–Based Resource Discovery. In *Proceedings of Heterogeneous Computing Workshop 2000, to appear*, 2000.

23. K. Jun, L. Bölöni, D. Yau, and D. C. Marinescu. Intelligent QoS Support for an Adaptive Video Service. In *Proceedings of IRMA 2000, to appear*, 2000.

24. David Kotz and Robert S. Gray. Mobile code: The future of the Internet. In *Proceedings of the Workshop "Mobile Agents in the Context of Competition and Cooperation (MAC3)" at Autonomous Agents '99*, pages 6–12, May 1999.

25. D. B. Lange and M. Oshima. *Programming and Deploying Java Mobile Agents with Aglets*. Addison Wesley Longman, 1998. ,

26. Dejan Milojicic. Mobile Agent Applications. *IEEE Concurrency*, 7(3), 1999. ,

27. Hyacinth Nwana and Divine Ndumu. A perspective on software agents research. *The Knowledge Engineering Review*, January 1999.

28. Hyacinth Nwana, Divine Ndumu, Lyndon Lee, and Jaron Collis. Zeus: A tool-kit for building distributed multi-agent systems. *Applied Artifical Intelligence Journal*, 13 (1):129–186, 1999. ,

29. Object Management Group. *OMG Unified Modeling Language Specification*.

30. Krzysztof Palacz and Dan C. Marinescu. An agent-based workflow management system. In *Proc. AAAI Spring Symposium Workshop "Bringing Knowledge to Business Processes"*, 2000.

31. M. Paolucci, D. Kalp, A. Pannu, O. Shehory, and K. Sycara. *Lecture Notes in Artificial Intelligence, Intelligent Agents*, chapter A Planning Component for RETSINA Agents. Springer-Verlag Heidelberg, 1998.

32. Charles Petrie. Agent-based engineering, the web, and intelligence. *IEEE Expert*, 11(6):24–29, December 1996.

33. J. Smith, K. Calvert, S. Murphy, H. Orman, and L. Peterson. Activating Networks: A Progress Report. April, 1999.

34. P. Tsompanopoulou, L. Bölöni, D. C. Marinescu, and J. R. Rice. The Design of Software Agents for a Network of PDE Solvers. In *Workshop on Agent Technologies for High Performance Computing, Agents 99*, pages 57–68. IEEE Press, 1999.

35. W. M. P. van der Aalst and T. Basten. Inheritance of Workflows. An approach to tackling problems related to change. (draft).

36. D. Wetherall, J. Guttag, and D. Tennenhouse. ANTS: A Toolkit for Building and Dynamically Deploying Network Protocols. In *IEEE INFOCOM, San Francisco*, 1998.

37. James E. White. Telescript technology: Mobile agents. In Jeffrey Bradshaw, editor, *Software Agents*. AAAI Press/MIT Press, 1996.

38. Agentbuilder framework. URL http://www.agentbuilder.com.

39. FIPA Specifications. URL http://www.fipa.org.
40. MASIF - The CORBA Mobile Agent Specification. URL http://www.omg.org/cgi-bin/doc?orbos/98-03-09.

MobiDoc: A Framework for Building Mobile Compound Documents from Hierarchical Mobile Agents

Ichiro Satoh

Department of Information Sciences, Ochanomizu University /
Japan Science and Technology Corporation
2-1-1 Otsuka Bunkyo-ku Tokyo 112-8610 Japan
ichiro@is.ocha.ac.jp

Abstract. MobiDoc is a framework for building mobile compound documents, where the compound document can be dynamically composed of mobile agents and can migrate itself over a network as a whole, with all its embedded agents. The key of this framework is that it builds a hierarchical mobile agent system that enables multiple mobile agents to be combined into a single mobile agent. The framework also provides several added-value mechanisms for visually manipulating components embedded in a compound document and for sharing a window on the screen among the components. This paper will describe the MobiDoc framework and its first implementation, currently using Java as implementation language as well as component development language, and then illustrate several interesting applications to demonstrate the utility and flexibility of this framework.

1   Introduction

Building systems from software components has already proven useful in the development of large and complex systems. Several frameworks for software components have been developed, such as COM/OLE [ ], OpenDoc [ ], Common-Point [   ], and JavaBeans [ ]. Among them, the notion of compound documents is a document-centric component framework, where various visible parts, such as text, image, and video, that are created by different applications can be combined into one document and be independently manipulated in-place in the document. An example of this type of frameworks is CI Labs' OpenDoc [ ] developed by Apple computer and IBM, although their development work on this framework has stopped.

However, there have been several problems in the few existing compound document frameworks. A compound component is typically defined by two parts: contents, and codes for modifying the contents. Contents are often stored in the component but not the codes for accessing them. Thus, a user cannot view or modify a document whose contents need the support of different applications, if the user does not have the applications themselves. Moreover, most existing

D. Kotz and F. Mattern (Eds.): ASA/MA 2000, LNCS 1882, pp. 113–   , 2000.
© Springer-Verlag Berlin Heidelberg 2000

frameworks assume that a user manually lays out components into a compound document. It is difficult to change a compound document autonomously. So, when a compound document arrives at a computer, the document is unable to dynamically change the layouts and combinations of its components, and it cannot be dynamically adapted to the user's requirements. A document is not designed for mobility and thus the document itself cannot determine where it should go next.

The goal of this paper is to propose a new framework for building mobile compound documents. Each document is built as a component that can be a container for components that is able to migrate over a network. Accessing compound documents over a network requires a powerful infrastructure for building and migrating, such as mobile agents. Mobile agents are autonomous programs that can travel from computer to computer under their own control. When each agent migrates over network, both the state and the codes can be transferred to the destination. However, traditional mobile agent systems cannot be composed of more than one mobile agent, unlike component technology. Therefore, we built a framework on a unique mobile agent system, called *MobileSpaces*, which was presented in an earlier paper [ ]. The system is constructed using Java language [ ] and provides mobile agents that can move over a network, like other mobile agent systems. However, it also allows more than one mobile agent to be hierarchically assembled into a single mobile agent. Consequently, in our framework, a compound document is a hierarchical mobile agent that contains its contents and a hierarchy of mobile agents, which correspond to nested components embedded in the document. Furthermore, the framework offers several mechanisms for coordinating visible components so that these components can effectively share visual real estate on a screen in a seamless-looking way.

This paper is organized in the following sections. Section 2 surveys related work and Section 3 presents the basic ideas of the compound document framework, called *MobiDoc*. Section 4 details its first implementation and Section 5 shows the usability of our framework based on real-world examples. Section 6 gives some concluding remarks.

2   Background

Among the component technologies developed so far, OpenDoc and JavaBeans are characterized by allowing a component to contain a hierarchy of nested components. Although there are few hierarchical components available in the market today, their advent appears to be necessary and unavoidable in the long run.

OpenDoc is a document-centric components framework and has several advantages over other frameworks, but it has been discontinued. An OpenDoc component is not self-configurable, although it is equipped with scripts to control itself, and thus a component cannot migrate over a network under its own control. JavaBeans is a general framework for building reusable software components designed for the Java language. The initial release of JavaBeans (version

1.0 specified in [ ]) does not contain a hierarchical or logical structure for JavaBean objects, but its latest release specified in [ ] allows JavaBean objects to be organized hierarchically. However, the JavaBeans framework does not provide any higher level document-related functions. Moreover, it is not inherently designed for mobility. Therefore, it is very difficult for a group of JavaBean objects in the containment hierarchy to migrate to another computer.

A number of other mobile agent systems have been released recently, for example Aglets [ ], Mole [ ], Telescript [ ], and Voyager [ ]. However, these agent systems unfortunately lack a mechanism for structurally assembling more than one mobile agent, unlike component technologies. This is because each mobile agent is basically designed as an isolated entity that migrates independently. Some of them offer inter-agent communication, but they can only couple mobile agents loosely and thus cannot migrate a group of mobile agents to another computer as whole. Telescript introduces the concept of places in addition to mobile agents. Places are agents that can contain mobile agents and places inside them, but they are not mobile. Therefore, the notion of places does not support mobile compound documents.

To solve the above problem in existing mobile agent systems, we constructed a new mobile agent system called MobileSpaces [ ]. The system introduces the notion of agent hierarchy and inter-agent migration. This system allows a group of mobile agents to be dynamically assembled into a single mobile agent. Although the system itself has no mechanism for constructing compound documents, it can provide a powerful infrastructure for implementing compound documents to network computing settings.

ADK [ ] is a framework for building mobile agents from JavaBeans. It provides an extension of Sun's visual builder tool for JavaBeans, called BeanBox, to support the visual construction of mobile agents. In contrast, we intend to construct a new framework for building mobile compound documents in which each component can be a container for components and can migrate over a network under its own control. Our compound document will be able to migrate itself from one computer to another as a whole with all of its embedded components to the new computer and adapt the arrangement of its inner components to the user's requirements and its environments by migrating and replacing corresponding components. The HyperNews framework [ ] provides an electronic newspaper system to the WWW by using mobile agents to encapsulate and update articles. It does not offer any any general framework for building mobile compound documents, but can provide an architecture for electronic documents based on mobile agents.

3   Approach

This section outlines the framework for building compound documents based on mobile agents called *MobiDoc*.

3.1 Compound Documents as Mobile Agents

To create an enriched compound document, a component or document must be able to contain other components, like OpenDoc. We intend to provide such a component through a hierarchical mobile agent. Our framework is therefore constructed on the MobileSpaces system presented in our earlier paper [ ] which can dynamically assemble more than one mobile agent into a single mobile agent. The system supports mobile agents that are computational and itinerant entities, like other mobile agent systems. Also, the MobileSpaces system incorporates the following concepts:

- **Agent Hierarchy:** Each mobile agent can be contained within one mobile agent.
- **Inter-agent Migration:** Each mobile agent can migrate between other mobile agents as a whole, with all of its inner agents.

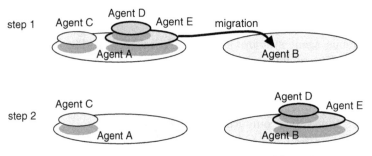

Fig. 1. Agent Hierarchy and Inter-agent Migration

The first concept enables each component to be a group of mobile agents organized hierarchically. The second concept enables a compound document to migrate itself and its components as a whole. Fig.   shows an example of an inter-agent migration in an agent hierarchy. Our agent model is similar to a process calculus for modeling process migration called Mobile Ambients [ ]. The containment hierarchy for components in a document is organized directly in the agent hierarchy in the MobileSpace system.

3.2 Compound Document Framework

The MobileSpaces system is a suitable infrastructure for mobile compound documents, but it does not provide any document-centric mechanisms for managing components in a compound document. We offer a compound document framework for supporting mobile agent-based components, including graphical user interfaces for manipulating visible components. This framework, called *MobiDoc*, is given as a collection of Java objects that belong to one of about 40 classes. It defines the protocols that let components embedded in a document communicate with each other. It also deals with in-place editing services similar to those provided by OpenDoc and OLE. The framework offers several mechanisms for effectively sharing a visual estate of a container among components embedded and for coordinating their use of shared resources, such as keyboard, mouse, and window.

4   Implementation

Next, we will describe our method for using the MobileSpaces system to construct mobile compound documents. The system can execute and migrate mobile agents that are incorporated with the two concepts presented in the previous section. It has been incorporated in Java Development Kit version 1.2 and can run on any computer that has a runtime compatible with this version.

4.1   The Runtime System

The MobileSpaces runtime system is a platform for executing and migrating mobile agents. It is built on a Java virtual machine and mobile agents are given as Java objects [ ]. Each component is given as a mobile agent in the system and the containment hierarchy of components in a document is given as an agent hierarchy managed by the system. The runtime system has the following functions:

Agent Hierarchy Management: The agent hierarchy is given as a tree structure in which each node contains a mobile agent and its attributes. The runtime system is assumed to be at the root node of the agent hierarchy. Agent migration in an agent hierarchy is performed just as a transformation of the tree structure of the hierarchy. In the runtime system, each agent has direct control of its inner agent. That is, a container agent can instruct its embedded agents to move to other agents or computers, serialize and destroy them. In contrast, each agent has no direct control over its container agent. Instead, each container can offer a collection of service methods which can be accessed by its embedded agents.

Agent Execution Management: The runtime system is at the root node of the agent hierarchy and can control all the agents in the agent hierarchy. Furthermore, it maintains the life-cycle of agents: initialization, execution, suspension, and termination. When the life-cycle state of an agent is changed, the runtime system issues events to invoke certain methods in the agent and its containing agents. Moreover, the runtime system enforces interoperation among mobile agent-based components. The runtime system monitors the changes of components and propagates certain events to the right components. For example, when a component is added to or removed from its container component, the system dispatches specified events to the component and the container.

---

[1] Details of the MobileSpaces mobile agent system can be found in our previous paper [ ].

Agent Migration: Each document is saved and transmitted as a group of mobile agents. When a component is moved inside a computer, the component and its inner components can still be running. When a component is transferred over a network, the runtime system stores the state and the codes of the component, including the components embedded in it, into a bit-stream formed in Java's JAR file format that can support digital signatures for authentication. The system provides a built-in mechanism for transmitting the bit-stream over the network by using an extension of the HTTP protocol. The current system basically uses the Java object serialization package for marshaling components. The package does not support the capturing of stack frames of threads. Instead, when a component is serialized, the system propagates certain events to its embedded components to instruct the agent to stop its active threads.

Extensibility: The MobileSpaces system is characterized by offering its own facilities through mobile agents, so that these subcomponents can be dynamically added to and removed from the system by migrating and replacing the corresponding agents. Therefore, the system itself can dynamically extend and adapt its new functions, such as inter-agent communication, agent persistency, and agent migration between computers to its execution environments. For example, the system can migrate agents through unreliable, unsecured, and temporally disconnected networks, that may not have been initially supported.

4.2   Agent Model

In our compound document framework, each component is a group of mobile agents in the MobileSpaces system. They consist of a body program and a set of services implemented in Java language. The body program defines the behavior of the component and the set of services defines various APIs for components embedded within the component. Every agent program has to be an instance of a subclass of the abstract class `ComponentAgent`, which consists of some fundamental methods to control the mobility and the life-cycle of a mobile agent-based component.

```
 1: public class ComponentAgent extends Agent {
 2:   // (un)registering services for inner agents
 3:   void addContextService(ContextService service){ ... }
 4:   void removeContextService(ContextService service){ ... }
 5:   ....
 6:   // (un)registering listener objects to hook events
 7:   void addListener(AgentEventListener listener) { ... }
 8:   void removeListener(AgentEventListener listener) { ... }
 9:   ....
10:   void getService(Service service) throws ... { ... }
11:   void go(AgentURL url) throws ... { ... }
12:   void go(AgentURL url1, AgentURL url2) throws ... { ... }
13:   byte[] create(byte[] data) throws ... { ... }
14:   byte[] serialize(AgentURL url) throws ... { ... }
15:   AgentURL deserialize(byte[] data) throws ... { ... }
16:   void destroy(AgentURL url) throws ... { ... }
17:   ....
18:   ComponentFrame getFrame() { ... }
19:   ComponentFrame getFrame(AgentURL url) { ... }
20:   ....
21: }
```

The methods used to control mobility and lifecycle defined in the
`ComponentAgent` class are as follows:

- An agent can invoke public methods defined in a set of service methods offered by its container by invoking the `getService()` method with an instance
  of the `Service` class. The instance can specify the kind of service methods,
  arbitrary objects as arguments, and deadline time for timeout exception.
- When an agent performs the `go(AgentURL url)` method, the agent migrates
  itself to the destination agent specified as `url`. The `go(AgentURL url1,
  AgentURL url2)` method instructs the descendant specified as `url1` to move
  to the destination agent specified as `url2`.
- Each container agent can dispatch certain events to its inner agents and
  notify them when specified actions happened within their surroundings by
  using the `dispatchEvent()` method.

Our framework provides an event mechanism based on the delegation-based
event model introduced in the Abstract Window Toolkit of JDK 1.1 or later,
like Aglets [ ]. When an agent is migrated, marshaled, or destroyed, our runtime
system does not automatically release all the resources, such as files, windows,
and sockets, which are captured by the agent. Instead, the runtime system can
issue certain events in the changes of life-cycle states. Also, a container agent
can dispatch specified events to its inner mobile agent-based components at the
occurrence of user-interface level actions, such as mouse clicks, keystrokes, and
window activation, as well as at the occurrence of application level actions, such
as the opening and closing of documents. To hook these events, each mobile
agent-based component can have one or more listener objects which implement
specific methods invoked by the runtime system and its container component. For
example, each component can have one or more activities which are performed
by using the Java thread library, but needs to capture certain events issued
before it migrates over a network and stop its own activities.

4.3   The MobiDoc Compound Document Framework

The *MobiDoc* framework is implemented as a collection of Java classes to enforce
some of the principles of component-interoperation and graphical user interface.

Visual Layout Management: Each mobile agent-based component can be
displayed within the estate of its container or a window on the screen, but
it must be accessed through an indirection: *frame* objects derived from the
`ComponentFrame` class as shown in Fig. . Each frame object is the area of
the display that represents the contents of components and is used for negotiating the use of geometric space between the frame of its its container component
and the frame of its component.

---

[2] Although the `ComponentFrame` class is a subclass of the `java.awt.Panel` class, we
call them *frame* objects because many existing compound document frameworks
often call the visual space of an embedded component *frame*.

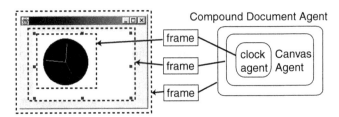

Fig. 2. Components for Compound Document in Agent Hierarchy

The frame object of each container component manages the display of the frames of the components it contains. That is, it can control the sizes, positions, and offsets of all the frames embedded within it, while the frame object of each contained component is responsible for drawing its own contents. For example, if a component needs to change the size of its frame by calling the `setFrameSize()` method, its frame must negotiate with the frame object of its container for its size and shape and redraw its contents within the frame.

```
 1: public class ComponentFrame extends java.awt.Panel {
 2:    // sets the size of the frame
 3:    void setFrameSize(java.awt.Point p);
 4:    // gets the size of the frame
 5:    java.awt.Point getFrameSize();
 6:    // sets the layout manager for the embedded frames
 7:    void setLayout(CompoundLayoutManager mgr) {
 8:    // views the type of the component, e.g. iconic, thumbnail, or framed,
 9:    int getViewType();
10:    // gets the reference of the container's frame
11:    ComponentFrame getContainerFrame();
12:    // adds an embedded component specified as frame
13:    void addFrame(ComponentFrame frame);
14:    // removes an embedded component specified as frame
15:    void removeFrame(ComponentFrame frame);
16:    // gets all the references of embedded frames
17:    ComponentFrame[] getEmbeddedFrames();
18:    // gets the offset and size of the inner frame specified as cf
19:    java.awt.Rectangle getEmbeddedFramePosition(ComponentFrame cf);
20:    // sets the offset and size of the inner frame specified as cf
21:    void setEmbeddedFramePosition(ComponentFrame cf, java.awt.Rectangle);
22:    ....
23: }
```

When one component is activated, another component is usually deactivated but is not necessarily idle. To create a seamless application look, components embedded in a container component need to coordinately share several resources, such as keyboard, mouse, and window. Each component is restricted from directly accessing such shared resources. Instead, the frame object of one activated component is responsible for handling and dispatching user interface actions issued from most resources, and can own these resources until it sends a request to relinquish its resource.

In-Place Editing: The MobiDoc framework provides for document wide operations, such as mouse click and keystrokes. It can dispatch certain events to its components to notify them when specified actions happen within their surroundings. Moreover, the framework provides each container component with a set of built-in services for switching among multiple components embedded in the container and for manipulating the borders of the frame objects of its inner components. One of these services offers graphical user interfaces for in-place editing. This mechanism allows different components in a document to share the same window. Consequently, components can be immediately manipulated in-place, without the need for opening a separate window for each component.

To directly interact with a component, we need to make the component *active* by clicking the mouse within its frame. When a component is active, we can directly manipulate its contents. When clicking the boundary of the frame, the frame becomes *selected* and then has eight rectangle control points for moving it around and resizing it, as shown in Fig. . The user can easily resize and move the selected components by dragging their handles.

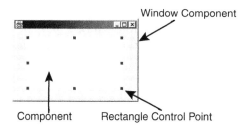

Fig. 3. Selected Component and Its Rectangle Control Points

Structured Storage and Migration: When migrating over a network and being stored onto a disk, each component must be responsible for transforming its own contents and codes into a stream of bytes by using the serialization facility of the runtime system. However, the frame object of each component is not stored in the component. Instead, it is dynamically created and allocated in its container's frame, when it becomes visible and restored. The framework automatically disposes frame objects of each component from the screen and stores specified attributes of the frame object in a list of values corresponding to the attributes, because other frame objects may refer objects which are not serializable, such as several visible objects in the Java Foundation Class package. After restoring such serialized streams as components at the destination, the framework appropriately redraws the frames of the components, as accurately as possible.

4.4   The Current Status

The MobiDoc framework has been implemented in the MobileSpaces system using the Java language (JDK1.2 or later version), and we have developed various components for compound documents, including the examples presented in this paper. The MobileSpaces system is a general-purpose mobile agent system. Therefore, mobile agents in the system may be unwieldy as components of compound documents, but our components can inherit the powerful properties of mobile agents, including their activity and mobility. Security is essential in compound documents as well as mobile agents. The current system relies on the Java security manager and provides a simple mechanism for authentication of components. A container component can judge whether it accepts a new inner component or not beforehand, where the inner components can know the available methods embedded in their containers by using the class introspector mechanism of the Java language. Furthermore, since a container agent plays a role in providing resources for its inner agent, it can limit the accessibility of its inner components to resources such as window, mouse, and keyboard, by hiding events issued from these resources.

5   Examples

The MobiDoc compound document framework is powerful and flexible enough to support radically different applications. This section shows some examples of compound documents based on the MobiDoc framework.

5.1   Electronic Mail System

One of the most illustrative examples of the MobiDoc framework is for the provision of mobile documents for communication and workflow management. We have constructed an electronic mail system based on the framework. The system consists of an inbox document and letter documents as shown in Fig. . The inbox document provides a window that can contain two components. One of the components is a history of received mails and the other component offers a visual space for displaying the contents of mail selected from the history. The letter document corresponds to a mobile agent-based letter and can contain various components for accessing text, graphics, and animation. It also has a window for displaying its contents. It can migrate itself to its destination, but it is not a complete GUI application because it cannot display its contents without the collaboration of its container, i.e., the inbox document.

For example, to edit the text in a letter component, simply click on it, and editor program is invoked by the in-place editing mechanism of the MobiDoc framework. The component can deliver itself and its inner components to an inbox document at the receiver. After a moving letter is accepted by the inbox document, if a user clicks a letter in the list of received mail, the selected letter creates a frame object of it and requests the document to display the frame object within the frame of the document. The key idea of this mail system is that it composes different mobile agent-based components into a seamless-looking compound document and allows us to immediately display and access the contents of the components in-place. Since the inbox document is the root of the letter component, when the document is stored and moved, all the components embedded in the document are stored and moved with the document.

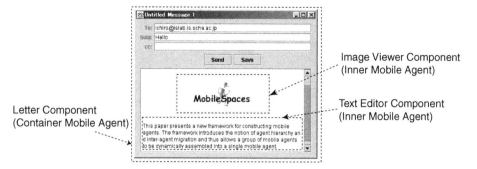

Fig. 4. Structure of a Letter Document

5.2 Desktop Teleporting

We constructed a mobile agent-based desktop system similar to the Teleporting System and the Virtual Network Computing system. These systems are based on the X Window System and allow the running applications in the computer display to be redirected to a different computer display.

In contrast, our desktop system consists of mobile agent-based applications and thus can migrate not only the surface of applications but also the applications themselves to another computer (Fig.). The system consists of a window manager document and its inner applications. The manager corresponds to a desktop document at the top of the component hierarchy of applications separately displayed in their own windows on the desktop on the screen. It can be used to control the sizes, positions, and overlaps of the windows of its inner applications. When the desktop document is moved to another computer, all the components, including their windows, move to the new computer. The framework tries to keep the moving desktop and applications the same as when the user last accessed them on the previous computer, even when the previous computer and network are stopped. For example, the framework can migrate a user's custom desktop and applications to another computer the user is accessing.

6 Conclusion

We have presented a new approach for building mobile compound documents. The key idea of the approach is to build compound documents from hierarchical mobile agents in the MobileSpaces system, which allows more than one mobile agent to be dynamically assembled into a single mobile agent. Our approach allows a compound document to be dynamically composed of mobile components and to be migrated over a network as a whole with its inner components. We design and built a framework, called MobiDoc, to demonstrate the usability and flexibility of this approach. The framework provides value-added services for coordinating mobile agent-based components embedded in a document. We be-

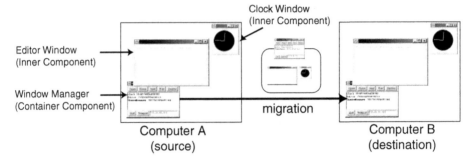

Fig. 5. A Desktop Teleporting to Another Computer

lieve that the framework can provide a realistic and useful application of mobile agents.

Finally, we would like to point out further issues to be resolved. To develop compound documents more effectively, we need a visual builder for our mobile components. We plan to extend a visual builder tool for JavaBeans, such as the BeanBox system included in the Bean Development Kit (BDK) [ ], so that it has the ability to support mobile agent-based compound documents. In the current system, resource management and security mechanisms were incorporated relatively straightforwardly. These now should be designed for mobile compound documents. Additionally, the programming interface of the current system is not yet satisfactory. We plan to design a more elegant and flexible interface incorporating with existing compound document technologies. The MobileSpaces system is a general-purpose mobile agent system and thus can easily be used to build the framework. However, it may be unwieldy as an infrastructure for compound documents, and thus we are interested in investigating a lightweight system, which is optimized to handle mobile compound documents.

References

1. Apple Computer Inc., OpenDoc: White Paper, Apple Computer Inc., 1994.
2. K. Arnold and J. Gosling, The Java Programming Language, Addison-Wesley, 1998.   ,
3. J. Baumann, F. Hole, K. Rothermel, and M. Strasser, Mole - Concepts of A Mobile Agent System, Mobility: Processes, Computers, and Agents, pp.536–554, Addison-Wesley, 1999.
4. K. Brockschmidt, Inside OLE 2, Microsoft Press, 1995.
5. L. Cardelli and A. D. Gordon, Mobile Ambients, Foundations of Software Science and Computational Structures, LNCS, Vol. 1378, pp. 140–155, 1998.
6. L. Cable, Extensible Runtime Containment and Server Protocol for JavaBeans, Sun Microsfystems, http://java.sun.com/beans, 1997.
7. T. Gschwind, M. Feridun, and S. Pleisch, ADK: Building Mobile Agents for Network and System Management from Resuable Components, Proceedings of Symposium on Agent Systems and Applications / Symposium on Mobile Agents (ASA/MA'1999), pp.13–21, 1999.

8. G. Hamilton, The JavaBeans Specification, Sun Microsfystems, http://java.sun.com/beans, 1997.   ,
9. B. D. Lange and M. Oshima, Programming and Deploying Java Mobile Agents with Aglets, Addison-Wesley, 1998.   ,
10. J. Morin, HyperNews, a Hypermedia Electronic-Newspaper Environment based on Agents, Proceedings of HICSS-31, pp.58–67, 1998.
11. ObjectSpace Inc, ObjectSpace Voyager Technical Overview, ObjectSpace, Inc. 1997.
12. M. Potel and S. Cotter, Inside Taligent Technology, Addison-Wesley, 1995.
13. I. Satoh, MobileSpaces: A Framework for Building Adaptive Distributed Applications Using a Hierarchical Mobile Agent System, Proceedings of IEEE International Conference on Distributed Computing Systems (ICDCS'2000), pp.161-168, April, 2000.   ,   ,   ,
14. Sun Microsystems, The Bean Development Kit, http://java.sun.com/beans/, July, 1998.
15. C. Szyperski, Component Software, Addison-Wesley, 1998.
16. J. E. White, Telescript Technology: Mobile Agents, Mobility: Processes, Computers, and Agents, pp.461–492, Addison-Wesley, 1999.

Distributed Collaborations Using Network Mobile Agents*

Anand Tripathi, Tanvir Ahmed, Vineet Kakani, and Shremattie Jaman**

Department of Computer Science
University of Minnesota, Minneapolis MN 55455
{tripathi,tahmed,kakani,jaman}@cs.umn.edu

Abstract. This paper describes a mobile agent-based approach for supporting coordination of user activities in distributed collaborations. The approach presented here uses XML to specify a collaboration plan in terms of various participants' roles, access rights based on roles, and the coordination actions to be executed when certain events occur. Using this plan an agent-based distributed middleware system provides each user an interface to perform the tasks pertaining to the collaboration. The actions of a user transparently create and dispatch coordination agents to other users. The middleware also enforces the security constraints defined in the collaboration plan. We illustrate our approach with an example system for collaborative authoring implemented using the Ajanta mobile agent system.

1   Introduction

The focus of this paper is on building distributed collaborations using mobile agents. Mobile agents provide a new paradigm for building distributed applications. A mobile agent is an object capable of migrating autonomously from node to node, and performing tasks on behalf of a user. The main advantages of the mobile agent paradigm lie in its ability to move client code and computation to remote server resources, and in permitting increased asynchrony in client-server interactions. A distributed collaboration involves a number of physically distributed users, who cooperate on some common tasks and share an environment composed of objects. In such an environment, a user may participate in multiple roles and may have different levels of access privileges based on his roles.

As discussed below, there are several motivations for exploring the use of mobile agents in building distributed collaborations. With the use of mobile agents as user-interface objects, which a user obtains from the collaboration group's coordinator, one can ensure that the members participate only by using the prescribed protocols. Such interface agents can encapsulate coordination protocols and appropriate privileges based on a member's role in the collaboration.

* This work was supported by National Science Foundation grants ANIR 9813703 and EIA 9818338.
** The author's participation was supported by REU supplement funds to NSF grant ANIR 9813703.

D. Kotz and F. Mattern (Eds.): ASA/MA 2000, LNCS 1882, pp. 126–   , 2000.
© Springer-Verlag Berlin Heidelberg 2000

Moreover, the coordinator can dynamically upgrade its agents at participants' nodes to alter the coordination policies. Another use of mobile agents in distributed collaborations is for executing remote coordination operations. This is particularly attractive for supporting collaborations in intermittently connected environments. Mobile agents can also be used in workflow systems as shared objects, which can move from one participant to another at various processing stages. Additionally, by implementing a user's interaction environment in a collaboration as a collection of mobile agents, it is possible for a user to physically move to a different node by simply migrating its agents to that node.

The main contribution of this paper is in developing a methodology for building a distributed collaboration environment starting with its specification in a high level form and then interfacing such a specification with a mobile agent based middleware. This middleware uses mobile agents to facilitate coordination actions. We present here an approach for specifying a collaboration plan using XML [ ]. Such a specification needs to describe shared objects, coordination operations, roles of various people involved in a collaboration, and security policies based on roles. The security and coordination policies specified in the XML plan are implemented by the agent-based middleware. An important aspect of our work is the fact that the designer of a collaboration needs to specify only the XML plan without being concerned about the management of the mobile coordination agents and the security issues.

We present the details of our approach through an example based on a collaborative authoring system, which we implemented as a proof-of-concept experiment, using the Ajanta mobile agent system [ ]. The functions of this example system are described in Section 2. Section 3 presents our approach for specifying a collaboration plan. Section 4 describes how this plan is interfaced with an agent-based middleware to build the desired distributed collaboration environment. Section 5 presents related work, and section 6 discusses the conclusions and future directions of our work.

2   Overview of the Approach

2.1   Design Steps

In the proposed approach, building a distributed collaboration system using mobile agents involves three steps. The first step involves the specification of a *collaboration schema*, using XML Document Type Definition (DTD) for defining roles, shared objects, and operations associated with a collaborative task. It also provides rules for associating privileges with roles, and coordination actions with operations. The second step is the specification of a collaboration plan, using XML, in conformance with the rules given by the DTD. The designer of the collaboration plan, whom we refer to as the *convener*, is responsible for preparing this specification.

This step involves defining the following elements in a collaboration:

Shared Objects: A collaborative activity involves use of a set of shared objects, whose operations are executed by the participants based on their roles.

Participant Roles: A role defines a set of responsibilities and tasks for a participant towards the goal of the collaborative activity. The participants involved
in a collaboration are identified by their roles.

Privileges: The security policies in a collaboration are based on the participants'
roles. Privileges are associated with each role.

Coordination operations: A coordination operation defines the actions to be executed when a certain task is executed in the collaboration. For example,
the completion of a task by a participant may require some objects to be
made available to other participants based on their roles.

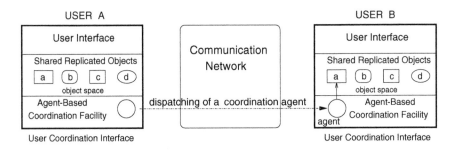

Fig. 1. System level view of agent-based collaboration

The third step is illustrated by Figure , which shows the typical structure
for realizing a distributed collaboration using agents. The collaboration plan is
securely distributed to each user's computer. Each user participates by executing
an agent-based coordinator on his computer. We refer to this as the *User Coordination Interface (UCI)*. A UCI maintains copies of the shared objects that
are required as per the user's roles. It provides suitable interfaces to its user
to facilitate execution of operations on the shared objects. The user interface
component of a UCI is constructed as a collection of mobile agents obtained
from the convener, based on the user's roles. When a certain task is executed,
the UCI transparently dispatches agents to other UCIs to perform coordination
actions. Also, it receives and executes the agents that are sent to it by the other
UCIs.

One could use RPC or message-passing to perform such coordination actions.
However, the agent-based coordination mechanism used here is particularly at-
tactive for collaborations in intermttently connected environments. While a user
is disconnected from the environment, its agents can migrate in the connected
backbone network to perform coordination actions at other users' nodes. Other
researchers have also proposed the use of mobile agents in intermittently connected environments [ ]. Another advantage of using mobile agents arises while
waiting to ensure the precondition for a coordination operation at a remote
node. In contrast to RPC or message-passing model, the agent-based approach

obviates the need of either maintaing a connection or making repeated attempts until the required precondition is satisfied.

When installed and initialized on a user's computer, a UCI parses and verifies the collaboration plan and creates a collection of objects defining the shared workspace. We refer to these local copies as the user's *object-space.* Some of the objects in the shared workspace may not be present in the participant's object-space, if disallowed by the security policy. In Figure , objects a and c are present at user A's object-space, whereas objects a, c and d are present at user B's object-space.

2.2 Example: A Collaborative Authoring System

We use a collaborative authoring system as an example to experiment with the central concepts discussed in this paper. The collaborative authoring environment considered in this paper supports the activities of a group of people jointly developing a document. In this example, the participants perform tasks related to writing, reviewing, and editing different parts of the document to be developed. The central entity in the shared workspace is the document object to be produced. Three roles are defined for the authoring system: *author*, *editor*, and *reviewer*. The document object contains one or more chapter objects. A chapter contains three objects that are shared: the chapter's contents, the reviewer's comments and the editor's comments.

Following are some of the coordination operations defined for this authoring system. The first operation in the collaboration occurs at the chapter level. When the author of a chapter completes a draft of the chapter's contents, it is published to the chapter's reviewer and editor by invoking the "publish" operation. This results in the coordination actions of making the chapter's contents available to the participants in these two roles. This operation also enables a reviewer to write a review of the chapter's text. The reviewer of the chapter cannot compose the review until the chapter's contents have been written and received. The next operation occurs at the reviewer level. Upon completion of the review, the reviewer publishes the review to make it available to the author and the editor. The editor of the chapter composes his comments based on the chapter's contents and the review. The editor publishes the comments to the author. The author can then read the review and the editor's comments, and modify the chapter accordingly.

3 Description of a Collaboration Plan

This section presents an XML schema that we developed for specifying a collaboration plan. In section 3.1 we introduce the schema for generic collaboration environments. Using the authoring system as an example, we illustrate our approach in the following section. Figures , , and   show, in three parts, a simplified version of the DTD specification for a generalized collaboration environment. The corresponding examples of an XML plan to collaboratively compose a document object are shown in Figures , , and .

```
<!DOCTYPE PLAN [
<!ELEMENT PLAN (ROLE+, OBJECT+,
              OPERATION+)>
<!ELEMENT ROLE (PARTICIPANT+)>
<!ATTLIST ROLE
  ROLE_ID ID #REQUIRED
  ROLE_NAME CDATA #REQUIRED
  OBJECT_REF IDREF #IMPLIED
  ROLE_INTERFACE NMTOKEN #IMPLIED
>
<!ELEMENT PARTICIPANT EMPTY>
<!ATTLIST PARTICIPANT
  URN CDATA #REQUIRED
>
. . . . . .
]>
```

```
<PLAN>
  <ROLE ROLE_ID="doc:author"
        ROLE_NAME="author"
        ROLE_INTERFACE="AuthorUI">
    <PARTICIPANT URN="URN:ans:A">
    </PARTICIPANT>
  </ROLE>
  <ROLE ROLE_ID="doc:reviewer"
        ROLE_NAME="reviewer">
    <PARTICIPANT URN="URN:ans:B">
    </PARTICIPANT>
    <PARTICIPANT URN="URN:ans:C">
    </PARTICIPANT>
  </ROLE>
. . . . . . . . .
</PLAN>
```

Fig. 2. DTD for a Collaboration Environment and Role Specification

Fig. 3. Example: Collaboration Plan and Role

3.1   A Schema for Collaboration Specification

The XML DTD defines a generic specification of the collaboration environment to be supported by the agent-based collaborative system. Figure   defines a collaboration environment under the element named PLAN, which is composed of one or many roles, objects, and operations. This definition can be used to specify a plan for any desired collaboration environment: it is not limited to the authoring system presented here. As shown in Figure   , a role has a unique id, a name, an object reference, and a role-interface. The object reference can be specified by the convener if a role is associated with an object. The role-interface can be a Java class supplied by the convener or implied by the collaborative system. This role specific interface can provide different views of the same object to different participants based on their access privileges. Each role is assigned to one or more participants, who are identified uniquely using their Uniform Resource Names (URN) [   ] in the Ajanta naming scheme.

According to the DTD specification in Figure   , an object must have a unique id, a name, a type, and can have a codebase which specifies the class implementing this object. Moreover, an object can have methods and can be composed of other nested objects. As a part of the method definition, access control is specified based on roles. For simplicity, the details of the method parameter specification are omitted from the DTD.

Figure   shows the specification of an operation whose execution is controlled by the UCI. Each operation has a name, access control entries, and one or more agent-actions. The attribute OPERATION_STATUS is implicitly maintained by the UCI to keep track of the status of the operation. These operation status values are also used for workflow coordination. The access control entries of an

```
<!ELEMENT OBJECT ( METHOD*,
                   OBJECT*)>
<!ATTLIST OBJECT
  OBJ_ID ID #REQUIRED
  OBJ_NAME CDATA #REQUIRED
  OBJ_TYPE CDATA #REQUIRED
  CODE_BASE NMTOKEN #IMPLIED
>
<!ELEMENT METHOD(ACCESS_CONTROL*,
                 PARAMETER*)>
<!ATTLIST METHOD
  METHOD_NAME NMTOKEN #REQUIRED
>
<!ELEMENT ACCESS_CONTROL EMPTY>
<!ATTLIST ACCESS_CONTROL
  ROLE_REF IDREF #REQUIRED
>
```

```
<OBJECT OBJ_ID="doc"
        OBJ_NAME="Document"
        OBJ_TYPE="Composite">
 <OBJECT OBJ_ID="doc:ch1"
         OBJ_NAME="Chapter1"
         OBJ_TYPE="Text"
         CODE_BASE="doc.Chapter">
  <METHOD METHOD_NAME="update">
   <ACCESS_CONTROL
        ROLE_REF="doc:author">
   </ACCESS_CONTROL>
  </METHOD>
   .......
 </OBJECT>
</OBJECT>
```

Fig. 4. DTD Specification for Objects

Fig. 5. Example: XML Specification for an Object

operation specify, for various roles, the permissions to execute this operation. The AGENT_ACTION element defines the coordination actions that need to be performed when the given operation is executed. An agent-action is composed of a remote method and one or more targets, which are references to roles. The remote method is uniquely identified by a reference to the desired object, a method name, and a parameter list. In general, these are the methods of the shared objects that an agent would invoke when visiting the UCIs of the users corresponding to the target roles.

3.2   An Example of Collaboration Plan Specification

In this section, we discuss an example of a plan for a collaborative authoring system. Figures   and   present a collaboration plan for preparing a document with a single chapter, three participants and two roles: author and reviewer. In Figure , the author role has a participant urn:ans:A and the reviewer role has two participants: urn:ans:B and urn:ans:C. The Java class of the author's interface is AuthorUI, which is specified by the convener. The interface object is implemented using mobile agents, and such an implementation enables the convener to impose desired restrictions on access to shared objects. The review and editor comments of the chapter are omitted from this example, as the given chapter specification is enough for the basic illustration of our approach. The type of the document is declared as Composite, as it may contain several chapter objects. Moreover, the chapter object has a codebase doc.Chapter and a method update, which can be executed only by the author role. This update method

```
<!ELEMENT OPERATION                <OPERATION
    (ACCESS_CONTROL*,AGENT_ACTION+)>      OBJECT_REF="doc:ch1"
<!ATTLIST OPERATION                    OPERATION_NAME="publish">
  OBJECT_REF IDREFS #REQUIRED        <ACCESS_CONTROL
  OPERATION_NAME NMTOKEN #REQUIRED      ROLE_REF="doc:author">
  OPERATION_STATUS NMTOKEN #IMPLIED   </ACCESS_CONTROL>
>
<!ELEMENT AGENT_ACTION             <AGENT_ACTION>
    (TARGET*, REMOTE_METHOD)>         <TARGET
<!ELEMENT TARGET EMPTY>                 TARGET_REF="doc:author"/>
<!ATTLIST TARGET                      <TARGET
  TARGET_REF IDREFS #REQUIRED           TARGET_REF="doc:reviewer"/>
>                                     <REMOTE_METHOD
<!ELEMENT REMOTE_METHOD                  OBJECT_REF="doc:ch1"
        (PARAMETER*)>                    METHOD_NAME="update">
<!ATTLIST REMOTE_METHOD               </REMOTE_METHOD>
  OBJECT_REF IDREFS #REQUIRED         </AGENT_ACTION>
  METHOD_NAME NMTOKEN #REQUIRED     </OPERATION>
>
```

Fig. 6. DTD Specification for Operations

Fig. 7. Example: XML Specification for an Operation

is executed either locally by a user or remotely by a mobile agent through the UCI.

Figure   presents the plan for an operation specification. The author role has the access right to perform the **publish** operation on the **chapter1** object. The corresponding agent-action of the **publish** operation contains a list of roles as targets and specifies the **update** method of the **chapter1** object for remote action. Here, the remote method does not require any parameters. The operation status values, maintained by the UCI, ensure that the reviewer is not permitted to publish a review until the author has published the chapter text. In the current implementation, a coordination agent visits various participants' UCIs in a sequential order to execute the specified methods. It should be noted that each operation can have multiple agent-actions, each of which can be performed in parallel by different agents.

4 Collaboration Using Network Mobile Agents

In this section we describe how the XML specification of a collaboration plan is integrated into a mobile agent-based middleware to build a distributed collaboration environment. Section 4.1 presents a brief overview of Ajanta's agent programming model and facilities. Section 4.2 describes, using the authoring system as an example, how a plan is interfaced with the agent-based middleware to build UCIs.

4.1   Mobile Agents in Ajanta

Ajanta [ ] is a Java-based system for programming mobile agents in distributed systems. Ajanta agents are *mobile objects*, which encapsulate code and execution context along with data. The Ajanta system provides facilities to build customizable *servers* to host mobile agents, and a set of primitives for the creation and management of agents. Programming abstractions are provided to specify an agent's tasks and its migration path. Support for security is an integral part of the Ajanta system, which provides facilities for authentication, public key maintenance, access control, and host resource protection.

The base `AgentServer` class provides the generic functionality to host agents, create protected domains for their execution, transfer agents from one server to another, and respond to various agent control functions. An application specific agent server is implemented by inheriting from the base `AgentServer` class. It can be easily customized for specific services by creating appropriate resources (objects) and making them available to the visiting agents through its resource registry. Each agent carries with it credentials, which include the identity of the agent's owner. A visiting agent can request access to a resource through the server's resource registry. The resource then constructs a suitably restricted proxy based on its security policy, and gives the agent a reference to this proxy. The agent cannot access the resources directly, and the proxy object enforces the required access control based on the agent's credentials. Ajanta ensures that the proxy class is loaded from a trusted codebase.

The `Agent` class implements the generic functionality of a mobile agent. It defines protocols for handling arrival and departure events of an agent at a server. Each agent is bound to its host environment using which it can request various services from its local host. These services include obtaining access to local resources, registering itself as a resource, or requesting migration. An agent can request migration to another host, specifying the method to be executed there. The concept of itineraries is also supported by the Ajanta system. In its most simple form an itinerary defines a sequence of hops to various agent servers, and for each hop it defines a method to be executed at that server.

4.2   Implementation of the Collaborative Authoring System

Each user performs his tasks in the collaboration through the UCI process executing on the user's desktop. Our approach is to implement a UCI by extending Ajanta's `AgentServer` class. Figure shows the structure of a UCI for the example authoring system. It contains a *document manager* object and a *user interface* object. The document manager reads the XML plan and maintains the shared object space. Its interface enables the user and the visiting agents to read, write, edit, and publish any parts of a document. The document manager is registered as a resource in the agent server's resource registry. The user performs the tasks through the user interface, which is implemented as a collection of mobile agents obtained from the convener based on the user's roles in the collaboration. Through the user interface, operations of the document manager are executed, which may result in the creation and launching of coordination agents. A visiting agent, launched by another UCI, requests access to the document manager using the agent server's resource access protocol.

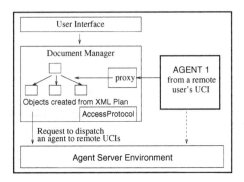

Fig. 8. UCI Implementation as an Agent Server

The document manager maintains the information derived from the XML plan. At the time of its creation and initialization, the document manager parses the XML specification and creates a tree structure storing various objects. In our example system, the root of the tree is the document object, which contains chapter objects as descendents, and so forth. It maintains the copies of the shared objects in the user's object-space. It also maintains objects corresponding to the OPERATION element, and these *operation objects* contain the specifications of the associated agent-actions. The access rights and workflow constraints are checked and maintained by the document manager.

When an operation is executed, the corresponding operation object is examined by the document manager. If any agent-action is specified as a part of this operation, the document manager creates an agent to execute the methods at the specified user's UCIs. For each such agent-action, an agent is created with an itinerary to visit each participant's UCI. An itinerary entry contains an object reference, a method name, and the destination URN which is determined from the role definitions in the XML plan.

Agent servers, in our context the UCIs, provide protected execution domains for hosting agents. When an agent arrives at a host, the agent-server checks its credentials and verifies the agent's identity. Upon success, the agent-server creates an exclusive proxy of the document manager for this agent and embeds the identity of the agent's owner in the proxy. Later, when the agent invokes a method in the proxy, the proxy transparently invokes the corresponding method in the document manager using the agent owner's identity.

5   Related Work

The work presented here relates to many existing ideas from a number of areas, such as mobile agent systems, computer-supported collaborative work, coordination specifications, workflow management, and role-based security. Our work integrates these ideas into a mobile agent based middleware for distributed collaborations.

An agent-based workflow system architecture based on the HTTP protocol and Web is presented in [ ], but there the agent mobility is limited to Java applets. In [ ], agent enhanced workflow is discussed, where an agent layer is wrapped around existing workflow applications. In contrast, our work uses an agent based distributed middleware in which agents are used to support workflow applications. The use of mobile agents has been discussed in the evolution of workflow implementation architectures [ ] but no specific models or systems are cited there. Also their use in workflow systems has been investigated in [ ], where mobile agents are referred to as "worklets" and are written in JPython; the workflow rules are encapsulated in the scripted agents. A worklet is similar to an Ajanta agent. The worklets project does not provide a high level abstraction for specifying global workflow activities. In contrast, the focus of our work is on developing a broad based methodology for constructing distributed collaborations from their high level specifications, including security and coordination requirements. Based on these specifications, the generic agent-based collaboration facility transparently creates and launches mobile agents for workflow coordination. In our approach the agents are implicitly derived from XML specifications.

Coordination specifications indicate how the dependencies between activities should be managed in a workflow or collaboration. In a workflow design, a process language is used to define the workflow activities [ ]. A number of groups have proposed process definition meta models. These include UML [ ] and Wfmc [ ] process definition meta-language. In our approach, the XML based plan description corresponds to a process level description, and the agent-based middleware is the execution infrastructure. Our work is fundamentally different from Wfmc [ ], which is concerned with process descriptions for interoperability of workflow systems, and OMG's XMI (XML Meta Data Interchange)[ ] which mainly focuses on data exchange related issues.

Several general purpose systems have been developed for building collaboration environments using library modules and interfaces [ ]. However, in these systems coordination policies still need to be programmed using procedural languages. COCA [ ] is a framework for collaborative objects coordination, separating specification of coordination from computation. Our work is related to COCA in that it also uses roles to specify policies for collaboration. However, our approach differs from COCA in that we use XML for specification of various coordination policies and description of roles, unlike a first order logic language used in COCA. Our approach decouples the specification and the underlying implementation framework. Also, XML is more readily understood by both the human users and the software systems.

Role based security models [ ] have been widely investigated in the past for distributed collaborations [ ] [ ], distributed object systems [ ], and enterprise workflow systems. In the context of agent based systems, a discussion of role based modeling techniques is presented in [ ]. Our work uses role based security models for specifying security constraints. The agent based middleware implements these constraints at two levels. First, from the role based security policies the convener constructs a user's interfaces for the environment as mobile agents that encapsulate required security restrictions. Second, during any coordination action the middleware uses Ajanta's security infrastructure to ensure that the agents executing at a server on behalf of a remote user can perform only those operations for which the user is authorized.

6   Conclusion

The main contribution of this paper is in developing a methodology for building a distributed collaboration system using a high level specification in XML, and then interfacing this specification with a mobile agent based middleware to realize the desired system. The collaboration plan is specified in XML in terms of shared objects, operations, user roles, role-based security requirements, and coordination constraints. The mobile agent based middleware provides a set of generic capabilities for implementing these specifications. It interprets the XML specification of the environment, and transparently launches agents to other users' nodes when coordination actions need to be performed.

We have presented our approach using an example system to support collaborative authoring of a document. This proof-of-concept implementation was developed using the Ajanta system. Based on this work, we make the following observations. Mobile agents provide a powerful facility for performing coordination actions asynchronously. Moreover, XML provides a high level abstraction for agent programming, which includes building itineraries, and creating and launching agents. Especially noteworthy is the use of a secure agent programming system such as Ajanta because it relieves the programmer from the burden of building a security infrastructure and agent management protocols. Such an approach also provides customized user interfaces based on the participants' roles.

There are several directions that we plan to investigate in our future research. A general application level exception handling model needs to be developed which can be integrated with a collaboration plan in XML. Currently, we rely on Ajanta's system level exception handling mechanism to handle application level exceptions. Also, we plan to develop a more general collaboration specification in XML that can specify plans other than simple workflows.

References

1. Jin W. Chang and Colin T. Scott. Agent-based Workflow: TRP Support Environment (TSE). In *Fifth International World Wide Web Conference*, May 1996.

2. S. A. Demurjian, T. C. Ting, and B. Thuraisingham. User-Role Based Security for Collaborative Computing Environments . *Multimedia Review*, 4(2):40–47, Summer 1993.

3. Prasun Dewan and HongHai Shen. Access Control for Collaborative Environments. In *Proceedings of the ACM Conference on CSCW*, pages 51–58, 1992.

4. Gail Kaiser, Adam Stone, and Stepher Dossick. A Mobile Agent Approach to Lightweight Process Workflow. Technical Report CUCS-021-99, Columbia University, 1999. Available at URL ftp://ftp.psl.cs.columbia.edu/pub/psl/CUCS-021-99.pdf.

5. Elizabeth A. Kendall. Role Modelling for Agent Sysems Analysis, Design, and Implementation. In *Proc. of the First Intl. Symp. on Agent Systems and Applications and the Third Intl. Symp. on Mobile Agents*, pages 204–218, October 1999.

6. David Kotz, Robert Gray, Saurab Nog, Daniela Rus, Sumit Chawla, and George Cybenko. Agent TCL: Targeting the Needs of Mobile Computers. *IEEE Internet Computing*, pages 58–67, July-August 1997. Available at http://computer.org/internet/.

7. Du Li and Richard Muntz. COCA: Collaborative Objects Coordination Architecture. In *Proceedings of CSCW'98*, pages 179–188, 1998.

8. OMG . XML Meta Data Interchange. http://www.omg.org.

9. Rational Software. UML Documentation. Available at URL http:www.rational.com/uml/resources.

10. Mark Roseman and Saul Greenberg. Building Realtime Groupware with GroupKit, A Groupware Toolkit. In *ACM SIGCHI'96*, March 1996.

11. Ravi Sandhu, Edward Coyne, Hal Feinstein, and Charles Youman. Role-Based Access Control Models. *IEEE Computer*, 29(2):38–47, February 1996.

12. Marc-Thomas Schmidt. The Evolution of Workflow Standards . *IEEE Concurrency*, 7(3):44–52, July-September 1999.

13. J. W. Shepherdson, S. G. Thompson, and B. R. Odgers. Cross Organisational Workflow Coordinated by Software Agents. Available at URL http://www.zurich.ibm.com/ hlu/WACCworkshop/papers/Shepherdson/.

14. Amit Sheth, Wil van der Alst, and Ismailcem B. Arpinar. Processes Driving the Networked Economy. *IEEE Concurrency*, 7(3):18–31, July-September 1999.

15. Karen Sollins and Larry Masinter. RFC 1737: Functional Requirements for Uniform Resource Names. Available at URL http://www.cis.ohio-state.edu/htbin/rfc/rfc1737.html, December 1994.

16. Anand Tripathi, Neeran Karnik, Manish Vora, Tanvir Ahmed, and Ram Singh. Mobile Agent Programming in Ajanta. In *Proceedings of the 19th International Conference on Distributed Computing Systems*, May 1999.   ,

17. W3C. Extensible Markup Language (XML) 1.0, W3C Recommendation 10. Available at URL http://www.w3.org/TR/, February 1998.

18. Workflow Management Coalition. Interface 1 - Process Definition Interchange V 1.0 Final . Technical Report WfMC TC-1016-P, October 1999. Available at URL http://www.wfmc.org.

19. N. Yialelis, E. Lupu, and M. Sloman. Role-based Security for Distributed Object Systems . In *Proceedings of the 5th IEEE Workshops on Enabling Technologies: Infrastructure for Collaborative Enterprises (WET ICE '96)*, pages 80–85, 1996.

Using Adaptation and Organisational Knowledge to Coordinate Mobile Agents

Steven Willmott and Boi Faltings

Laboratoire d'Intelligence Artificielle, Department Informatique, Swiss Federal
Institute of Technology
IN (Ecublens), CH-1015 Lausanne, Switzerland
{willmott,faltings}@lia.di.epfl.ch

Abstract. Quality of Service (QoS) routing generally requires fast reaction times, tight coupling of interactions between routing systems and
mechanisms for ensuring that actions taken throughout the network are
coherent. [ ] showed how an agent based QoS routing approach can benefit significantly from making controller agents mobile and allowing them
adapt the information and control distribution in the network over time.
This paper discusses how giving mobile agents organisational models can
bridge the gap between the need for tight, fast coordination and freedom
to move around the network. Furthermore coordination is achieved without imposing any globally or external controls on the mobile agents in
the system.

1 Introduction

[ ] describes how groups of agents performing Quality of Service routing can
be made to adapt their working relationships over time with respect to the state
of their environment. The resulting system is based on mobile controller agents
moving around the network as resource availability patterns change. This paper
describes how giving mobile agents models of their relationships to other agents
in the system:

- Builds up an organisational structure
- Speeds up coordination for solving routing problems
- Controls agent mobility to ensure that the routing service is provided effi-
  ciently throughout the network

Section   of the paper gives an overview of an agent based Quality of Service
routing approach, Section   describes the use of organisational models. Section
briefly covers preliminary results and Section   discusses the importance of the
organisational approach. Section   concludes the paper.

D. Kotz and F. Mattern (Eds.): ASA/MA 2000, LNCS 1882, pp. 138–   , 2000.
© Springer-Verlag Berlin Heidelberg 2000

2   Hierarchies of Agents for Quality of Service Routing

On-line, state-based Quality of Service (QoS) routing presents challenging problems in the distribution of information and control. As the network state changes, information for routing decisions needs to be propagated and routing decisions made which respect current constraints. Hierarchical models (such as the ATM forum's PNNI architecture [ ]) are often proposed to help deal with the complexity of the problem:

- The network is divided up into disjoint *regions* $r \in L_1$, each region grouping together one or more network nodes
- Subsets of these first tier regions are then grouped together at the next level up (L_2 into *meta-regions*)

This process continues recursively until a complete hierarchy is formed. Aggregation techniques can be used to generate summarised models of the network state at higher levels in the hierarchy. This aggregation abstracts away the detailed link state information to produce more manageable information models.

Going one step beyond the standard hierarchical models, the regions and meta-regions can be controlled by *controller agents* $c_{i/j}$ responsible for resource allocation decisions in each region $r_{i/j} \in L_j$. Agents controlling regions $r \in L_1$ are responsible for actual physical resources, agents controlling regions at levels L_2 and above have an aggregated view of the network state and are responsible for coordinating the actions of agents visible to them in the level below.

2.1   Static Hierarchy

To solve routing problems which traverse more than one region, controller agents need to interact with one another. The hierarchy created by the regions $r \in L_1$, $r \in L_2$ etc. can be used to define relationships between controllers which determine how information is propagated and how agents work together to solve individual routing problems. These temporally stable relationships are often called *organisational* relationships [ ] whereas interactions carried out by agents to jointly solve individual routing tasks are classified as *coordination* (see [ ] for example).

A basic agent based routing scheme for a hierarchy is shown in Figure . (Note that standard hierarchical routing schemes such as [ ] and [ ] for example often have non-hierarchical control flow.)

2.2   Adapting the Hierarchy to the Network State

The division of regions between agents and controllers represents a static distribution of information (local controller $c_{i/j}$ keeps track of the state in its part

---

[1] See [ ] for a good overview of existing techniques, issues and discussion of the need for on-line state based approaches.

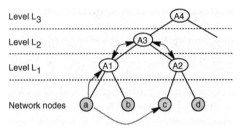

Fig. 1. Agents A1 and A2 are responsible for regions containing nodes a and b and c and d respectively. When A1 receives a demand for a route from node a to node c it is not able to allocate resource immediately since c is not in its own region. A3 is then requested to help, which it does by allocating resources between A2 (the owner of node c) and A1 before requesting both A1 and A2 to complete the remainder of the routes in their own regions

of the network $r_{i/j}$) and control ($c_{i/j}$ is responsible for all resource allocations in $r_{i/j}$). As has often been pointed out however, no distribution is optimal for every situation [ ] - this is especially true in an environment as challenging and dynamic as a communications network. To address this problem, [ ] describes an agent based approach which is able to change distribution of information and control according to the remaining bandwidth available on the links in the network. The division of the network into regions is based on a *blocking islands* clustering described in [ ]. The clustering scheme defines a unique structure $AH(R)$ for any given configuration R of bandwidth availability on the network links. Briefly:

- Regions in the network are formed by grouping together nodes which are *mutually reachable* at a specified bandwidth level βMbit/s
- Clustering is repeated at predetermined levels of the hierarchy with β decreasing at successively higher levels. The lowest level (L_1) therefore contains the smallest regions, clustering nodes connected by very high available bandwidth. Regions at higher levels are connected at progressively lower available bandwidths

The decomposition at any given moment is therefore dependent on R and changes over time as resources are allocated and de-allocated in the network. The abstraction proved very successful for off-line resource planning (see [ ]).

The Need for Mobility: As described in [ ], the blocking islands approach can also be applied to the on-line, state-based routing problem, extending the idea of a static hierarchy of routing agents (Section   ) and making the hierarchy adaptive to the network state. The added dimension of change over time adds the requirement that the previously stationary controller agents become mobile. Each region controller stays resident on one of the nodes in its domain to:

- Reduce the resources needed to propagate state data
- Minimise reaction time for routing decisions
- Make the system more robust by ensuring that the controller is co-located with its resources

These reasons make agent mobility an essential part of the approach, allowing the agent based routing service to adapt its configuration to the network state over time.

Coordination Problems: Unlike previous mobile agent approaches to routing which targeted telephone [,], IP style [ ] and ad-hoc [ ] networks the approach described above requires a high degree of coordination between the agents providing the routing service. Previous approaches were able to minimise contact between agents by leaving markers in the environment to build up information about the network state (which is then used by an on-line packet forwarding or call allocation using routing tables). In none of the systems were single agents themselves responsible for making routing decisions. On-line, state-based QoS routing however, presents a rather different set of problems: 1) each demand must be routed individually as it arrives in the network (on-line), 2) Routing decisions are made on the basis of an up to date model of the network state (state-based) and 3) Resource allocation along the entire route must be coordinated (since each link in the chosen path must support the allocation and end-to-end constraints such as delay and cell loss must be checked).

These problems boil down to finding an effective distribution of information and control in the network. Dividing up the routing task to be performed as a service provided by a set of mobile agents therefore raises a number of serious coordination issues which must be addressed:

- Agents need to be free to move and adapt the information and control distribution to follow $(AH(R)$ in this case)
- Routing decisions need to be made very quickly, with a minimum of time spent locating agents with relevant state information and resources on offer
- Problem solving requires tight synchronisation between agents (to access all relevant information, ensure that the correct resources are reserved and check end-to-end constraints)
- Ensure that the routing service is available throughout the network at all times (an agent should not be able to renaige responsibility for routing in a region $r_{i/j}$ without finding a replacement controller for the nodes concerned)

The remainder of the paper goes on to discuss how this level of coordination can be achieved without imposing external control structures on the agents in the system.

3   Introducing Organisational Knowledge

Dealing with the coordination problems identified in Section   is non-trivial. A further constraint is to keep any mechanisms added "agent centric", that is to allow agents complete and local control over the coordination mechanism rather than imposing an *external* structure. This is vital for robustness and scalability. The approach introduced in [ ] achieves this by providing each agent $c_{j/i}$ with three models:

- Information model $c_{j/i}(I)$
- Control model $c_{j/i}(C)$
- Organisational model $c_{j/i}(O)$

The information model represents the current network state of the $r_{j/i}$ and the control model represents the types of action $c_{j/i}$ is able to take during resource allocation tasks. These alone are sufficient for the agent to complete routing tasks autonomously in its own region $r_{j/i} \in L_i$. The organisation model $c_{j/i}(O)$ shown in Figure   represents $c_{j/i}$'s relationships to other controllers. The ensemble of the information contained in all the organisational models of all the agents at any one instant in time describes the state of the whole organisational structure.

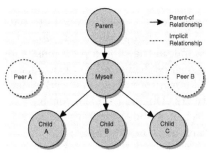

Fig. 2. In its organisational model, the agent maintains explicit relationships to its current child agents (the agents controlling regions in the level below its own) and its parent (the agent responsible for it in the level above). There are also implicit relationships to peer agents in its own layer, these are not maintained in the model - when contact is needed, the location and identity of the peer agent in question is provided by the parent agent

Each $c_{j/i}$'s three I, C and O models are linked as follows:

- I determines the resources the C applies to
- Local changes in the I prompt the agent to change its relationships in O to its fellow agents (driving adaptation in the organisation)
- C determines which actions can be taken when allocating traffic (which influences I)
- C determines the actions which can be taken when cooperating with other agents in the I to solve routing problems
- O determines which agents are relevant when solving routing problems outside the scope of C (supporting coordination)

– Changes in O update the scope of I (managing coverage of the network with the routing service)

The organisational model is also the key to mobility in the agent system and adapting the routing mechanism to best match the network resources. As the environment (bandwidth state) changes, the agents have the option of locally updating the organisational structure in two ways:

– **Split:** an agent may decide to split the region $r_{j/i}$ into several new regions in L_i
– **Merge:** an agent may decide to merge its region $r_{j/i}$ with the region of an adjacent controller $c_{k/i}$

These two actions are all that is needed for agents themselves to gradually change the organisation to make it more like the uniquely defined structure $AH(R)$ for any given R.

3.1   Splitting into Several Regions

As resources inside a region are allocated to traffic demands, the region may become disconnected at the bandwidth level the controller is working at (the β mentioned in Section   ). This change prompts the controller to consider dividing the region into two or more new regions which themselves connected at bandwidth β.

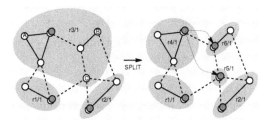

Fig. 3. The figure shows network with two types of link: links with less than β bandwidth remaining (dashed) and links with β or more bandwidth remaining (solid). The dark circles represent controller agents and the dotted arrows agent migration. During the split action, one large region is divided up between three new controllers

Figure   shows the transition involved in a split. In this case, region $r_{3/1}$ is no longer connected at bandwidth level β (no traffic demand with a bandwidth requirement of β or more could be allocated between any of nodes A, B and C). This prompts the controller of region $r_{3/1}$ to consider splitting the region into three pieces. The splitting process involves the following steps:

- The agent determines the new regions $r_{4/1}$, $r_{5/1}$ and $r_{6/1}$ (this is uniquely defined by the bandwidth available on the links - known from $c_{3/1}(I)$)
- Creates a new controller agent for each region (these new agents will subsequently be peers of the current region controller)
- The new agents $c_{5/1}$ and $c_{6/1}$ each migrate to node which is in their new region, $c_{3/1}$ updates its I, C and O models and becomes $c_{4/1}$

The newly created regions are now once more internally connected at bandwidth level β (the organisational structure is equal to $AH(R)$ for bandwidth level β). Each new region controller has its own new I, C and O models which represent their place in the network and organisation.

3.2   Merging with a Neighbouring Region

As resources between two regions are freed up, these become candidates for a merger (since they could form a larger connected cluster). The parent agent supervising the two regions is able to detect this in its information model (which consists of nodes made up of the regions at the lower level and the links between them). The parent agent then sends a suggestion to one of the regions concerned to merge with the other.

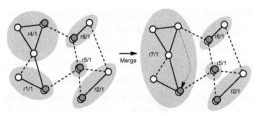

Fig. 4. Executing the merge action, the controller of $r_{4/1}$ moves to join up with the controller of $r_{1/1}$ to form region $r_{7/1}$

On receiving a suggestion to merge, the agent considers its current state and workload before deciding what to. If the agent decides to merge it:

- Contacts the other controller involved ($r_{1/1}$ in Figure) and requests a merger
- If the merge can go ahead, $c_{4/1}$ moves to the same node as $c_{1/1}$ and takes over its role and information model (merging $c_{4/1}(I,C,O)$ with $c_{1/1}(I,C,O)$)
- Thus the two mobile agents themselves merge - leaving only one controller with an enlarged region ($r_{7/1}$)

Figure   shows the transition involved in such a merge. The social interaction between $c_{4/1}$ and $c_{1/1}$ is very important to ensure that both parties are prepared for the merger to happen, $c_{1/1}$ might refuse a merger for several reasons including mergers or splits of its own or a large number of open routing tasks.

4   Implementation and Experimental Results

All testing was carried out in a distributed Java based test environment with the following core components:

- A purpose built agent platform supporting agent local/remote communication, management and configuration
- Agents running on each platform to model the roles in scenarios to be tested. Services modelled as agents include: network resources (implementing the ATM PNNI protocol suite (see [ ]) for connection setup and tear down), traffic generation, standard QoS routing mechanisms, data collection, monitoring and the resource allocation organisations themselves

Mobility was implemented as simply as possible by caching the code for mobile agents at each node and transmitting only memory state between platforms. The benefits which would be achieved by true code mobility (flexibility, robustness and simplified code updates) are orthogonal to the results described in this paper. A final important feature of the platform (and one of the primary reasons for custom building the testbed and not using an existing framework such as [ ]) is that all messages between platforms (network nodes) incur send delays equal to those they would incur if they took the shortest path in the real network (calculated using the known network link delays). Thus *all* network actions carried out by agents, including controller mobility, experience the appropriate network communication conditions.

Preliminary tests were carried on a model of the Compuserve USA backbone which has 11 nodes, 14 (45Mbit/s) ATM links and approximate links delays varying between 5 and 60ms. Figure   compares results for the static hierarchy (SH), the adaptive hierarchy (AH) for a simple traffic scenario using increasing random traffic over a 10 hour simulation period. The graph summarises rejection percentages   for both approaches averaged over 16 test runs (see [ ] for preliminary comparisons with other techniques).

The results show that even though both hierarchies (SH and AH) had access to the same state information and worked under the same network conditions the mobility enabled AH performs significantly better than SH. The reasons behind the difference between SH and AH are discussed in detail in [ ]. Briefly however, the differences are primarily due to the fact that SH agents often do not have access to pertinent network state information. For AH, bandwidth information is captured implicitly in the organisational structure of the agents and agents are able to focus on the other QoS parameters (in this case delay only). AH's organisation supports coordination more effectively than SH by maintaining links between agents which reflect their available network resources (and hence whether they might be part of a team solving a particular routing problem).

---

[2] Source: http://www.caida.org/Tools/Mapnet/.

[3] Comparisons using the percentage of offered bandwidth accepted give comparable results.

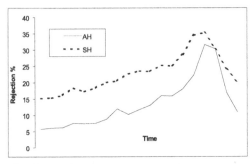

Fig. 5. AH rejects significantly less demands that SH (13% average v's 22% average over the whole period). Standard deviations (for variance between experiment runs) vary between 3% and 9% (larger variances at increased traffic load)

5   Achieving Globally Coherent Behaviour

The split and merge actions are purely local. That is, based on one or more agents' local models of their regions. Despite the local nature of the changes however, splitting and merging throughout the network leads to globally coherent behaviour. This is because the unique configuration $AH(R)$ is not simply a global network property but can be applied to any subset of nodes in the network. A local controller is therefore able to apply simple rules to its information model to check if the local organisational model requires an update. There are only two possible types deviations from the local part of $AH(R)$ which corresponds to $c_{i/j}$'s region:

1. The region is no longer connected at the specified bandwidth level β for the current level L_j. This can be solved by splitting the region as described in Section
2. The region contains subregions which are connected at a bandwidth level equal to or higher that the β for the level below (L_{j-1}). This can be addressed by suggesting the subregions to merge as describe in Section

Both of these types of deviation from $AH(R)$ can be detected simultaneously and occur multiple times in an agent's information model. In this case choosing any of the possible corrective actions eliminates one or more of the deviations and moves the local structure closer to $AH(R)$. Thus for any fixed R', actions considered or taken by the agents in the network will always move the global structure closer to $AH(R')$. Agents are free to move around inside its own region but required to agree any other movement which might imply organisational change with the agents in adjoining agents. This coordination ensures that:

- No agent moves without handing over control of the nodes it is responsible for to the control of another agent. Information and control models are maintained continually cover the whole network

- The ensemble of the organisational models always forms a complete consistent hierarchy. Routing tasks herefore can always be carried out because links to agents relevant to solving the routing problem are always valid

Clearly however, as the agents make local changes to their organisational models to move towards $AH(R')$, R' may be changing. Organisational updates also incur communication costs and are therefore not instantaneous. Thus, in a highly dynamic network, $AH(R)$ may never be reached. However, as the results in Section   show, the agents get close enough to $AH(R)$ to perform significantly better than a static hierarchy SH (see [ ] for more details on the speed of change in the network scenario tested). Although the target $AH(R)$ is a moving one, it provides a focus for the organisational changes considered by the agents throughout the network.

5.1   The Importance of Organisation

Work on coordination in Distributed Artificial Intelligence can be divided into three broad categories:

- **Coordination Media and Languages:** these approaches support communication about coordinated action in various ways. Mobile agent related work includes Linda-like tuple spaces [,   ], simple blackboards [ ] or using the environment to support communication [ ]
- **Coordination Mechanisms:** this includes protocols and conventions which agents can use to coordinate their actions for a single task or task episode. Whilst [ ] gives an overview of multi-agent systems approaches to this problem, most of the mobile agent related work in this area is confined to simple examples describing the use of the coordination media above
- **Organisational Approaches:** organisational techniques are defined as building relationships between agents which last for more than one problem solving episode [ ]. Very little work has been done in applying these techniques to mobile agent systems. One reason is perhaps that organisational structures are generally too restrictive to make good use of the mobile agent paradigm

The organisational approach presented here is vital to the QoS routing task because:

- It provides a way to maintain relationships between moving agents which can be used to tightly couple interactions between subsets of agents for brief periods of time
- The only medium that is required to support this is a shared point to point messaging system (provided by the agent platforms), there is no need for a blackboard (as in [ ]) or message broadcasts (as in several multi-agent system coordination mechanisms)
- the organisation constrains the mobility of the agents to ensure that the information and control they hold in the network is always effectively distributed to cover the whole network

This goes beyond what can be achieved using coordination mechanisms based on single tasks since these require significant initial overhead for each task before beginning work (agents would need to continually keep re-finding each other). It also has certain advantages over proposed mobile agent coordination media since these provide mainly asynchronous communication (information is posted in a common space such a tuple space or on a blackboard) for other agents to find. This incurs a significant speed penalty over explicitly addressing individual agents, and in the case of blackboards has strong centralising effect on the system.

5.2   On-Going Work

Current work on the approach is focused on the following main areas:

- Extensive testing using larger networks, more realistic traffic scenarios and comparing the routing techniques to other standard routing approaches
- Adapting the ATM routing techniques for use in IP networks
- Investigating the dynamics of the organisation

An important weakness in the current approach is that organisational change can only occur *explicitly* through the exchange of messages. This means that if a message or an agent is lost, the whole organisation may be out of step and never recover. An significant area of work is therefore adapting the agents to detect organisational relationships by themselves and allow them to recover from such failures.

6   Conclusion

This paper describes how giving mobile agents organisational models of their relationships to fellow agents enables them to perform tasks as complex as on-line, state-based QoS routing. The relationships maintained by the agents:

- Tightly couple interactions for individual tasks at given instants in time
- Enable fast coordination
- Ensure that the global behaviour of all agents is coherent

This coordination is achieved without imposing an external framework on the agents. As they move around the network, the agents are themselves responsible for keeping track of their relationships and all organisation, information and control knowledge is encapsulated in the agents themselves.

Acknowledgements

This work is partly supported by the Swiss National Science Foundation under project number 21-59081.99.

References

1. S. Appleby and S. Steward. Mobile Software Agents for Control in Telecommunications Networks. *British Telecom Technology Journal*, 12(2), 1994.   ,

2. ATM-FORUM.   P-NNI V1.0 - ATM Forum approved specification, af-pnni-0055.000. *ATM FORUM*, 1996.

3. M. Breugst and T. Magedanz. On the Usage of Standard Mobile Agent Platforms in Telecommunication Environments. In S. Trigila et al., editor, *Proceedings of 5th Int. Conference on Intelligence in Services and Networks (IS&N)*, Lecture Notes of Computer Sciences 1430, Intelligence in Services and Networks: Technologies for Ubiquitous Telecom Services, pages 275–286, Antwerp, Belgium, May 1998. Springer Verlag.

4. L. Cardelli and D. Gordon. Mobile Ambients. In M. Nivat, editor, *Foundations of Science and Computational Structures*, pages 140–155. Springer Verlang, LNCS 1378, 1998.

5. Shigang Chen and Klara Nahrstedt. An Overview of Quality of Service Routing for Next-Generation High-Speed Networks: Problems and Solutions. *IEEE Network*, pages 64–79, November/December 1998.

6. Christian Frei and Boi Faltings. Abstraction and Constraint Satisfaction Techniques for Planning Bandwidth Allocation. In *IEEE INFOCOM'2000*, Tel-Aviv, Israel, March 2000. In print.

7. L. Gasser. Social Concepts of Knowledge and Action. *Artificial Intelligence*, 47:107–138, 1991.

8. L. Gasser. DAI Approaches to Coordination. In N. M. Avouris and L. Gasser, editors, *Distributed Artificial Intelligence: Theory and Praxis*, pages 31–51. Kluwer, 1992.

9. N. R. Jennings. Coordination Techniques for Distributed Artificial Intelligence. In F. M. P. O'Hare and N. R. Jennings, editors, *Foundations of Distributed Artificial Intelligence*, pages 187–210. John Wiley & Sons, 1996.

10. N. Minar, K. H. Kramer, and P. Maes. Cooperating mobile agents for dynamic network routing. In A. L. G. Hayzelden, editor, *Software Agents for Future Communications Systems*, chapter 12. Springer-Verlag, Berlin Germany, 1999.

11. A. Omicini and F. Zambonelli. Coordination of mobile information agents in tucson. *Journal of Internet Research*, 8(5), 1998.

12. R. O. Onvural and R. Cherukuri. *Signalling in ATM Networks*. Artech House, 1997.

13. Gian Pietro Picco, Amy L. Murphy, and Gruia-Catalin Roman. LIME: Linda meets mobility. In *Proceedings of the 21st International Conference on Software Engineering*, pages 368–377. ACM Press, May 1999.

14. Ruud Schoonderwoerd, Owen Holland, and Janet Bruten. Ant-like agents for load balancing in telecommunications networks. In W. Lewis Johnson and Barbara Hayes-Roth, editors, *Proceedings of the 1st International Conference on Autonomous Agents*, pages 209–216, New York, February5–8 1997. ACM Press.

15. Y-P. So and E. H. Durfee. Designing Organisations for Computational Agents. In M. J. Prietula, K. M. Carley, and L. Gasser, editors, *Simulating Organisations*, pages 47–64. AAAI Press, 1998.

16. D. Subramanian, P. Druschel, and J. Chen. Ants and Reinforcement Learning: A Case Study in Routing in Dynamic Networks. . In *Proc. of IJCAI'97*, pages 832–838. 1997.

17. W. T. Tsai, C. V. Ramamoorthy, W. K. Tsai, and O. Nishiguchi. An Adaptive Hierarchical Routing Protocol. *IEEE Transactions on Computers*, 38(8):1059–1075, August 1989.
18. S. Willmott and B. Faltings. The Benefits of Environment Adaptive Organisations for Agent Coordination and Network Routing Problems. In *Proceedings of the Fourth International Conference on Multi Agent Systems (ICMAS-2000)*, page tba. IEEE Press (in print), 2000.   ,   ,   ,   ,
19. N. R. Wooldridge, M. J. amd Jennings. Formalizing the Cooperative Problem Solving Process. In *Proceedings of the 13th International Workshop on Distributed Artificial Intelligence (IWDAI'94)*, pages 403–417. 1994.

Multiple Agent-Based Autonomy for Satellite Constellations

Thomas Schetter[1], Mark Campbell[1], and Derek Surka[2]

[1] University of Washington
Box 352400, Seattle WA 98195-2400, USA
mcamp@aa.washington.edu
[2] Princeton Satellite Systems
33 Witherspoon St, Princeton NJ, 08542, USA
dmsurka@psatellite.com

Abstract. There is an increasing desire to use constellations of autonomous spacecraft working together to accomplish complex mission objectives. Multiple, highly autonomous, satellite systems are envisioned because they are capable of higher performance, lower cost, better fault tolerance, reconfigurability and upgradability. This paper presents an architecture and multi-agent design and simulation environment that will enable agent-based multi-satellite systems to fulfill their complex mission objectives, termed TeamAgent^{TM}. Its application is shown for TechSat21, a U.S. Air Force mission designed to explore the benefits of distributed satellite systems. Required spacecraft functions, software agents, and multi-agent organisations are described for the TechSat21 mission, as well as their implementation. Agent-based simulations of TechSat21 case studies show the autonomous operation and how TeamAgent can be used to evaluate and compare multi agent-based organisations.

1 Introduction

Interest in dividing the functions of a single large satellite among several smaller and simpler units working in tandem is gaining more momentum for an increasing number of space applications. Satellite clusters that include several smaller satellites that collaboratively work together on a satellite mission, thus forming a "virtual" satellite, are commonly referred to as *Distributed Satellite Systems (DSS)*. Multiple, distributed agent-based satellite systems are envisioned because they are capable of higher performance, lower cost, better fault tolerance, reconfigurability and upgradability.

The cost of operating spacecraft after launch is a considerable portion of the overall mission cost of the mission. For commercial satellites, operations consist of monitoring the spacecrafts health and status, taking corrective measures when necessary, and performing maneuvers. Military and scientific satellites require additional ground personnel to process the tremendous amount of payload data gathered. Automating these activities through the use of agents will reduce the cost of missions and make spacecraft more robust, reliable, and efficient.

D. Kotz and F. Mattern (Eds.): ASA/MA 2000, LNCS 1882, pp. 151–   , 2000.
© Springer-Verlag Berlin Heidelberg 2000

Most intelligence on current satellites is non-existent. Current space flight software only measures sensors, acts on ground commands, and gracefully reboots when an anomaly occurs. In 1999, the first attempt to use agents for satellite autonomy was launched in NASA's Deep Space 1 (DS1) mission. The DS1 researchers developed Remote Agent [ ], an autonomous agent architecture based on model based programming, on-board deduction and search, and goal-directed closed loop commanding. The DS1 work is slightly different than this work for several reasons. First, it was for one satellite, not a group of satellites. Second, DS1 was still based on traditional flight software rather than a hierarchy of intelligent agents. In addition, because of technical difficulties, much of the Remote Agent software was stripped off the satellite prior to launch, although it was planned to uplink part of its functionality at a later date [ ].

The most relevant work in autonomy for distributed systems has been in robotics and autonomous underwater vehicles. There has been a recent interest in emergent behavior [ ], where robot colonies work together, even though no single robot knows the group objectives. Though this approach has had much success for robots and simple tasks, many useful tasks for multiple satellites will require the ability to plan. The MAUV/CoDA Project [ ] focuses on controlling autonomous oceanographic networks, including autonomous underwater vehicles. The work uses two organizations: a task-level organization to control the system during the actual mission, and a meta-level organization to self-organize the system. The work to date is missing many pieces to the full architecture has only been implemented in simulation.

The purpose of this paper is to present an multiple agent based software (MAS) architecture that will enable agent-based multi-satellite systems to fulfill their complex mission objectives. Termed TeamAgent, this system is applied to TechSat21, a space based radar demonstration. First, a short outline of the TechSat21 mission is given. Then, required functional agents are identified and possible agent-based organisations are presented. Next, implementation within the TeamAgent framework is described. Finally, agent-based simulations of several TechSat21 case studies show the autonomous operation and how multi agent-based organisations can be evaluated and compared.

2   TechSat21

The TechSat21 mission is an Air Force mission designed to explore the benefits of a distributed approach to satellites. The initial demonstration is currently being designed to be a space based distributed radar [ ]. The ability to perform a space based radar mission, which historically has required very large, high-power satellites, is seen as an extreme test of this concept. TechSat21 takes advantage of the DSS by using a sparse aperture array for radar imaging, which allows improved resolution because of the satellite spacing, Figure .

In order to accomplish distributed aperture radar imaging, the satellites in the cluster must cover the Earth's surface area of particular interest with a more or less uniform distribution. Given the very strict constraints on the fuel

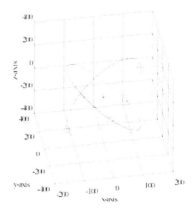

Fig. 1. Left: TechSat21 - a revolutionary approach to space based sensing. Right: a 3D-animation of the TechSat21 mission, where '*' is the virtual center of the cluster, and the spacecraft '△'s are in two planes of four

available, the only conceivable approach for the cluster is to have the satellites be in *force free* or "natural" orbits while in formation. The current configuration for the TechSat21 mission has focused on clusters of spacecraft in two local ellipses, tilted at ± 30 degrees from the z-axis in the Hill-frame. The Hill's equation [ ] describe the relative motion of spacecraft by the use of linearized equations. The nominal orbit for the cluster (or cluster center) is a circular, polar orbit.

For ease and simplicity of the simulation, a constellation of eight satellites was chosen, with four satellites placed in each ellipse. Figure   shows a 3D-Animation of the simulation, where spacecraft movements are shown with respect to the Hill-coordinate frame. The '*'-symbol locates the center of the Hill-frame, i.e. the trajectory of the circular, polar reference orbit.

3   Agent Definitions for Multiple Satellites

In the following section, agent descriptions are presented at both the spacecraft and functional levels. The fomer is referred to as a *spacecraft-level agent*. The term "skill" refer to the software functions that describe each agent.

3.1   Spacecraft-Level Agents

In order to narrow the scope of study of agents for multiple spacecraft, spacecraft-level agents as a function of their level of intelligence. Based on the sum of capable spacecraft functions, four levels of intelligence have been identified, where I_1 denotes the highest level of intelligence and I_4 the lowest level (Figure   ).

The spacecraft-level agent I_4 represents the most "unintelligent" agent. It can only receive commands and tasks from other spacecraft-level agents in the

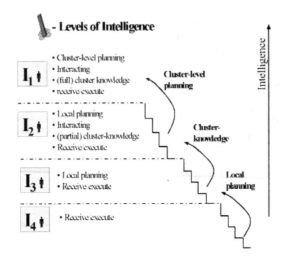

Fig. 2. Identification of spacecraft-level agents based on levels of capable intelligence

organisation or from the ground and execute them. An example includes receiving and execution of a control command sequence to move to a new position within the cluster. This type of intelligence is similar to what is being flown on most spacecraft today.

The next higher spacecraft-level agent is I_3, with local planning functionalities on board. "Local" means the spacecraft-level agent is capable of generating and executing only plans related to its own tasks. An example includes trajectory planning for orbital maneuvers in case of a cluster reconfiguration. This type of intelligence is similar to DS1 [ ].

Agent I_2 adds a capability to interact with other spacecraft-level agents in the organisation. This usually requires the agent to have at least partial knowledge of the full agent-based organisation, i.e. of other spacecraft-level agents. It must therefore continuously keep and update (or receive) an internal representation of the agent-based organisation. An example includes coordinating/negotiating with other spacecraft-level agents in case of conflicting requirements.

The spacecraft-level agent I_1 represents the most "intelligent" agent. The primary difference between I_1 and the spacecraft-level agents outlined thus far is that it is capable monitoring all spacecraft-level agents in the organisation and planning for the organisation as a whole. This requires planning capabilities on the cluster level as well as having full knowledge of all other spacecraft-level agents in the organisation. An example includes calculation of a new cluster configuration and assigning new satellite positions within the cluster.

3.2   Lower Level Functional Agents

In order to demonstrate the usefulness of MAS applied to multiple satellite clusters in general, and TechSat21 specifically, four high-level tasks are defined:

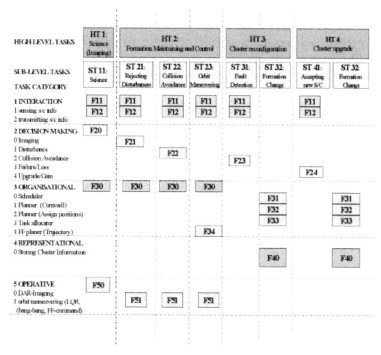

Fig. 3. Functional breakdown of the task structure specifically for Techsat21

- HT1: Performing science (Imaging),
- HT2: Formation maintaining and control,
- HT3: Cluster reconfiguration,
- HT4: Cluster upgrade.

These high-level tasks were then used to identify all necessary sub-level tasks, along with the elementary functional blocks required to implement these tasks. Figure   shows the functional breakdown from high level tasks to lower level agents. The columns correspond to four high level tasks, and the rows to sub-tasks and functional blocks. The functional blocks, or particular agents, are denoted with a two digit number. The first digit refers to the task category (i.e. 2-decision-making function) and the second to the sub-partition within the task category (i.e. 3-failure/loss).

F11 (sensing agent) continuously obtains the state and health from the spacecraft, and makes it available for the entire cluster. The state x includes satellite position and velocity, and the health h includes the status of the science h_s, power h_p, and thrust h_t subsystems, as well as the remaining fuel h_f.

Decision-making agents periodically make decisions or monitor specific system parameters for changes. F20 (decision-making agent science) decides which satellites acquire which targets, and how many satellites are required to monitor changing points of interest. F21 (decision-making agent station keeping) decides whether it is necessary to station keep or to perform an orbit correction maneuver due to external disturbances. F22 (decision-making agent collision avoidance) detects when collisions may occur between the spacecraft in the cluster. F23 (decision-making agent cluster downgrade) monitors the health status $\underline{h}$ of the spacecraft to detect failures on-board, and, if required, start a cluster reconfiguration. F24 (decision-making agent cluster upgrade) decides if there is a new spacecraft to be added to the cluster.

In the case of a failure or adding of a new spacecraft to the cluster, F31 (cluster reconfiguration planner agent) is called, which optimizes a new spacecraft position within the cluster based on maximizing its usefulness for science (imaging). Once a new cluster configuration is known, F32 (cluster allocation planner agent) assigns new spacecraft positions within the cluster. This can be done in many ways, but the approach here is to equalize fuel use across the cluster. F33 (task allocation planner agent) distributes tasks for the cluster based on a predefined cost. F34 (trajectory planner agent) generates a fuel and/or time optimized control maneuver for each spacecraft.

F40 (representational agent) keeps and continuously updates the internal cluster description. This description contains the number of active spacecraft in the cluster; a description of the particular tasks that the spacecraft are capable/allowed to carry out (i.e. passive, partial active and active); and a description of the relative position for each spacecraft within the cluster.

F50 (science agent) performs the radar imaging task. F51 (orbit maneuvering agent) performs the physical orbital maneuver.

3.3   Agent Skills

Table   shows the implemented skills for the corresponding agents. Shown are also the priority assignments, the update period and tools which are used by the corresponding skills. These can be variable.

All decision-making skills are implemented using Fuzzy logic [ ]. The ideal `PlanReconfigSkill` uses the *Cornwell Metric* to calculate new optimal cluster positions based on radar imaging, Ref. [ ]. A contract net bidding mechanism is used to implement the cluster assignment (`PlanAssignSkill`) and task allocation (`TaskAllocSkill`). The trajectory planner `PlanFFSkill` is implemented with a Linear Program (LP) [ ]. The `OrbitManSkill` uses a dynamic simulation of the relative spacecraft motion (Hill's equations) with an LQR controller.

4   Multi-Agent Based Organisations for Satellites

The type of multi-agent organization is a complex design process. The organization must be adaptable to prevent of faults, avoid bottlenecks, and allow reconfiguration. It must be efficient in terms of time, resources, information exchange and processing. And it must be distributed in terms of intelligence, capabilities, resources. Figure   shows a summary of options as a function of individual, capable spacecraft-level agent intelligence. Note that lower level functional agents

Table 1. Implemented software agents in TeamAgent

Skill	Identification	Priority	Update Period	Tool
SensingSkill	F11	fix	fix	-
ScienceSkill	F20	fix	fix	-
StatKeepSkill	F21	variable	variable	Fuzzy Control
CollAvoidSkill	F22	variable	variable	Fuzzy Control
DecMakFailSkill	F23	fix	variable	Fuzzy Control
DecMakAddSkill	F24	fix	fix	Fuzzy Control
Scheduler	F30	-	fix	-
PlanReconfigSkill	F31	fix	on demand	Cornwell Metric
PlanAssignSkill	F32	fix	on demand	Contract net
TaskAllocSkill	F33	fix	on demand	Contract net
PlanFFSkill	F34	fix	on demand	Linear Program
OrbitManSkill	F40,F51	variable	on demand	LQR

are implied. Ref. [ ] presents a comparison of these organizations based on the TechSat21 mission.

As can be seen, the number and composition of the different spacecraft-level agents I_1-I_4 determines the organisational architecture. The top-down coordination architecture includes only one single (highly intelligent) spacecraft-level agent I_1 and the other spacecraft are (non-intelligent) I_4 agents. The centralized coordination architecture requires at least local planning and possibly interaction capabilities from each spacecraft, requiring I_3 or I_2 agents. The distributed coordination architecture consists of several parallel hierarchical decision-making structures, each of which is "commanded" by intelligent spacecraft-level agent I_1. In the case of a fully distributed coordination architecture, each spacecraft in the organisation represents a spacecraft-level agent I_1, resulting in a totally "flat" organisation.

5   TeamAgent Software Architecture for MAS

5.1   TeamAgent

TeamAgent is a MATLAB toolbox [ ] for design and simulation of multi-agent systems, especially spacecraft. In TeamAgent, *agents* represent software and remote terminals and *remote terminals (RT)* connect the agents with hardware.

TeamAgent MATLAB is based on a *message passing architecture*, meaning that all agent-to-agent and agent-to-RT communication is done through messages that pass through message centers (MC). The function of the MC is to:

- register and validate agents,
- process messages for itself,
- pass messages to registered agents, RT's, and other MC's for processing,
- allocates processor time for each agent. Messages can be passed over several MC's; therefore it does not matter where the agent or RT is located. The MC functional process is shown in Figure .

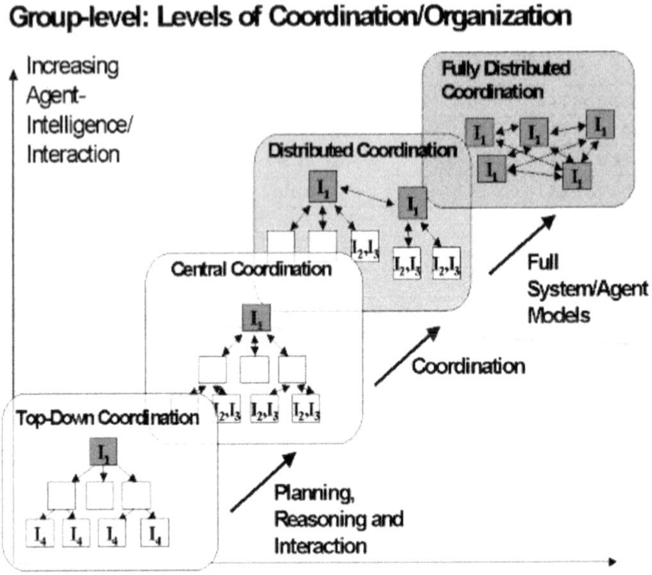

Fig. 4. Coordination architectures for coordination of multiple spacecraft-level agents

The basic building blocks of agents and remote terminals within TeamAgent are *skills*. Agents and RT's are created in TeamAgent by assigning a set of skills, or software functions. These are special MATLAB files that represent agent functions. For example, a skill required by all agents is to register with the MC, represented by the `RegisterSkill.m` function. Generally, each skill corresponds to one basic function, has inputs and outputs, and triggers one or more actions. The primary action for each skill is a `update` action, or that the skill is run periodically based on a pre-defined update period. Each skill contains a data structure field that describes the assigned priority, the update period, the input and output interfaces and the communication method.

Messages and tasks are identical in TeamAgent, and therefore have the same data structure. The `message.content` data structure is used by special *verb* functions to perform appropriate actions. The first element of `message.content` determines which verb function is called. Other entries describe the object of the verb, sender and receiver agent and associated skills. When skills are added to an agent, tasks associated with that skill are automatically generated. These tasks, when processed, can cause a message to be created and sent, and/or actions to be taken by agents that change the internal state. Figure shows an example, where the task "update `CollAvoidSkill`" creates the message "`MoveCollAvoid sc_4 | To: OrbitManAgent4(OrbitManSkill4)`" (m1), because a possible collision involving spacecraft #4 was detected. The message m1 is then sent to message center 4. The verb function `MoveCollAvoid` is called

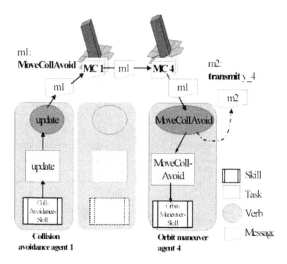

Fig. 5. Example of the relationship between skills, messages, and verbs

which triggers the same named action of the `OrbitManeuverSkill`. Additionally, message m2 is transmitted back to the collision avoidance agent 1.

5.2   Information Flow Architecture

Figure   shows the information flow architecture for a central coordination architecture, and the distribution of the functional agents onto spacecraft-level agents. A "passive" spacecraft level agent (such as passive I_1) indicates a redundant agent, or an agent with more intelligent capability (I_1), but acts with lower intelligence (I_3). Also, "m" refers to a message, and "d" refers to data.

Shown are an active spacecraft-level agent I_1, a passive spacecraft-level agent I_1, and an active spacecraft-level agent I_2. Each lower level spacecraft agent performs local planning and decision-making, and interacts with the higher-level agent I_1 in the case of a reconfiguration. Each spacecraft-level agent performs its own station keeping, F21, monitors the relative position error (d13) and produces, if required, a `RejectDist` message (m21) that triggers a station keeping task. Additionally, each spacecraft-level agent runs its own trajectory planner agent (F34) for the generation of the feed forward control sequence (d32). The primary difference lies in the case of a cluster reconfiguration, where each spacecraft-level agent interacts with the central spacecraft-level agent I_1. To assign new positions within the cluster, the spacecraft-level agent I_1 requests bids from each spacecraft by transmitting a `CalculateDeltaV` message (m32). Each spacecraft then submits a bid to the cluster allocation planner agent (F32) on the central spacecraft-level agent I_1 in form of the velocity increment (d31) required to move to these new positions. The latter then decides upon an optimal cluster assignment based on the received bids. If a failure within an intelligent I_1 level agent occurs, a dynamic reconfiguration mode is used to create a new

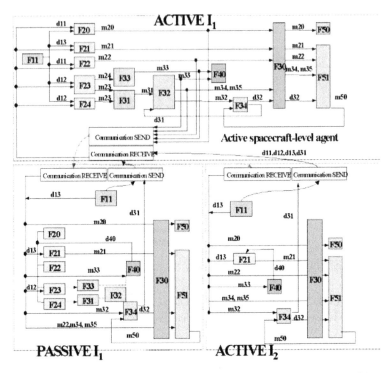

Fig. 6. Information flow architecture for a distributed coordination architecture, with active and passive spacecraft-level agents I_1, and spacecraft-level agent I_2

organization of spacecraft-level agents using the task allocation planner agents (F33). A summary of messages and agents is given in Table .

6   Simulation Results

The spacecraft and functional agents for TechSat21 described previously were then integrated and implemented in the TeamAgent environment. The following two sections show two case studies for the simulation.

6.1   Reconfiguration of an Agent-Based Organisation

The first case study is the reconfiguration of a system when a high level, intelligent spacecraft agent I_1 has failed. This is shown in Figure for a distributed coordinated organization, each with I_1 spacecraft level agents. The top of the figure depicts the nominal operation for the organisation, while the bottom figure shows the case where the active spacecraft-level agent I_1 in cluster 2 (spacecraft #5) has failed, and the organization must be reconfigured.

Table 2. Messages within TeamAgent with corresponding verbs, sources and sinks

Identification	Verb Required	Action	Source	Sink
m21	RejectDist	Station Keeping	F21	F51
m22	MoveCollAvoid	Collision avoidance	F22	F51
m23	ReconfigureCluster	Cluster reconfiguration	F23	F31
m24	AssignRole	Assigning of roles/tasks	F23	F33
m31	AssignCluster	Cluster assignment	F31	F32
m32	CalculateDeltaV	$\triangle V$ calculation	F32	F34
m33	UpdateClusterInformation	Update internal state	F32,F33	F40
m34	MoveNewPos	Move to new position	F32	F51
m35	DeOrbit	De-orbit S/C	F32	F51
m40	CalculateFFControl	FF control generation	F51	F34

Two primary approaches exist for organization reconfiguration: static and dynamic reconfiguration. *Static reconfiguration* is based on a logic rule base, while *dynamic reconfiguration* makes use of distributed task allocation techniques such as the contract net protocol [ ], or negotiation techniques [ ] to nominate the "optimal" candidate spacecraft-level agent.

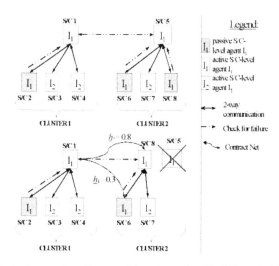

Fig. 7. Distributed coordination architecture for TechSat21. Top: nominal organisation, bottom: reconfiguration example where spacecraft #5 has failed

For the case of a static reconfiguration, a logic rule base is used. For instance, if there is one passive I_1 agent in each cluster, then the logic rule base could contain several priority levels for the nomination, such as:

```
IF (passive I₁ agent is alive in cluster of failed I₁ agent)
THEN (nominate new active I₁ in own cluster)
ELSEIF (passive I₁ agent is alive in other cluster)
THEN (nominate active I₁ (old passive) agent in other cluster)
ELSEIF (active I₁ agent from other cluster is alive)
THEN nominate active I₁ (old passive) agent from other cluster
```

Note that if there were more I_1 agents, such as two passive I_1 level agents shown in cluster 1 of Figure , then a more complicated logic rule base would be required to select between the two. This selection could be made based on spacecraft health or other factors.

For the case of a dynamic reconfiguration, the contract net protocol is applied to a reconfiguration based on a failure within spacecraft #5. In this case, spacecraft #1, which is a spacecraft-level agent I_1, acts as contractor in nominating a new leader agent, and the other (passive) spacecraft-level agents I_1 act as bidders. The following steps detail the contract net protocol to this problem:

1. Intelligent spacecraft-level agent I_1 on spacecraft #1 is nominated as contractor for the contract net protocol using a logic based rule base.
2. The contractor sends out requests to all passive spacecraft-level agents I_1 in the cluster, i.e. to spacecraft #2, #6, and #8, which act as bidders.
3. The bidders can either accept or deny the request. In the case of an accept, the bidder transmits the bid in the form of their spacecraft health values $\underline{h}$, i.e. health values for science, power, thrust and the remaining fuel to the contractor.
4. The contractor selects a new active spacecraft-level agent I_1 based on the smallest cost from the bidders. An example could be

$$C = \frac{c_1}{h_s} \cdot \frac{c_2}{h_p} \cdot \frac{c_3}{h_t} \cdot \frac{c_4}{h_f} \tag{1}$$

   where c_1 - c_4 are weighting factors, chosen on the importance of the different subsystems and the h's correspond to the health values of the different monitored spacecraft subsystems. Spacecraft #8 is chosen, because it has the smallest cost ($C = 1/0.8$).
5. The contractor updates the internal cluster description of the organisation.
6. The new active master spacecraft-level agent begins its operation.

6.2   Conflict Resolution

The second case study is that of conflict resolution between more than one agent. Conflictual relationships between tasks and agents arise when they can be run in parallel. The sub-level tasks ST11 (science) , ST21 (rejecting disturbances), ST22 (collision avoidance) and ST23 (orbit maneuvering) occasionally require execution at the same time. A conflict resolution is therefore required.

The resolution of conflictual relationships between tasks is implemented using an approach similar to the subsumption architecture ([ ], [ ]). When a conflict occurs, the most dominant task inhibits the output of the less dominant tasks. A task with a higher priority value therefore suppresses a task with a lower priority.

Figure   shows the priority for the tasks `PerformScience` (m20), `RejectDist` (m21), `MoveCollAvoidance` (m22), and `ReconfigureCluster` (m23) as a function of the degree of membership of a fuzzy output variable. This variable is the prime factor within the decision-making skill. The science task and the cluster reconfiguration task have a fixed priority because the science is always performed in a healthy situation, and the cluster is always reconfigured as new targets arise. The collision avoidance and disturbance rejection tasks, however, have a dynamic priority, depending on whether a collision is imminent or if a disturbance has been measured and requires action. Collision avoidance and cluster reconfiguration can have a higher priority than disturbance rejection or science because they must be accomplished prior to all other tasks.

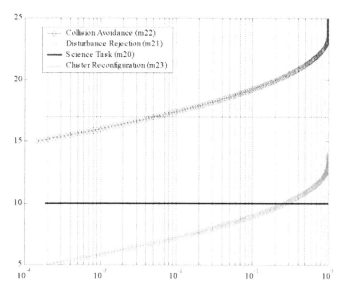

Fig. 8. Resolution of the conflictual relationships between different tasks using dynamic allocation of the priority of the corresponding tasks

Using different values for membership functions, the intersection points for the task priorities (points "A" and "B" in the figure) can be regulated. For example, it is natural that the relative distance between two spacecraft can become smaller during a reconfiguration maneuver. However, the collision avoidance task is activated only when the relative distance between the spacecraft reaches a certain limit (A). Similarly, the science task must be canceled if the error between actual and reference position of the spacecraft reaches a point at which the radar imaging task is not possible (B).

7   Conclusions and Future Work

A software architecture for multiple satellite autonomy using a message passing simulation environment (TeamAgent) for MAS has been presented. The required software agents along with possible agent based organisations for TechSat21, which is a distributed multi-satellite mission, have been identified. Tools such as fuzzy control, linear programming and the contract net have been used for the implementation of the spacecraft-level agents and agent-based organisations in TeamAgent. Conflict resolution between the agent is accomplished by using of a dynamic priority allocation for the tasks. TeamAgent is well suited for the simulation of multi-agent based systems applied to the space domain. The multi-agent approach is complicated, yet promising. Thus, quick comparisons and design evaluations are critical, all of which can be accomplished in the TeamAgent environment.

Future steps include the evaluation of the "optimal" agent based organisation for the TechSat21 mission, as well as design and implementation for the TechSat21 mission. The message center concept will be evaluated further because it will need improvement/streamlining for eventual implementation.

References

1. Nicola Muscettola; P. Pandurang Nayak; Barney Pell; Brian C. Williams. Remote Agent: To Boldly Go Where No AI System Has Gone Before, 1998 Artificial Intelligence. Invited Talk, IJCAI-97, Nayoga, Japan.   ,
2. Dornheim, M. A., Deep Space 1 Launch Slips Three Months. Aviation Week and Space Technology, April 27, 1998, p. 39.
3. Brooks, R. A., A Robust Layered Control System for a Mobile Robot, IEEE Journal of Robotics and Automation, RA-2v1 (1986), 14-23.
4. Turner, R., Turner, E., Blidberg, D. Organization and reorganization of autonomous oceano-graphic sampling networks, IEEE Robotics and Automation (ICRA'98), Leuven, Belgium, 1998.
5. Alok Das; Richard Cobb; Michael Stallard. A Revolutionary Concept in Distributed Space Based Sensing. In *AIAA Defense and Civil Space Programs Conference & Exhibit*, pages p. 1–6, Huntsville, AL, 1998.
6. Hill, G. W. 1978. Researches in the Lunar Theory. *American Journal of Mathematics, Vol 1, No. 1*, pages p. 5–26.
7. Rodney A. Brooks. Achieving Artificial Intelligence through Building Robots, 1986.
8. Rodney A. Brooks. Elephants Don't Play Chess. In *Robotics and Autonomous Systems 6*, pages p. 3–15, 1999.
9. R. Davis; and R. Smith. Negotiation as a Metaphor for Distributed Problem Solving. In *Artificial Intelligence*, pages p. 63–109, 1983.
10. Shaw Green; Leon Hurst; Brenda Nangle; Dr. Padraig Cunningham; Fergal Somers; Dr. Richard Evans. *Software Agents: A Review*. Trinitiy College Dublin, Broadcom Eireann Research Ltd., version 1.0 edition, May 1997.
11. Princeton-satellite systems web-page. http://www.psatellite.com.
12. Techsat21: Advanced Research and Technology Enabling Distributed Satellite Systems. http://www.vs.afrl.af.mil/VSD/TechSat21/.

13. Edmund M. Kong; Mark V. Tollefson; James M. Skinner; Jeremy C. Rosenstock. TechSat21 Cluster Design Using AI Approaches and the Cornwell Metric. In *AIAA Paper AIAA-99-4635*, 1999.

14. M. E. Campbell; T. Schetter. Formation Flying Mission for UW Dawgstar Satellite. IEEE Aerospace Conference, March 2000.

15. T. Schetter;M. E. Campbell. *Comparison of Agent Organizations of Multiple Satellite Autonomy.* Flairs AI Conference, Orlando, FL, May 2000.

16. Hung T. Nguyen; Michio Sugeno; Richard Tong; and Ronald R. Yager. *Theoretical Aspects of Fuzzy Control.* John Wiley Sons, Inc., 1995.

Saving Energy and Providing Value Added Services in Intelligent Buildings: A MAS Approach

Paul Davidsson[1] and Magnus Boman[2]

[1]Department of Computer Science, University of Karlskrona/Ronneby
Soft Center, 372 25 Ronneby, Sweden
pdv@ipd.hk-r.se
http://www.ide.hk-r.se/~pdv
[2]Department of Computer and Systems Sciences, Stockholm University and
the Royal Institute of Technology, Electrum 230, 164 40 Kista, Sweden
mab@dsv.su.se
http://www.dsv.su.se/~mab

Abstract. In a de-regulated market the distribution utilities will compete with added value for the customer in addition to the delivery of energy. We describe a system consisting of a collection of software agents that monitor and control an office building. It uses the existing power lines for communication between the agents and the electrical devices of the building, such as sensors and actuators for lights, heating, and ventilation. The objectives are both energy saving and increasing customer satisfaction through value added services. Results of qualitative simulations and quantitative analysis based on thermodynamical modeling of an office building and its staff using four different approaches for controlling the building indicate that significant energy savings, up to 40 per cent, can be achieved by using the agent-based approach. The evaluation also shows that customer satisfaction can be increased in most situations. In fact, this approach makes it possible to control the trade-off between energy saving and customer satisfaction (and actually increase both in comparison with current approaches).

1   Introduction

In a de-regulated market the distribution utilities will compete with added value for the customer in addition to the delivery of energy. We will here describe a system consisting of a Multi-Agent System (MAS) that monitors and controls an office building in order to provide services of this kind. The system was developed as a part of the ISES (Information/Society/ Energy/System) project [12]. The goal of ISES was to assess and demonstrate new business opportunities for future service-centric utilities.[1]

---

[1] The ISES project was a collaboration between a number of Swedish universities and some of the leading players in the European energy market, such as, EnerSearch AB (owned by

D. Kotz and F. Mattern (Eds.): ASA/MA 2000, LNCS 1882, pp. 166-177, 2000.

The system uses the existing power lines for communication between the agents and the electrical devices of the building, i.e., sensors and actuators for lights, heating, ventilation, etc. The objectives are both energy saving and increasing customer satisfaction through value added services. Energy saving is realized, e.g., by lights being automatically switched off, and room temperature being lowered in empty rooms. Increased customer satisfaction is realized, e.g., by adapting temperature and light intensity according to each person's personal preferences.

In the MAS, which will be described in detail below, different agents control different parts of the building, as well as different aspects of the environmental conditions of the building. Other agents represent the persons in the building in order maintain their preferences concerning temperature, light intensity, etc. The goal is to make the system transparent to the people in the building in the sense that they do not have to interact with the system in any laborious manner. By using an active badge system [5], it is possible for the MAS to automatically detect in which room each person is at any moment and adapts the conditions in the room according to that person's preferences.

In order to evaluate the MAS approach to control environmental parameters such as temperature and light in office buildings, we have run a number of qualitative simulations as well as made quantitative calculations comparing two versions of the approach to the two currently most used methods for this type of control. In addition, fielded experiments at our test site—the Villa Wega building in Ronneby, Sweden— have been made to assure that the performance of power line communication is sufficient for controlling, e.g., radiators [12].

2   The Building Infrastructure

A typical office building contains an electrical network and a number of electrical devices that constitute an important part of its infrastructure. At the Villa Wega test site, communication with the devices at the hardware level is facilitated by LonWorks technology (cf. www.echelon.com). Each electrical device in the system is connected via special purpose hardware nodes to the LonWorks system, allowing the exchange of information over the electrical network.

Some of the devices are sensory and some are actuator devices. The sensory devices we use in the work presented here are temperature, light intensity, and an active badge system. It is of course possible to include also other types of sensors, e.g., presence sensors and fire detectors. The active badge system makes it possible to know which persons are in each room at any moment. There are alternative types of sensor systems for doing this, but we will not discuss the pros and cons of different approaches in this paper.

The actuator devices differ from the sensory devices in that it is possible, besides reading the state of the device, to change the state of the device (in order to change the state of the building). The actuator devices in the current application are lamps, radiators, and generic mobile devices (such as ARIGO Switch Stations, cf.

Sydkraft and IBM Utility & Energy Services), ABB Network Partner AB, Electricité de France, and PreussenElektra.

`www.arigo.de`) that can be connected to an arbitrary electrical device, e.g., a coffee machine, or a personal computer. It is possible to switch on and off the device connected to the generic mobile device and to read its state. These devices interact with, and are controlled by, the MAS. The sensory devices provide input to the MAS and the actuator devices occasionally receive instructions from the MAS.

3   The Multi-agent System

Each agent is intuitively linked to a particular entity in the building, e.g., an office, a meeting room, a corridor, a person, or an electrical device. The behavior of each agent is determined by a number of rules that express the desired control policies of the building conditions. The occurrence of certain events inside the building (e.g., a person moving from one room to another) will generate messages to some of the agents that will trigger some appropriate rule(s). The agents execute the rule(s), with the purpose of adjusting the environmental conditions to some preferred set of values. The rule will cause a sequence of actions to be executed, which will involve communication between the agents of the system and eventually with an actuator device. For the format of the messages a KQML-like [4] approach was adopted. The language used to implement the MAS was April [8] together with its extension April++.

The agent-based approach provides an open architecture in the given context, i.e., agents can be easily configured and even dynamically re-configured. It is possible to add new agents at run-time without the need of interrupting the normal operation of the system. Such changes reflect changes in the infrastructure of the building or among the staff.

There are four main categories of agents in the MAS:

Personal Comfort (PC) agents, which each corresponds to a particular person. It contains personal preferences and acts on that person's behalf in the MAS trying to maximize customer value. Thus, the agent does not model the behavior of a person, but tries to act in that person's interest.

Room agents, which each corresponds to and controls a particular room with the goal of saving as much energy as possible. Taking into account the preferences of the persons currently in the room, it decides what values of the environmental parameters, e.g., temperature and light, are appropriate.

Environmental Parameter (EP) agents, which each monitors and controls a particular environmental parameter in a particular room. They have access to sensor and actuator devices for reading and changing the parameter. For instance, a temperature agent can read the temperature sensor and control the radiators in a room. The goal of an EP agent is to achieve and then maintain the value of the parameter decided by the Room agent.

Badge System Agent (BSA), which keeps track of where in the building each person (i.e., badge) is situated and maintains a data base of the PC agents and their associations to persons (badges).

We make no assumptions about the agents' locations in the network. For instance, the PC agents may reside on the individuals' desktop computers and interact locally with the corresponding person, e.g., in order to change the preferences. Normally, the preferences are set when the agent is initiated, i.e., when the person visits the building for the first time, and then rarely changed.

To illustrate agent control, we describe what happens when a person moves from one room to another. When a person movement is detected by a badge sensor and forwarded to the BSA, the BSA informs the appropriate PC agent about this. The PC agent informs the appropriate room agents, i.e., the agent of the room the person is leaving and the agent of the room the person is entering. The PC agent also provides the room agent with the personal preferences. The room agent decides, based on these preferences and on energy saving considerations, the new desired environmental conditions and pass them on to the EP agents. The EP agents then try to achieve and keep the values decided by the room agent by monitoring the relevant sensors and sending commands to the relevant actuators.

Using the approach described in [13], each agent contains a number of components contributing to the overall functionality of the agent. The architecture of the room and PC agents is depicted in Figure 1. (The EP and BSA agents, on the other hand, have got a simpler structure and are implemented as April processes.) Some of the components (rectangular boxes) are included in each agent by default, but it is possible to add other domain dependent components (rounded boxes).

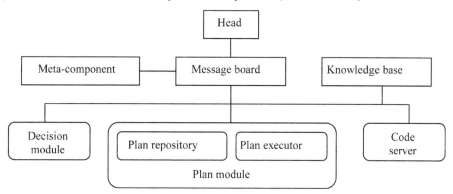

Figure 1. The architecture of the room and PC agents

One generic module is the *head* that plays the role of the communication interface of the agent. All messages directed to the agent are sent to the head and are subsequently forwarded to the internal modules. In this way external entities do not need direct access to the agent's modules. Also, a shared *knowledge base* is included that can be used to store shared information. The *meta-component* is used for administrative purposes during the addition and deletion of components. Finally, the communication between the components is facilitated by the *message board*.

Depending on the situation, an agent needs to execute a sequence of actions, i.e., a plan. The *plan module* is responsible for maintaining such plans and consists of a *plan repository* and a *plan executor*. The plan repository stores the plan descriptions, which include the name of the actions involved in the plan, their temporal relationships, and descriptions of the information they manipulate. Requests for executing single plans are received by the plan executor. The executor fetches the code that implements the specific actions from the *code server* and executes them. The code stored on a code server can be supplied on demand. An alternative approach would be to have the actions hard-wired in the decision module. Although our approach requires some additional communication among the components in order to retrieve the code, it simplifies the configuration of the agents. New actions are simply added to the code server and new plans can be added to the plan repository. Exactly which plan to be executed at a particular moment is decided by the *decision module* based on the agent's current state and any external event. More details about the MAS software can be found in [1].

The MAS conforms to a number of general rules (constraints) that are programmed into the agents. Some examples are listed below:

> When a particular person is in her office, the room agent must adapt temperature, light, etc. to her preferences, otherwise the default conditions are maintained. If an irrelevant person (i.e., another person than the one that normally works in that office) enters, this does not affect the environmental conditions (except for the light being turned on if the room was empty).

> For meeting rooms, the temperature condition is adjusted to the mean value of all the meeting participants, and the light intensity to the highest preference value.

> For other common rooms, like corridors, the temperature remains steady regardless whether there are people in the room or not. The light is turned on only when at least one person is in the room, otherwise it is off.

> Every room with no persons in it must maintain some default environmental conditions.

> It must always be possible to over-rule the decisions of the agents in the MAS by physical interaction with the electrical equipment. For instance, even if an EP agent has decided that the light in a room should be on, it must be possible for a person to turn off the light using the switch in the actual room.

These constraints are not hard-wired into the MAS and can be changed easily. With regard to the last constraint, it is worth mentioning that the concept of manual overrides is becoming increasingly important to systems in which human and artificial agents both act [10]. The agents in the MAS must display *adjustable autonomy*. Interestingly, human operation of the hardware in Villa Wega is viewed as a form of interference by the agents controlling the building. At the same time, a difficult object from the design point of view is to make the agent operations transparent to the people in the building, and in doing so prevent persons from viewing agent action on hardware as a form of interference.

Usually, the goals of the room agents and the PC agents are conflicting: the room agents maximizing energy saving and the PC agents maximizing customer value. Another type of a conflicting goal situation is the adjustment of temperature in a meeting room in which people with different preferences regarding temperature will meet.

We have begun investigations into the role of *pronouncers*, i.e. real-time decision support to the agents [2], and we are currently investigating the combination of pronouncers and technical norms. This combination in turn allows for agents to abandon elaborate plans and increases efficiency by freeing agents from the burden of plan revisions (cf. [14]). A pronouncer can be seen as a decision module located outside the agents themselves, providing normative advice in generic situations, and typically using only information provided by the agents themselves at query time, e.g., in the form of decision trees with probability and utility assessments. The intelligent building domain is suitable for pronouncer use, since the size of the agents must be kept reasonably small.

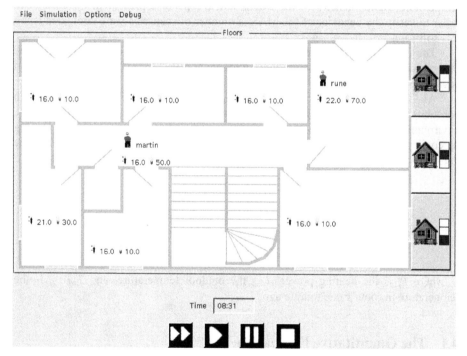

Figure 2. A snapshot of the environment visualization GUI

4   Evaluation

Although much of the hardware necessary to evaluate the approach outlined above is actually installed in the Villa Wega building, it would be quite expensive to make the installation complete. Since communication over the electrical network is a new technology and devices currently are produced in small numbers, the required hardware is expensive at the moment, but we expect that this situation will change drastically in the next couple of years. Therefore, we have made the evaluation of the approach (i.e., the MAS) through qualitative simulations [1, 3] as well as through quantitative analytical computations.

The total system can be divided into three parts; the hardware, i.e., the building including sensors and effectors, the software, i.e., the MAS, and the people working in the building. Thus, we simulate the hardware and the behavior of the people, and let the actual MAS, which would be used in a fielded application, interact with these simulated entities instead of the actual building and people. (This simulation of the behavior of the people should be contrasted to the PC agents in the MAS which serves the persons, i.e., are agents in the true sense of the word.)

In order to monitor the simulations, a graphical user interface (GUI) visualizing the building environment was implemented. Figure 2 shows a snapshot of the environment visualization GUI that visualizes the state of the building in terms of temperature, light intensity of the rooms and the persons present in the rooms. In order to verify the behavior of the MAS, a number of scenarios were simulated using this software.

The physical properties of the building were modelled using the thermodynamical models described by Incropera and Witt [7]. These were discretized according to standard procedures (cf. Ogata [11]).

All the thermodynamical characteristics of a room are described by two constants: the thermal resistance, R, which captures the heat losses to the environment, and the thermal capacitance, C, which captures the inertia when heating up/cooling down the entities in the room. (In the quantitative evaluation below we use the sample time 1 minute.). The temperature, T_{xi}, in room x at time i is described by:

$$T_{xi} = \frac{1}{1+\dfrac{1}{R_x C_x}}\left(T_{x(i-1)} + \frac{P_i + \dfrac{T_{outi}}{R_x}}{C_x}\right)$$

where P_i is the heating power, T_{outi} the outdoor temperature, and $T_{x(i-1)}$ is the temperature in room x one minute ago.

4.1   The Quantitative Evaluation

A number of simplifications were made:

   only energy used for heating is taken into account, not for lighting etc.

   constant outdoor temperature is assumed (10°C)

   negligible radiation from the sun (i.e., cloudy weather)

   the heat produced by persons in the room is ignored

   the heat produced by computers, lamps, and fluorescent tubes is ignored

Note that if we were to take into account any of these aspects, the performance of the MAS approach would probably have been even more favorable compared to the other approaches. For instance, since the MAS approach would take into account and make use of the outdoor sunlight, both energy saving and customer satisfaction would increase if we were to control also the lighting.

The building has five small offices (each used by one person), two large offices (3-5 persons), and one meeting room, and one corridor at each of the three floors. We use $R = 0.1$ and $C = 3000$ for the small offices in the building, $R = 0.05$ and $C = 5000$ for the large offices, and $R = 0.05$ and $C = 3000$ for the meeting room. (Larger rooms have greater losses to the environment than smaller rooms and there are fewer entities to heat up/cool down in the meeting room.) In the small offices there is one 1000W radiator, whereas in the large offices and the meeting room there are two such radiators.

In the scenario used in the calculations there are 12 persons working in the building who share the following characteristics:

> prefer 22°C both at their offices and when in the meeting room

> the working day is normally nine hours with a one hour lunch break, i.e., on average eight hours are spent in the building. However, there is a 20 per cent probability that a person does not show up at all during a day (because of meetings in another city, illness etc.)

> on average there are five meetings in the meeting room each week

> the length of a meeting is two hours on average

We assumed that the radiators use a simple (ideal) temperature control algorithm: To raise the temperature, they use the maximal effect (i.e., 1000W) to heat up the room to the desired temperature. To maintain the desired temperature, they produce just the right amount of heating power. Finally, to lower the temperature, the radiators are turned off.

4.2 The Results – Energy Saving

Four different approaches were compared:

1. *The thermostat approach*: This is the current method of controlling the environmental parameters of the Villa Wega building (and most other buildings in the industrialized world). The people working in the building set the desired temperature manually. However, since most people do not lower the temperature in their offices when they go home, we assume that the temperature is always set to 22°C both in the offices and in the meeting room.

2. *The timer-based approach*: This is a bit more sophisticated (in fact, it may well be the smartest approach in current use). A timer starts raising the temperature at 7 a.m. to 22°C in all rooms, and at 7 p.m. it starts to lower the temperature to 16°C, i.e., the thermostat is set to 22°C and 16°C respectively.

3. *The reactive MAS approach*: When a person is in the building, the temperature of her office is set to 22°C, and when she is not, the temperature

is set to 16°C. Similarly, when the meeting room is empty the temperature is set to 16°C, and otherwise to 22°C.

4. *The pro-active MAS approach*: makes use of the electronic diaries of the persons working in the building in order to heat up the rooms to the preferred temperature in advance. (Thus, it requires that the individuals keep their electronic diaries updated.)

The results are described in the Table 1.

Table 1. The average weekly energy consumption of the four control approaches

Control approach	Average weekly energy consumption
1. Thermostat	221.8 kWh
2. Timer-based	154.3 kWh
3. Reactive MAS	136.2 kWh
4. Pro-active MAS	137.0 kWh

Thus, compared to first approach, we save almost 40% energy by using the MAS approach and almost 12% compared to the timer-based approach. Note also that the pro-active approach is only slightly more energy consuming than the reactive, but will increase customer temperature satisfaction (see next section).

4.3   The Results – Customer Satisfaction

The saving of energy was only one goal of our system. Now we turn to the evaluation of how the MAS fulfils the second goal of increased customer satisfaction. We will here concentrate on the persons who work in the small offices. We use a simple linear model of the degree of satisfaction with respect to temperature where 16 °C corresponds to 0% satisfaction and 22 °C corresponds to 100% satisfaction.

In order to make an appropriate comparison we have to specify the distribution of working time of the persons involved. We have assumed the distribution illustrated in Figure 3 on weekdays, i.e., no work at all during weekends.

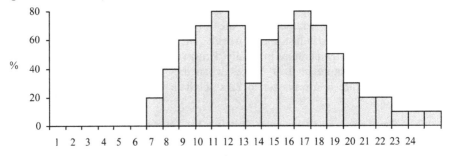

Figure 3. The distribution of working time of the persons involved (the height of a bar corresponds to the probability that the person is working in the building during that hour)

The results are described in Table 2.

Table 2. The average degree of temperature satisfaction of the four control approaches

Control approach	Average degree of temperature satisfaction
1. Thermostat	100.0 %
2. Timer-based	91.8 %
3. Reactive MAS	97.7 %
4. Pro-active MAS	100.0 %

Thus, we see that the thermostat approach of course yields the maximal degree of customer satisfaction since it keeps the desired temperature at all times. However, as we have seen, the price for this is a very high energy consumption. The current method to lower the energy consumption, i.e., using a timer-based approach, on the other hand, has a significantly lower degree of customer satisfaction than the MAS-based approaches. In addition, the MAS-based approaches enable us to control the trade-off between energy saving and customer satisfaction in a much more sophisticated manner than, e.g., the timer-based approach. Notice also that the assumed distribution of working time is quite favorable to the timer-based approach. For instance, if we were to include over-time work during weekends the results would be much worse while the performance of the MAS-based approaches would be the same as before.

Admittedly, this evaluation of customer satisfaction is very coarse, ignoring many aspects that would influence the degree of satisfaction experienced by the people working in a building actually equipped with such a system, e.g., personal integrity issues, and the extra work of keeping the diary updated. Privacy and integrity are very interesting aspects, however, we believe that empirical studies based on field-tests are necessary to assess these aspects properly. Actually, we are currently working with a psychologist concerning these issues.

Also, developing more complex "contracts" with the customers would be a possibility for the providers. For instance, the contract could be stated in the following way: the average "satisfiability factor" should be 0.95 and/or it should not drop below 0.5 for more than ten minutes. Such contracts would open up further possibilities to save energy.

5   Related Work

The research efforts on intelligent buildings and environments have increased rapidly during the last couple of years. However, much work has been spent on either developing infrastructures supporting such applications or finding solutions to particular sub-problems, rather than on general control mechanisms on the system level. Also, most current work do not make use of the flexibility that agent technology offers and therefore we believe that its potential in this domain has not been sufficiently explored.

For instance, Hasha [14] describes a platform based on distributed active objects and has many characteristics in common with a normal multi-agent system platform. However, in the existing fielded implementation of this platform (the Gates Estate in Medina, Washington, USA), both hardware and installation costs were very high. Since it is based on a large number of computers (more than 120) connected via a dedicated network, rather than on (potentially cheap) smart sensors and actuators equipped with minimal processing capability and communicating with each other via the existing power lines, we believe that this approach probably will be too expensive to be widely used also in the future.

Another interesting piece of work is the Intelligent Room project at the MIT AI lab [13]. Its main focus is on the interaction between the users and the system, in particular how to integrate different sensor modalities, such as, vision, gestures and speech. In contrast, our approach is to make this interaction as simple and transparent as possible for the users (i.e., by just wearing a badge).

One of the approaches most similar to ours is the ACHE system [9], which also aims at energy saving and increased personal comfort. While we have assumed that the persons working in the building enter their preferences manually, ACHE learns these automatically by observing the behavior of the persons of the building, e.g., when they manually adjust the settings of lights or thermostats. An interesting idea would be to use this adaptability to learn, or at least fine-tune, the preference settings of our systems. However, ACHE does not have any system for locating and identifying individual persons and is thus unable to deal with personal preferences.

6   Conclusions

We have given a high-level description of a project aimed at investigating the usefulness of the agent metaphor and the notion of multi-agent systems for the design of control systems for intelligent buildings. The use of the agent approach was initially motivated by the close mapping that it offered between the entities of the application domain and the entities of the software. The concurrent non-deterministic nature of the activities inside the building was another factor that led to the development of concurrent autonomous entities.

We have presented a general multi-agent system architecture, which we argue can be easily adapted to almost any building. Moreover, the agent system was designed to allow for dynamic re-configuration of the agents, without any disruptions of the operation of the system. This is a useful feature when changes in the building infrastructure or of the persons in the building occur. Finally, we evaluated the approach by means of qualitative computer simulations and quantitative analyses based on thermodynamical models. Our results indicate that the approach is viable and that considerable energy savings are possible while at the same time providing added value for the customer. In addition, the approach enables a much more fine-grained control of the trade-off between energy saving and customer satisfaction than is possible with current approaches.

It is also worth mentioning that an agent-based approach permits even more advanced control mechanisms than previously mentioned in this paper. For instance, it is possible to let the agents take into account that the price of energy is not constant.

We have also been experimenting with more complex functionality, e.g., when a person enters the building in the morning, her monitor is switched on and the coffee machine starts making coffee. While the study of such functionalities is beyond the scope of the work presented here, we believe that they will be very important when developing future intelligent buildings.

Acknowledgements

We thank Christoffer Dahlblom, Martin Fredriksson and Mikael Svahnberg who implemented the environment visualization GUI, Marko Krejic for helping us with hardware-related issues, Dr. Nikolaos Skarmeas and Professor Keith L. Clark who helped us with the implementation of the MAS, and Dr. Fredrik Ygge for the help with the thermodynamical modeling.

References

1. Boman M., Davidsson P., Skarmeas N., Clark K., and Gustavsson R., "Energy Saving and Added Customer Value in Intelligent Buildings", *Third International Conference on the Practical Application of Intelligent Agents and Multi-Agent Technology*, pp. 505-517, 1998.
2. Boman M., Davidsson P., and Younes H.L., Artificial Decision Making under Uncertainty in Intelligent Buildings, *Fifteenth Conference on Uncertainty in Artificial Intelligence*, pp. 65-70, Morgan Kaufmann, 1999.
3. Coen M., Design Principles for Intelligent Environments, *Fifteenth National Conference on Artificial Intelligence (AAAI'98)*, pp. 547-554, 1998.
4. Finin T., Fritzson R., and McKay D., et al., An Overview of KQML: A Knowledge Query and Manipulation Language, Technical report, Department of Computer Science, University of Maryland, Baltimore County, USA, 1992.
5. Harter A and Hopper A, A Distributed Location System for the Active Office, *IEEE Network 8(1)*, 1994.
6. Hasha R., Needed: A common distributed-object platform, *IEEE Intelligent Systems*, March/April, pp. 14-16, 1999.
7. Incropera F.P. and Witt D.P., *Fundamentals of Heat and Mass Transfer* (3rd edition), Wiley and Sons, 1990.
8. McCabe F. G. and Clark K. L., April: Agent Process Interaction Language, in Wooldridge M. J. and Jennings N. R. (eds.), *Intelligent Agents (Lecture Notes in Artificial Intelligence 890)*, pp. 324-340, Springer-Verlag, 1995.
9. Mozer M., The Neural Network House: An Environment that Adapts to its Inhabitants, *AAAI Spring Symposium on Intelligent Environments*, pp.110-114, 1998.
10. Musliner D. and Pell B. (eds.), Agents with Adjustable Autonomy, AAAI Spring Symposium, Technical Report SS-99-06, AAAI, 1999. ISBN 1-57735-102-9.
11. Ogata K., *Modern Control Engineering* (2nd edition), Prentice-Hall, 1990.
12. Ottosson H., Akkermans H., and Ygge F. (eds.), *The ISES Project*, EnerSearch, 1998, ISBN 91-9753567-0-0.
13. Skarmeas N., "Agents as Objects with Knowledge Base State", PhD Thesis, Imperial College, Department of Computing, January, 1997.
14. Verhagen H., and Boman M., Norms can replace plans, *IJCAI'99 Workshop on Adjustable, Autonomous Systems*, 1999.

CarPAcities: Distributed Car Pool Agencies in Mobile Networks[1]

Steffen Rothkugel and Peter Sturm

System Software and Distributed Systems, University of Trier
D-54286 Trier, Germany

Abstract. CarPAcities provides a highly dynamic, easy to use, cost effective and safe approach to car sharing. It is designed to be tightly integrated into today's mobile network infrastructure. The underlying model as well as an agent-based prototype implementation employing the Jini technology for service management are described throughout this paper. Simulation results underpin the effectiveness of CarPAcities.

1   Introduction

The steadily increasing traffic volume is one of the most demanding ecological problems. German studies for the period between 1988 and 2010 expect a 32% increase of passenger traffic and about 78% growth in the area of freight traffic [1]. Researchers as well as politicians not only predict a traffic collapse but a significant drop of economic growth [2].

A couple of strategies tackling this problem using modern computer and communication technologies exist. Among them are changing traffic signs controlled by traffic volume measurements and navigation systems taking traffic jams into account [3]. Some proposals strive for reducing the traffic volume. Telework is one example [4], but it is only applicable to a limited extent. Sharing cars is another prominent way, coming in different flavors. For instance, persons may share their own car with other people, e.g. by picking up hitchhikers. However, there are some drawbacks of pure hitchhiking. Whom do you trust? And what about the costs? Ride boards as known for example from universities reduce the risks and allow for preliminary cost negotiation, but at the expense of significant organizational overhead. This scheme is not well suited for spontaneous trips either. Car pool agencies are still another possibility for efficient and safe car sharing. In this approach, the cars are the property of the agency. However, largely due to their inconvenient usage, the acceptance of car pooling is still limited. People want to be free to move from one place to another nearly spontaneously, without much organizational overhead, at low costs and in a safe manner. Any approach has to take these prerequisites into account for being successful [5].

---

[1]This work was funded in parts by Nortel Networks, Center of Network Optimization (CNO)

D. Kotz and F. Mattern (Eds.): ASA/MA 2000, LNCS 1882, pp. 178-191, 2000.
© Springer-Verlag Berlin Heidelberg

In this paper, we propose CarPAcities, a car sharing system combining the advantages of the sharing schemes described above. The dynamics and low effort of hitchhiking are joined with the safety gained through professional car pool agencies, while maximizing cost effectiveness through extensive sharing. Furthermore, by explicitly designing the system to allow for a seamless and tight integration into today's infrastructure of mobile networks, its ease-of-use is guaranteed.

After outlining the model behind CarPAcities, we will describe its prototypical implementation in the third section. Section 4 will discuss strategies for the integration of the system into an existing mobile network infrastructure. Summary and conclusions are presented in the section that follows. Section 6 will discuss future work.

2 CarPAcities: The Model

The rationale behind CarPAcities is to provide an easy-to-use, scalable, self-organizing and highly dynamic car sharing system. Some basic assumptions and fundamental strategies are applied in our first prototypical implementation. A couple of different enhancements of the initial model are possible and will be described in a subsequent section. We will first describe the basic abstractions of CarPAcities in conjunction with some typical usage scenarios.

2.1 Basic Abstractions

Three different parties may participate in the system—people looking for a ride, those willing to share their own car with others as well as car rentals providing cars for pooling. This leads to the basic abstractions `Passenger` and `Car`.

From an organizational point of view, it makes no difference whether the `Car` is owned by a private individual or belongs to a car pool. It is only the duration of its participation in the system that differs. Persons willing to share their car may make it available temporarily for dispatch on a trip by trip basis.

`Itinerary` is the third basic abstraction. An `Itinerary` describes the planned path from a starting point to an endpoint together with a possibly incomplete schedule. When an `Itinerary` is created, only the starting time has to be known, perhaps including an additional waiting time. The waiting time specifies the maximum amount of time a `Passenger` is willing to wait for a ride to begin. As `Itineraries` are travelled along, the schedule will be completed.

Note that in our initial prototype, `Itineraries` are automatically generated by the system. In a real-world implementation, CarPAcities should be used in conjunction with a GPS-based navigation system for route planning. This not only allows to take traffic jams into account, but it enables the system to dynamically react on changing conditions. For example, `Passengers` booked a trip with a late `Car` may be informed automatically, possibly resulting in cancelling the trip and starting the negotiation anew.

2.2   Interaction with CarPAcities

Passengers looking for a ride register with the system. The same applies to Cars of private individuals offering rides. Cars from the pool are registered statically with the system. Passengers and Cars are both mobile entities and therefore should need to be connected only temporarily. After registering, they are represented in the system through agents acting autonomously on their behalf. When necessary, the agent calls back its originator.

Passengers as well as Cars, represented by their respective drivers, must be identifiable to the system for meeting safety needs. Logging information about booked rides greatly reduces the risks for all participants. Criminal abuses as known from hitchhiking are obviated. Additionally, absorption of costs is warranted due to non-repudiation.

2.3   Ride Negotiation

The system is responsible for mapping Passengers to Cars based on their re-spective Itinerary. We decided to let CarPAcities perform solely a preselection driven by preference parameters provided by the Passengers and the Cars via their agents. For example, a Passenger might be willing to wait only a small amount of time for a cheap private ride offer. Thereafter, the Passenger might want to accept a Car from the pool, which is typically more expensive.

When an appropriate private ride offer has been found, the system can calculate a proposal for a place to meet. It then will establish a direct connection between the two potential partners. If they agree on the ride, thereby doing the ultimate negotiation e.g. about the concrete meeting point, the system will be informed about the booking. Otherwise, the system will continue to look for suitable ride offers. Thus, CarPAcities can be augmented with the user's heuristics while still leaving enough room for human interaction.

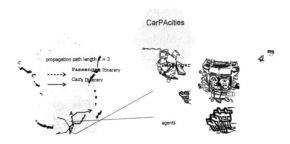

Fig. 1. CarPAcities scenario showing the Itineraries of two Cars and one Passenger just starting their trips. At the zoomed cell, the Passenger may change to the second Car. Information about the parties is propagated to the next k=3 cells in this example

Because most Passengers are assumed to be willing to wait only a certain amount of time, their interest is limited in Cars in their vicinity. The whole negotiation process therefore is bound to a local scope, making a cell-based design of the CarPAcities infrastructure obvious. However, limiting the visibility of Cars to a single cell would be much too restrictive. Propagating information about Cars and their Itineraries to the next k cells is a sensible approach. The selection of k is a critical design factor. It not only has a direct influence on the communication effort, k also determines the amount of time the system will be able to do pre-planning.

As Cars move along their Itinerary from cell to cell, each cell change triggers some actions. The cell just left may forget about the Car. Additionally, information about the Car will be propagated to the next k cells. This allows the subsequent k-1 cells to update their local state associated with a Car, e.g. by adjusting the estimated arrival time. The k-th cell will learn about a new Car, possibly starting new negotiation processes for registered and waiting Passengers.

2.4   Structural Properties

A cell-based organization is in favor of scalability. Not only the amount of negotiation processing is influenced by the cell structure. In order to be able to propagate information about Cars to the next k cells, each cell only needs to know the adjacent cell as dictated by the Itinerary. This restricts the information needed in each cell about the global infrastructure to its neighbor cells. Changing the cell structure, e.g. in order to split overloaded cells, requires only local updates on affected cells.

The cell-based organization furthermore is advantageous in case of failures, as only a limited area will be out of service. However, additional provisions have to be made for the system to be fault tolerant. The knowledge of a Car's Itinerary, for example, is locally held in the Car itself. Information about Passengers on a trip is stored in the corresponding Car, respectively. Only Passengers still waiting for a trip offer are stored in the cell itself and are therefore affected by the outage.

CarPAcities does not strive for globally optimal planning, but for semi-optimal decisions based on local knowledge from adjacent cells. Due to the large number of cars and people on their way at any point in time, limiting decisions to a local scope doesn't seem to be restrictive but rather necessary. Obviously, the more participants, the better the overall profit of the system will be.

3   CarPAcities: The Simulation

When implementing our first prototype, we wanted to achieve two different goals. Firstly, we wanted to be able to quantify the effects of our car sharing model. Secondly, we wanted to investigate technologies we found most appropriate to apply in our context, in particular the Jini technology [6], [7].

3.1   Introduction to Jini

Jini is a technology for spontaneous networking. It tries to combine some vital properties of distributed systems under a set of Java-based application programming interfaces. Jini allows networked devices to setup an impromptu community without the need for device specific drivers to be installed in advance while being resilient to failures. Jini services are offered to clients in a manner that allows clients to dynamically download the code needed to talk to the service. A set of services locally available forms a Jini community. The basic abstractions of Jini are Discovery, Lookup, Leasing, Remote Events, and Transactions.

Discovery is the process of finding a Jini community. Jini communities are identified by a symbolic name, allowing to establish groups of similar services. The result of the discovery process is a set of so-called lookup services. A lookup service essentially is a directory service, holding representatives of Jini services in form of proxies. These proxies are downloaded into the client dynamically. This way, the driver for the service doesn't need to be known to the client in advance. Querying the directory service is termed Lookup in Jini speech.

Leases are the Jini concept to handle failures of any kind. Consumers of a service are forced to first apply for a lease. Leases are granted for a limited time only. If a consumer wants to stick to the service, it has to reapply the lease periodically. Therefore, due to network failures or ill-behaved clients forgetting to release their link to a service, resources are blocked at most for the duration of one lease.

Remote Events are a means of asynchronous communication between two parties possibly residing on different hosts. Due to their generic nature, Remote Events allow the decoupling of event producers from event consumers. For example, event channels may be used for tunneling and/or deferred delivery purposes. Jini Transactions encompass interfaces to implement a distributed two-phase commit protocol.

3.2   Jini Services in CarPAcities

CarPAcities makes use of the Jini technology to implement its service infrastructure. Four services are provided: the AgentRuntimeService, the RegistrationService, the NavigationService and the ConnectionService. Each service is available in every cell.

The NavigationService is responsible for Itinerary planning. It provides methods to retrieve the next cell on the path to a specified destination. The ConnectionService is used to setup a communication channel between two parties, possibly residing in different cells.

The RegistrationService acts as the primary contact point for Passengers and Cars. Passengers register their interest in rides with this service. They provide an agent to be downloaded to the registration server. This agent implements the user specific heuristics to be applied in ride negotiation. Passengers remain registered with the service until they accept a ride offer or cancel their registration themselves. Cars are registered with the service either if they are available in a local car pool or if they are in transit at most k cells away from the current one. Additionally, each `Car` is associated with an agent used for negotiation purposes. This agent knows about the `Car`'s `Itinerary`, the available seats along this `Itinerary`, and estimated arrival times.

The `AgentRuntimeService` provides a secure runtime platform for the execution of the various agents within their respective lease interval. The `RegistrationService` collaborates with the `AgentRuntimeService` during ride negotiation. New ride offers, for example, are dispatched to the registered `Passenger` agents. If necessary, agents call back their originator by means of Jini remote events.

3.3   Lease Considerations

The Jini concept of leasing is used extensively throughout the implementation. `Passengers` and `Cars`, for example, hold leases to the `RegistrationService`. If their leases expire, their registration is removed from the system.

Leases can help much in the self-healing nature of Jini communities [8]. Especially in the presence of ill-behaved clients, the negative effects due to unsolicited resource consumption is limited. However, in scenarios like ours, where mobile users are only temporarily connected and network links are unreliable, leases may be counterproductive when applied too frequently. It is not always sensible to force a mobile user to setup a connection periodically just to renew a lease. Jini itself provides utility classes to bypass this situation. A helper class that may run in its own process is delegated the task of lease renewal. The lifetimes of the client and the lease renewal process in this scenario are completely independent.Thus, if a delegating client crashes, its leases may still be renewed, eliminating the self-healing effect of leases completely.

However, third party leasing is not necessary in our application, because appropriate lease durations can be derived directly from known or measurable attributes. The cell size in combination with the `Car`'s average velocity gives a sensible hint on the time span the `Car` is expected to reside in a cell. The average velocity, in turn, can be calculated by monitoring `Car` movement via GPS. If no unforeseen events occur, leases do not have to be renewed at all. Traffic jams, if not already known to the system by different means, can be detected via GPS monitoring either and the durations of renewed leases can be adjusted accordingly. Expired leases trigger the deletion of obsolete data in the cell's services.

3.4   The SimulationCore

The `SimulationCore` encompasses the functionality needed to setup the CarPAcities infrastructure and to drive the simulation of `Cars` and `Passengers`. The infrastructure is described in a file containing the underlying map. On startup, the Jini services are initialized and registered with their corresponding lookup services.

Furthermore, the simulation is parameterized with the length of the propagation path k.

Passengers and Cars entering the simulation follow the model's rules as described above. They start a discovery process, query the lookup service, and contact the local RegistrationService, respectively. Passengers register their agents with the RegistrationService. Cars only have to register their agent when beginning a trip. The RegistrationService will propagate the Car's agent automatically along its Itinerary as the NavigationService dictates.

Note that in our first prototype simulation, some additional rules apply. None of them are crucial, but clear decisions had to be made to resolve a couple of cases. For example, Cars—or actually their drivers—are assumed not to wait for any Passengers. Thus, if a Car A, carrying a Passenger that has booked a ride with Car B, arrives later than expected, Car B may leave. The Passenger will have to look for a new ride. Additionally, Cars are assumed not to drive any detours. Furthermore, there are no traffic jams simulated yet. Passenger groups are supported by booking more than one seat thru a single Passenger representing the group.

Because of the resource requirements for Java/Jini applications, it was not sensible to implement CarPAcities with a realistic number of Cars and Passengers and within a sufficiently large cell structure as threaded clients and servers executed in their respective virtual machines. Instead, the prototype has been implemented as a combination of event- and time-driven simulation. The execution time of events is correlated with real-time by a runtime parameter. When simulated in real-time, the simulation allows for the integration of true Jini clients and services that interact with the simulated entities. In order to mimic the geographical distribution, all simulated services require the cell identification as the first argument. By these means, e.g. a real Jini implementation of a Car communicates with the different RegistrationServices etc. in the various cells en route.

3.5   Effectiveness of Car Sharing in CarPAcities

During the run of a simulation, Cars and Passengers are generated according to predefined random distributions. In our first prototype, start- and endpoints of the Itineraries follow an equipartition while the speed of the Cars follows a normal distribution. New Passengers and Cars are generated with respect to an exponential distribution.

Two different negotiation strategies are currently implemented. In the *first arrival* strategy, the first Car driving in the Passenger's direction is accepted. The *longest path* strategy chooses the Car whose Itinerary contains the longest coverage of the Passenger's Itinerary. In both strategies, if no Car driving in the Passenger's direction arrives within a specified amount of time, a Car from the pool is accepted.

The simulation results indicate that the share of successfully booked rides easily exceeds 75% even with a short propagation path length of k=5, provided that enough

Cars offer rides. As table 1 shows, a Passengers-to-Cars ratio of about 1:11 is sufficient to allow 75.2% of all Passengers to arrive at their destination without needing a Car from the pool. Furthermore, table 1 shows that the average duration a Passenger has to wait for an appropriate Car is relatively short. In the aforementioned example, a Passenger has to wait less than 14 minutes on the average. Because in a real-world scenario, most probably there will be even more Cars than Passengers, waiting times can be assumed to be even less than 5 to 10 minutes.

Table 1. Results of first simulation runs showing the effect of different Passengers-to-Cars ratios. The underlying map consists of 253 cities. The negotiation strategy is *longest path* with a propagation path length k=5. The row headed *share of booked rides* indicates the percentage of Passengers not needing a Car from the pool

Passengers-to-Cars ratio	1:1.5	1:3.7	1:7.7	1:11.4	1:29.9	1:60.7
Cars	14,352	36,174	73,711	109,836	203,768	407,704
Passengers	9,764	9,706	9,614	9,673	6,806	6,717
share of booked rides	23%	46.2%	67.5%	75.2%	80.8%	87.2%
average waiting time	22'18	19'10	15'28	13'39	7'47	5'59

Table 2. Influence of the waiting time on the share of booked rides, investigating different negotiation strategies and propagation path lengths. The Passengers-to-Cars ratio is 1:10 in all cases

selected average passenger waiting time / deviation [sec]	propagation path length k = 5				k = 20	
	longest path		next arrival		longest path	
	share of booked rides	average changes	share of booked rides	average changes	share of booked rides	average changes
240 / 60	21.4%	1.0	17.7%	1.3	39.5%	1.2
500 / 200	44.3%	1.1	42.5%	1.8	65.4%	1.2
1200 / 600	75.2%	1.2	71.9%	2.1	84.7%	1.1
2000 / 600	92.3%	1.1	90.9%	2.3	95.7%	1.0
7200 / 600	99.7%	1.1	99.8%	2.5	99.8%	0.9

The impact of the waiting time, the negotiation strategy, and the propagation path length k on the system's effectiveness is shown in table 2. The time Passengers are willing to wait apparently influences the share of booked rides. The negotiation strategy has only a small influence on the results, except for the number of necessary

`Car` changes. While in the case of the *longest path* strategy, Passenger have to change Cars only once, the *next arrival* strategy forces people to change `Cars` approximately twice.

3.6   The CarPAcities Demonstration

Part of the simulation is a graphical user interface visualizing the `Cars` and `Passengers` on their `Itinerary`. With a mouse click on any item, the user is presented additional information about this entity. For example, clicking on a `Car` shows its current position, the start- and endpoint of its `Itinerary` and its current velocity.

Single `Cars` and `Passengers` may be simulated with a dedicated application, respectively. Both applications are augmented with their own graphical user interface, giving detailed information about every action, down to lookup service discovery. Furthermore, the `Car` application can remote control a Lego Mindstorm miniature car via an infrared link. The whole model has been presented on the German CeBIT 2000 exhibition [9].

4   CarPAcities in the Real World

The results of the simulation have shown that CarPAcities is a suitable model for car sharing. Ideas and suggestions for its integration into the infrastructure of today's mobile networks are discussed in this section.

The cell-based structure of the model allows a natural mapping onto existing mobile phone networks, making CarPAcities a perfect candidate for a future value-added service to be offered by mobile network providers. Especially in areas with a high population and along highways, where CarPAcities will be most commonly used, mobile networks are well deployed. The dense cell structure in those areas leads to a reasonable small number of mobile units to be handled by a single base station. Due to the automatic hand-over between cells, the detection of cell changes comes for free. Additionally, mobile phone networks can be integrated perfectly with Jini lease management. Assuming the mobile phone is a lease holder, lease renewal can be coupled directly with periodically pinging the mobile phone, as is already done in today's mobile phone networks.

`Passengers` may use their mobile phones to interact with the system. A SIM application could provide a simple frontend for registering interest in rides. The starting point could default to the current cell and the starting time to the current time. The endpoint could be entered via the key panel. Preferences like the maximum waiting time could likewise be supplied through the phone's number pad. Ride offers could be sent back from the provider to the SIM application, possibly supplemented with additional information like the overlapping part of both parties' `Itineraries` and a cost estimation.

Fig. 2. Photo of the demonstration at the CeBIT 2000 fair. The highlighted on screen map corresponds to the printed plan on which the Lego Mindstorm model drives

Using plain mobile phones has several advantages. First of all, being a ubiquitous device nowadays, CarPAcities would be available immediately to a large user community. Additionally, relying solely on mobile phones would preserve a person's mobility. For example, a `Passenger` may continue shopping while waiting for proper ride offers. Furthermore, mobile phones combine ease of use with a sufficiently sophisticated frontend and a suitable implementation platform. Particularly, SIM application toolkits being compliant with current GSM standards 11.11 [10] and 11.14 [11] permit the use of public key encryption as well as digital signatures. Thus, authentication and non-repudiation can be accomplished easily.

However, more sophisticated frontends allowing for a higher degree of functional flexibility are also conceivable. PDAs are a prominent example. For example, downloading a map with the meeting point highlighted would be highly convenient. As Java virtual machines become available for these devices, like the KVM [12] for the Palm Computing Platform, downloading agent code from the user's device will be no more a technological vision only.

`Cars` may interact with the system through an enhanced GPS-based navigation system in combination with a mobile phone. Entering `Itineraries` could be done by augmenting the navigation system's frontend with some additional options, e.g. for providing the number of available seats and loading capacity. The mobile phone would be used similar to the `Passenger`'s one, e.g. for an authenticated negotiation process.

5   Related Work

Traffic simulations have been implemented in various forms. SIM-ENG [13], for example, is an engine for discrete-event traffic simulation. Traffic models are described using a special methodology called MMTS [14]. A parallel traffic simulator presented in [15] applies PVM-based algorithms in a network of workstations. Yet another simulation described in [16] was implemented for a Cray T3E. The focus of all this work is on the simulation of large amounts of traffic data using load balancing schemes striving for a highly efficient implementation. The simulation core of CarPAcities rather concentrates on the incorporation of the agent programming paradigm as well as the Jini technology.

An evaluation of mobile agent technology in the area of vehicular traffic management is presented in [17]. This work introduces a general application partitioning model which facilitates the combination of asynchronous and autonomous operation, data filtering and scheduling in a user specific manner. The model is applied in a prototypical implementation of a *Proactive Route Planning System*, which is based on the ObjectSpace Voyager core technology API [18]. Performance results demonstrate "the feasibility and applicability of an integrated approach of mobile computing and mobile agent technology for application partitioning in a traffic telematics scenario" as employed in CarPAcities.

In the Praxitele project, a simulation environment for a new kind of transportation in an urban environment was developed [19]. A "fleet of electric public cars [...] capable of autonomous motion on given journeys between stations" form the basis of this work. In contrast to this virtual environment, CarPAcities is a more pragmatic approach incorporating today's infrastructure as-is.

The German Ministry for Education and Research [20] supports, among others, a project called MOBINET. Its goal is to preserve mobility in congested urban areas through an integrative traffic management. Intelligent traffic control, traffic information systems, park and ride, public means of transportation carrying people from start points to their destination instead of from stop to stop are examples of the underlying concepts. Remarkably, car sharing as promoted by CarPAcities is no integral part of MOBINET.

Mobility CarSharing [21] is a company located in Switzerland, currently offering about 1300 cars for rent to over 33000 registered customers. Cars located at locked parking sites in over 300 cities can be booked via phone or Internet. The customer is informed immediately about car availability at the nearest location. The rates are relatively low if the car is returned to its original location after usage. It is possible to return the car at a different point, but at significantly higher costs. Mobility CarSharing clearly demonstrates that people are willing to share cars in order to reduce costs if only the overhead is sufficiently low.

6   The Future of CarPAcities

We plan to do additional simulations in a more realistic scenario, based on statistical data as is available e.g. from the Federal Statistical Office [22]. Those simulations are expected to give substantial hints for tuning the system's effectiveness.

Special investigations related to commuters have to be performed. Commuters are predestined clients of CarPAcities. They play a significant role in today's car sharing. In Germany, for example, special parking sites reserved for commuters exist, e.g. located near highway exits. Currently, groups of commuters are often fixed, having the disadvantage for the participants of being timely inflexible. The dynamic nature of CarPAcities could provide additional advantages here. Due to the large amount of people participating, simulation results may be significantly influenced.

Additionally to the effectiveness of CarPAcities, we have to evaluate its communication overhead as well as its overall resource consumption and its resistance to failures. The simulation has to be instrumented accordingly. The characteristics of mobile networks have to be taken into account appropriately. Although we designed CarPAcities with mobile networks in mind, we currently have no concrete measurements of its communication behavior.

Furthermore, some prerequisites currently hardcoded into the simulation have to be relaxed. For instance, cars currently do not wait for passengers. In a real-world scenario, such decisions wouldn't be so clear-cut. An additional parameter influencing the car's maximum waiting time would help improving simulation results. The simulation specific rule that cars do not drive any detours is a comparable restriction. On a long trip, a small detour could still significantly reduce costs and therefore most probably would be accepted by the driver. Additionally, traffic jams have to be incorporated into the simulation.

The integration of public means of transportation is another necessary extension of CarPAcities. In a real-world scenario, this integration seems to be mandatory for the acceptance of the whole approach. If no suitable ride offer can be found, many people would prefer taking a bus or a train rather than a pooled car. Especially the first and last sections of an itinerary are eligible candidates, respectively.

7   Summary and Conclusions

In this paper, we introduced CarPAcities, a model for efficient car sharing. The system can be used both passively by persons looking for a ride as well as actively by private individuals offering their cars for sharing. Car pools are also an integral part of the system, allowing passengers to fallback on the typically more expensive car rental solution if no appropriate ride offer can be found in a specified time.

CarPAcities is explicitly designed to be tightly integrated into existent mobile networks. The cell-based structure allows for a highly dynamic and scalable way of ride negotiation. The utilization of mobile phones not only makes CarPAcities available to a large user community, it also permits for a high degree of safety. Participants are unambiguously identifiable by the system, thereby greatly reducing risks as known for example from hitchhiking, where partners typically remain anonymous. Payment for booked trips can be undeniable authorized.

We implemented a prototype simulation and investigated the effects on car utilization and saved miles. The simulation was based on statistical distributions and an imaginary map. The results showed that a reasonable amount of Passengers, about 87% in our simulation runs, found an appropriate ride offer, saving approximately 37% driven miles overall.

Our simulation applied agent technology to represent passengers and cars in the system. This allows for the real entities to being connected only temporarily for registering their agent with CarPAcities while still getting continuous service.

For resource management, we used Jini [6], [7]. In essence, Jini does not provide anything really new. It is just a merge of well-known, practically working techniques under a consistent application programming interface. As we have shown, the Jini concept of leasing is well suited for our application scenario. However, Jini is no prerequisite in the system's design, so a real-world implementation could freely decide to use a different technology.

Acknowledgements

We would like to thank Markus Lütticken for the implementation of the first Java/ Jini prototype version of CarPAcities. We also want to thank Jürgen Ballmann and Alexander Greiml for developing these nice looking Lego Mindstorm cars and connecting them with the simulation core. Thanks to Christian Hutter and Johannes K. Lehnert for their help in putting all the pieces together. Last but not least we want to thank again Markus Lütticken and Christian Hutter for surviving one week CeBIT 2000 fair while presenting and defending the prototype.

References

1. Kreibich, Rolf, Nolte, Roland: *Umweltgerechter Verkehr.* Springer-Verlag (1996)
2. Bundesminister für Verkehr: *Bundesverkehrswegeplan* (1992)
3. Boes, Hans: *Telematikanwendungen im Güterverkehr—Einstieg in den Ausstieg aus der Stoffwirtschaft.* In: Nolte, R., Kreibich, R.: Verkehr und Telematik— Konzepte für eine umweltfreundliche Mobilität (1994) 67-75
4. Nolte, Roland: *Verkehrliche Substitutionspotentiale der Telematik—Mit Hochtechnologie aus der Verkehrskrise?* In: Nolte, R., Kreibich, R.: Verkehr und Telematik—Konzepte für eine umweltfreundliche Mobilität (1994) 88-97
5. Haefner, Klaus: *Verkehrs-System-Management in deutschen Kommunen—Ein reales Projekt zur Lösung vieler Verkehrsprobleme.* In: Nolte, R., Kreibich, R.: Verkehr und Telematik— Konzepte für eine umweltfreundliche Mobilität (1994) 67-75
6. Sun Microsystems, Inc.: *Jini Architectural Overview.* Technical White Paper (1999)
7. Sun Microsystems, Inc.: *Jini Connection Technology.* http://www.sun.com/jini (2000)
8. Waldo, Jim: *The Jini Architecture for Network Centric Computing.* Communications of the ACM, Vol. 42, No. 7, July 1999, pg. 76-82 (1999)
9. CeBIT 2000 Fair, Hannover. http://www.cebit.de (2000)
10. European Telecommunications Standards Institute: *Digital cellular telecommunications system (Phase 2+); Specification of the Subscriber Identity Module—Mobile Equipment (SIM-ME) interface (GSM 11.11 version 7.4.0 Release 1998).* http://www.etsi.org (1999)
11. European Telecommunications Standards Institute: *Digital cellular telecommunications system (Phase 2+); Specification of the SIM Application Toolkit for the Subscriber Identity Module—Mobile Equipment (SIM-ME) interface (GSM 11.14 version 7.3.1 Release 1998).* http:/ /www.etsi.org (2000)

12. Sun Microsystems, Inc.: *K Virtual Machine (KVM)*.
    http://java.sun.com/products/kvm (2000)
13. Creagh, John M.: *SIM-ENG: A Traffic Simulation Engine*. Proceedings of the
    Thirty-Second Annual Simulation Symposium, April 11-15, San Diego,
    California (1999)
14. Creagh, John M.: *MMTS: A Modelling Methodology for Traffic Simulation*.
    Proceedings of the SCS 1998, Summer Computer Simulation Conference, Reno,
    Nevada (1998)
15. Tibaut, Andrej: *Dynamic Load-Balancing for Parallel Traffic Simulation*. Fifth
    Euromicro Workshop on Parallel and Distributed Processing (PDP '97), January
    22-24 (1997)
16. Johnston, Charles M., Chronopoulos, Anthony T.: *The Parallelization of a
    Highway Traffic Flow Simulation*. Proceedings of the Seventh Symposium on the
    Frontiers of Massively Parallel Computation, Annapolis, Maryland, February 21-
    25 (1999)
17. Schill, A., Held, A., Böhmak, W., Springer, T., Ziegert, T.: *An Agent Based
    Application for Personalized Vehicular Traffic Management*. Proceedings of the
    Second International Workshop on Mobile Agents, Stuttgart, Germany,
    September 9-11 (1998)
18. ObjectSpace, Inc.: *Voyager Core Technology User Guide, Version 2.0 Beta 1*
    (1997)
19. Donikian, Stephane: *Multilevel Modelling of Virtual Urban Environments for
    Behavioural Animation*. Proceedings of Computer Animation '97, Geneva,
    Switzerland, June 4-7 (1997)
20. German Ministry for Education and Research, bmb+f: http://www.bmbf.de (2000)
21. Mobility CarSharing. http://www.mobility.ch (2000)
22. German Federal Statistical Office. http://www.statistik-bund.de (2000)

Quantitative Evaluation of Pairwise Interactions between Agents

Takahiro Kawamura[1], Sam Joseph[2], Akihiko Ohsuga[1], and
Shinichi Honiden[3]

[1] Corporate Research and Development Center, TOSHIBA Corp.,
`Takahiro@isl.rdc.toshiba.co.jp`,
[2] ValueCommerce Co.,Ltd.,
[3] National Institute of Informatics, Japan

Abstract. Systems comprised of multiple interacting mobile agents provide an alternate network computing paradigm that integrates remote
data access, message exchange and migration; which up until now have
largely been considered independently. This paper focuses on basic one-
to-one agent interactions, or paradigms, which can be used as building blocks; allowing larger system characteristics and performance to
be understood in terms of their combination. This paper defines three
basic agent paradigms and presents associated performance models. The
paradigms are evaluated quantitatively in terms of network traffic, overall
processing time and size of memory used, in the context of a distributed
DB system developed using the Bee-gent Agent Framework. Comparison
of the results and models illustrates the performance trade-off for each
paradigm, which are not represented in the models, and some implementation issues of agent frameworks.

1 Introduction

Agent-based distributed systems that incorporate techniques such as mobility
and message exchange promise to handle the increasing complexity of our expanding computer networks. One of the goals of Mobile Multi-Agent systems
is to integrate the varied and, up till now, independent agent interaction models. Selecting an appropriate interaction paradigm is important because it can
greatly affect system performance, and is complicated because of the huge number of possible design combinations. Thus, this paper focuses on a small number
of fundamental agent interaction paradigms to try and understand the relationship between paradigm, performance task and network conditions.

In section 2, we consider the three agent paradigms with their performance
model. Section 3 illustrates the paradigms implemented under the Bee-gent via
a series of database (DB) interaction examples. Quantitative evaluation of each
system is presented in section 4. In section 5, comparison between the models and
the quantitative results highlights the characteristics of each paradigm, which
are not represented in the models, and we assess the generality of these results
in order to identify any implementation issues of agent frameworks. Section 6
presents related work and finally section 7 summarize our experience.

D. Kotz and F. Mattern (Eds.): ASA/MA 2000, LNCS 1882, pp. 192–   , 2000.
© Springer-Verlag Berlin Heidelberg 2000

2   Fundamental Agent Design Paradigms

2.1   Basic Concepts

In this paper, we take the smallest conceptual unit of a distributed system to be an interaction between two hosts, one of which has a data processing need, and the other has the data required to fulfill that need. Fig.   presents a conceptualization of a distributed system, in which each host has bi-directional access to the other hosts in the network. We consider three basic agent interaction paradigms called Direct Access, Stationary agents Access and Mobile agent Access. We take the term "agent" to refer to any object that can perform a process on the behalf of some other agent or person.

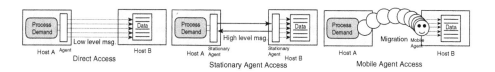

Fig. 1. Basic design paradigms

Direct Access (DA). An agent of Host A directly accesses data at Host B, and subsequently executes a process on the assembled data. For example, a search engine at Host A performs a search of a DB on Host B, by directly accessing all the tables of the DB using simple SQL queries. This corresponds to the traditional client server approach of a server having all the data and the clients having access to the server. Fetching HTML documents and SNMP are examples of this paradigm.

Stationary agents Access (SA). A stationary agent on Host A requests a stationary agent residing on Host B to execute a process related to the local DB, using an Agent Communication Language (ACL) based message. A stationary agent on Host B returns the result message to Host A. For example, a search engine at Host A searches a Host B DB by generating a message which contains the conditions of the search, fields required etc. (e.g. name, attribute.) and passes it to the stationary agent on Host B. The stationary agent parses the message and locally assembles the data that matches the conditions as specified by the message. Lastly, the stationary agent sends the results to Host A. This situation consists of servers having both data and related processes while clients are still restricted to simply accessing the servers.

The Stationary Agent (SA) approach is really a variation of the client server setup. However in this paper we assume that a distinction can be made according to the granularity of the messages involved, and the complexity of the processes that can be invoked on the server side. The distinction rests upon whether a search process is executed on the server side (SA) or client side (DA).

Mobile agent Access(MA). Host A generates a mobile agent based on a particular process. The mobile agent migrates from Host A to Host B to execute the process and returns with the result. For example, a search engine at Host A performs a search of a DB on Host B, generating a mobile agent which contains a search routine particular to Host A. The mobile agent migrates to Host B and applies the routine and returns to Host A with any results. Mobile agents are able to dynamically configure the process executed on a server by providing the specifications of that process, e.g., a process that requires modification at run time or a process that needs to be differentiated depending on different clients. Mobile agents can also maintain execution state and thus continue processing at a remote host that was suspended prior to migration.

2.2   Models of Basic Paradigms

This section presents models for network traffic and overall processing time that provide a qualitative analysis of the above three paradigms. The network traffic models represent the sum of the data being sent between Host A and Host B and are also a function of the number N of DBs being simultaneously accessed from Host A. Our models are based on using TCP/IP to establish connections, and although there are many possible protocols, we use TCP for reliability and because of its ubiquity. However, it is important to note that if UDP was being used, the models of network traffic might be significantly affected since queries would be broadcasted to all databases. The overall processing time is taken from the beginning of the process on Host A to the end of that process which assumes the conclusion of communication with Host B has taken place and thus represents the sum of the communication time and the processing time on Host A and B. Note that we represent all processes executed on Host A as dependent on the number N of DBs being simultaneously accessed.

In the following equations, N is the number of simultaneously connected DBs and Q is the number of queries. $I_q n$ is the size of a query from Host A to Host B, while $R_q n$ is the size of the reply. The actual amount of data is represented here as ηX where the overhead coefficient η and the size of the data to be transmitted is X. $\tilde{\eta} X$ is overhead coefficient for data flowing in the reverse direction. DA, SA, MA network traffic can be represented by the following equations respectively.

$$S_{DA} = \sum_{n=1}^{N} \sum_{q=1}^{Q} (\eta_{DA} I_{qn} + \tilde{\eta}_{DA} R_{qn}) \tag{1}$$

$$S_{SA} = \sum_{n=1}^{N} \sum_{p=1}^{P} (\eta_{SA} M_{pn} + \tilde{\eta}_{SA} A_{pn}) \tag{2}$$

$$S_{MA} = \sum_{n=1}^{N} (\eta_{MA}(C_n + O_n) + \tilde{\eta}_{MA}(O_n + D_n)) \tag{3}$$

---

[1] In the simplest case it could be $\frac{1}{N}$.

[2] ηX is represented as $\eta(X)X = \alpha(X) + \beta(X)X$ [ ]. The first term corresponds to the control information exchanged during a TCP/IP setup phase, while the second term corresponds to the overhead introduced by message encapsulation.

In the above equations, $M_{p}n$ is the size of a message from Host A to Host B. $A_{p}n$ is the size of a reply message. Also P corresponds to the number of messages $0 < P \leq Q$ from Host A to Host B. $P = 1$ indicates that one message can include the contents of Q queries. $P = Q$ indicates that one message can include contents of only *one* query. Therefore, we can regard DA as a special form of SA where $P = Q$ at all times. In equation (3), C_{n} is the size of classes (CodeBase) of the mobile agent and O_{n} is the size of execution state of the mobile agent. D_{n} is the size of the result brought back by the mobile agent. When a mobile migrates to Host B, it is necessary to transmit any classes that do not exist at Host B. However, this expense will not be incurred on the return trip.

We can represent the processing time of each paradigm by taking the size of data to be transmitted per second as $U(N)$ where N is the number of DBs being simultaneously accessed. From equation (1) it follows that the DA communication time for single Host B access is T_{comm}. Equation (2) can be used to derive $T_{comm'}$ for the time taken for SA round trip message. Moreover, we get $T_{comm''}$ as the time for a round trip migration of mobile agent referring equation (3) in MA.

$$T_{comm} = \frac{\eta_{DA} I_{q}}{U(N)} + \frac{\tilde{\eta}_{DA} R_{q}}{\tilde{U}(N)}$$

$$T_{comm'} = \frac{\eta_{SA} M_{p}}{U(N)} + \frac{\tilde{\eta}_{SA} A_{p}}{\tilde{U}(N)}$$

$$T_{comm''} = \frac{\eta_{MA}(C+O)}{U(N)} + \frac{\tilde{\eta}_{MA}(O+D)}{\tilde{U}(N)}$$

Therefore, the overall processing time of each paradigm is represented as the sum of the above communication time $T_{comm}, T_{comm'}, T_{comm''}$ and the processing time at both hosts.

$$T_{DA} = \sum_{q=1}^{Q}(T_{comm_{q}} + T_{proc_{q}}(N) + T_{resp_{q}}) \tag{4}$$

$$T_{SA} = \sum_{p=1}^{P}(T_{comm'_{p}} + T_{ge_{p}}(N) + T_{pa_{p}} + T_{ge_{p}} + T_{pa_{p}}(N) + \sum_{q=1}^{Q/P}(T_{proc'_{q}} + T_{resp'_{q}}))\tag{5}$$

$$T_{MA} = T_{comm''} + T_{se}(N) + T_{de} + T_{se} + T_{de}(N) + \sum_{q=1}^{Q}(T_{proc''_{q}} + T_{resp''_{q}}) \tag{6}$$

$T_{proc_{q}}$ in DA is the execution time for a process on Host A, such as computing some function of the data gathered from Host B. $T_{resp_{q}}$ in DA is the time for the execution of the process at Host B, such as the database access time. $T_{proc'_{q}}, T_{resp'_{q}}$ in SA is the time taken for the interaction between the stationary agent and the DB at Host B. $T_{proc''}, T_{resp''}$ in MA is the time taken for the interaction between the mobile agent and DB on Host B. Communication time between entities residing on the same host is considered negligible. Also, $T_{ge_{p}}$

---

[3] $U(N)$ also depends on the throughput of disk access and network interface cards being used. Here, we assume all hosts are using similar devices.

is the time consumed generating ACL messages M. T_{pa_p} is the time consumed parsing ACL messages M. T_{se} is the time consumed serializing mobile agents. T_{de} is the time consumed deserializing mobile agents.

The next section introduces some distributed DB systems based on the basic agent paradigms.

3   Distributed Database Systems Implemented in Bee-gent

3.1   Bee-gent Framework

The Bee-gent Framework is summarized below to the extent necessary to support understanding of the experiments in the next section. Further information about Bee-gent can be found elsewhere[,]. The Bee-gent is a development framework that supports the construction of efficient distributed systems. The Bee-gent consists of applications that are elements of a distributed system, agent-wrappers to enable the applications to connect to the network and mediation-agents whose role is facilitating cooperation between the agent-wrappers.

The system is implemented in the Java language and operates on any platform supporting JDK1.1 or higher. The agent-wrappers also operate to host the mediation-agents. To this end, the agent-wrappers are HTTP Servers and the mediation-agents are Java threads executed on the servers. The migration function of the mediation-agents comprises of object serialization and HTTP. During migration, instances of mediation-agents are serialized at any state and pushed to a destination agent-wrapper by the HTTP POST method. If there is no code related to the instance, a destination agent-wrapper pulls the code via HTTP GET method. The language of the messages is described as XML/ACL, which is FIPA ACL[ ] mapped onto XML.

3.2   Basic Paradigms Applied to Distributed Databases

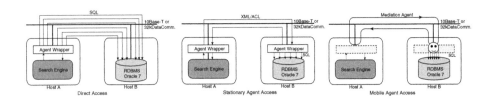

Fig. 2. Distributed DB systems based on basic paradigms

In order to evaluate the basic agent interaction paradigms we employ a distributed DB system as an example. Many of these distributed DB systems use

SQL. However, SQL functions cannot be used in non-SQL DBs and CSV file based DB structures. In such a heterogeneous environment the support of an agent framework like Bee-gent becomes all the more valuable, and allows integration with all sorts of other systems that are not sharing the same tool set, e.g., SNMP and HTTP-based systems can be incorporated into a single encompassing framework. We implemented distributed DB systems under each design paradigms by configuring the appropriate applications, agent-wrappers and mediation-agents in Bee-gent(Fig.). There is a search engine in Host A and a DB in Host B. The SA stationary agent is an agent wrapper, while the MA mobile agent is a mediation-agent. In the DA paradigm, the Host A agent-wrapper directly accesses the DB on Host B.

We try to place the three systems on an even footing and thus find the characteristic features of each paradigm as a result. Thus, we use the same code to realize the same functionalities and remove code if it is not necessary. We use simple SQL statements (SELECT, UPDATE) to query local or remote DBs. These are equals to the GET/POST methods of HTTP or the get/set of SNMP. We have decided not to use the high level functionalities of SQL so that our three paradigms maintain their distinctive abilities, i.e., the SA interaction paradigm cannot start moving code about. The implementation details were as follows; the RDBMS was an Oracle7 Workgroup Server R7.3 and the purpose-built search engine shared between all interaction paradigms. Host A and Host B ran Windows NT4.0 on 133MHz Pentium. The network between Host A and Host B was a 10Base–T LAN.

The next section presents the experimental assessment of each paradigms performance.

4   Performance Assessment of Paradigms

4.1   Experiments

We assess the DB access effectiveness in terms of the following three conditions:

- the amount of data access
- the size of network bandwidth
- how the search processing is distributed over the hosts (shared/localized)

Table. shows four experiments which examine a range of different experimental conditions. The DB contents were product information from a manufacturing industry database. A "Shared" process is searching for lowest priced product in all tables. A "Localized" process is getting product information and calculation of a discount rate for each product. However, the routine for calculating the discount rate is different for each host. All data is either a string value or a numerical value. Each product is represented by its own table. The DB contents were not duplicated from Host B to Host A in any of the experiments.

In DA of experiment 1, an agent of Host A remotely fetches the tables of the Host B DB using individual SQL queries. The agent then extracts the prices from

Table 1. Experiments

	Data access	Bandwidth	Search Process
Experiment 1	Small (1000 tables)	High (LAN 10Base–T)	Shared
Experiment 2	Small (1000 tables)	Low (PHS 32k)	Shared
Experiment 3	Large (10000 tables)	High (LAN 10Base–T)	Shared
Experiment 4	Small (1000 tables)	High (LAN 10Base–T)	Localized

the table for comparison. In SA, Host A sends an ACL message to a stationary agent at Host B. The message describes a request for the product information of the least expensive product over all tables. The Host B stationary agent parses the message and locally searches the tables on Host B. Finally, the stationary agent summarizes the product information into a message and sends it to Host A. In MA, a mobile agent migrates from Host A to Host B and locally searches the tables on Host B. The mobile agent then returns with the product information.

In experiment 2, the network is replaced with a PHS (Personal Handyphone System, a wireless telephone in Japan) 32k data communication.

Experiment 3 was identical to experiment 1 except for the volume of data access, specifically that the number of tables accessed was increased to 10000.

Experiment 4 assumes that the search process being used to access the Host B database cannot be specified in advance, e.g. that it is a process to be changed at run time or a process that must be adjusted depending on the client that is accessing the database. The discount rate calculation routine is specific to Host A (another host would employ a different routine). The Host B stationary agent does not have access to the routine. A further assumption is that this is a routine that cannot be requested through the use of ACL messages because the content language in the ACL message cannot represent the same function as the routine. We do not assume the content language which can represent arbitrary functions because it is extremely difficult to implement agent systems to be able to take advantage of such expressive power. In DA, Host A remotely searches the tables of the Host B database using SQL queries to access information about particular products. Subsequently, Host A calculates the discount rate and compiles the result into a table. It follows that each table requires two accesses per table. In SA, Host A performs the same process as in DA. Host A requests the stationary agent on Host B to retrieve product information from a table using a message. Host A then calculates a discount rate from the product information and requests (via message) that the stationary agent on Host B put the discount rate in a table. In the MA paradigm, a mobile agent that has the routine particular to Host A migrates from Host A to Host B. The mobile agent accesses the product information and calculates the discount rate, and writes the result for each product to a table. Finally it returns to Host B.

The following performance was assessed in each of the four experiments.

Network Traffic The total amount of IP packets (Kbyte) and the total number of IP packets (packets) transferred between Host A and Host B

Table 2. Results of experiments

	experiment 1			experiment 2		
	DA	SA	MA	DA	SA	MA
Amount(Kbyte)	1105.1	3.5	23.9	na	na	na
Num.(packets)	8059	22	69	na	na	na
Time(sec)	40.058	45.505	55.349	1413.5	50.040	76.180
Memory(Kbyte)				na	na	na
Host A	340.0	1220.6	min 331.8	na	na	na
			max 1208.3	na	na	na
Host B		1482.7	min 331.8	na	na	na
			max 905.2	na	na	na
	experiment 3			experiment 4		
	DA	SA	MA	DA	SA	MA
Amount(Kbyte)	11004.8	3.5	23.9	16004.8	73589.0	23.8
Num.(packets)	80067	22	69	120057	466012	71
Time(sec)	286.192	278.485	286.402	605.020	40336.099	563.551
Memory(Kbyte)						
Host A	340.0	1220.6	min 331.8	340.0	1359.9	min 331.8
			max 1208.3			max 1294.3
Host B		1482.7	min 331.8		1527.8	min 331.8
			max 905.2			max 905.2

Processing Time Overall processing time to get final result (sec)
Memory Size Size of heap memory used (Kbyte)

4.2 Experimental Results

The results of experiments 1–4 are shown in Table . In experiment 2 only processing time was measured. The processing time for each paradigm is summarized in Fig. , where the DA processing time is taken to be 100%, with the other paradigms shown as percentages of that.

5   Comparing Paradigms Performance

This section presents a comparison of the qualitative aspects of the models and the quantitative experimental results, in order to try and discern the details particular to the individual paradigms. Additionally, we try to identify which aspects of the results are a consequence of the Bee-gent implementation and which can be generalized to other agent systems.

5.1   Comparing Paradigms in Experiment 1

Experiment 1 involved a small to medium amount of data access with a large network bandwidth, and the search process was shared between the hosts.

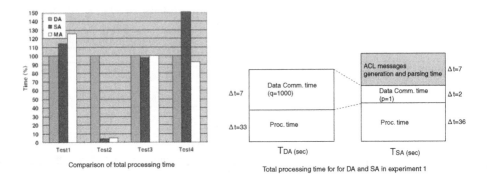

Fig. 3. Comparison of total processing time and its breakdown

In terms of overall processing time, the results indicate that DA was the fastest, while conversely SA can greatly reduce the communication cost for local searches. As we can see in equations (4)–(6), the reason that SA takes longer than DA is because of the time $T_{ge_p}(N) + T_{pa_p} + T_{ge_p} + T_{pa_p}(N)$ taken up generating and parsing ACL messages. Thus, comparison with the qualitative models shows that the difference between the communication time and the time consumed generating and parsing ACL messages is a key issue.

Moreover, comparison with the quantitative results indicates that the communication time consumed under the DA paradigm (T_{DA}) was 7 (sec) ($Q = 1000$), while the communication time consumed for SA (T_{SA}) was 2 (sec) ($P = 1$), giving a difference of five seconds. On the other hand, the time consumed by the ACL message under SA (T_{SA}) was the followings:

$$T_{ge_p}(N) + T_{pa_p} + T_{ge_p} + T_{pa_p}(N) \simeq 7(sec).$$

As a result, the comparison of the models and the results provides us with the insight that the difference between the time taken to transmit an individual DA message and the time taken to generate and parse ACL messages reaches double figures, so that counter-intuitively DA has an advantage over SA given that a broadband network like 10Base–T is being used. Fig. itemizes the processing times involved. In this figure the processing time of SA is larger than that of DA, because the response time $T_{resp'}$ of the database is reduced by the operation of the stationary agent.

Thinking about how the above is dependent on aspects of the Bee-gent system, it is important to note that Bee-gent uses specially designed interfaces based on SAX (Simple API for XML) to handle XML documents. When XML documents are generated and parsed in Bee-gent additional processes are applied

---

4 The communication time involves library loading and negotiations for establishing connections.

to perform DTD validation, use SAX to make temporal tables include all pairs of tags and values, and to obtain the appropriate tag values through access to the table methods. Other systems may have different implementations of these functions, but any system making use of a high level semantic language like ACL is likely to lead to processes that consume similar amounts of time, i.e., syntax checking and semantic content retrieval.

In terms of network traffic, SA performed the best and DA performed the worst. Comparing the models, we can see that this is caused by the $Q = 1000$ factor in equation (1) while in (2) $P = 1$ (i.e., a message corresponds to Q queries) given that the stationary agent in Host B is using a shared search process (search for the least expensive product in all tables). If we assume $\eta_{DA} \simeq \tilde{\eta}_{DA} \simeq \eta_{SA} \simeq \tilde{\eta}_{SA} \simeq \eta_{MA} \simeq \tilde{\eta}_{MA}$ in (1)–(3), we can represent the experimental result $S_{DA} \gg S_{MA} > S_{SA}$ by the following relation.

$$\sum_{q=1}^{1000}(I_q + R_q) \gg C + 2O + D$$

$$> M + A$$

Additionally, based on the experimental results, we can also calculate the conditions that would make the traffic for all paradigms equal:

$$\sum_{q=1}^{9}(I_q + R_q) \simeq M + A$$

$$\sum_{q=1}^{25}(I_q + R_q) \simeq C + 2O + D$$

Although this matches our intuition that DA has the worst performance in terms of network traffic, the quantitative results indicate that if the number of individual DA queries that can be replaced by an alternate paradigm transmission is low enough then DA has an advantage due to the small size of each of its individual transmissions.

Further, the quantitative results show that the MA paradigm most effectively uses the network bandwidth, which is not shown by the network traffic models. The volume of data transferred is not proportional to the number of IP packets shown in Table . SA and MA create much larger packets than DA. The larger the packets become,the smaller the network traffic overhead becomes, such as the IP headers that are introduced when actual data is segmented. We can estimate values of η for a 20 byte IP header: $\eta_{DA} \simeq 1.17$, $\eta_{SA} \simeq 1.14$, $\eta_{MA} \simeq 1.06$, assuming $\eta = \tilde{\eta}$. For the transmission of 100 Kbyte of actual data, DA adds 17 Kbyte extra data against only 6 Kbyte for MA. Something not covered by the models above is the special "sliding window" TCP function, which in some sense approximates the MA paradigm. The MA paradigm sends a large amount of data at once, so that the average packet size is larger than the other paradigms. In a burst mode transmission, a sliding window which clusters data together for dispatch can effectively reduce communication time. This implies that $U(N), \tilde{U}(N)$ in $T_{comm}, T_{comm'}, T_{comm''}$ are not necessarily equal in reality.

In terms of size of memory used, DA had the best performance. This is because Host B needs not support a stationary agent or a platform for mobile agents. Furthermore, MA makes more effective use of memory than SA. MA uses the same size of memory (max in the tables) as SA on Host B while the mobile agent is at Host B. But following migration, MA uses the less memory (min in the tables) than SA. The above result endorses the intuitional merit of mobile agents, although assumes that the JavaVM unloads objects that are no longer required. Many agent systems have been implemented in Java and thus can take advantage of this. However, it is difficult to know in advance whether the garbage collection mechanisms will necessarily release the memory after mobile agents have migrated to other hosts.

5.2   Comparing Paradigms in Experiment 2

In experiment 2 the network bandwidth is more restricted than in experiment 1.

In terms of overall processing time, the SA paradigm was superior. Comparison with the qualitative models indicated that the difference between the communication time and the ACL generating/parsing time was as pivotal as in the previous experiment. Comparison with the quantitative results showed that the communication time consumed under the DA paradigm was 1380 (sec) ($Q = 1000$), while for SA it was 7 (sec) ($P = 1$), making the difference 1373 (sec). It seems clear that in the case of limited network bandwidth, such as with a mobile device (PDA, Cellphone, etc.) that individual transmission times become larger causing the ACL generating/parsing time of the SA paradigm to be outweighed by the increased communication time under DA.

5.3   Comparing Paradigms in Experiment 3

Experiment 3 is similar to experiment 1, but the amount of data access required was increased.

In terms of overall processing time, SA performed the best, as in experiment 2. That is because $Q = 10000$ in equation (4) increases the communication times of the DA paradigm exceeding the ACL message related times of the SA paradigm.

In terms of network traffic, although the DA traffic levels increased in proportion to the increase in data accesses, SA and MA maintain similar levels to before.

5.4   Comparing Paradigms in Experiment 4

In experiment 4 the data access and the available bandwidth were both large, while the search process was particular to the host that was accessing the database.

MA created the minimum network traffic, while SA created the most. SA has $P = 20000$ (10000 tables × 2 access) in equation (2) because Host A is unable to request the calculations using ACL messages. On the other hand, the mobile agent in MA can finish the process in a single round trip because it carries a search routine specific to calculating the Host A discount rate. If we assume $\eta_{DA} \simeq \tilde{\eta}_{DA} \simeq \eta_{SA} \simeq \tilde{\eta}_{SA} \simeq \eta_{MA} \simeq \tilde{\eta}_{MA}$ in (1)–(3), we can represent this experimental result $S_{SA} > S_{DA} \gg S_{MA}$ by the following relation.

$$\sum_{p=1}^{20000} (M_p + A_p) > \sum_{q=1}^{20000} (I_q + R_q)$$
$$\gg C + 2O + D$$

It should be pointed out that the Bee-gent agent migration mechanism splits the agent state O and classes C before agent migration so that only the classes that are needed at the destination can be transmitted. Thus, as indicated by equation (3), no classes need to be transferred along with the results when they are sent back. Some existing agent systems do not make this split and send both state and all associated classes together. In such agent systems we might expect the network traffic of MA to increase. In this experiment the size of the agent classes was about 7 Kbytes and comprised one third of the MA network traffic, which is likely to be larger in practical applications.

In terms of overall processing time, MA had the best performance. Comparison with the qualitative models of DA and MA indicates the importance of the difference in the communication time and the mobile agent (de)serialization time $T_{se}(N) + T_{de} + T_{se} + T_{de}(N)$ which draws parallels with the DA and SA comparison in section 5.1. The experimental results, however, indicate that there is a big difference in its figures between the time taken for one DA transmission and MA (de)serializing events. The results of experiments 1,3,4 are shown in Fig. , which also illustrates the relationship between T_{DA} and T_{MA}. In this figure, the overall processing time becomes $T_{DA} \simeq T_{MA}$ when the number Q of queries of DA exceeds 10000. Note that the time for the search process in MA is larger than DA because mobile agents active at Host B reduce the speed of the database search process.

The Bee-gent serialization mechanism incorporates the process of encryption/decryption as well as the conversion between objects and byte arrays. Concern has often been expressed about the security of mobile agents, leading us to include this aspect while evaluating mobile agent performance. Serialization costs can be avoided by using specific implementations (such as scripts transmitted as ASCII strings), however many agent systems share the serialization.

5.5 Results Summary

Processing time. Comparison with the models shows the important factors are the DA communication time, the SA XML/ACL generating/parsing time and the MA (de)serializing time. Further comparison with the experimental results shows that a time for a simple DA query in a broadband network is much

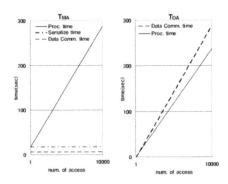

Fig. 4. Total processing time for DA and MA

smaller, under double figures, than the time for an XML/ACL message or a mobile agent. As a consequence the DA paradigm can offset its poor network traffic performance with its greater speed, at least until CPU or JavaVM speeds increase by a factor of ten. This also suggests that these aspects are the implementation issues for agent frameworks which should be investigated further if one wished to improve the processing time performance of the DA and SA paradigms. However, the situation changes in lower bandwidth environments, where the overall DA processing time suffers due to an order of magnitude increase in the DA communication time. Therefore SA becomes the most effective option, and this also applies to situations in which the number of data accesses is large. Finally, when processes that must be dynamically modified at runtime, or machine resources are severely restricted the SA paradigm cannot be implemented effectively making the MA paradigm the best option.

Network traffic. The network traffic is, as shown in the models of DA, SA and MA, the total amount of the data passed through the network, giving SA a general advantage. If dynamically modified processes are required that prevent realization of the SA approach then MA paradigms provide the best performance. However, the quantitative results show that if the number of queries is a one-figure number, then the DA paradigm can be used effectively. In addition, the experimental results illustrate something not obvious from the network traffic models. The MA approach increases the average packet size, leading to smaller overhead compared with DA and SA. Thus one might suggest that the MA paradigm is most effectively using network bandwidth.

Memory. In terms of the memory consumed the quantitative measurements contradict the qualitative expectation that the MA paradigms are the most advantageous, indicating that memory consumption should be considered in terms of the particular agent framework implementation.

6   Related Work

Most of the related work concerning agent paradigms and their evaluation is closely related the the particular system in question or the range of performance aspects assessed is limited. Stamos et al.[ ] presented mobile code paradigms in their most basic form as REV (Remote Evaluation) and evaluated RPC (Remove Procedure Call) processing time. However the REV system is implemented using LISP and while it is important work, it operates on a different level of granularity to our own system, and fails to discuss other performance aspects and make application-based distinctions. Picco et al.[,] derived models of network traffic and evaluate them within a network management application. They compare four paradigms: CS, COD, REV, MA. However, different performance aspects or experimental measures are not investigated. We owe much to the work of Picco et al.[,], upon which we based our model derivation. In this paper, we have presented our models along with a series of quantitative experiments, assessing overall processing time and memory usage in addition to network traffic. The process of comparing the models and the experimental results has illuminated the characteristics of each paradigm which are not obvious from the models and some of the issues associated with agent frameworks implementation.

7   Conclusion

In this paper, we focused on the basic agent paradigms. Comparison of the models we had constructed with our experimental results highlighted the characteristics of each paradigm, in a way that went beyond what could be gathered from just the models. Further, our experiments indicated that the critical issues for agent framework are the message-exchange and mobility mechanisms; or in other words the generating/parsing of ACL messages and the serialization/memory management issues associate with mobility. In the future, we hope to increase the number of basic agent paradigms, such as including mobile agent itineraries and application specific paradigms. At the same time we would like to apply the results of this paper to practical system development, and thus improve the performance of these systems.

References

1. T. Kawamura, T. Hasegawa, A. Ohsuga, S. Honiden: Bee-gent : Bonding and Encapsulation Enhancement Agent Framework for Development of Distributed Systems, Proceedings of 6th Asia-Pacific Software Engineering Conference, pp. 260–267 (1999).
2. Multi-agent Framework Bee-gent, http://www2.toshiba.co.jp/beegent/ (2000).
3. A. Carzaniga, G. P. Picco, G. Vigna: Designing Distributed Applications with Mobile Code Paradigms, Proceedings of the 19th International Conference on Software Engineering (1997).
4. M. Baldi, G. P. Picco: Evaluation the Tradeoffs of Mobile Code Design Paradigms in Network Management Applications, Proceedings of the 20th International Conference on Software Engineering (1998).   ,
5. J. W. Stamos, D. K. Gifford: Remote evaluation, ACM Transactions on Programming Languages and Systems, Vol. 12, No. 4, pp. 537–565 (1990).
6. FIPA98 Specification, http://www.fipa.org/ (2000).

A Reliable Message Delivery Protocol
for Mobile Agents

Mudumbai Ranganathan, Marc Bednarek, and Doug Montgomery

Internetworking Technologies Group
Advanced Network Technologies Divsion
National Institute of Standards and Technology
100 Bureau Drive, Gaithersburg, MD 20899
{mranga,bednarek,dougm}@antd.nist.gov

Abstract. The abstractions and protocol mechanisms that form the
basis for inter-agent communications can significantly impact the overall
design and effectiveness of Mobile Agent systems. We present the design and performance analysis of a reliable communication mechanism
for Mobile Agent systems. Our protocols are presented in the context of
a Mobile Agent system called AGNI . We have developed AGNI communication mechanisms that offer reliable peer-to-peer communications,
and that are integrated with our agent location tracking infrastructure
to enable efficient, failure-resistant networking among highly mobile systems. We have analyzed the design parameters of our protocols using
an in-situ simulation approach with validation through measurement of
our prototype implementation in real distributed systems. Our system
assumptions are simple and general enough to make our results applicable to other Agent systems that may adopt our protocols and/or design
principles.

1 Introduction

Mobile Agents are a convenient and powerful paradigm for structuring distributed systems. Using the Agent paradigm, work can be assigned to sequential,
event-driven tasks that cooperate with each other to solve a distributed problem.
In such systems, Agents roam the network accessing distributed information and
resources while solving pieces of the problem. During the course of these computations Mobile Agents need to communicate among themselves to exchange state
and status information, control and direct future behavior, and report results.

The abstractions and protocol mechanisms that form the basis for inter-agent
communications can significantly impact the overall design and effectiveness of
Mobile Agent systems. Numerous approaches to inter-Agent communications

---

[1] AGNI stands for Agents at NIST and is also Sanskrit for fire.

[2] This work was supported in part by DARPA under the *Autonomous Negotiation
Teams* (ANTS) program (AO # 99-H412/00). The work described in this paper is
a research project and not an official US. Government endorsement of any product
or protocol.

D. Kotz and F. Mattern (Eds.): ASA/MA 2000, LNCS 1882, pp. 206–   , 2000.
© Springer-Verlag Berlin Heidelberg 2000

are possible including RPC and mailboxes [ ]. In this work we present a simple, ordered, reliable, one-way message protocol on top of which other abstractions can easily be built.

Reliable, ordered one-way communication mechanisms greatly simplify the construction of most distributed applications. In traditional distributed applications, TCP [ ] provides such services. Through decades of experience and re-engineering, TCP has evolved into a protocol that is highly effective at providing reliable end-to-end data delivery over the conditions found in today's Internet (e.g., link failures, variable latencies, congestion loss).

In this paper, we examine how to build a TCP-like reliable communication mechanism for Mobile Agent systems. The first question to be addressed is "Why we don't use the existing TCP?" We argue that Mobile Agent systems impose new communication requirements and problems that are not adequately addressed by conventional TCP, nor its potential minor variants. In particular, we are concerned with building failure resistant, rapidly re-configurable distributed systems. We view these system properties as a primary motivation for dynamic Agent creation and mobility mechanisms, and as posing significant requirements on inter-Agent communications mechanisms. As such, we require that Agent systems be able to (1) detect and recover from failures in the end-to-end transport mechanism and (2) accommodate efficient communication among mobile end-points. Neither of these capabilities can be provided using standard TCP.

In the remainder of this paper we present the design and performance analysis of a reliable communication mechanism for Mobile Agent systems. Our protocol is presented in the context of a Mobile Agent system called AGNI, whose general design and capabilities have been described earlier [ ]. Our communication mechanism offers reliable peer-to-peer communications that are integrated with our Agent location tracking infrastructure to enable efficient, failure-resistant networking among highly mobile systems. Our system assumptions are simple and general enough to make our results applicable to other Agent systems that may adopt our protocol and design principles. We have analyzed the design parameters of our protocols using an in-situ simulation approach with validation through measurement of our prototype implementation operating in real distributed systems.

The rest of this paper is organized as follows. Section   presents an overview of our system design and describes a sliding window protocol for mobile end-points that is the focus of this paper. Section   presents results that show the importance of efficient location tracking and message buffering as they relate to the efficiency of the protocol. Section   presents related work and finally we conclude with a summary of our findings in Section   .

2   Mobile Streams and AGNI

We begin by providing an overview of our system model. The specifics of this model are pertinent to our AGNI Mobile Agent system; however, the model is general enough to fit several existing Mobile Agent systems. The basic abstractions, constructs and components of our system are summarized in the following paragraphs.

A Mobile Stream (*MStream*) is a named communication end-point in a distributed system that can be moved from machine to machine while a distributed computation is in progress and while maintaining a sender-defined ordering guarantee of message consumption with respect to the order in which messages are sent to it.

An MStream has a globally unique name. We refer to any processor that supports an MStream execution environment as a *Site*. The closest analogy to an MStream is a mobile active mailbox. A mailbox, like an MStream has a globally unique name. MStreams provide a *FIFO* ordering, ensuring that messages are consumed from MStream in the same order as they are sent to it. Usually mailboxes are stationary. MStreams, on the other hand, have the ability to move from Site to Site. Usually mailboxes are passive. In contrast, message arrival at an MStream can trigger the concurrent execution of message consumption event handlers (*Append Handlers*). Such handlers that are registered with the MStream process the message and can send messages to other MStreams.

An AGNI distributed system consists of one or more *Sites*. A collection of Sites participating in a distributed application is called a *Session*. Each Site is assigned a *Location Identifier* that uniquely identifies it within a given Session. New Sites may be added and removed from the Session at any time. An MStream may be located on, or moved to any Site in the Session that allows it to reside there. MStreams may be opened like sockets and messages sent (*appended*) to them. Multiple event handlers may be dynamically attached, to and detached from, an MStream. Handlers are invoked on discrete changes in system state such as message delivery (append), MStream relocations, new Handler attachments new Site additions and Site failures.

Handlers can communicate with each other by *appending* messages to MStreams. These messages are delivered asynchronously to the registered Append Handlers in the same order that they were issued . A message is *delivered* at an MStream when the Append Handlers of the MStream has been activated for execution as a result of the message. A message is *consumed* when all the *Append* handlers of the MStream that are activated as a result of its delivery have completed execution.

An application built on our system may be dynamically extended and reconfigured in several ways while it is in execution (i.e., while there are pending un-delivered messages). First, an *Agent* can dynamically change the handlers it has registered for a given Event. Second, new Agents may be added and existing Agents (and their handlers) removed for an existing MStream. Third, new MStreams may be added and removed. Fourth, new Sites may be added and removed, and finally, MStreams may be moved dynamically from Site to

---

[3] By asynchronous delivery we mean that the sender can continue to send messages even when previously sent messages have not been consumed. Synchronous delivery of messages is supported as an option but asynchronous delivery is expected to be the common case. We do not discuss synchronous delivery in this paper.

Site. These changes may be restricted using resource control mechanisms that are described in greater detail in our earlier paper [ ].

All changes in the configuration of an MStream, such as MStream movement, new Agent addition and deletion, and MStream destruction are deferred until the time when no Handlers of the MStream are executing. We call this the *Atomic Handler Execution Model*. Message delivery order is preserved despite dynamic reconfiguration, allowing both the sender and receiver to be in motion while asynchronous messages are pending delivery.

2.1   Requirements for Reliable Message Passing between Agents

When one needs to provide reliable in-order end-to-end communications, the first issue to be addressed is "Can we use the existing TCP ?" We argue that highly Mobile Agent systems impose unique communication requirements that are not easily addressed by conventional TCP. In particular: (1) Agents need the ability to detect and recover from failures in the end-to-end transport mechanism. If we use conventional TCP and the Site where a receiver is located fails, the sender would have no idea of what packets have been delivered. To accommodate for this, we would have to build application level protocols that address reliability beyond the existence of a single TCP connection. (2) Agents need to communicate while moving from machine to machine and TCP does not handle moving endpoints. Even in mobile TCP [ ], the communication stack and the connection state remains fixed to a given machine - only the packets are re-routed as the machines move around. Mobile Agents, on the other hand are mobile applications. When the application moves, the connection has to move. (3) Agent communications need to be optimized for mobility. If we addressed mobility by creating new TCP connections to each location an Agent visited, we would suffer the connection setup cost for each move and the inability to transmit to Agents while they are in motion. In our work, we adopt many of the design features and mechanisms of TCP, but embody them in a UDP-based protocol that accommodates highly mobile end-points and extended reliability semantics. We describe our protocol in the next section.

2.2   A Sliding-Window Protocol for Reliable Agent Communication

Within our AGNI framework, messages are sent to MStreams using an in-order, sender-reliable delivery scheme built on top of UDP. All messages are consumed in the order they are issued by the sender despite failures and MStream movements. When the target of a message moves, messages that have not been consumed have to be delivered to the MStream at the new Site. There are two strategies one may consider in addressing this problem (1) Forward un-consumed messages from the old Site to the new Site or (2) Re-deliver from the sender to the new Site. Forwarding messages has some negative implications for reliability and stability. If the Site from which the MStream is migrating dies before buffered messages have been forwarded to the new Site, these messages will be lost. Also, if the target MStream is moving rapidly, forwarding will result in un-consumed messages being retransmitted several times before final consumption. Hence, we followed the second strategy. In our system, the sender buffers each message until it receives notification that the handler has run and the message has been consumed, re-transmitting the message on time-out.

In our system, when an MStream moves, it takes various state information along with it. Clearly, there is an implicit movement of handler code and Agent execution state, but in addition, the MStream takes a state vector of sequence numbers. There is a slot in this vector for each live MStream that the MStream in motion has sent messages to or received messages from. Each slot contains a sent-received pair of integers indicating the next sequence number to be sent or received from a given MStream. This allows the messaging code to determine how to stamp the next outgoing message or what sequence number should be consumed next from a given sender.

Our protocol uses a sliding-window acknowledgement mechanism similar to those employed by TCP. The sender buffers un-acknowledged messages and com-putes a smoothed estimate of the expected round-trip time for the acknowledg-ment to arrive from the receiver. If the acknowledgment does not arrive in the expected time, the sender re-transmits the message. The sender keeps a transmit window of messages that have been sent but not acknowledged by the receiver and adjusts the width of this window depending upon whether an ACK was received in the expected time. The receiver keeps a reception window that it ad-vertises in acknowledgements. The sender transmit window is the minimum of the reception window and the window size computed by the sender. As in TCP, the sender uses ACKs as a clock to strobe new packets into the network. When an MStream moves, a *Location Manager* is informed of its new location. Mes-sages from senders that are pending delivery to the MStream that has moved use the information stored by the Location Manager to re-send messages to its new location. The slow start algorithm is adapted from the TCP and is as follows:

- Each sender has, as part of its mobile state, information pertaining to each MStream that has been opened by its Agents. This state information includes a buffer of messages that has been sent but not acknowledged, a sender congestion window for each receiver cwnd[receiver] and a pair of sequence numbers corresponding to the next message to send to (or receive from) a given sender (or receiver).

- When starting set cwnd[receiver] to 1. When the receiver has been de-tected as having moved by the sender, set its corresponding congestion win-dow to 1. When a loss is detected (i.e. sender ACK does not arrive in the estimated round-trip time or a NAK arrives from the sender), halve the current value of the congestion window.

- For each new ACK from a receiver, increase the senders congestion window for the receiver
(cwnd[receiver]) by one until the sender-established maximum or the max-imum advertisement of the receiver is reached.

Besides integration with the Location Manager, we depart from TCP in another important regard - the receiver sends an acknowledgement for a message only after the handler has completed execution at the receiver. We adopt this strategy for two reasons (1) if the receiver moves while there are still unconsumed but buffered messages, the site from which the move originated may elect to discard these messages and the sender is responsible for retransmission and (2) if the receiver site fails before buffered messages are consumed, the sender has to detect this occurrence and re-transmit un-consumed messages.

While we have described our basic mechanism for reliability and mobility, there are several performance and scaling questions that need to be addressed at this point. First, how does the efficiency of movement notifications affect the performance of message delivery? Second, how does the receiver window get established? Third, what do we do with packets that are sent to locations where a receiver does not reside? We examine the answers to these questions in the sections that follow by using a simulation studies.

3   Performance Analysis of Basic Protocol Mechanisms

The reliable peer-to-peer protocol achieves its efficiency through pipelining message production with the delay caused by link latency and message consumption. The critical issue for Mobile Agents is the performance of the protocol when the system is re-configured and the pipeline is broken as a result of end-point motion. In order to evaluate our algorithms under a variety of conditions, we constructed a detailed system simulation using an in-situ approach. This approach wraps a simulated environment around the actual AGNI system and application code using the CSIM [ ] simulation library. We replace thread creations, semaphore locking and message sends and receives with simulated versions of these, but leave the rest of the code unmodified. We inserted simulated delays into the code at various locations and tuned these with the goal of matching real and simulated performance for various parameters of interest.

3.1   The Importance of Efficient Location Tracking

If multiple Mobile Agents are to cooperate by sending messages to each other, there has to be a means of tracking where the Agents reside so that they can find each other efficiently. In the context of highly mobile systems, the capabilities and the responsiveness of name-to-location mapping services are of critical importance in the design and performance of Agent communication protocols. In this section, we examine the interaction of location tracking mechanism with our protocol for reliable messaging among MStreams.

We assume that applications can be dynamically reconfigured at any time resulting in situations with both the sender and receiver moving while there are still pending, un-delivered messages. In our design, when an MStream moves, a Location Manager is informed of the new Site where the MStream will reside. This information needs to be propagated to each Agent that has opened the MStream. Three notification strategies were considered: (1) a lazy strategy where the propagation of such information is deferred and made available on a reactive basis by informing senders after their next attempt to transmit to the old location, (2) an eager strategy where the Location Manager informs all sites about the new MStream location by disseminating this information via multicast or multiple unicast messages and (3) a combined strategy, which informs all senders on an eager basis and redirects misdirected messages if the need should arise.

In our protocol, the sender expects to get an acknowledgement back from the target location for a given message in 1.5 times the expected round-trip time. The estimated round-trip time is computed by keeping a running estimate of expected round trip time to each target site for each open MStream and recomputing it on each acknowledgement using a smoothing estimator similar to the one employed by TCP [ ] (i.e. $RTT_i = RTT_{i-1} + \alpha * MeasuredRTT$). As in TCP, we use an α value of 0.75. The expected round-trip time includes the time for the handler to run as the acknowledgement only returns after the handler is executed at the target MStream. If the acknowledgement does not arrive in the expected time, the sender attempts a re-transmission of the message. This is re-tried k (currently set to 3) times before the sender sends the message to the Location Manager to be forwarded to the new destination for the MStream and drops its congestion window `cwnd[receiver]` to 1. The Location Manager forwards the message to the current Site where the receiver resides and sends a notification back to the sender informing it about the new location of the receiver. Both the combined and the lazy schemes adopt this forwarding strategy. However, in the combined scheme, in addition to this forwarding service, the Location Manager informs all Sites that have an open MStream handle for the MStream in motion, immediately as soon as a movement takes place.

Location update messages can be delayed in transit, or lost. The delay in location notifications is important to consider as it affects the performance of message delivery in highly mobile systems. We have a classic case of scalability versus responsiveness and it is important to study the effect of this tradeoff to determine the cost of scalable structures. Note that we do not rely on the Sites propagating location information themselves for two reasons : (1) the Sites are assumed to be unreliable and the links are lossy so the location update message may be lost and never reach the senders (2) if multiple Sites are sending location update information, the information may be out of sync and lead to instability for rapidly moving targets.

Our first simulation scenario involves a single sender and a single receiver that is moving randomly between a set of locations. The sender sends messages to the receiver who moves after m messages. The receiver moves round-robin between 10 locations. Each time the receiver moves, the location manager sends a notification of the move to the senders. We examine the effect of delaying this notification on the average time to consume each message and on the number of retransmissions per move. We present the retransmission results for two cases - a perfect link with no loss and a lossy link with 5% drop in Figure . The interactions between the various mechanisms are a bit more complex than one might expect at the outset. For example, note that in the case of the rapidly moving endpoint (move interval of 5) the sender window never gets a chance to open up so there is no message pipeline. As the receive window never gets filled, fewer messages get dropped at the receiver. The message drop percentages are thus lower than in the other cases as no messages are dropped when the receiver moves - especially with the low location latencies.

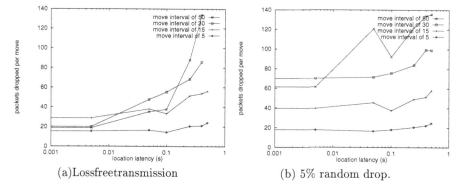

(a) Lossfreetransmission   (b) 5% random drop.

Fig. 1. Effect of location latency on messages dropped per move. Early messages are cached for 1 second at the receiver. The sender remains fixed. The *move interval* is the number of messages per move of the receiver

As may be observed, with the TCP-like sender reliable protocol, location latency has a significant impact on message drop when the MStreams move frequently. When an MStream moves, the senders get notification of the new location of the MStream. If move notification to senders is delayed, the pipeline is broken for a longer period of time and hence the receiver remains idle. The sender has to transmit its full window to the new location again when the receiver has arrived. This effect is illustrated in Figure   which shows the effect of different propagation delays of the Location Manager on the sequence numbers of the messages sent by the sender and consumed by the receiver. The effect is as expected. A higher location latency results in the pipeline being disrupted for a longer period of time and hence greater loss and reduced performance.

3.2   Caching Mis-delivered Messages

When a move notification is received, the sender starts transmitting messages to the new location for the MStream. Note that the MStream may not have arrived at its new site by the time the sender is notified. One interesting design issue is what to do with the packets that arrive at a site prior to the arrival of the receiving MStream. The simplest strategy is to drop the packets, but in highly mobile systems, other optimizations may result in better performance. If the

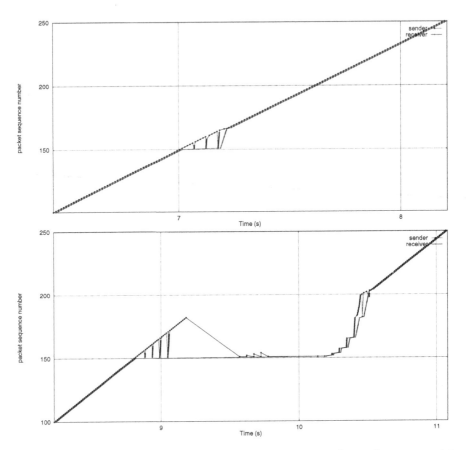

Fig. 2. The top figure shows the sequence number of sender and receiver with a location latency of 0.1 sec. and the bottom figure shows sequence numbers of sender and receiver with a location latency of 1.0 seconds. Sender is producing a message once every 0.01 seconds and the receiver handler runs for 0.001 seconds. Link latency is 0.01 seconds. The effect of increased pipeline disruption with higher location latency is evident

target Site of the move holds on to early packets for some time before discarding them, the MStream may arrive in that time and successfully consume these packets. This simple optimization has a significant effect on performance as can be seen in Figure . As expected, the benefit from this optimization displays a step behavior. After a threshold, holding packets for additional time does not yield greater benefit as the pipeline starvation effect caused by the move is already masked beyond this threshold.

The sequence number plots of the sender and receiver shown in Figures illustrate some interesting effects. In the top figure, there is no caching of packets. The pipeline shows starvation after the move. This effect can be explained by

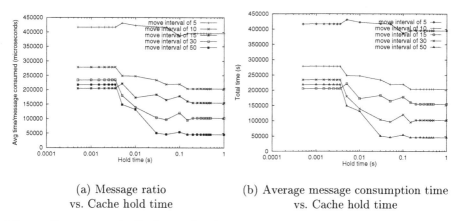

(a) Message ratio
vs. Cache hold time

(b) Average message consumption time
vs. Cache hold time

Fig. 3. Opportunistic Caching - Sender is producing a message every 0.005 seconds and receiver is consuming a message every 0.001 seconds. Location latency is 0.5 seconds. The connections loss-free

considering what happens to the send buffer right after the move. As previously described, the sender retransmits a packet 3 times to the receiver and if it does not receive an ACK in that interval it sends the packet to the location manager for forwarding and shrinks its send window down to 1. If the receiver simply discards each packet, the system goes into a state where the sender is unable to increase its send window as each successive packet reaches its maximum count and gets sent to the Location Manager for forwarding. On the other hand, if the target location holds on to the packets for a while before discarding them, this gives the receiver a chance to consume the message and send an ACK back to the sender. As can be seen from the bottom two plots in Figure , the pipeline is less severely disrupted by caching the packets rather than immediately discarding them after a move and hence the throughput is significantly improved.

This experiment illustrates a larger problem of stability of such a protocol. As this example shows, without damping, the system can be driven into a state of starvation. By adding buffering at the receiver, what we are doing is damping the system and this leads to quicker re-stabilization of the pipeline and a consequent improved throughput.

Our experiments indicate that a hold time of twice the expected relocation time of the receiver is an adequate hold time. In the following section, we implement a caching strategy with a hold time of 1 second, which is well above this limit.

3.3   Optimizing the Receiver Window Advertisement

In TCP, the receiver advertises a window that is used to compute the sender window size. The receiver window size is the advertised buffer size for the receiver. The larger this window, the greater the possible overlap between sender,

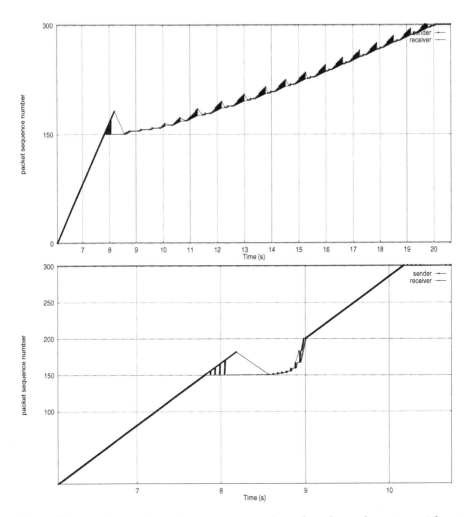

Fig. 4. The top figure shows the sequence number of sender and receiver without opportunistic caching, and the bottom figure shows the sequence number plot with 0.1 seconds cache residency. Sender is producing a message every 0.01 seconds and the receiver's append handler runs for 0.001 seconds seconds. Location latency is 0.5 seconds. Link latency is 0.01 seconds

as the receiver is able to buffer these messages while the sender produces more. If the receiver moves around frequently, in our protocol, the messages in the receive window of the receiver are discarded and the receiver relies on the sender to retransmit these packets to the new site.

Figure   shows the effect of receiver window sizes on the packet drop and the average delivery time per packet. We kept the receiver window sizes constant for this experiment. As the plots show, it is more efficient to have a small receiver window advertisement, particularly when the receiver is moving around frequently. If the window size is set too large, the performance degrades. Our experiments indicate that a window size set equal to the expected move frequency works well and we are experimenting with a dynamic scheme where the receiver window advertisement is related to the move frequency.

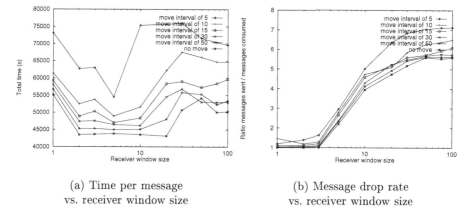

(a) Time per message
vs. receiver window size

(b) Message drop rate
vs. receiver window size

Fig. 5. Effect of receiver window size on throughput and message loss

3.4   Handling Failures

Our protocol ensures that messages are delivered in order to the receiver despite failure of the site where the receiver is located. The mechanism works as follows. MStream are assigned a reliable *Failure Manager* Site. The Failure Manager has a copy of the MStream Agent code, and has knowledge of the current Sites that have opened the MStream. Failure occurs when a Site disconnects from its Failure Manager. When such a failure occurs each of the MStreams located at the Site that has failed are implicitly relocated to its Failure Manager Site where its *Failure Handlers* are invoked. Failures may occur and be handled at any time - including during system configuration and reconfiguration. If the Site housing an MStream should fail or disconnect while a message is being consumed or while there are messages that have been buffered and not yet delivered, re-delivery is attempted at the Failure Manager. To ensure in-order delivery in the presence of failures, the message is dequeued at the sender only after the *Append Handlers* at the receiver have completed execution and the ACK for the message has been received by the sender.

After a failure has occurred at the site where an MStream resides, a failure recovery protocol is initiated at the Failure Manager that re-synchronizes sequence numbers between all Agents that have opened the failed MStream. The sequence number vector for the failed MStream is reconstructed by querying each potential sender for its next expected sequence number. We assume that the Sites being queried may fail while this process is ongoing but that the Failure Manager site itself remains reliable.

4   Related Work

There are two other efforts in Mobile Agent communication that are closely related to our efforts. Murphy and Picco [ ] present a scheme for communication in Mobile Agent systems. Our work differs in from this scheme in the following respects: (1) We have assumed that losses and failures are possible on the network. (2) We have a windowed scheme with sender-initiated retransmission for point to point messages that is fundamentally different in its operation than theirs. (3) Their scheme works for both multicast and unicast. Ours works only for unicast.

Okoshi et al. describe a mobile socket layer which is similar to our work and present details of their model in [ ]. Our scheme most resembles their *Explicit Redirection* scheme. However, the focus of our work is different from theirs. They have presented a formal protocol description, while we have concentrated more on performance and tuning aspects as they relate to mobility.

While we share several similarities with the systems mentioned above, our communication scheme differs significantly from those employed by these systems. Specifically, we do not employ forwarding pointers to redirect messages from the home location. MStreams need to rendezvous at a Site to communicate, nor do we employ RPC or rendezvous. In their examination of Mobile Agent Communication paradigms, Cabri et al. [ ] argue that direct co-ordination or message passing between Mobile Agents is not advisable for the following reasons: (1) the communicating Mobile Agents need to know about each others existence (2) routing schemes may be complex and result in residual information at the visited nodes and (3) if Mobile Agents need to communicate frequently they should be co-located anyway. They suggest black-boarding style of communication for Mobile Agents. They also note that direct message passing has the advantage of being efficient and light-weight. We concur with their comments for free-roaming disconnected Agents but we have targeted our system towards distributed interacting systems rather than disconnected operations and have presented a protocol for one-way reliable message passing that we feel is appropriate and efficient for this class of applications. We agree with the observation by Cabri et al. [ ], that forwarding messages when Agents are rapidly moving can result in messages traversing the visited locations and effectively chasing the moving Agent around over several hops before being finally consumed.

van Steen et al. [ ], present a global mobile object system called *Globe* that has a scalable, hierarchical location manager. This system is suitable for slow moving objects such as those associated with people moving around from one location to another. However, Mobile Agents, can in general, move much more rapidly and as we have shown in this paper, latency of location management is an important factor communication efficiency.

5   Conclusions and Future Work

In this paper we presented an application level, modified sliding window protocol for which functions much like TCP, but is able to handle some special requirements for Mobile Agent systems such as stack mobility, site and link failures and rapid re-configuration. We examined the effects of different location management strategies and in particular presented the effect of the latency of location resolution. Our conclusions from this study are as follows: (1) The Location Manager plays a key role in communication efficiency of a reliable protocol for Mobile Agents. For our simulations, a combined location propagation strategy worked better than a lazy one. (2) In a highly dynamic environment where Agents are frequently moving around and sending messages to each other, early messages should not be immediately discarded. We found that holding messages for several seconds for possible deferred consumption aided the protocol by reducing the number of re-transmissions. Examination of message traces revealed that this improved performance was because buffering masks the propagation of location and other information as the system is being dynamically reconfigured and allows the pipeline to continue to function while these actions are taking place. (3) Receiver window size has a significant effect on the protocol. A big receive window causes higher losses because messages in the window are discarded on move. Too small a receive window reduces throughput as no overlap is possible. A strategy that has shown promise, but that we need to examine further is to allow the receiver to set the receive window to equal the number of messages between moves. This receiver advertisement is adjusted dynamically, based on consumption rate.

We hope that our implementation and simulation environment will be useful for others designing algorithms and applications for Mobile Agent systems and we make it available for public download from http://www.antd.nist.gov/itg/agni or via email from the authors.

References

1. Ajay Bakre and B. R. Badrinath. I-TCP: Indirect TCP for Mobile Hosts. Technical Report DCS-TR-314, Rutgers University, October 1994.
2. G. Cabri, L. Leornardi, and F. Zambonelli. Coordination in Mobile Agent Systems. Technical Report DSI-97-24, Universita' di Modena, October 1997.   ,
3. Van Jacobson. Congestion Avoidance and Control. In *Proceedings ACM SIG-COMM*, pages 157–173, August 1988.
4. Amy Murphy and Gian Pietro Picco. Reliable Communication for Highly Mobile Agents. In *Agent Systems and Architectures/Mobile Agents (ASA/MA) '99*, pages 141–150, October 1999.
5. Tadashi Okoshi, Masahiro Mochizuki, Yoshito Tobe, and Hideyuki Tokuda. MobileSocket: Session Layer Continuous Operation Support for Java Applications. *Transactions of Information Processing Society of Japan*, 1(1), 1999.
6. M. Ranganathan, V. Schaal, V. Galtier, and D. Montgomery. Mobile Streams: A Middleware for Reconfigurable Distributed Scripting. In *Agent Systems And Architectures/Mobile Agents '99* , October 1999.   ,

7. Mesquite Software. Csim-18 simulation library. http://www.mesquite.com.
8. W. Richard Stevens. *TCPIP Illustrated, Vol 1: The Protocols*. Addison-Welsley, Reading, MA, 1994.
9. M. van Steen, P. Homburg, and A. S. Tanenbaum. The Architectural Design of Globe: A Wide-area Distributed System. Technical Report IR-422, Vrije University, March 1997.

Monitoring-Based Dynamic Relocation of Components in FarGo

Hovav Gazit, Israel Ben-Shaul, and Ophir Holder

Technion, Israel Institute of Technology
Haifa 32000, ISRAEL,
`issy@ee.technion.ac.il`

Abstract. We present a programming model and system support for
the development of self-monitoring distributed applications, which sense
changes in their networked environment and react by dynamically re-
locating their components. The monitoring service provides two unique
capabilities. First, it enables to perform application-level monitoring, as
opposed to only conventional system-level monitoring, without interfering with the basic application logic. Second, it enables dynamic relocation of the monitoring components, in addition to the migration of
the monitored components, again, without requiring changes inside application components. The monitoring service and programming model
were implemented as a subsystem of FARGO, a programming environment for dynamically-relocatable distributed application. In addition to
a programming language interface, relocation can be programmed using
a high-level script language, and manually controlled using a graphical
tool that tracks component relocations.

1 Introduction and Motivation

Object mobility is the capability to dynamically relocate the data state and behavior of a computational object from one host to another. It is distinct from mobile code, in which only static code is moved (e.g., Java applets), and is distinct
from mobile processes (e.g., as in Sprite [ ]), in which independent whole processes migrate. Object mobility has been widely used to implement autonomous
agent systems. We are mostly interested in a different use of mobility, namely for
improving the design and implementation of distributed applications in general.

An important distinction between these two uses of mobility is with respect
to the initiation of movement. In the autonomous agent model, movement is
often part of the logic of the application, and hence encoded inside the migrating component. In contrast, in the context of a general distributed application,
mobility is used to tune the application's performance and reliability, and thus
involves a separate facet of application design, which we term *relocation policies*.

Effective middleware support for designing relocation policies introduces several challenges. First, it requires distributed monitoring facilities that are themselves relocatable. That is, the monitoring primitives should be able to track

D. Kotz and F. Mattern (Eds.): ASA/MA 2000, LNCS 1882, pp. 221–   , 2000.
© Springer-Verlag Berlin Heidelberg 2000

(possibly remote) monitored mobile objects, and they should also be migratable to remain closer to the migratable monitored components.

Second, it requires two levels of monitoring: system-level and application-level. The former kind is more commonly supported, and includes standard properties such as machine load, memory usage, average network delay between two nodes, etc. Application-level monitoring complements the former, and is less common and harder to achieve, but is clearly important for relocation. For example, it may be important to know how two remote application components use a given connection in order to determine whether or not to co-locate them.

Third, it requires a programming model that cleanly separates the encoding of relocation policies from the encoding of the application logic, since, as mentioned above, such relocations are not driven by the application logic. In fact, it is desirable to even allow the external encoding of a relocation policy after the application has been deployed. The separation between relocation and logic programming is particularly challenging given the need for application-level monitoring. It implies that a relocation policy component may need to monitor the behavior of application components and their interactions with no understanding of or access to their code.

In previous work [,] we have presented the FARGO system, which introduced a third facet of programming (in addition to application logic and relocation policies) termed *dynamic layout*. Dynamic layout allows a designer to specify various co- and re-location relationships between FARGO components that are invariant despite movement. Thus, upon an explicit movement of a certain component, the system implicitly (thus automatically) migrates other components and extends (or shrinks) inter-component references in order to comply with the relocation constraints. Two important objectives were to provide: 1. a non-intrusive programming model that decouples the encoding of the application logic from the layout rules, and 2. effective runtime support for this model.

This paper presents FARGO's support for relocation policies, similarly focusing on: 1. a decoupled programming model, and on 2. effective system support. FARGO is implemented and is freely available for download from

.

The rest of the paper is organized as follows. Section   presents an overview of FARGO. Section   presents the monitoring-based programming model. Section   contains the major contributions of this paper, including system support for application level and relocatable monitoring. Section   evaluates the monitoring overhead. Section   overviews related work, and Section   summarizes our contributions and points to future work.

2   FarGo Overview

FARGO is a Java-based platform for the development of mobile-component-based distributed applications. The system's runtime infrastructure is composed of a collection of stationary components called *cores*. Each core runs within an instance of a Java virtual machine, which in turn runs inside a single operating system process. The core can receive mobile components from other cores, execute their code inside its process, and send them to other cores.

The design and implementation of a FARGO application is divided into three, typically consequent, facets. The first facet involves the design of the application logic by defining the components of the application and their interactions. FARGO components, termed *complets* are similar to components in other frameworks, such as Java Beans [ ]. A complet is a collection of objects that perform a certain task, and is accessed through a well-defined interface object (termed *anchor*). All external references into a complet point to the anchor, and the closure of the complet is defined as the directed graph of objects and references, starting from the anchor, except for references to other anchors (i.e., other complets).

In addition to their role as ordinary components, complets define the smallest unit of relocation. Thus, all objects within the same complet instance always share an address space and all intra-complet references are local, but complets may migrate during their lifetime. Therefore, inter-complet references, (henceforth *complet references*), may at times be local and at times remote. In order to provide clean semantics for method invocation, complets are always considered remote to each other with respect to parameter passing. Thus, regular objects are passed by value along a complet reference, and complets are passed by (complet) reference. The complet programming model is similar to plain Java. In particular, complets are instantiated, referenced, and relocated using regular Java syntax and semantics, and more importantly, following closely the Java object model. This is facilitated by the FARGO stub compiler, which pre-processes objects that implement the complet interface and generates for them objects that realize the complet reference (explained in Section).

The second facet is layout programming. Layout semantics are specified on complet references. They allow a designer to state how a complet reacts to the movement of a related complet. FARGO provides various primitive reference types, similar in concept to the classification of bindings between objects as presented in [ ]. For example, the basic default type is the `link` reference, which is a remote reference that additionally keeps track of the (possibly moving) target complet. Another frequently-used type is `pull`, which means that whenever the source complet moves, the target complet automatically moves along (similar to *attachment* of one mobile object to another in Emerald [ ]). A `stamp` reference means that when the source complet relocates, a complet with an equivalent type of the original target complet should be looked-up and connected at the new location of the source complet. This is useful for linking mobile complets with stationary complets (e.g., complets that represent physical devices such as a printer). Finally, FARGO enables to change the reference semantics at runtime using a reflective reference mechanism. For more details on FARGO see [,]. The third facet, relocation policy programming, is the subject of this paper.

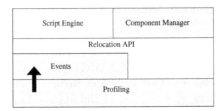

Fig. 1. Monitor Subsystem Architecture

3 Monitoring-Based Relocation Programming Model

Relocation programming is based on the monitoring subsystem, shown in Figure . The monitor consists of three layers. The bottom layer provides *profiling* services, which, upon request from applications, measures various aspects of the environment and returns the result to the caller. Profiling services may be directly accessed by the application, in which case the service is *synchronous*, or the application may access it indirectly by registering at an intermediate *event* layer, in which case the service is *asynchronous*. Since quite often relocation is driven by environmental changes that are not necessarily related to a specific application, and which are detected only over time, asynchronous notification is an important alternative to polling directly the profiling services. Finally, the top *application* layer uses the relocation API, and consists of user-defined applications and two FARGO components: A script interpreter for high-level encoding of relocation policies, and a distributed graphical utility for visually monitoring and manually managing complet relocations. The application layer is beyond the scope of this paper, however, which is focused on the lower levels (see [ ]).

3.1 Application Level Profiling

Like other profiling services (e.g., Sumatra [ ], discussed in Section), the FARGO profiler is capable of measuring various system properties, except the measured entities are at the FARGO level (e.g., complets, complet references, etc.), and the focus is on properties that are likely to impact relocation decisions. For example, the `NetworkDelay` property measures the round-trip time to send an empty message between two FARGO sites. Another example is the `CompletCount` property, which returns the number of complets that are currently hosted by a given site; together with the `CompletSize` property, the total memory usage at a given core can be estimated. For each measurable property, FARGO provides both instantaneous and continuous interfaces. The former refers to a single sampling that returns the current value of the measured resource, whereas the latter refers to periodic sampling, and the returned value represents an average of the samplings over a given interval.

In addition to this standard system profiling, FARGO provides unique *application profiling* services. Application profiling complements system profiling by measuring properties of specific (distributed) applications, thereby enabling an application to self-adapt its placement based on its own behavior. For example, the `InvocationRate` property measures the current (average) rate at which invocations are made along a reference between two complets. Combined with the `NetworkDelay` property, an application may encode the following composite relocation rule. Given two complets, α and β, that reside in sites A and B, respectively, if the invocation rate along the reference from α to β goes up beyond a certain threshold value *and* the network delay between sites A and B drops below a certain threshold value, then move β to α's site. Clearly, using only the second system condition as a relocation criterion might lead to wasteful movement if α and β happen to be in a "low-interaction" mode.

Unlike system-level profiling, application-level profiling could be implemented by the application programmer. However, this would require immense efforts and expertise on behalf of the programmer. Our goal was to provide generic support that enables applications to measure their behavior with minimal extra programming. Notice that such support is actually harder to achieve than system-level profiling, since it requires the monitor to examine the application internals at runtime, with no access to its source code. The solution to this problem is discussed in Section .

An example of continuous application-level monitoring is shown in Figure . The profiler object as obtained from the complet (as opposed to the case of system-level monitoring, whereby the single profiler is obtained from the system core), and monitoring begins by invoking the proper `start` method on the profiler and ends upon invocation of the corresponding `stop` method. At any time between those invocations, a `getAverage` method may be invoked to get the accumulated average value since the beginning of the monitoring session. The default calculated value is an exponential average that gives larger weights to more recent sampling. For more details on the profiling API, see [ ].

```
// receive a profiler for a given complet reference
Complet c = someComplet;
CompletProfiler profiler = Core.getMetaRef(c).getProfiler(metaRef);
// start continuous monitoring
profiler.startInvocationRate();
...
// get the average rate so far
int rate =  profiler.getAverageInvocationRate();
...
// stop monitoring
profiler.stopInvocationRate();
```

Fig. 2. Continuous Application-Level Profiling

3.2 Events and Filters

The profiling mechanism enables applications to examine the state of resources in a synchronous fashion. However, quite often applications need to be notified asynchronously when certain resource levels change, instead of having to continuously poll the resources. Furthermore, the polling approach might lead to excessive network overhead and consume CPU resources on the polling host. Thus, FARGO provides a distributed event mechanism (an extension of Java's event model) that enables components to be notified when changes in the system or in the application occur.

Specifically, every profiling service has a corresponding event to which complets can register to as listeners. Once registered, the system starts a profiling thread (if not already started) that monitors changes in the value of the profiled property. To avoid redundant profiling of the same property, each property is monitored by (at most) a single thread, and all listeners for the same property are effectively registered at the same profiling thread. When a change is traced by the profiling thread, an event is fired to all listeners, and each listener is invoked with a separate thread. This design enables the monitoring entity to conduct relocation operations separately from the "application" complets, although it still requires proper synchronization.

The above scheme does not take into consideration one important issue, however. If applications would be notified upon every single change, this could incur tremendous processing overhead on applications. This problem is further exacerbated in a distributed monitoring system, in which the monitoring component can be remote to the event source, incurring additional network cost for event transfer. Finally, fine-grained monitoring may be unnecessary. Indeed, as observed in [ ], mobility decisions for wide-area applications are often more effective when based on coarse-grained changes, to reduce jitter in resource levels.

The natural solution in FARGO is to augment events with *filters* that are evaluated against event contents and reduce the flow of events to listeners. Only events that pass the filter test are sent to listeners. This is similar in concept to the filtering support in the CORBA Notification service [ ], which augmented the Event service [ ] to address the problem of superfluous events at the clients.

FARGO supports both built-in and user-defined filters. An example of the former is ClassFilter, which filters events based on the class of the event object. User-defined filters are plain Java methods that are evaluated by simply invoking them with the event object as a parameter.

In addition to profile-based events, the core constantly fires non-measurable events that reflect changes in the state of the environment, including changes to the layout. For example, whenever a complet gets relocated, a CompletDepartured event is fired at the source site, and a CompletArrived event is fired at the destination site. Another example is the CoreShutdown event, which can be used to relocate complets to remote sites before the local core is shutting down, thereby keeping the application alive.

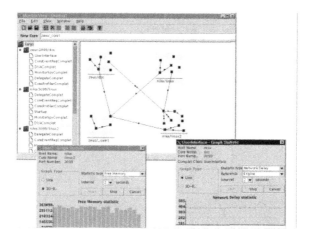

Fig. 3. The Visual Manager

3.3 High-Level Monitoring

Finally, FARGO provides two high-level facilities: a scripting language that augments the low-level API, and a graphical manager. The scripting language is event-driven, allowing to specify a set of event-action rules, with the events mapped to the lower-level events, and actions typically mapped to movement of complets. The visual manager, shown in Figure , is itself a FARGO application. It enables users to examine complets and their connections, as well as perform manual relocation operations. For example, the Figure shows four cores (the large squares at the top window), each of which is hosting several complets (the small dark squares), and the complet references that connect them.

4 System Support for Monitoring-Based Relocation

The realization of monitoring-based relocation programming model introduces the following main challenges:

1. Application-level monitoring that is decoupled from the application logic.
2. Relocatable monitoring, enabling independent relocation and remoteness of both monitoring and monitored entities, at the system and application levels.

4.1 Application Level Monitoring

Recall that application-level monitoring is difficult since it requires the monitor to examine the application internals without modifying its source and with minimum overhead. Our solution is based on intercepting access to complets through the complet reference. The structure of a complet reference is shown in Figure .

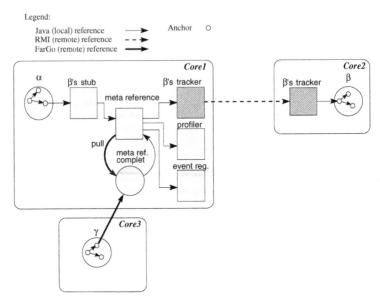

Fig. 4. Complet Reference with Meta-Ref Complet

It is generated automatically by the `fargoc` compiler, and is similar to a conventional remote reference (e.g., RMI reference), except the client-side proxy is split into two separate objects: a stub and a tracker. The stub object is pointed by the source object using a regular local reference and its interface is identical to the interface of the target complet interface object. The tracker is responsible for tracking the target complet and for actually performing invocations. The separation facilitates syntactic transparency (since the target complet is accessed as if it was local), and supports scalability, since only one tracker per target complet need to be kept in a single core.

The upper left rectangle in Figure shows a complet, α, and its exposed reference to complet β. The tiny diagrams inside α and β represent intra-complet objects that are part of their closure. β's stub has an outgoing regular (local) reference to the (local) tracker of β for passing all invocations (not shown in the Figure for clarity) and another reference to a system object called the *meta-reference*, or meta-ref for brevity.

The role of the meta-ref is to reify the reference semantics and to enable to change these semantics dynamically. It plays a key role in the monitoring design. In particular, it contains all application-level monitoring capabilities, which are encapsulated in two objects: the profiler object, which profiles access to the complet via the reference, and the event object for registering for events that are generated by the profiling results. Since every inter-complet invocation goes through the system objects that comprise the reference, profiling data can be inspected and gathered without interfering with the application's code. Returning to Figure , it can be seen how the meta-ref is used by the application to access the profiling object.

Although all monitoring services are initiated at the meta-ref, different services are performed in different objects. For example, the `InvocationRate` measurement is performed in the core of the source complet, whereas `completSize` profiling is performed in the core of the target complet, since it might be remote to the core in which the meta-ref resides.

Finally, the introspection capabilities of the complet-reference can be used to enable an application to find out what to monitor. For example, the `getOutgoing References` operation returns all outgoing references of a complet. It can be used together with `completSize` to determine whether the relocation of a complet would imply relocation of other (`Pull`) complets, and their weights.

4.2   Relocatable Monitoring

Recall that an important design objective of the monitor was to provide monitoring that is itself independent of physical location, enabling transparent relocation of both the monitor and the monitored (mobile) entities. As for system-level monitoring, the solution is simple. Since cores are stationary, they need only support remote access to them. This is achieved using a stationary complet that is generated on demand in any profiled core. The use of a complet for profiling the core provides remote access to the profiling information of any core regardless of the (current) location of the monitoring object. This is depicted in Figure by the `coreProfiler` object inside `Core2`.

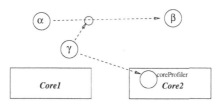

Fig. 5. Remote Profiling

Relocatable monitoring at the application level is more challenging. In the most general case, we would like one complet (e.g. complet γ in the Figure) to monitor the reference between two other complets (α and β), where each of the three complets can move independently. But since reference monitoring requires access to the internal meta-ref, this would imply that the monitoring object needs to always be co-located with the meta-ref (and hence with the source complet) because the meta-ref is a local Java object that is not accessible remotely. Such a constraint is clearly not always desirable, and is even unacceptable in cases where the monitoring complet monitors several relocatable complets (as is the case with FARGO's visual manager tool).

To address this limitation, we raised the meta-ref from a regular Java object into a (system) complet, thereby applying FARGO functionality to its own design. Thus, as a complet, the meta-ref can be accessed from remote (monitoring) complets, and relocated. However, it is desirable to bind the location of the meta-ref complet to the (re)location of the source complet, since many monitoring operations assume locality between the profiling and the profiled entities. Fortunately, this is supported in FARGO by defining a pull reference from the meta-ref object to the meta-ref complet, as shown in Figure . The meta-ref complet is actually used for all accesses to the meta-ref, for either reification or monitoring purposes. However, for regular invocations only the meta-ref object is accessed, and in fact the meta-ref complet is created only on demand, upon the first request to access the reference. The rationale behind this design is performance. By not passing through the reference complet for normal non-reflective use, several levels of indirection are avoided.

Finally, it might seem circular that a complet reference contains a complet. But since complet reference complets are created only on demand, and not upon creation of *every* complet reference, there is no such circularity. In particular, it is hardly the case that an application would want to monitor or reify a (complet) reference to a complet-reference complet. Although not impossible, it is probably not a practical use of the meta-ref complet. To summarize, the meta-ref complet enables a complet to continuously monitor another complet (through one of its incoming references) as well as monitor the reference between any two complets, while supporting independent relocation of all involved complets.

5   Evaluation of Monitoring Overhead

There are two main levels in which monitoring overhead should be discussed: the "basic" FARGO architecture as it was influenced by the need to support monitoring, and the monitoring architecture itself. As for the basic architecture, the main issue is the structure of the (compiler-generated) complet reference. Although it has been designed to address other issues too (including tracking and layout programming), the ability to intercept invocations for application-level monitoring was an important design consideration.

We evaluated the overhead method invocation along complet references through a simple benchmark, and compared FARGO to two other mobile-code systems, Voyager [ ] 3.1, and Aglets [ ] 1.0.3. The experiment was conducted using five PentiumII-400MHz PCs with 128 MB of RAM, each running Windows NT 4.0 (Service Pack 4) with Java 1.1.8. Each PC was connected to a local Ethernet network through a 10mbps interface. The invocation benchmark consisted of two remote complets, each of which invoked (empty) methods of the other one. Figure shows the average overhead of 20 invocations, where the weight correspond to the size of arguments that were passed (i.e., copied) along the invocation. FARGO outperformed Aglets but was inferior to Voyager. We believe that the reason for Voyager's advantage stems from the fact that it uses an optimized remote invocation mechanism instead of Java RMI, which is used by Aglets and FARGO. In fact, with no multi-hop tracking and when passing ordinary objects as parameters, FARGO's overhead over plain RMI was negligible. Multi-hop tracking is addressed in FARGO by using the chain-cutting technique, which reduces the hop-length to one after the first invocation (the Figure indeed shows measurements starting from the second invocation, thus not including multi-hop tracking). Overhead due to argument passing is non-negligible when the passed argument is a complet, since it involves a more expensive marshaling process, including the transmission of trackers over the network.

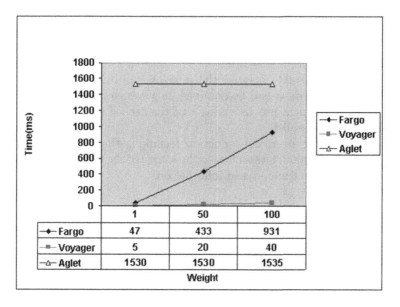

Fig. 6. Invocation Overhead

The second level in which overhead should be discussed is the monitoring architecture. First, if no monitoring features are enabled, there is no monitoring-related overhead (beyond the general structure overhead as introduced above). When monitoring is enabled, the overhead usually depends on the specific feature that is requested. In terms of space, each service maintains only few recent values for each measurements in the profiler object, and in any case all operations have a tight space bound of few kilobytes. The meta-ref complet is also a system complet with fixed size (of approximately 2K). In terms of time overhead, we distinguish between monitoring of inter-complet activities and intra-complet (single-site) activity. Two representative inter-complet activities are the application-level InvocationRate measurement and the system-level NetworkDelay measurement. The former has no overhead since it involves incrementing counters in the meta-ref. The system-level NetworkDelay measurement involves periodic "pinging" through a method invocation on a remote core. The average invocation of such operation is approximately 50msec, thus the default polling period was set to 5 seconds to retain the overhead below 1%.

Another important transport-related overhead concerns the meta-ref complet. Recall that our solution to remote monitoring (shown in Figure) was based on adding a meta-ref complet and attaching it with a `pull` reference to the internal meta-ref object. This means that every movement of a source complet incurs an overhead for pulling the meta-ref complet, in the order of hundreds milliseconds. However, the meta-ref complet is generated only when monitoring is requested from a remote core. Otherwise, no such complet gets generated.

The overhead of intra-complet measurements is typically directly related to the structure of the specific complet. A representative operation is CompletSize. It involves serialization of the complet and returning the size of of the serialized object. This might be an expensive operation, but unfortunately there are no better ways to obtain this value, since unlike inter-complet measurements, no interception is possible because the references are normal Java references. A significant improvement can be obtained, however, by caching previous measurements for subsequent use, assuming that the cached value approximates the current size of the complet.

Finally, recall the overhead reduction technique that FARGO provides by enabling to deploy remote filters close to the source of the event, thereby avoiding unnecessary transfer of unmatched information.

6   Related Work

Numerous frameworks for programming mobile distributed systems were developed in recent years, including Aglets [ ], Concordia [ ], Mole [ ], and Voyager [ ]. To the best of our knowledge, the only mobile object system besides FARGO that provides monitoring of distributed applications for relocation purposes is Sumatra [ ]. There are major differences between FARGO's monitor facilities and Sumatra's. Both Sumatra and FARGO monitor network latencies and resource use. FARGO goes one step ahead, however, and monitors also application specific attributes. As shown earlier, the ability to profile the application, for example to measure its use of a given link (as opposed to overall system profiling) may be crucial in determining component relocation.

Like Sumatra, FARGO supports both on-demand monitoring as well as continuous monitoring. Both systems give the application the choice between polling the monitor and getting notified asynchronously. In Sumatra the notification service is based on platform-specific UNIX signals while in FARGO we used a distributed event model which gives movement flexibility to the notified object as well as to the monitored object.

Unlike Sumatra, FARGO measures network latencies between complets, not between sites. This enables continuous measurement of the latencies between two components even if the components are migrating during the monitoring process. Thus, an application can get sense of the latencies between the components over time regardless of relocation of its components.

In Sumatra, relocation policies can be encoded only using an API. FARGO includes, in addition to the API, a Java-like event model that maps monitoring results and a high-level scripting language with the capability to attach layout scripts to active applications. Although Sumatra is also Java-based, unlike FARGO most of its monitoring support in implemented natively, either by changes to the JVM, or by external non-Java processes that intimately interact with the operating system using Unix-specific mechanisms (e.g. Unix sockets). While this approach has several advantages, e.g., supporting strong mobility from the interior of the (modified) JVM, it implies that Sumatra is non-portable. In contrast, FARGO supports weak mobility, but the entire core of FARGO including its monitoring layer, is completely implemented over standard JVM, which makes it large-scale deployment more feasible.

7   Conclusions and Future Work

Programming relocation policies for distributed components that execute in dynamically changing environments require monitoring facilities, both at the application and at the environment levels. A separation between the application logic and the relocation policy is desirable to enable the programmer to focus on each aspect separately. But keeping the relocation policy inside the application is also crucial when the logic of the application may impact relocation decisions. FARGO reconciles this conflict by enabling to monitor the internals of the application, but without requiring access to the source code, hence supporting syntactic transparency. The programming model is similar to conventional Java programming, while allowing sophisticated layout programming and monitoring-based relocation with orthogonal interfaces. Another unique contribution of this work is relocatable monitoring, which further enables monitoring and monitored entities to freely relocate while monitoring is in progress.

There are several future directions. We intend to extend the monitoring service by adding the capability to test the possible outcome of a layout change without actually performing the change by means of built-in simulations. Another enhancement is the capability to record layouts persistently such that later the core could be ordered to apply a last known "good" layout to an application that was restarted. Finally, we are investigating the integration of our work on security mechanisms for relocatable component [,], with monitoring-based relocation policies.

Acknowledgments

This research is supported by the Israeli Ministry of Science, Basic Infrastructure Fund, Project 9762. We would like to thank Boris Lavva for invaluable discussions and advice throughout the project. Idan Zach and Udi Shitrit have implemented the graphical monitor. Yoad Gidron is working on adaptive resource negotiation and allocation schemes. Tamir Ronen is working on a location-independent naming-scheme. Miki Abu is working on multi-threading and concurrency, and Yaron Weinsberg is working with us on disconnected operation and persistence schemes.

References

1. A. Acharya, M. Ranganathan, and J. Saltz. Sumatra: A language for resource-aware mobile programs. In *Mobile Object Systems: Towards the Programmable Internet*, pages 111–130. Springer-Verlag, April 1997. Lecture Notes in Computer Science No. 1222.   ,
2. A. Black. Fine-grained mobility in the emerald system. *ACM Transactions on Computer Systems*, 6(1):109–133, February 1988.
3. F. Douglis and J. Ousterhout. Process migration in the sprite operating system. In *Proceedings of the 7th International Conference on Distributed Computing Systems*, pages 18–25, Berlin, Germany, September 1987.
4. A. Fuggetta, G. P. Picco, and G. Vigna. Understanding Code Mobility. *IEEE Transactions on Software Engineering*, 24(5):342–361, May 1998.
5. H. Gazit. Monitoring-based dynamic relocation of components. Master's thesis, Technion — Israel Institute of Technology, August 2000.   ,
6. Y. Gidron, I. Ben-Shaul, and Y. Aridor. Dynamic configuration and enforcement of access control for mobile components. In *Proceedings of the 4th International Workshop on Next Generation Information Technologies and Systems (NGITS'99)*, Zikhron Yaakov, Israel, July 1999. to appear.
7. Y. Gidron, I. Ben-Shaul, Y. Aridor, and O. Holder. Dynamic configuration of access control for mobile components in fargo. 2000. Accepted for Publication.

8. Object Management Group. Event service specification.
   ftp://www.omg.org/pub/docs/formal/97-12-11.pdf.
9. Object Management Group. Notification service specification.
   ftp://ftp.omg.org/pub/docs/telecom/99-07-01.pdf.
10. O. Holder, I. Ben-Shaul, and H. Gazit. Dynamic layout of distributed applications in FarGo. In *Proceedings of the 21st International Conference on Software Engineering (ICSE'99)*, pages 403–411, Los Angeles, CA, May 1999.   ,
11. O. Holder, I. Ben-Shaul, and H. Gazit. System support for dynamic layout of distributed applications. In *Proceedings of the 19th International Conference on Distributed Computing Systems (ICDCS'99)*, pages 163–173, Austin, TX, May 1999.
    ,
12. D. B. Lange and D. T. Chang. IBM Aglets Workbench: Programming mobile agents in Java. A white paper. Technical report, IBM, Tokyo Research Lab, September 1996. Available at   .   ,
13. Mitsubishi Electric ITA Horizon Systems Laboratory. Concordia: An infrastructure for collaborating mobile agents. In *Proceedings of the First International Workshop on Mobile Agents (MA '97)*, Berlin, April 1997.
14. ObjectSpace Voyager core package: Technical overview, December 1997. Available at   .
    ,
15. M. Ranganathan, A. Acharya, S. Sharma, and J. Saltz. Network-aware mobile programs. In *Proceedings of USENIX*, 1997.

16. M. Straßer, J. Baumann, and F. Hohl. Mole — A Java based mobile object system. In *Proceedings of the 2nd ECOOP Workshop on Mobile Object Systems*, Linz, Austria, July 1996.

17. Sun Microsystems, Inc. *JavaBeans Specification Version 1.01*, July 1997. Available at :   .

Agent-Based Negotiations for Multi-provider Interactions

Monique Calisti and Boi Faltings

Laboratoire d'Intelligence Artificielle
Swiss Federal Institute of Technology (EPFL)
CH-1015 Lausanne, Switzerland.
Tel. +41 21 6936677, Fax. +41 21 6935225
{calisti,faltings}@lia.di.epfl.ch

Abstract. A particular challenging area where agent technology is increasingly applied is the Communication Networks field. As networks become increasingly complex, hard to manage and control the ideal of a distributed, intelligent network management and control system is becoming more and more of a necessity. This paper concentrates on the allocation of service demands spanning network domains owned and controlled by distinct operators. In particular, the focus is on an agent-based solution that has been defined in order to allow automatic *intra-domain* resource allocation and *inter-domain* negotiations between peer operators. Self-interested agents interact in order to define consistent end-to-end routes that satisfy Quality of Service requirements, network resources availability and utility's maximisation.

1 Introduction

Recently, many researchers have been investigating the potential of introducing autonomous software agents for distributing *communication network control* and *management* tasks. Even though for an effective deployment of agents within communication networks several obstacles need to be overcome [ ], the increasing availability of agent-based development tools and agents' standards [ ], [ ] is accelerating this process. Furthermore, experimental results evaluating the deployment of agents and their integration within real frameworks represent one of the most effective ways of building confidence in agent technology.

The *Network Provider Interworking* (NPI) paradigm is an agent-based approach for the allocation of service demands spanning distinct providers networks, i.e., networks under the control of different operators [ ]. Nowadays, the world-wide communication infrastructure is a network of domains controlled by self-interested authorities, therefore, carrying traffic across multiple domains usually requires cooperation of several operators. In particular, when traffic has to satisfy Quality of Service (QoS) requirements, this leads to even more complex negotiation problems. Currently, multi-provider cooperation is regulated by

D. Kotz and F. Mattern (Eds.): ASA/MA 2000, LNCS 1882, pp. 235–   , 2000.
© Springer-Verlag Berlin Heidelberg 2000

fixed long-term agreements. In the future, increasingly dynamic network protocols will make it possible to negotiate and implement agreements at very short time scales. Based on this assumption, the NPI architecture provides a flexible and efficient paradigm for automated inter-domain negotiations. After the conceptual definition of a new formalism to represent the multi-provider service demand allocation as a *Distributed Constraint Satisfaction Problem* (DCSP), and the development of specific algorithms for a consistent end-to-end routing [ ], the *NPI-multi agent simulator* (NPI-mas) [ ] has been implemented. In this context a service demand is specified in terms of source node, destination node and QoS requirements. Whenever the source and destination nodes belong to distinct networks, distinct Network Provider Agents (NPAs) acting on behalf of human operators, need to coordinate their actions and negotiate in order to select a unique end-to-end connection satisfying all QoS requirements.

This paper concentrates on the negotiation process that enables the inter-domain coordination among distinct networks. By describing the infrastructure of the simulator and by showing how the NPI paradigm could support humans, the aim is to prove the potential of negotiating agents for a more effective allocation of Telecom and IP services. The conceptual arguments are validated by experimental results. This concrete evaluation is a preliminary step in proving that it is not only possible, but also desirable to integrate agent technology within existing network infrastructures. However, the main limit of this work is in the lack of more realistic data for evaluating more precisely the impact of the NPI techniques in a real scenario. Furthermore, pricing mechanisms need more work to determine stable network providers' coalitions.

Section introduces some background in multi-provider management, presents the NPI paradigm and describes the simulator's structure. Section focuses on agents' interactions and some of the main concrete challenges encountered for the implementation of the NPI-mas system. Experimental results obtained by simulation are reported in Section , where the NPI-mas system is also evaluated vis-a-vis of other solutions. Section concludes the paper with final remarks and comments about ongoing work.

2   The Multi-provider Framework

Today, many aspects of inter-domain networks' interactions are statically fixed by long-term contracts, and many steps of the interaction are regulated by human operators via fax, e-mail, etc. Boundary network resources are allocated according to what established in these contracts and depending on the underlying technology, specific signalling techniques are used for establishing physical interconnectivity. This makes the overall coordination process very slow and inefficient. The inefficiency is mainly due to the difficulty humans have considering aspects which complicate the interworking process: an increasing number of actors with different roles from those of the traditional Telecom operators, the use of different and heterogeneous technologies and the need to map between intra- and inter-domain management aspects.

In order to overcome such limitations and improve the multi-provider service demand allocation, a distributed agent-based paradigm has been defined. Autonomous software entities representing customers, service and network providers have the potential of accelerating many steps of the interworking by automating many intra- and inter-domain resource allocation tasks and negotiation steps. Agents use DCSP [ ] techniques to find the space of possible routes for a given traffic demand, thus creating a concise representation of all possible routes. This set provides the basis for subsequent negotiation about which specific route to select and which price to fix.

2.1   The NPI Paradigm

The NPI paradigm supplies a set of procedures and interaction protocols to achieve connectivity across several domains independently on the under-laying network technology. The main goal is to provide a *network-to-network operator* paradigm for improving multi-provider interactions. Figure   shows the conceptual model behind the NPI approach. A final end-user is represented by an *End User Agent* (EUA) that can contact one or several *Service Provider Agents* (SPAs). Every SPA can then contact one or several *Network Provider Agents* (NPAs). Whenever a service demand spans multiple network domains, several NPAs must coordinate their actions. A final end-user specifies a service demand

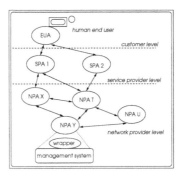

Fig. 1. The NPI conceptual model: an agent-based service provisioning scenario

through a graphical user interface. The service demand requirements are then interpreted by the EUA, that can contact one or several SPAs. An SPA represents both the client of the network services offered by the NPAs and the provider of a variety of telecommunications services to customers. The SPA acts as a (currently very simple) *matchmaker*, finding suitable agents (NPAs), and accessing them on behalf of the requesting agent (EUA). In the future, this entity will be enhanced by introducing more sophisticated *brokering* and *recruiting* capabilities. Every network provider is represented by a distinct NPA. Distributed NPAs have to coordinate their actions whenever demands span several domains, since all knowledge about network topologies and resources availability cannot be gathered into one agent. First of all, collecting information about a problem implies communication costs and it can become very inefficient or even impossible for scalability reasons. Furthermore, a centralised structure would lack robustness, since any kind of failure damaging the centralised control unit would compromise the whole system. Finally, collecting all the information into one agent is not always feasible because of security and privacy limitations.

2.2   The NPI-mas Simulator Structure

The NPI-mas simulator is entirely implemented in Java. JATLite has been adopted as the main framework for the agent development. There are 3 main components. The *Agent Management Interface* (AMI) is a graphical interface that allows the selection of a multi-domain scenario, the creation of agents, and the visualisation of simulations' outputs. The *agents' community* consists of several EUAs, SPAs and NPAs. In particular, a distinct NPA is associated with every network provider in the simulated scenario. The *router* receives messages from all the registered agents and routes them to the correct recipient.

The Agent Communication Language (ACL) currently deployed by NPI agents is KQML [ ], since KQML facilities are integrated within JATLite. In order to increase the potential of the NPI-mas paradigm, we developed communication facilities for FIPA ACL to be used within JATLite. FIPA ACL is in fact gaining more and more consensus in the agent community since it has a stronger semantic basis than KQML. Concerning the knowledge representation, we have focused on Virtual Private Network (VPN) services and the VPN-cl content language that allows the representation of objects, propositions and actions has been developed. For portability and re-usability reasons, the syntax of the VPN-cl language has been defined in XML. The common *ontology*, i.e., the *VPN-ontology*, that all NPI agents implicitly refer to, collects terms and definitions such as *connections, services, offers, service level agreements, quality-of-service*, etc. In the current VPN-ontology specification, the definitions are not strictly dependent on any specific network technology. An IP oriented version of the ontology, that is based on the Differentiated Services framework [ ], is currently under development.

First of all, the AMI enables the selection of a randomly generated network environment and the creation of all the agents populating it. Each agent automatically registers its identity with the *router*. In addition, every NPA recovers the data describing the network topology from dedicated *management information databases*. From the AMI, a text window displays the simulation outputs such as the computed end-to-end paths from the source to the destination net-

---

[1] JATLite is a set of packages that facilitates the agent framework development using Java. On-line documentation can be found at: http://piano.stanford.edu/.

[2] More details can be found at http://liawww.epfl.ch/~calisti/ACL-LITE/.

[3] More details about the *VPN-cl* content language and the *VPN-ontology* can be found at: http://liawww.epfl.ch/~calisti/ACL-LITE/VPN/.

work, the results of intermediate steps of the demand allocation process and final negotiation outcomes.

The Internal NPA Structure. Since the main goal of our simulator is to make use of algorithms and techniques designed for the inter-domain QoS-based routing, the focus is on the development of Network Provider Agents. For an NPA the perceptions or input can be either messages coming from other agents or human user commands. The *central controller* is a fundamental NPA's component responsible for the coordination of several parallel activities, for processing inputs, for interfacing the agent world with human operators, for getting data characterising the network state. In our simulated scenario, the data is stored in a database that is dynamically updated during the simulation. In a real network, the data would be retrieved directly from the network management platform through the use of ad hoc wrappers. The NPA *communicator module* parses agents' messages, maintains communication channels, controls and manages all ongoing conversations. The NPA *CSP expert* is a specialised sub-structure responsible for DCSP modelling and for applying typical DCSP consistency and searching techniques. The NPA *negotiator module* generates strategies for the controller. Considering the current state of the network, the various constraints, the utility function and the interaction protocol, this module produces the strategy to be followed at every step of the negotiation process. Possible outputs of the NPA activity are either ACL messages to other agents, or internal actions, such as changes in the data configuration, or presentation of options to human operators.

3   Agent-Based Interactions

Ongoing agent conversations expect certain message sequences, which are fixed by the *interaction protocols*. In NPI-mas, agents make use of specific standard FIPA protocols, e.g., *fipa-request* [ ], and more specific negotiation protocols that we have designed. Considering to bypass the SPA entity, since at the current stage of the NPI-mas development it is mainly acting as a proxy agent that forwards messages, two main agent interactions are considered in the following: the *EUA-to-NPA* and the *NPA-to-NPA* relationships (see Figure   for a compact representation).

3.1   EUA-to-NPA Interaction

The EUA receives inputs and commands from the end user mainly through a graphical interface. This information is used to build a *user profile* and to formulate specific service demands for network providers. These kinds of functionalities require two main sub-modules: a *User Dialogue Management Service*, UDMS, and a *User Personalisation Service*, UPS [ ]. The UDMS wraps the graphical interface allowing to translate from/to a human language to/from an ACL. The UPS maintains a user model and supports its construction either by accepting

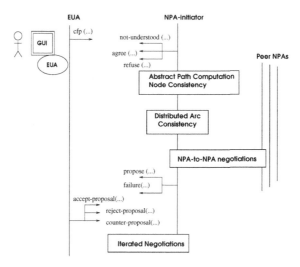

Fig. 2. A schematic summary of the main NPI-mas agents interactions

explicit information about the user or by learning from observations of the user's behaviour.

- Every time an end user formulates a service demand the associated EUA generates a *call for proposal* message for network providers. Specific *negotiation parameters*, such as negotiation protocol, timeout, budget, strategy, etc., can be introduced. Part of this information determines the *agent's behaviour* that will be followed during the negotiation with an NPA.
- The NPA that first receives a *call for proposal* for a multi-provider service demand, contacts one or several peer NPAs. Parallel bi-lateral negotiations can be started. This allows the definition of a unique global end-to-end route that will be offered under certain conditions to the EUA (see next Section).
- Based on the negotiation behaviour that has been selected and on the internal *negotiation strategy*, the EUA examines the offers coming from the NPA. First of all, the EUA verifies that the offers have been received on time, i.e., within a given timeout. Then, the *evaluation function* allows the computation of a *score* associated with every received offer. Next, the *interpretation module* processes the score for deciding if an offer is *acceptable* or *unacceptable*. If one or several acceptable offers exist, the one maximising the EUA's utility is selected.
- If one or several acceptable offers exist, the one maximising the EUA's utility is selected. The EUA accepts the NPA's proposal and concludes the negotiation by sending an *accept-proposal* message to the NPA. If all offers are unacceptable, the EUA's reaction depends on which negotiation protocol governs

---

[4] As already mentioned before, for brevity's sake, the SPA is bypassed in this description.

the interaction between the EUA and the NPA. (1) If no counter-offers are possible, the EUA can decide whether accepting or not the *unacceptable* offer by relaxing or not some service demand requirements, or by eventually increasing the budget for that specific service. (2) If counter-offers are possible a *counter-proposal function* generates a *counter-offer* that is sent to the NPA. Several counter-proposals from both negotiating agents can occur, if the negotiation protocol allows further iterations.

- When a NPA receives a counter-offer, an *evaluation function* and an *interpretation method* are used for deciding how to proceed. Eventually, peer NPAs are further contacted in order to refine the end-to-end offer for the EUA.

3.2 NPA-to-NPA Interactions

- Every NPA has an *aggregated* view of the multi-domain network topology, that is referred when computing the abstract paths. An *abstract path* is an ordered list of distinct providers' networks between the source and the destination network, without any pre-selected access point. The NPA that first receives a call for proposal for allocating a service demand d_k is called *initiator*. The computation and the selection of a specific abstract path P are based on the Dijkstra's algorithm and on the use of heuristics that take into account both demand requirements and network utilisation [ ].
- Next, the *initiator* requests all NPA agents along the abstract path P to locally determine the set of possible internal routes for allocating d_k. This means that every NPA checks internal resource availability and determines the intra-domain or *node* consistency. The protocol used for this interaction is the *fipa-request* [ ].
- If all providers are locally consistent, i.e., at least one local feasible route for allocating the service demand exists, the *initiator* starts the *arc consistency* phase. During this step, all involved NPAs exchange information about inter-domain constraints. All incompatible network access points are discarded, so that every NPA reduces the set of possible local routes to allocate d_k. This process implies a propagation of messages among neighbours, in order to revise the set of possible local routes for every access point that has been discarded because of inter-domain constraints.
- If the arc consistency is successful, i.e., all NPAs have a non empty set of local routes consistent with inter-domain constraints, the negotiation for selecting a specific end-to-end route takes place. The *initiator* starts parallel bi-lateral negotiations with every NPA along P. Every contacted NPA elaborates an offer consisting of a specific local route with certain characteristics at a fixed price.
- The *initiator* evaluates all received offers and elaborates possible global end-to-end offers for the end-user. During this computation, pricing mechanisms and utility maximisation guide the *initiator*. The NPA-to-EUA negotiation is successful if the global offer is accepted by the EUA (several iterating counter-proposals can be exchanged). The *initiator* confirms to the NPAs the results of the transition. If the negotiation fails and the end-user does

not modify its requirements the demand request is rejected and the initiator notifies all other NPAs.

3.3   Agents Interactions Facilities

Standard problems that developers encounter when implementing agents concern *naming and addressing* issues, *agent communication* facilities (including *message transport* and *message encoding*), *coordination*, usually supplied through the use of standard interaction protocols, *integration* of agents with non-agent components, etc. The use of JATLite simplified our tasks concerning the transport of messages: the *router* is delivering messages to the appropriate recipient by using addressing tables and TCP/IP sockets. Message routing is based upon the use of agents' identifiers (the router verifies their uniqueness at the agent's registration). Further challenges encountered during the NPI-mas implementation are closely related to the integration of market-based techniques for Telecom service provisioning purposes.

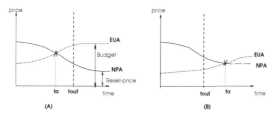

Fig. 3. If the price curves of the NPA and EUA agents converge before the timeout expiration (tout), the negotiation terminates with an agreement (case (A)). The negotiation fails either if $Resellprice > Budget$ or if the price curves do not converge before the timeout expiration, i.e., $ta > tout$ (case (B))

At the agent communication level there are three main needs to consider: the deployment of a known *agent communication language*, the use of a common *content language* and the implicit or explicit reference to a common ontology. **The solution:** Currently, by default, NPI agents make use of KQML, but they could optionally decide to adopt FIPA ACL. This double choice increases the potential interoperability of NPI agents with agents developed in other frameworks. For the specific field our application is targeting, the content language that is used is the *VPN-cl*. The design and the development of this language aim to: (1) collect the most recurrent and strategic *objects*, *actions* and *propositions* needed by agents negotiating for Telecom service provisioning, (2) provide a language with a semantic which is coherent with the current Telecom and IP specifications and that is compliant with the semantic of the ACL used by agents, (3) deploy a flexible and efficient syntax for the concrete language encoding, namely the XML syntax. Finally, terms and definitions that are implicitly referred or explicitly used during agent conversations, belong to the *VPN-ontology*. The specification currently in use is quite generic, i.e., not dependent on any specific network technology, but its expressiveness is capable to support the NPI paradigm.

Agent interaction protocols should appropriately reflect economic transactions, but this is not always trivial to achieve in virtual environments. Timing rules and policies can be difficult to implement and important communication overheads, that increase as the number of agents scales up, can take place. Furthermore, even though a number of well-known game theory, auction theory, and bargaining mechanisms in the economic field promise to find optimal solutions, this is not always feasible in real systems because of the limited rationality of software entities and the limited amount of computational resources. **The solution:** The guarantee that all negotiations will terminate is given by the deployment of *timeouts* [ ]. Furthermore, given that the sets of NPAs' feasible offers are finite and discrete (since network resources are finite) the possible iterations, i.e., counter-proposals, are also finite. For terminating a negotiation with an agreement, buyers and sellers utility functions should converge before the timeout expiration (Figure , case (A)). For this reason, both EUA and NPA agents take into account the time left before the timeout expiration in order to modify their attitude when making or evaluating an offer [ ]. They, become in principle, more conciliatory when the timeout is about to expire. However, NPAs further deploy *resource dependent* techniques, i.e., mechanisms that verify the current network resource utilisation. Furthermore, a dynamic modification of the NPA's utility function can occur, taking into account concurrent incoming demands for the same network resources.

4 Simulation Results

The performance metrics that have been observed for evaluating the NPI-mas paradigm and the DCSP-based techniques are the average demand allocation time, T_{tot}, and the allocation rate, $A_r := nbsuccess/nbdemands$, with $nbsuccess$ the number of demands successfully allocated, and $nbdemands$ the total number of service demands generated by the EUAs. Simulations with a variable number N_D of networks (Figure), and therefore of NPAs , have been run in order to check the scalability of our algorithms and in parallel the usability of communicating agents for the multi-provider service allocation purpose.

The average values that has been obtained for T_{tot}, i.e., [25, 40] seconds, can be considered a positive result when compared to the current delays required by human operators to negotiate solutions and topology changes. Given a fixed number N_D of providers' networks, we then tested the influence of a different number $|L|$ of inter-domain links. Increasing $|L|$ has a double effect: (1) The complexity of the solving process increases by augmenting the number of possible access points combinations between neighbour networks, therefore T_{tot} increases, see Figure . However, the increment of T_{tot} is smaller than 1/3, since

---

[5] In our simulations $N_D \in [4, 15]$, which correspond to a realistic multi-provider environment. However, we are testing the NPI paradigm for greater values of N_D.

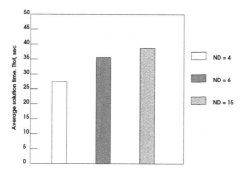

Fig. 4. Three different simulated scenarios have been considered. T_{tot} has been computed over a set of 300 randomly generated demands

the addition of new links does necessarily increases the search space for all service demand allocations. (2) The probability that at least one end-to-end path satisfying the QoS requirements of demands to be allocated exists augments so that A_r increases, see Figure . Adding $1/3$ of $|L|$ does not lead to an equivalent increment of A_r, since new links do not always facilitate the allocation for all possible service demands.

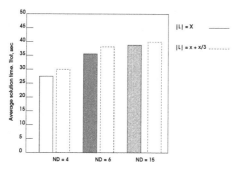

Fig. 5. T_{tot} increases when increasing the number of inter-domain links, since the search space become larger

Similar results have been obtained when varying the complexity of the internal topology of every network. A greater number of network nodes and intra-domain links can augment the search space and introduce an additional computational overhead. However, similarly to the augmentation of $|L|$, if the topological changes correspond to an increment of available network resources, the number of demands successfully allocated increases.

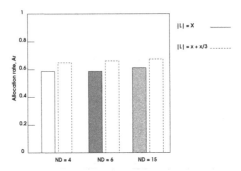

Fig. 6. The graphic shows the increment of demands successfully allocated, when increasing the inter-domain capacity

4.1 Evaluation of the NPI Paradigm

In the networking community, several bodies have already considered various problems in the area of the multi-provider network management. The Telecommunication Management Network (TMN) architecture [ ] defines conceptual layers that address different needs to the organisation of a provider's operations. In particular, there are different *reference points* that can exist between the different types of functional units and between functional units inside and outside of the same organisational domain. The reference points provide the support for building interfaces between specific functional units. More specifically, distinct network operators exchange limited information concerning boundary network elements through the TMN-X interface [ ]. Another major contribution is given by the *Telecommunications Information Networking Architecture Consortium*, TINA-C. The *Layer Network Coordinator*, LNC, is an object responsible for interconnecting termination points in a subnetwork defined as a domain. If several domains need to interconnect to each other the horizontal communication between LNCs is called federation [ ]. However, in face of the today's growing and changing technology requirements these low level interfaces are becoming increasingly inadequate. For this reason, the TMForum is giving contributions in this direction with the "SMART-TMN". In particular the work is on supplying: the customer-to-provider interface, the service provider-to-service provider interface and the service provider-to-network operator interface. However, the network-to-network operator interface is still not properly considered and this is where NPI-mas aims to bring innovative contributions.

In parallel with the work done by the networking community, several agent-based paradigms for routing multimedia traffic over distributed networks have been conceived and/or developed. FIPA envisaged the *Network Management* scenario as a main agent application field [ ]. However, FIPA documentation gives the basic guidelines about the functionalities that software entities should provide, but the details of how to integrate different agents and to improve the service provisioning process with intelligent techniques, i.e. coordination, collaboration etc., is left to application developers. The FACTS project addressed many of these issues, but did not consider dynamic provider-to-provider negotiations. *Nakamura et al.* [   ] consider more in detail pricing and accounting mechanisms for connection-less services requiring QoS guarantees. In their framework, the provider who first receives a demand computes the end-to-end route until the destination node, i.e., all intermediate nodes and access points to be crossed are pre-selected. This implies that every provider has a detailed view of all neighbour domains details. It is not clear if this kind of approach is scalable or not. Secondly, no dynamic negotiation about different local routes can take place, therefore it is not clear if utility and resource utilisation could be dynamically optimised inside every network. *Stamoulis et al.* [   ] have built an agent-based paradigm very similar to the NPI architecture, but the main difference concerns the *inter-domain protocol.* They assume that long-term bilateral agreements exist between neighbour networks to establish the amount of aggregated traffic that is supposed to be routed through pre-designed access points. A *Bandwidth Broker* agent controls how to optimise intra-domain resource allocation, so that inter-domain aggregated level of traffic is respected, but there is no way to influence or dynamically modify the inter-domain routing.

NPI-mas has the potential to speed up multi-provider service demands allocations. Agents could either support human decisions, or, in a more future scenario, replace human operators. The approach enables dynamic inter-domain transactions and parallel intra-domain optimisation processes. Moreover, by using DCSP technique, it is possible to calculate consistent solutions without the need of revealing internal and confidential data (such as network topologies, negotiation strategies, pricing mechanisms) [ ]. During service provisioning, agents only exchange constraints' details, which are used to prune out local inconsistent solutions. Off-line, agents periodically exchange aggregated information about *boundary resources*, i.e., access points and inter-domain resources. The NPI approach, by means of common and standardised agent communication languages facilities, supplies a standard middle-ware layer that provides an abstracted view of low-level technical details. Finally, NPI agents can negotiate about more than one path at a time: *constraint* agents can in fact offer a set of solutions by simply expressing all the constraints over their variables domains.

5   Conclusion

This paper describes the structure of an agent-based simulator for the allocation of multi-provider demands and focuses on agents interactions. The experimental results obtained so far prove the potential of the NPI-mas paradigm and can be considered as a valuable contribution for several reasons. First of all, they concretely show the potential of deploying agent technology in communication networks and secondly despite the lack of more realistic data, they give a rough estimate of NPI performance. Moreover, the integration of specific economic techniques within software agents increases the chance of an efficient electronic

---

[6] http://www.labs.bt.com/profsoc/facts

commerce of both Telecommunication services and IP bandwidth. Finally, auxiliary components of the NPI-mas simulator, such as the *VPN-cl* content language and the *VPN-ontology*, can potentially be reused in other frameworks by other researchers and agent developers. Those components are in fact completely independent on the NPI paradigm. In parallel, the work done so far also revealed some major limits of our solution. First, the need of developing ad hoc wrappers for integrating agents with specific network management platforms, that could be potentially quite complex. Second, considering an high number of parallel incoming demands more sophisticated reservation mechanisms need to be defined in order to ensure the availability of network resources for those demands that are successfully negotiated.

Beyond more realistic simulations and more exhaustive data analysis, several directions are currently under investigation: the introduction of more complete and realistic representations of networking data and multi-provider service demands, the development of more sophisticated pricing mechanisms based on the creation of stable NPAs coalitions.

References

1. M. Calisti and B. Faltings. A multi-agent paradigm for the Inter-domain Demand Allocation process. *DSOM'99, Tenth IFIP/IEEE International Workshop on Distributed Systems: Operations and Management*, 1999.
2. M. Calisti, C. Frei, and B. Faltings. A distributed approach for QoS-based multi-domain routing. *AiDIN'99, AAAI-Workshop on Artificial Intelligence for Distributed Information Networking*, 1999.
3. P. Faratin, C. Sierra, and N. R. Jennings. Negotiation decision functions for autonomous agents. *Int. Journal of Robotics and Autonomous Systems*, 24(3-4):159–182, 1998.
4. Tim Finin. Specification of the KQML Agent-Communication Language – plus example agent policies and architectures, 1993.
5. Fipa. Agent communication language, specification 97, part 2. *Foundation for Intelligent Physical Agents*, 1997.
6. Fipa. Specification 97, v2.0. *Foundation for Intelligent Physical Agents*, 1997.
7. Fipa. Human-agent interaction, specification 98, part 8. *Foundation for Intelligent Physical Agents*, 1998.
8. Foundation for Intelligent Physical Agents. Specifications, 1997. http://www.fipa.org/spec/.
9. A. Hopson and R. Janson. Deployment scenarios for interworking. Engineering Notes TP_AJH.001_0.10_94, TINA-C, 1995.
10. ITU-T, editor. *ITU-T Recommendation Principles for a Telecommunications management network, M3010*. Genf, 1996.
11. S. Kraus and J. Wilkenfeld. Multiagent negotiation under time constraints. Technical Report CS 2649, Institute for Advanced Computer Studies, University of Maryland, 1993.
12. T. Li and Y. Rekhter. RFC 2430: RA provider architecture for differentiated services and traffic engineering (PASTE), October 1998. Status: INFORMATIONAL.

13. S. Murthy and A. Vernekar. TMN-Based Interoperability Administration Interface. *Journal of Network and System Management*, 3(2):217–227, 1995.
14. M. Nakamura, M. Sato, and T. Hamada. A Pricing and Accounting Architecture for QoS Guaranteed Services on a Multi-Domain Network. In *Proceedings of GLOBECOM'99, Global Telecommunication Conference*, pages 1984–1988, 1999.

15. OMG. http://www.omg.org.
16. G. D. Stamoulis, D. Kalopsikakis, and A. Kirikoglou. Efficient-Based Negotiation for Telecommunication Services. In *Proceedings of GLOBECOM'99, Global Telecommunication Conference*, pages 1989–1996, 1999.
17. S. Willmott and M. Calisti. An Agent Future for Network Control? *Swiss Journal of Computer Science (Informatik/Informatique)*, 2000(1), January 2000.
18. M. Yokoo, E. H. Durfee, T. Ishida, and K. Kuwabara. Distributed Constraint Satisfaction for Formalising Distributed Problem Solving. *Proceedings 12th IEEE International Conference on Distributed Computing Systems.*, pages 614–621, 1992.

Modeling Soccer-Robots Strategies through Conversation Policies

Pierre-Yves Oudeyer[1] and Jean-Luc Koning[2]

[1] Sony CSL Paris
6 rue Amyot, 75005 Paris, France
[2] Leibniz-Esisar
50 rue Laffemas - BP 54, 26902 Valence cedex 9, France
http://www-leibniz.imag.fr/MAGMA/People/koning/koning.html

Abstract. Straightforward approaches to team coordination with the expressive power of finite state automata are doomed to fail under a wide range of heterogeneity due to the combinatorial explosion of states. In this paper we propose a coordination scheme based on operational semantics, which allows an extremely compact and modular way of specifying soccer-robot team behaviors. The capabilities of our approach are demonstrated on two examples, which, though just being simple demo implementations, perform very well in a simulator tournament.

1   Soccer Strategies as Interaction Protocols

Building a strategy for a team of soccer-robots amounts to specifying the overall system's intention as far as its operational mode. A strategy encompasses general goals and features one may want to see arise during the course of a game, especially the main goal of winning the game. This naturally impacts on the robots cooperation/coordination.

In the multiagent system community communication and coordination issues are typically addressed by means of interaction protocols that give more or less flexible guidelines to the agents in their communication with each other [ ]. Given its knowledge bases, what it perceives from its outside world and the possible messages it gets from teammates, an agent communicates with others both through message passing (direct communication) and modification of the world (indirect communication). In the former case, where messages are exchanged, interaction protocols are referred to as *conversation policies* [ ]. The aim of these policies is to impose a number of constraints over what agents may say, interpret or do during a conversation. This paper presents a formalism, called POS (*Protocol Operational Semantics*), that allows, among other things, for the description of these conversational constraints as well as their implementation since it is also a universal computational model. Thus, the description of conversation policies will be the main aspect presented in this paper, but POS also allows for the description of coordination policies that are not conversations (example of section   shows such an example).

D. Kotz and F. Mattern (Eds.): ASA/MA 2000, LNCS 1882, pp. 249–   , 2000.
© Springer-Verlag Berlin Heidelberg 2000

When dealing with an open multiagent system such as a soccer-robot system, agents are allowed to quit or enter their team at any time during the course of the game. This flow can be forced or intentional. It is for example forced by the break-down of a robot or noisy radio-communication. It is intended when a certain type of player gets replaced with another one—to strengthen the defense after a decent lead in the score for example. Furthermore, we assume that the ontologies are predefined and known to all of the team agents. In other words, they all know the allowed message types and are fully capable of interpreting them. They do not have to depend on a learning mechanism in order to process them.

For our system, protocols may be manifold thus enabling the agents to embody different roles and possibly dynamically change it during the course of the game. For instance, at some point a same robot may shift from a forward to a defender type of protocol. This assumption imposes the various protocols involved in the conversation between two agents to be compatible at a given time. That is, it is necessary for the messages being sent by an agent to be interpretable by the other one.

Following the approach presented in [ ], conversational policies should be viewed as constraints. Two types of constraints exist: syntactical constraints that restricts the possible sequences of messages and conversational states, and semantic constraints that define what actions external to the protocol an agent may perform at certain conversational states or when receiving certain messages. A policy should not presuppose any kind of implicit assumptions such as termination, synchrony or uptake acknowledgment, but rather make everything explicit.

Classically, the syntactic constraints may be modeled and implemented using finite state machines (FSA) whose vertices represent the system's conversational states and edges correspond to conversational events. Petri nets are also sometimes used [ ], and like FSA, they basically consist in specifying by extension all possible sequences of states and messages. Such basic transition net approach has a number of straightforward drawbacks. Because of the definition by extension, they can quickly lead to a combinatoric explosion of their representation, hence difficulties to engineer them. They also lack expressive power, as for instance, FSA can only specify sequences of possible messages that belong to the class of regular languages. On the contrary, the system presented here, inspired by the Structural Operational Semantics [ ] in programming languages [ ] allows to define the syntax of a conversation both operationally and by intention . This is made possible by the use of patterns: transitions cannot only be specified between particular states or upon the exchange of particular messages, but also between patterns of states (which are structured objects) upon the exchange of

---

[1] Let us note that objects defined by intention are not usually operationally defined which prevents them to be often computed. A definition by intention means the list of state or message sequences are not described in an exhaustive way (definition by extension), but by more generic "constraints".

patterns of messages. Patterns additionally confer to our system universal power, which means that it can express arbitrarily complex protocols.

Semantic constraints are also addressed by POS. This is achieved by specifying a number of predicates and behavior interfaces that agents should invoke when required. This allows for a clean separation of a protocol's specification from the internal architecture of agents, upon which no other assumption is made except for their interfaces and their ability to handle protocols. Thus, making such protocols operational requires each agent to possess a general and quite flexible protocol execution algorithm, namely primitives for reading, processing, and sending messages. Such piece of code should be totally independent from any specific protocol which for instance could be downloaded from some repository.

A number of closely related works exist in the literature. [ ] defines a programming environment that very much resembles the general architecture implied by POS, but it can not be used as a specification formalism and relies on FSA. [ ] shows similarities with POS in that it enables to use message patterns in rules and to neatly compose several protocols, but conversational states are finite and there is no semantic counterpart. [ ] defines a formalism that allows for the specification of what they call *action level semantics*. This corresponds to what we call syntactic constraints which also relies only on finite states (they acknowledge that they may need a way to represent states with structured information, which POS does). Yet, they give examples of coupling these specifications with the intentional level ("intentional semantics") which corresponds to our concept of semantics, but their system is commited to BDI agents. There is also a common view between this system and POS in that they can not only specify conversation policies, but they define ACLs as well .

Section   briefly presents the POS model. In section   we examine several basic behaviors of the JavaSoccer simulation environment as it is later used along with JavaBots to demonstrate POS' capabilities. In section   , two team strategies are modeled using POS. We demonstrate how POS is a suited theoretical tool and leads as well to extremely compact and modular code due to its high expressive power. We also show that the two strategies defined perform very well in a JavaSoccer tournament against other predefined strategies.

2   Overview of the POS Model

Basically, making use of the Protocol Operational Semantics (POS) consists for each agent in specifying a set of rules (called a protocol) that will monitor the use of basic behaviors depending on evaluations of the world and messages exchanged with other agents. The abstract architecture of an agent using a protocol is thus the coupling of two subparts: the set of rules defining the protocol and the set of basic behaviors and evaluations the agent can perform.

---

[2] They can of course rely on an existing ACL and cast it into their representation language in order to specify constraints over its use. But in general one defines ACLs and the constraints over their use at the same time with both systems.

POS' strength and specificity is that it uses algebraic data types and pattern-matching, allowing to describe powerful protocols (i.e., stronger than those based on finite state automata) in a very compact way. It is important to understand that this model is not only a theoretical framework, but also to a computational one due to the existence of adequate programming languages, like Pizza/Java [   ] and other ML languages [   ].

In a theoretical paper [   ] we have extensively developed the POS model. The current section briefly summarizes its main characteristics.

The three kinds of rules available in POS are:

$$
\begin{array}{ll}
\textbf{type 1} & \overbrace{\langle(sk, par), \phi(world)\rangle}^{\text{trigger}} \xrightarrow{[Send]} \overbrace{\langle(sk', par'), [\mathcal{A}(world)]\rangle}^{\text{consequence}} \\
\textbf{type 2} & \langle(sk, par), \phi(world)\rangle \xrightarrow[msg]{} \langle(sk', par'), [\mathcal{A}(world)]\rangle \\
\textbf{type 3} & \langle(sk, par), \phi(world)\rangle \xrightarrow{\varepsilon} \langle(sk', par'), [\mathcal{A}(world)]\rangle
\end{array}
$$

where:

- sk and sk' are skeletons in a string format for enhanced readability
- par and par' are parameters in form of objects with an algebraic data type on which pattern-matching can be performed. It may contain a number of pattern variables, which may basically mean anything. The rest of the rule refers to such patterns through their variable name. Thus, pattern-matching can be seen as a unification procedure which fails if the pattern does not match and which possibly binds a number of variables if it succeeds. A pair made of a skeleton and a parameter represents a parameterized state
- msg is a message pattern, which is also given in the form of an object with an algebraic data type on which pattern-matching can be performed
- $\phi(world)$ is a logical combination of predicates over the world. Such a predicate is defined as a procedure that returns "nil" if false or a non-nil value otherwise, that can additionally be linked to a variable
- $\mathcal{A}(world)$ is a list of side-effects performed by the agent onto the world; here this corresponds to the activation of a basic behavior
- $send$ is a list of message sendings with one of the following possible types
  - *SendToId id msg*: sends the message *msg* to agent *id*
  - *SendToGroup list msg*: sends the message *msg* to a group of agents listed in *list*
  - *SendToAll msg*: sends the message *msg* to all agents

Type 1 rules correspond to the sending of messages, hence they are called sending rules. Type 2 rules correspond to the reading of a message from the agent's FIFO mailbox, so they are denoted as receiving rules. With type 3 rules no message is exchanged, they are denoted as ε rules.

A rule is fired when its parameterized state matches the current agent state and its predicate is true. Then, the corresponding list of messages is sent and the side-effects are performed upon the world. Furthermore, the agent state changes to the parameterized state indicated by the rule. The rule engine we use here, is as follows:

```
repeat:
While (FIFO mailbox is not empty)
        read first message;
        try to interpret it (try to fire a receiving rule);
        throw it;
endWhile
try to fire a sending rule or an ε-rule;
```

This is not the most general engine, but we have found it sufficient for our purpose. It is suited for protocols where either a read message can always be interpreted, or a loss of uninterpreted messages is not important. As mentioned, we have found it sufficient so far, yet it can easily be changed to fit protocols that do not have these properties.

As indicated above, POS' major feature lies in the notions of abstract data-types and pattern matching capabilities on agent states and message patterns. This has lead to a high expressive power, and therefore offers the possibility to get a very compact and modular code.

3   The JavaBots Simulation Environment

The so-called JavaBots [ ], freely available via [ ], along with a soccer world (JavaSoccer) are an excellent tool-kit suited for several purposes within the RoboCup framework [ ]. First the nice graphical interface of the JavaBots allows to easily display what each part of the system "believes", in terms of where the robots are and what they are doing, and so on. Second, JavaBots are an excellent simulation tool with which strategies can be easily prototyped and tested. We use this property here to demonstrate the expressive power of POS.

JavaSoccer is different from quite many other simulators. Whereas common types of simulations are rather abstract and only remotely linked to the physical world, JavaBots tries to reproduce the robots' "body" and the soccer field with their physical laws. Nevertheless, JavaBots is relatively simple to use, which is very important in terms of ease to perform a high number of experiments. In concrete terms, the user is given access to the many robot's sensors and actuators.

The JavaSoccer proceeds in time steps as follows. Each robot is given the new sensor values and computes a vector move, which determines the direction the robot should try to take, as well as the speed the robot should try to reach.

The following basic behaviors are the basis for the team behaviors or strategies of our demo-teams as presented later on, and are implemented using a behavior-based architecture:

Attacking with the ball. This behavior *driveBall()* results in an attack on the opponents' goal: if the robot is behind the ball and oriented towards the goal, then the robot starts charging the goal and kicks the ball when it is

---

[3] The Robot World Cup Soccer Initiative (RoboCup), is an annual event which is supposed to be a standard problem for Artificial Intelligence research [ ] [ ].

close enough to the opponents' goal; otherwise it gets behind the ball and avoids colliding with other players.

Shooting and receiving passes. Passes mainly rely on three behaviors running on different robots, namely *passBall(destination)*, *WaitPass()* and *Intercept()*. The behavior *passBall(destination)* gets the robot behind the ball in relation to the *destination* and then the robot kicks the ball. The *WaitPass()* behavior means to stop moving. The *Intercept()* behavior consists in trying to get behind the ball in relation to the opposite goal.

Spreading on the field. In real soccer, not every player runs after the ball. Instead, the team is spread over the field along some strategic position. The *Demarcate()* behavior can be useful to implement according strategies on soccer-robots. This behavior gets a robot to find a place on the field where it is more or less alone, while following the progression of the ball.

Predicates. Together with the basic behaviors, the following predicates are used to form the building-blocks of different strategies that can easily be implemented with POS: *ballIsInRadius()*, *opponentInRadius()*, *ballIsDangerous()*, *ballIsInteresting()*, *AmIclosest()*, *findClosest()*. These predicates are self-explaining.

One fundamental thing that needs to be understood is that the protocols we are going to describe do not specify a particular implementation of these behaviors and predicates. They only specify an interface. For simplicity sake, we are simply presenting here an example where all robots have identical behaviors and predicates. In fact, they may be implemented very differently by heterogeneous internal architectures: some robots could use symbolic planning to achieve them, some others could use neural nets. Additionally, the robots could have very different mechanical features.

4   Modeling Strategies

4.1   A Straightforward POS Strategy

The first strategy we are presenting here is rather straightforward. Let us remind that in this article, our main intention is to demonstrate how POS can be used to describe complex situations, and not to present a highly successful team strategy for RoboCup. Nevertheless, despite its simplicity this first team performs quite well as we shall see later on.

All robots in this team are heterogeneous with respect to the team's behaviors or roles they can take and dynamically change. The possible roles are: *Demarcate*, *Defend*, *Attack*, *Pass*, *WaitPass*, *Intercept* and *Possessor* (of the ball).

Different phases in the game are classified into the following three categories:

Phase 1: An agent tries to get the ball towards the opponent goal. But upon seeing there might be a difficulty, the agent tries to pass the ball to a teammate, while other agents try to demarcate.

Phase 2: If the ball gets really interesting (i.e., close to the opponent goal), a squad of two forwards launches an attack and repeatedly try to shoot the ball into the opponent's goal.

Phase 3: If the ball looks too threatening, a squad of two defenders is (dynamically) formed and comes to help the goal keeper.

At the beginning of a match, an arbitrary robot is set to the state *Possessor* and the others are set to the *Demarcating* state. In the following presentation of the protocols, b :=beh is used for denoting the action of taking up the behavior *beh* by the robot. Two patterns variable appear: State s and Behavior be.

Let us note how easy it is to specify encapsulated set of rules in POS since each of them leads to a well-defined and meaningful behavior.

Phase 1:

(1) $\langle Demarcating, True\rangle \xrightarrow[PassToYou]{} \langle WaitingPass, b := WaitPass\rangle$

(2) $\langle WaitingPass, True\rangle \xrightarrow[Go]{} \langle Intercepting, b := Intercept\rangle$

(3) $\langle Intercepting, ballIsInRadius()\rangle \xrightarrow{\varepsilon} \langle Posessor, b := DriveBall\rangle$

(4) $\langle Posessor, (opponentInRadius())and(v = findDest())\rangle \xrightarrow{sendTo(v,PassToYou)}$
$\langle Passing(v), b := Pass(v)\rangle$

(5) $\langle Passing(dest), (IHaveKicked()||!ballIsInRadius())\rangle \xrightarrow{sendTo(dest,Go)}$
$\langle Demarcating, b := Demarcate\rangle$

This set of rules alone is already self-sufficient for defining a powerful group behavior. Robots tend to get the ball closer to the opponent's goal while keeping it away from these opponents by passing the ball among themselves. However, their behavior can be made more competitive by making them more offensive when arriving near the goal:

Phase 2:

(6) $\langle State\ s, True\rangle \xrightarrow[Attack]{} \langle Attack(s, b(old)), b := Attack\rangle$

(7) $\langle Passing(dest), (ballIsInteresting())and(v = findDest())\rangle \xrightarrow{sendTo(v,Attack)}$
$\langle AttackPos(Passing(dest), Pass(dest), v), b := Attack\rangle$

(8) $\langle Posessor, (ballIsInteresting())and(v = findDest())\rangle \xrightarrow{sendTo(v,Attack)}$
$\langle AttackPos(Posessor, DriveBall, v), b := Attack\rangle$

(9) $\langle Attack(State s, behavior\ be), True\rangle \xrightarrow[AttackFinished]{} \langle s, b := be\rangle$

(10) $\langle AttackPos(State\ s, behavior\ be, dest), !ballIsInteresting()\rangle$
$\xrightarrow{sendTo(dest,AttackFinished)} \langle s, b := be\rangle$

As far as this new set of rules let us point out two remarks. Has we decided to get all robots to attack (as it is the case in the strategy presented in the next section) instead of having the current possessor along with another robot as only attackers, only two rules would have been sufficient.

Second, these rules are only enter/exit rules with a simple attack scheme: just the two forward most robots try to score, regardless of the other ones. An additional or new set of rules, i.e., a sub-protocol dedicated to cooperation of these two robots can easily be added without bothering about the rest of the entire protocol. Here again, we see POS' modularity potential.

Finally, this strategy is improved with a way to handle a dangerous ball. These rules are symmetrical to the attacking rules in phase 2.

Phase 3:

(11) $\langle State\ s, True\rangle \xrightarrow[Help]{} \langle Defend(s, b(old)), b := Defend\rangle$

(12) $\langle Defend(State\ s, behavior\ be), True\rangle \xrightarrow[Finished]{} \langle s, b := be\rangle$

(13) $\langle Posessor, (ballIsDangerous())and(v = findDest())\rangle \xrightarrow{sendTo(v(),Help)}$ $\langle DefendPos(Posessor, DriveBall, v), b := Defend\rangle$

(14) $\langle Passing(dest), (ballIsDangerous())and(v = findDest())\rangle \xrightarrow{sendTo(v,Defend)}$ $\langle DefendPos(Passing(dest), Pass(dest), v), b := Attack\rangle)$

(15) $\langle DefendPos(State\ s, behavior\ be, dest),$ $(!ballIsDangerous())and(v = findDest())\rangle \xrightarrow{sendTo(v,Finished)} \langle s, b := be\rangle$

Let us notice the relatively small size for the strategy's description, namely 15 rules. This is also very small in terms of actual code with a suited programming language. In some other recent work [ ]⁴ we have detailed a concrete transition from POS formula to ML which is a language that naturally allows for the implementation of algebraic data types and pattern matching. Here we use the Pizza language, a super-set of Java adding these two fundamental features needed for a POS implementation. The generated code is completely Java-compliant so that the type of work presented here can be repeated in any Java framework. An example showing the ease for implementing the rules as well as their interpretation is given below:

```
public void FireReceive(CoreAgent coreag,message mess,agentTeam t)
{
    // rule (1)
    switch(Pair(currentState,mess)) {
    case Pair(Demarcating,PassToYou):
            currentState = WaitingPass; // new parameterized state
            coreag.behave = WaitPass; // side effect
            break; };

    // rule (2)
    switch(Pair(currentState,mess)) {
    case Pair(WaitingPass,Go):
            currentState = Intercepting;
```

---

⁴ In that paper, we implemented the Collect protocol which makes a fleet of little and possibly heterogeneous agents cooperate in order to achieve a joint task. This type of protocol applies to a world where several kinds of tasks exist and where no one agent is capable of handling all of them.

```
        coreag.behave = Intercept;
        break; };
```

```
// rule (11)
switch(Pair(currentState,mess)) {
case Pair(stateProt s,Help):
        currentState = Defend(s,coreag.behave);
        coreag.behave = Defending;
        break; };
```

```
// rule (12)
switch(Pair(currentState,mess)) {
case Pair(Defend(stateProt s,behavior b),Finished):
        currentState = s;
        coreag.behave = b;
        break; };
```
...

The related engine is also straightforward:

```
public void engine(CoreAgent coreagent,agentTeam t) {
  while ( !box.is.empty() ) {
    FireReceive(coreagent,box.take(),t); };
 FireSend(coreagent,t); }
```

The benefits of using the expressive power of algebraic data types and pattern matching compared to finite state automata with conventional if-then-rules is demonstrated best on an example. With conventional approaches, rules (6) and (11) would each require 12 additional transitions, and accordingly the formulation of rules. Rules (7), (8) or (10) would be even more difficult to implement with a standard finite state automata (or even with Petri nets) because they basically store the current states as in order to be able to retrieve them at a later stage. Besides, as shown in the COLLECT protocol in [ ] such rules can be nested as many times as wanted. In order to avoid the combinatoric explosion of states generated by such an approach, existing works introduce ad hoc external variables and tests over these variables. On the contrary, this kind of situation can be neatly dealt with in POS without any extensions. Also, this formalism allows for a clean and small description of exceptions. It is not rare to have to deal with exceptional messages that could possibly be received during any conversational state. Using finite state automata most often amounts to add *"enormous numbers of little used error handling transitions, often to the extent that the preferred conversational flow in the net is completely obscured"* [ ], whereas with POS rules resembling (6) can do the job elegantly. In a general framework, because POS is a calculus model with universal power [ ], there are many protocols or constraints over conversations that can be expressed in POS and that simply can not be described by finite state machines or Petri nets without serious extensions.

4.2   A Simpler Yet Stronger Strategy

This second strategy is simpler (in terms of the number of rules), but at the same time stronger (in terms of the performance). Coordination here is achieved entirely through direct perception of the world. Four roles are possible for the robots, namely *Demarcate*, *DriveBall*, *Defend*, and *Attack*. The basic idea is rather straightforward: the robot closest to the ball tries to get it closer to the opponent's goal while the others are trying to demarcate (phase 1); when the ball is dangerous, everyone comes in defense (phase 2); when it is interesting, everyone attacks (phase 3).

Phase 1:
$\quad$ (1) $\langle Demarcating, AmIclosest() \rangle \xrightarrow{\varepsilon} \langle DrivingBall, b := DriveBall \rangle$
$\quad$ (2) $\langle DrivingBall, !AmIclosest() \rangle \xrightarrow{\varepsilon} \langle Demarcating, b := Demarcate \rangle$
Phase 2:
$\quad$ (3) $\langle Statep, ballIsDangerous() \rangle \xrightarrow{\varepsilon} \langle Defending, b := Defend \rangle$
$\quad$ (4) $\langle Defending, !ballIsDangerous \rangle \xrightarrow{\varepsilon} \langle Demarcating, b := Demarcate \rangle$
Phase 3:
$\quad$ (5) $\langle Statep, ballIsInteresting() \rangle \xrightarrow{\varepsilon} \langle Attacking, b := Attack \rangle$
$\quad$ (6) $\langle Attacking, !ballIsInteresting() \rangle \xrightarrow{\varepsilon} \langle Demarcating, b := Demarcate \rangle$

$\quad$ The first remark is that again phase 2 and phase 3 are just enter/exit attack or defense, and we could easily refine both of them by independently designing a dedicated attack protocol and include it here for instance. A second remark is the really small size of the description. Here finite state automata would have been able to describe the protocol, but would still be much more complicated (because of rules (3) and (5) that would map to many states and transitions). It is important to remark that the superior expressive power of POS does not impose unnecessary complications when very simple protocols have to be described. Despite its extreme simplicity, this strategy leads to a really efficient team work as seen in section   .

4.3   Test Games

To demonstrate that team strategies modeled with POS are not only simple, in terms of compactness of code due to its expressive power, but also efficient, the two team strategies presented above are tested in a soccer tournament against the following other teams.

DTeam. The so-called *DTeam* (DT) provided in the JavaSoccer package is composed of heterogeneous robots who do not explicitly cooperate (but they do implicitly, in a way similar to that encoded in T2):
$\quad$ – an off-side player always sticking with the opponent goalie, trying to hinder it;
$\quad$ – one player constantly trying to get behind the ball and to push it in the direction of the opponent's goal;

- one robot playing backwards and defending when necessary;
- one player staying in the center and driving the ball to the opponent goal when it gets the opportunity;
- one robot is the goalie.

The specificity of this team is that four robots out of five are designated a more or less fixed location on the field. They always have the same role.

SchemaDemo. The *SchemaDemo* (Sch) team is also provided within the JavaSoccer package. All robots are homogeneous (except for the goalie). The individual behavior is: get behind the ball, then move to it and kick it, while keeping away from teammates. The specificity of this team is that robots are very mobile on the field and do not tend to keep the ball within a close range for dribbling, but they rather kick it ahead.

PyTeam. The *PyTeam* (PyT) is a team strategy we have designed. It is composed of heterogeneous robots with fixed roles:

- one robot is the goalie;
- one robot stays in defense, following the movements of the ball like the goalie, and defends when necessary with the *DriveBall()* behavior;
- a second robot stays also in defense, but it works differently: it tries to get behind the ball perpendicular to the heading of an attacking player with the ball; so, it tries to steal the ball;
- one robot always tries to get the ball closer to the opponent goal by passing it to more off-side mates or by using *DriveBallRear()*;
- one robot stays around the opponents' goal and launches an attack when the ball becomes interesting.

NopTeam. The *NopTeam* (Nop) is extremely simple, as all robots just do not move. It is of more significance than it might seem at a first glance, because this kind of situation is not too uncommon in the present state of art of RoboCup.

RandomTeam. The *RandomTeam* (R) is a variation where all robots just move randomly around.

4.4   Comparing the Performances

Before looking at the actual results of different soccer games, let us focus on some general properties shown by teams T1 and T2 which demonstrate POS' capabilities with strategies presented in sections   and   . First, both protocols never get into a deadlock, and they correctly perform the task they were designed for in every game against each other. This has been achieved right from the beginning without any trial-and-error debugging.

Second, the number and frequency of exchanged messages for the first protocol is low. On average there are 15 exchanged messages per minute for the whole team, while the player and the ball move in "real-time", i.e., similar to the speed of a real soccer game. This can be viewed as an indication of a low computational complexity, based on measures similar to the ones of communication protocols in distributed systems. In other words, this shows a high efficiency. In addition, the frequency with which the parameterized states change is also relatively low for both teams. On average this frequency is 15 times per minute for the first protocol, and 5 times per minute for the second one. This is an indication of a balanced relation between the dynamics of the strategies and the dynamics of the game.

Now let us summarize what we obtained after ten 10-minute runs of each match. The only team that never looses is *Team 2*. Three teams win 3 times out of 6: *Team 2*, *SchemaDemo*, and *DTeam*. But *Team 2* beats *SchemaDemo*, and *DTeam* has difficulties to win against *NopTeam* whereas *Team 2* has no such difficulties. Hence, *Team 2* is somehow the best one in this tournament.

Furthermore, we did an experiment to demonstrate the robustness of *Team 2*. In doing so, an arbitrary player is dis-activated, such that the team has always to get along with only three players against a complete adversary team. The results appeared to be the same except for the *DreamTeam* that can outrun this performance and outrun beat *T2*.

5   Conclusion

In a more theoretical and technical paper [ ] we have presented the Protocol Operational Semantics (POS), an interaction protocol model based on abstract data-types and pattern matching capabilities. Endowed with these special features, POS has a high expressive power which generally makes it an interesting approach for coordinating agents in multiagent systems. Furthermore, POS allows for an easy verification of semantic properties of protocols.

The resulting compactness and modularity is especially of interest for robot soccer teams as we have argued in this article. In this particular application, heterogeneity on several levels (roles, implementation of behaviors and predicates, mechanical features) can be very beneficial, as it allows to adapt to the almost unlimited number of potential opponent teams, game situations, and so on. But this so-to-say large scale heterogeneity leads to a combinatorial explosion with classical protocols, where graphs with conversational states as nodes are constructed.

The high expressive power of POS is not only a theoretical property, but it is reflected in actual implementations with suited programming languages like Pizza, a super-set of Java. In this article, we have presented two simple teams for the soccer world of JavaBots to illustrate the potential of POS. Though these teams are intended for demonstration purposes only, they perform very well in a tournament against other strategies.

Contrary to real time reactive robots as we are dealing with here, we have also used POS to handle information agents in knowledge base environments [ ]. This demonstrates POS' versatility in that it is applicable to completely different types of setting too.

References

1. T. R. Balch and A. Ram. Integrating robotics research with JavaBots. In *Working Notes of the AAAI 1998 Spring Symposium*, 1998.
2. Mihai Barbuceanu and Wai-Kao Lo. Conversation oriented programming in COOL: Current state and future directions. In *Autonomous Agents'99 Special Workshop on Conversation Policies*, 1999.
3. S. Cammarata, D. Mac Arthur, and R. Steeb. Strategies of cooperation in distributed problem solving. In A. H. Bond and L. Gasser, editors, *Readings in Distributed Artificial Intelligence*, pages 102–105. Morgan Kaufmann Publishers, Inc., San Mateo, CA, 1988.
4. R. S. Cost, Y. Chen, T. Finin, Y. Labrou, and Y. Peng. Modeling agent conversation with colored Petri nets. In Jeff Bradshaw, editor, *Autonomous Agents'99, Special Workshop on Conversation Policies*, May 1999.
5. Mark Greaves, Heather Holmback, and Jeffrey Bradshaw. What is a conversation policy? In *Autonomous Agents'99 Special Workshop on Conversation Policies*, 1999.   ,   ,
6. M. Hennessy. *The Semantics of Programming Languages: An Introduction Using Structured Operational Semantics*. Wiley, 1990. Out of print.
7. Javabots information page. http://www.cs.cmu.edu/trb/JavaBots.
8. Hiroaki Kitano, Minoru Asada, Yasuo Kuniyoshi, Itsuki Noda, and Eiichi Osawa. Robocup: The robot world cup initiative. In *First International Conference on Autonomous Agents (Agents-97)*. The ACM Press, 1997.
9. Hiroaki Kitano, Milind Tambe, Peter Stone, Manuela Veloso, Silvia Coradeschi, Eiichi Osawa, Hitoshi Matsubara, Itsuki Noda, and Minoru Asada. The robocup synthetic agent challenge 97. In *IJCAI-97*, 1997.
10. Jean-Luc Koning and Pierre-Yves Oudeyer. Introduction to POS: A protocol operational semantics. *International Journal on Cooperative Information Systems*, 2000. To be published.   ,   ,
11. Jean-Luc Koning and Pierre-Yves Oudeyer. Modeling and implementing conversation policies using POS. In B. d'Auriol, editor, *International Conference on Communications in Computing (CIC-00)*, Las Vegas, NV, June 2000. CSREA Press.
    ,
12. Kazubiro Kuwabara, Toru Ishida, and Nobuyasu Osato. AgenTalk: Describing multiagent coordination protocols with inheritance. In *Seventh IEEE International Conference on Tools with Artificial Intelligence*, pages 460–465, Herndon, Virginia, November 1995.
13. R. Milner. A proposal for standard ML. In *ACM Conference on Lisp and Functional Programming*, 1987.
14. Martin Odersky and Philip Wadler. Pizza into Java: Translating theory into practice. In *4th ACM Symposium on Principles of Programming Languages*, Paris, France, January 1997.
15. Jeremy Pitt and Abe Mamdani. Designing agent communication languages for multi-agent systems. In *European Workshop on Modelling Autonomous Agents and Multi-Agent World (MAAMAW-99)*, pages 102–114, 1999.
16. G. Plotkin. A structural approach to operationnal semantics. Technical Report DAIMI FN-19, Aarhus university, Computer Science Department, Denmark, 1981.
17. http://www.robocup.org.

Using Intelligent Agents and a Personal Knowledge Management Application

Marja Phipps, Jay Mork, and Mark McSherry

General Dynamics Information Systems,
8800 Queen Ave. S., Bloomington, MN 55431
{Marja.J.Phipps,Jay.E.Mork,Mark.A.McSherry}@gd-is.com

Abstract. General Dynamics Information Systems (GDIS), in cooperation with the U.S. Navy, has been applying agent-based technology to
intelligently retrieve distributed data and developing personalized tools
to assimilate and manage the knowledge inherent in that data. Our initial
hypothesis was that by filtering information based on user need, we
could greatly decrease the amount of remote information transferred and
increase the value of information locally available to the user. In evaluating our hypothesis, we found that the user's information needs were
implicit; that is not codified. By explicitly capturing the information requirements, we could repeat our initial experimentation and extend our
solution to a generalized set of knowledge management problems. As a
driving scenario for this research we worked with 3rd Fleet Staff to formalize and expedite the process of gathering and organizing information
for their daily situation briefs. Our experience includes a refined list of
knowledge management issues and lessons learned in applying agent-
based technology.

1   Introduction

With the expansion of the Web and other data stores, military analysts have gained
access to a wide variety of comprehensive information repositories. This, coupled with
the advent of broadband communications and Web "push" technology, has created a
dramatic increase in the amount of information available to these consumers, not however always to their benefit. Upon interviewing 3rd Fleet Staff personnel in the fall of
1998, we found that their biggest complaint was not one of too little bandwidth, but
rather the lack of tools that could quickly and efficiently narrow an information search
to the necessary set of data required for their particular task. New and improved information delivery systems, with the promise of providing even more data, were
viewed with apprehension. Tools were desperately needed to help filter and organize
the information.

Under a cooperative research and development effort with the U.S. Navy, GDIS
has been studying this problem and applying agent-based technology and desktop

D. Kotz and F. Mattern (Eds.): ASA/MA 2000, LNCS 1882, pp. 262-274, 2000.

knowledge management tools to help manage the information situation aboard the USS *Coronado*. To evaluate our research, we worked with a group of 3rd Fleet Staff personnel who were asked to support our experiments and to assess the technology. The selected application domain areas included Operations, Intelligence, and Logistics. Within these domain areas, we focused on the task of gathering and organizing information for daily situational briefs. While each area had unique tasks and different information requirements a common need for selective data gathering and desktop analytical tools was evident.

In this paper, we present our approach to addressing these issues as well as our lessons learned and continuing research direction. The next section describes the environment we found when we began this research and the end result after technology application. Subsequent sections highlight the technology framework and components, along with issues found, resolved, and deferred. We conclude with our experimental results and lessons learned.

2   Application State-of-the-Art

2.1   Manually Generating the Daily Situational Brief

Figure 1 illustrates the manual process that describes one aspect of the information problem when we began our research. In this example, an Anti-Submarine Warfare (ASW) staff officer spent nearly 4 hours each day gathering relevant information (documents, messages, imagery, etc) over constrained communications channels, extracting desired knowledge constructs, creating higher order concepts, and finally putting this knowledge in the daily ASW briefing for presentation to Commander 3rd Fleet. This manual process was not shared and the semantics of the information generated were not expressly maintained.

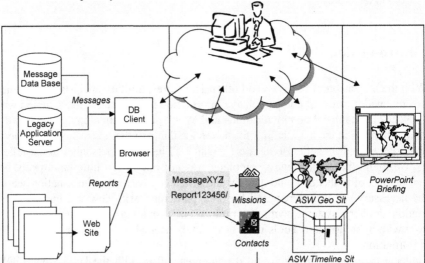

Figure 1. Manually generating the daily situation brief may require as much as 4-5 hours

2.2 Automating the Process Steps

The subsequent hypothesis for our research was that we could create a reusable system, leveraging intelligent agents and a knowledge management application, that would capture and automate the information gathering and organization process for the preparation of daily situation briefs. Our envisioned approach would greatly reduce the amount of information that the officer would need to review and at the same time capture shareable knowledge of the undertaking.

In our Managed Information Network Exchange Router (MINER™) research initiative, we developed a personal, Java-based, knowledge management application called Information Management Analysis and Presentation (IMAP). IMAP enables the specification of a user's context, organization of resulting knowledge concepts, and visualization of how these concepts are integrated together. An intelligent agent infrastructure, InfoSleuth, provides services for the location and gathering of pertinent information to feed into the knowledge management system. Client interfaces permit data retrieval through multiple communication mediums and the export of data to other applications such as MS PowerPoint. This integrated system allowed staff to:

- organize the information domain with a specific ontology relevant to the task;
- collect and map information against this ontology;
- route information over multiple communication mediums (e.g. asymmetric web channel);
- abstract concepts from the information;
- store and organize the concepts;
- view the concepts in a variety of contexts (e.g. geospatial, temporal);
- export the findings to other applications (e.g. Excel, PowerPoint, email);
- and replicate the information base to other users via XML.

Figure 2 graphically depicts how the various knowledge constructs relevant to the ASW brief generation process are now automatically derived.

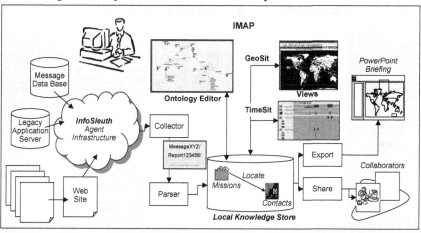

Figure 2. Utilizing intelligent agents and knowledge management tools, the brief may be generated in as little as 4-5 minutes

3   Application Framework

We built our application framework in an iterative fashion: identifying domain issues, applying technology, and executing experiments directly with the users. During a series of three at-sea trials, we demonstrated increasingly focused and robust knowledge management services, distributed across a variety of locations including California, Hawaii, and aboard the USS *Coronado*. In this section we list the primary issues found, the technology applied, and the experimental results.

3.1   IDM Framework

Our initial hypothesis was that by reducing information flows to a small set of desired knowledge concepts, we could significantly decrease the amount of information locally stored. Our solution began with an Information Dissemination Management (IDM) framework (Figure 3). Here, our implementation utilized an intelligent agent infrastructure for information access and awareness; leveraged state-of-the-art communication mechanisms and Commercial Off-The-Shelf (COTS) packages for distribution and source access; incorporated unique delivery handlers as required by the distribution infrastructure; and employed knowledge management clients on behalf of the users. To evaluate our hypothesis, we identified disparate remote information repositories, incorporated multiple communication paths, and employed a variety of end users. As shown in Figure 3, the information repositories included imagery and video clips in databases (e.g. Sybase, Oracle, SQL Server), documents (e.g. PowerPoint, Word, unformatted text, Web) on web sites, and formatted text naval messages from legacy applications. These repositories were distributed remotely across our California and Hawaii sites as well as locally aboard the USS *Coronado*. Communication mediums included the Global Broadcast Service (GBS) [4] and Internet Protocol networks. As mentioned previously, our selected end users were Intelligence, Operations, and Logistics officers from the Commander 3rd Fleet Staff.

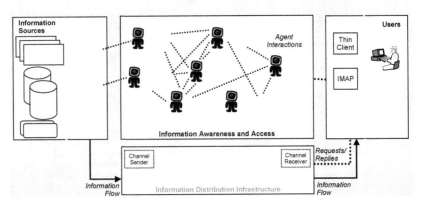

Figure 3. Intelligent agents, personalized clients, COTS packages, and required routers implement the Information Dissemination Management framework

3.2   Agent Architecture

In looking at the information awareness and access requirements in more detail, we find that the agent infrastructure must support:

- highly distributed agents;
- heterogeneous information access;
- and multiple information contexts.

The InfoSleuth agent architecture, developed as a collaborative research project at MCC since 1994, met these requirements. The InfoSleuth [1] project incorporates technologies that operate on heterogeneous information sources in open, dynamic environments. InfoSleuth views an information source at the level of its relevant semantic concepts, thus preserving the autonomy of its data. Information requests to InfoSleuth are specified generically, independent of the structure, location, or even existence of the requested information. InfoSleuth filters these requests, specified at the semantic level, flexibly matching them to the information resources that are relevant at the time the request is processed.

Specifically, InfoSleuth met our flexibility and interoperability requirements as follows.

- ***Agent Technology.***   Specialized agents that represent the users, the information repositories, and the system services cooperate to address information processing requirements, allowing for dynamic reconfiguration of system capabilities. The use of agent technology provides a high degree of decentralization of capabilities, which is the key to system scalability and extensibility.
- ***Ontology Specifications.***   Ontologies give a concise, uniform, and declarative description of semantic information, independent of the underlying syntactic representation or the data models of information repositories. To resolve the discrepancy between how the data is structured within the individual databases and how the user conceptualizes it, InfoSleuth utilizes a common ontology for a given application domain, and local mappings from individual repositories (e.g. database schemas) to the common ontology. InfoSleuth extends information accessibility by allowing multiple simultaneous ontologies belonging to common or diverse application domains.
- ***Brokering.***   InfoSleuth agents advertise semantic constraints about themselves to InfoSleuth brokers using a global InfoSleuth ontology. When queried, a broker reasons over these constraints to determine the minimal set of agents that can provide a solution to the query. Services include distributed multi-resource queries, location-independent single-resource updates, event monitoring by means of subscription/notification, statistical or inferential data analysis, and trend discovery in complex event streams. In its simplest case, brokering of resource agents allows distributed heterogeneous resources (information repositories) to be easily and dynamically (at run-time) brought on-line.
- ***Java Classes.***   Java and Java Applets are used extensively to provide users and administrators with system-independent user interfaces, and to enable ubiquitous agents that can be deployed at any source of information regardless of its location or platform.

To instantiate this framework, we first defined multiple application ontologies. Our approach was to take a source-centric view of the officer's information needs, namely web, message, and multi-media ontologies. We then configured resource agents to mediate between the ontologies and metadata attributes embedded within the information repositories. We demonstrated access to multiple JDBC-compliant databases (Sybase, Oracle, SQL Server) containing structured messages and imagery/video annotations and references. Web sites were scraped and metadata captured in a common repository using the Netscape Compass Server [7]. A specific agent was written, derived from a common resource agent shell, to comply with the Netscape Compass API for information access. Generic services such as subscriptions and brokering were enabled, based on the application-defined ontologies.

With the abundance of desktop browsers in the operational domain, we implemented a simple applet that allowed the users to interact with the agent infrastructure. This applet, or thin client, provided profiled access to information (based on the application-defined ontologies), heavyweight data (e.g. video clips, web pages) dissemination, and email notification.

While this agent infrastructure and client met the initial requirements of our information delivery research, we found that several issues prevented it from being extensively deployed as the encompassing framework in the area of knowledge management. These issues are described in the next section, along with their resolution approach.

3.3   Knowledge Management Client

Configuration of an agent infrastructure can be partitioned into two tiers: 1) defining the application-level parameters or the system semantics and 2) instantiating the executable or syntactic system parameters. To accomplish the latter, we simply use quality system engineering practices (e.g. load-balancing, environment variables, configuration files) to implement and evaluate the system. To accomplish the former, however, we find a set of challenges. First, we need to extract domain knowledge from the potential end users and information producers; and second, explicitly capture the knowledge in one or more ontologies. This requires a unique blend of software engineering pragmatism and application domain understanding.

With each application instance, we struggled to develop strawman ontologies, explain them to the producers/users, and incorporate their domain knowledge. We found that existing ontology tools did not meet our needs. Clearly, a tool was required which would allow the engineers and the users/producers to construct and visualize the application semantics. We met this need with IMAP, an object-oriented knowledge management application designed to dynamically generate, persistently store, and visualize information models using folders, templates, context mapping, and concepts [2] (Figure 4).

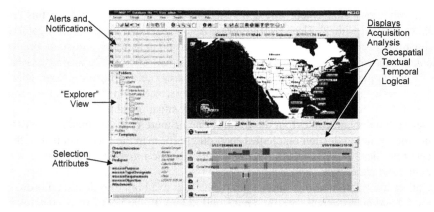

Figure 4. Users may edit templates, preferences, and profiles; visualize concepts in multiple displays; organize information in folders; modify selected elements; and manage all data persistently

In addition, we recognized the need for more prudent features, such as profile (i.e. query) and results organization, visualization tools, and unique information handlers. To enhance the visualization suite, IMAP incorporated a third-party cartography engine (SpatialX by Object/FX [5]), a browser (HotJava from Sun [6]), a multi-media player (Java™ Media APIs [12]), custom tables, sort, search, and highlight utilities, as well as a temporal display. A distinguishing feature included the coupling of objects across displays (e.g. temporal and geospatial).

Client interfaces were added to invoke the intelligent agent infrastructure and handle the results by concept type. Consequently, we were able to graphically depict the users' contexts (or information models), issue agent requests constrained within those contexts, and organize and visualize the returned results at varying semantic levels.

The dynamic and persistent features of IMAP greatly reduced the amount of effort expended collaboratively defining application ontologies, although further research is required in graphically depicting the information models as the ontologies increase in size and complexity. Also, as we implemented our applications, it became clear that we were only attacking a portion of the information processing problem. We accomplished the first step: information access, awareness, and delivery. The next step is to capture and control the processing flow itself.

4   Extending the Application Framework

In performing our intelligent information retrieval experimentation, we found it necessary to extend our base infrastructure and develop desktop tools to dynamically define the information models (or contexts) as well as organize and visualize the results. Consequently, we added the following hypothesis to our research. By explicitly capturing information needs, contextual models, and conceptual relationships in a persistent and visual manner, we can derive and share knowledge associated with a given information management role and function. As a driving scenario for this research we worked with 3rd Fleet Staff to formalize and expedite the process of gathering, organizing, and visualizing information for inclusion in their daily situation briefs. To look at this workflow problem in more detail, we identified the following generic steps. When implemented for a specific application area (i.e. Intelligence, Operations, and Logistics), these features enabled multiple users, acting in the context of that application area, to collaboratively generate the daily situational brief.

1. Define the domain context, in the form of one or more ontology models. Configure the agent application ontologies accordingly (or map the users' context to the agent application ontologies). *This enabled semantic interoperability across the agent and client infrastructures.*

2. Collect information against these ontologies. Retrieve both metadata (in a browse mode) and heavyweight data (in a push/pull mode). Route heavyweight data over alternate communication paths (e.g. GBS). *A browsing feature is critical to transferring information over constrained resources, i.e. do not transfer unnecessary data. Data delivered in a push or subscription mode enables more timely and automated delivery. Alternate communication paths allow data transport activities to be effectively partitioned from intelligent reasoning.*

3. Extract, organize, and store concepts from the collected information. Create visual displays of the resulting knowledge. *Manage the results according to the defined context. Allow user input to determine how the information is correlated and visualized. Capture the user preferences.*

4. Export the findings to other applications (e.g. PowerPoint). *Exploit the knowledge.*

Step 1 was accomplished in meeting our initial hypothesis, that of filtering the information retrieved using the constraints of a query defined within a user's context. Participating components include IMAP information modeling and mapping, InfoSleuth ontology agent and configuration tools.

Basic information retrieval mechanisms were also in place as a result of our initial experimentation. To handle heavyweight data in a separate execution thread, we modified the profiling segment of the IMAP client. The browse/push/pull features were implemented by partitioning the information in the ontologies into metadata attributes and references to heavyweight data. If the user queried the system in a browse mode, the matching metadata and references would be returned. If the user queried the system in a push/pull mode, the heavyweight data pointed to via the reference (i.e. URL) would be pushed/pulled. In addition to data partitioning, we added several dissemination mechanisms to the framework for executing multiple transportation paradigms. We employed standard HTTP protocols [8] and two GBS paths; a web cast channel and a near real-time replication channel. To execute these paradigms, we installed "forward" and "receive" data components on applicable host routers and we implemented "post" and "watch" clients within the profiling segment of the knowledge management application. Instead of modifying the communication protocol of the agents, we leveraged existing transportation services through custom client-side hooks.

To realize step 3, we implemented concept-based data handling, dynamic storage, and cross-display coupling within our knowledge management client application.

Dynamic templates were generated by user context specification. Agent infrastructure queries and results were formatted and parsed based upon the context-specific templates. Storage transactions were committed accordingly. Specialized panel displays were developed for geospatial, temporal, textual, and table visualization aids. Commercially available visualization packages were also employed as plug-ins for multimedia data: web, audio, imagery, and video files. As the data was persistently stored in a common repository, multiple display panels were able to simultaneously showcase selected data elements.

Exporting the data to external applications can be accomplished through standard or non-standard interface definitions. We chose to prototype both. An interface was implemented to export (and import) the contents of the database in an XML format. A portion of the database, representing formatted naval messages, was profiled for and pushed into a legacy application, the Lightweight Extensible Interface Framework (LEIF) [3], through implementation of a LEIF Application Programming Interface (API). To generate briefing material, we took a snapshot of the user-specified display (via an integrated COTS utility [9]) and automatically exported the resultant image to a user-configured PowerPoint file.

This extended framework exceeded the 3rd Fleet Staff's information processing expectations with its end-to-end knowledge management solution, ability to quickly and dynamically add/modify information types, and demonstrated interoperability features. As a result, our framework was successfully applied in the following domains aboard the USS Coronado: GBS Evaluation, Logistics, Intelligence, and Operations. In the case of the GBS Evaluation domain, we were able to facilitate performance testing of the broadband dissemination mechanism by profiling for information based on size, location, and data type; transferring the constrained data over the GBS medium; and assessing the timeliness and quality of the received data.

5   Lessons Learned

Our underlying "build a little, listen a little" philosophy, that is include the end users *early and frequently* in the research and development cycle, proved to be the key to our success in developing technology that addressed real problems and could potentially be transitioned into an operational environment. However, from an applied technology perspective, we find that many challenges remain.

Scalability, extensibility, configuration, tailoring, and training were the primary discriminators we found while applying intelligent agents and developing knowledge management clients in an operational domain. We will look at each of these in detail, exploring our application experience and subsequent lessons learned.

5.1   Scalability

We increased the breadth and depth of accessible information repositories with each iteration of our application evaluation cycle. In so doing, we found transport throughput problems (in the agents and the networks), client data management problems (database overload, cluttered displays), and invalid formatted data (highlighting a lack of error handling). In most cases, we implemented the short-term solution of constraining the information queries and results through configuration parameters. The long-term goal is clear. In addition to increasing the robustness of the code, we need to develop more complex data structures, processing, and displays. For example, most of the officers operate in a drill-down fashion. First they select a geographical area. Next, they select an object within that area and view its high-level characteristics (e.g. name, location, and status). Then they search for specific characteristics associated with that object relative to their role (e.g. intelligence). In this example, we can see a need for hierarchical abstractions and relationships between data sets. As such, ontology structures need to be extended, displays need to be multi-tiered, and content and processing relationships need to be coupled within and across user contexts.

5.2   Extensibility

As part of each evaluation, user needs were re-assessed and as a result, features were continuously modified and/or added. Modifying capabilities within the common agent infrastructure or the tightly coupled knowledge management toolkit were found to be unacceptable solutions. Instead, we hooked entities into existing interfaces and configured system threads to operate on a common semantic level.

For example, our web resource agent issued Verity searches against the Netscape Compass Server. The search queries incorporated an extended operator set beyond that provided in SQL. Our agent infrastructure required queries to be expressed in SQL2. Instead of modifying the agent query language, we built an ontology capable of carrying the extended search operators from the client to the web resource agent where the query could be translated into the Verity format. This was an appropriate near-term solution, but not extensible. Since the web resource agent only understands Verity and the multi-resource query agent speaks SQL, we could not easily join queries from relational repositories with the web. The long-term solution requires semantic interoperability among computing entities not for unique or single application threads but for the system infrastructure as a whole.

Data or service brokering across systems should be independent of the computing infrastructures. As our knowledge management application acted as an independent client to our agent framework, we found this paradigm to be successful and extensible. Our knowledge management application shared objects through inheritance in an extremely powerful manner (e.g. multiple views exploiting a single dynamic object), while our agents cooperated through message passing in a distributed and dynamic manner. Our system design proved to be an effective solution to the partitioned problem space. Yet from the perspective of developing the knowledge management application, the state of the object design and the extent of the coupling needs to be taken into account when determining where the boundary lines of the independent computing infrastructures are drawn.

5.3   Configuration

Installing and executing agents and clients in an operational environment requires knowledge of and conformance to a variety of potential platforms, middleware, and external applications. As our experiments shifted in location and across application domains, we found that platform-independence (e.g. Java) and standardized middleware interfaces (e.g. RMI, JDBC, HTTP, SMTP) were essential to our design. As a result, we were able to execute our capabilities in a broad range of application environments, primarily through configuration changes.

Much of the agent-based infrastructure is applied solely through the setting of configuration parameters. To bring a new information repository on-line, we simply generate one or more configuration files mapping its information schema or unstructured text to an ontology. Generic advertising capabilities are instantiated via a configuration file, bringing the agent into the applied infrastructure. Applicable system ontologies, ports, and addresses (of the brokers) are defined in the system configuration file. Agent specific configuration parameters (e.g. format, type, language) may also be defined in this file or in specific agent configuration files.

Client features, such as email notification or heavyweight data retrieval requires the setting of configuration parameters based on the operational environment (e.g. mail server address and port). Collection mechanisms, display preferences, and available pre-processed data are also dynamically defined based on configuration parameters. These selectable parameters enabled the user to reuse existing models, specify storage locations, request agent connections, and leverage unique data handlers to name a few of the tailorable options.

Using this configurable framework, we were able to instantiate a series of end-to-end operational applications in less than a day each. Given the ontology models were defined a priori, we

- ✓ configured the agent syntactic operating parameters in less than an hour
- ✓ configured the agent syntactic application parameters in a matter of hours, depending on the data complexity
- ✓ configured the client syntactic operating parameters in less than an hour
- ✓ configured the client syntactic application parameters in a matter of hours, again depending on the data complexity.

As discussed earlier, the time-consuming and difficult task relevant to our application effort was in defining the semantics of the application, i.e. the ontological models.

5.4   Tailoring

An early lesson learned in resource agent application was that little or no metadata existed for many of the information repositories. In some cases, we could annotate the metadata fields directly (e.g. Netscape Compass Server, databases under our auspices). In other cases, we had to write specific parsers to generate valid metadata (e.g. legacy applications). These options proved to be cumbersome. In the future, we assume that the information community will begin to correct the problem (e.g. geospatial metadata [11]) and that new tools (e.g. web summarizers [10]) will begin to alleviate the problem.

Another lesson found in applying knowledge management techniques was that the tools must be personalized. For example, the ability to request information, store and extract relevant concepts, and view those concepts geospatially (i.e. in a map display) is applicable to an Intelligence Officer, Operations Officer, and a Logistics Officer acting in a number of roles. Tasks may range from generating the daily situational brief to participating in a regional exercise. From the perspective of the user, the features and preferences maintained in the knowledge management system should be based on the action officer's role. This way, the action officer can explicitly store and share knowledge relevant to specific activities. As new officers are transitioned into a role, they will have the benefit of prior knowledge. Our agent infrastructure fully supports context-based access by allowing multiple simultaneous ontologies and execution threads. Within the knowledge management client, we enabled the user to dynamically generate the information models, organization, and views required of the action officer's role. In addition, we provided the ability to persistently store and share these knowledge contexts.

5.5   Training

System tools for generating and applying the configuration elements were developed for and utilized by engineers, and therefore, not necessarily appropriate for all users. In addition, the dynamics of our knowledge management client required system administrative type activities. Again, the tools for which were not appropriate for an all users. We found that to fully exploit the intelligent agents and the personal knowledge management application, we need to bridge the gap between the system implementers and the domain experts. To this end, we must train a new breed of end users capable of configuring the dynamic aspect of the system application.

6   Conclusions and Future Work

In this paper, we discussed the value of our easily extended and configured agent-based infrastructure, the power of our object-oriented technology for personalized knowledge management, and the evident necessity in leveraging information management features within commercial products and legacy applications. Throughout our strategic research effort, we elicited guidance on the future direction of agent-based knowledge management technology. Our conclusion is that the technology reviewed in this paper is necessary and sufficient for addressing information processing problems directly related to information overload and in capturing the end user's knowledge of a specific information processing domain. Future technology enhancements include semantic interoperability at the system level, automated and dynamic task execution, de-coupling of specialized knowledge management techniques (e.g. metadata generation), and richer ontological models.

According to this excerpt from a fleet message: "Based on these assessments, C3F strongly endorses these types of IM/KM tools to assist the staff in gaining control over continuously increasing volumes of information now available to the fleet.", our effort shows great promise to the U.S. Navy. As our extended system framework encompasses a wide range of generic capabilities, we plan on verifying the direction of this technology in other military and commercial ventures.

References

1. Marian Nodine, Brad Perry and Amy Unruh: Experience with the InfoSleuth Agent Architecture. Proceedings of AAAI-98 Workshop on Software Tools for Developing Agents (1998)
2. Rob Kremer: Visual Languages for Knowledge Representation. Eleventh Workshop on Knowledge Acquisition, Modeling and Management (1998)
3. DTAI: Lightweight Extensible Information Framework (LEIF) product description. http://www.dtai.com/products/leif/ (2000)
4. G.Blohm, R. Parikh, E. Davis, A. Bhatt and A. Ware: Information Dissemination Via Global Broadcast Service (GBS). IEEE MILCOM 96 Conference Proceedings (1996) 506-511
5. ObjectFX: ObjectFX Releases SpatialFX™2.0. http://www.objectfx.com/ (2000)
6. Sun: HotJava™Browser 3.0. http://java.sun.com/products/hotjava/ (2000)
7. Netscape: Netwcape Compass Server product description. http://www.netscape.com/compass/v3.0/ (2000)
8. W3C: HTTP – Hypertext Transfer Protocol. http://www.w3.org/Protocols/ (2000)
9. TechSmith: SnagIt® Windows Screen Capture. http://www.techsmith.com/products/snagit/default.asp (2000)
10. Charlotte Jenkins, Mike Jackson, Peter Burden, Jon Wallis: Automatic Metadata Generation for Resource Discovery. WWW8 Conference Refereed Papers (1999)
11. Federal Geographic Data Committee: Content standard for digital geospatial metadata. FGDC-STD-001-1998 (revised 1998)
12. Sun: Java™ Media APIs. http://jsp.java.sun.com/products/java-media/ (2000)

Author Index